THE
CATHOLIC CONTROVERSY

The 27-year-old St. Francis de Sales and his cousin, Canon Louis de Sales, pray to the Guardian Angel of the diocese as they enter the Calvinist district of the Chablais on their great mission of conversion. Louis returned home because of a critical lack of funds, and St. Francis then continued on alone. (Louis was to succeed St. Francis de Sales as Bishop of Geneva.)

THE
CATHOLIC CONTROVERSY

ST. FRANCIS DE SALES' DEFENSE
OF THE FAITH

By

St. Francis de Sales
1567-1622
BISHOP AND DOCTOR OF THE CHURCH

Translated by
Rev. Henry Benedict Mackey, O.S.B.
FROM THE AUTOGRAPH MANUSCRIPTS AT ROME AND AT ANNECY

Under the Direction of the
Right Rev. John Cuthbert Hedley, O.S.B.
BISHOP OF NEWPORT AND MENEVIA

*"He that heareth you, heareth me;
and he that despiseth you, despiseth
me; and he that despiseth me,
despiseth him that sent me."*
—Luke 10:16

TAN BOOKS AND PUBLISHERS, INC.
Rockford, Illinois 61105

Published by Burns and Oates, London and by Catholic Publication Society Co., New York, in 1886, as Vol. III of the series entitled *Library of St. Francis de Sales: Works of This Doctor of the Church Translated into English.* (This particular work is also known simply as *Controversies.*)

Reprinted by TAN Books and Publishers, Inc. in 1989 after arrangement with Burns & Oates, Tunbridge Wells, England. Typography is the property of TAN Books and Publishers, Inc., and may not be reproduced, in whole or in part, without written permission from the publisher.

Cover picture: 27-year-old St. Francis de Sales (left) and his cousin, Canon Louis de Sales, pray to the Guardian Angel of the diocese as they enter the Calvinist district of the Chablais on their great mission of conversion. Louis returned home because of a critical lack of financial support, and St. Francis then continued on alone. *(After a mural in the Visitation of Thonon in the Chablais.)*

ISBN: 0-89555-387-2

Library of Congress Catalog Card No.: 89-52138

Printed and bound in the United States of America.

TAN BOOKS AND PUBLISHERS, INC.
P. O. Box 424
Rockford, Illinois 61105

1989

TRANSLATOR'S PREFACE.

THE following Treatise is the message or teaching of S. Francis de Sales to the Calvinists of the Chablais, reluctantly written out because they would not go to hear him preach. The Saint neither published it nor named it. We have called it "The Catholic Controversy," partly to make our title correspond as nearly as possible with the title "Les Controverses," given by the French editor when the work was posthumously published, chiefly because its scope is to state and justify the Catholic doctrine as against Calvin and his fellow-heretics. It is the Catholic position, and the defence of Catholicism as such. At the same time it is incidentally the defence of Christianity, because his justification of Catholicism lies just in this that it alone is Christianity ; and his argument turns entirely on the fundamental question of the exclusive authority of the Catholic Church, as the sole representative of Christianity and Christ. This is the real point at issue between the Church and the sects, and therefore he, as officer of the Church, begins by traversing the commission of those who teach against her. He shows at length, in Part I., that she alone has Mission, that she alone is sent to teach, and that thus their authority is void, and their teaching but the vain teaching of men.

This teaching he tests in Part II. by the Rule of Faith. Assuming as common ground that the Word of God is the Rule of Faith, he shows that the so-called reformers have composed a false Scripture, and that they err also in rejecting Tradition or the un-written Word of God. And then, proceeding to the central point of his case, he shows that while the Word of God is the formal Rule of Faith, is the external standard by which faith is to be measured and adjusted, there is need of a judge who may explain, apply, and declare the meaning of the Word. That judge is the Holy Catholic Church. She is thus the necessary exponent of the Rule of right-believing, and each of the voices by which she utters her decision becomes also a part of the Rule of Faith, viz., her own general body, Councils, Fathers, and her supreme Head and mouthpiece, the Pope, the successor of S. Peter and Vicar of Christ. Miracles and harmony of doctrines may be considered the complement of the Rule of Faith. In all these matters the Saint proves conclusively that the Catholic Church alone fulfils the necessary conditions.

In Part III. he comes to the doctrines of the Church in detail, but of this Part there only remain to us three chapters on the Sacraments and an Essay on Purgatory.

This may suffice as to the aim and subject-matter of the Treatise. Of its intrinsic merits the author's name is sufficient guarantee, but we add more direct testimony because it is a new revelation of the Saint.

The Bull of Doctorate calls it "a complete demon-stration of Catholic doctrine." Alibrandi, in the *Pro-cessus*, speaks of "the incredible power of his words," and says in particular that no other writer, as far as he knows, has "so conclusively, fully, and lucidly explained the Church's teaching on the primacy, infallible *magisterium*, and other prerogatives of the successors of S. Peter." Hamon, in his Life of the Saint,* says: "If we consider it, not as disfigured by its first editor, who made it unrecognisable in trying to perfect it, but as it left its author's hands, we see that it is of inestimable value, that it presents the proofs of the Catholic Church with an irresistible force." Its first editor, Léonard, says: "We are entirely of the opinion that this book deserves to be esteemed beyond all the others he has composed." The Mother de Chaugy, superior of Annecy, in her circular letter of 1661 to the Houses of the Visitation, writes thus: "It is considered that this Treatise is calculated to produce as much fruit amongst heretics for their conversion as the *Introduction to a Devout Life* amongst Catholics for devotion. And their Lordships our Judges (for the cause of Canonization) say that S. Athanasius, S. Ambrose and S. Augustine have not more zealously defended the faith than our Blessed Father has done."

Cardinal Zacchetti, in introducing the cause of Beatification, gives a further proof of its excellence in describing the effect it had on the obstinate men for whom it was composed: "When the inhabitants of the Chablais were forbidden by magisterial decree to attend his sermons or frequent his company, he began to fight with his pen, and wrote to them a letter accompanied with certain selected arguments for the Catholic faith, by which he recalled so great a multitude of wandering souls to the Church that he happily

* I. 167.

raised up and restored first Thonon and then the other parishes."

And the power of the work lies not in its substance only but also in its manner. It is true controversy, yet unlike all other controversy. He seems to follow the same method as in his practical theology, making the difficult easy, turning the rough into smooth. What S. Thomas and the grand theologians have done for learned men, S. Francis has done for the general people. He ever seems to have little ones in his mind, to be speaking and writing for them. We see in this Treatise the leading of the same spirit which made him love to preach to children, and to nuns, and to the poor country people; which made him keep in his own establishment and teach with his own lips the poor deaf-mute of whom we read in his Life. It is in great measure this spirit which gives him such an affinity with our age in that sympathy with the weak and miserable which is one of its best and noblest tendencies. And here again we have a striking proof of his genius. "It is perhaps harder," say the Bollandists in their petition for his Doctorate (xxxv), "to write correctly on dogmatic, moral, and ascetic subjects in such a way as to be understood by the unlearned and not despised by the learned, than to compose the greater works of theology; it is a difficulty only overcome by the best men."

We must now satisfy our readers that we offer them a faithful text of a work of such extreme value. This is the more necessary on the ground that it is an unfinished and posthumous production, and it is especially incumbent upon us, because we put forward our edition as representing in English a *first edition*, the first printing of the true text. Ours is veritably a new work by S. Francis brought out in this nineteenth century.

The original was written on fugitive separate sheets, which were copied and distributed week by week, sometimes being placarded in the streets and squares. The Saint did not consider them of sufficient importance to be mentioned in the list of his works contained in the Preface to the *Love of God*, but they were carefully written, and he preserved a copy more or less complete which bears marks of being revised by him later, and which he speaks of to the Archbishop of Vienne (L. 170), as "studies" suitable for use in a future work on "a method of converting heretics by holy preaching."

The first we hear of a portion of these sheets is in the "Life" by his nephew, Charles Auguste de Sales, who gives a rather full and very accurate analysis of them. They are labelled in his "Table des Preuves" (63) as follows: "Fragment of the work of S. Francis de Sales, Provost of Geneva, on the Marks of the Church and the Primacy of S. Peter; written partly with his own hand when he was at Thonon for the conversion of the Chablais. We have the original on paper." These fragments were the chief part of the article on Scripture, the article on Tradition, the chief part of the article on the Pope, and half that on the Church. The parts "written with his own hand" were those on Scripture and Tradition.

This abstract was made before 1633 (the Saint died at the end of 1622), and exactly a quarter of a century after that date, when Charles Auguste had been bishop fourteen years, he "discovered" the whole manuscript as we have it now, except a comparatively small portion which was, and is, preserved at Annecy. The MS. was contained with other papers in a plain deal box which for greater security during those disturbed times had been cemented into the thick wall of an archive-chamber. Of this fact he gave the following attestation :—

"We testify to all whom it may concern that on the 14th May of the present year 1658, when we were in our château of La Thuille, from which we had been absent fourteen years, and were turning over the records of our archives, we found twelve large manuscript books, in the hand of the venerable servant of God and our predecessor, Francis de Sales, in which are treated many points of theology which are in controversy between Catholic doctors and the heretics, especially concerning the authority of the Supreme Roman Pontiff and Vicar of Jesus Christ and successor of Blessed Peter. We also found three other books on the same matters, which were written by another hand except as to three pages which are in the hand of the aforesaid servant of God. All these we consigned to the Rev. Father Andrew de Chaugy, Minim, Procurator in the cause of Beatification of the servant of God." *

Father de Chaugy, who sent, or probably took, them to Rome, gives the following attestation. The names of

---

* The Bishop does not mention the sheets he had handled before 1633, but we have no doubt, from internal evidence, that they formed part of what he found in 1658, though they were probably placed in the deal coffer by another hand. They are all together at the end of the MS., except that the part on the Pope has been brought next to that part of the autograph which treats of the same subject, thus placing the parts on Scripture and Tradition one step away from their companion sheets.

witnesses will easily be recognised by those who are familiar with the Saint's life :—

" I, Brother Andrew de Chaugy, Minim, Procurator of the Religious of the Visitation for the Canonization of the venerable servant of God, M. de Sales, Bishop and Prince of Geneva, certify that I have procured to be witnessed that these present Manuscripts, which treat of the authority and primacy of S. Peter and of the sovereign Pontiffs his successors, are written and dictated in the hand and style of the venerable servant of God, M. Francis de Sales.

" Those who have witnessed them are M. the Marquis de Lullin, Governor of the Chablais ; the Reverend Father Prior of the Carthusians of Ripaille ; M. Seraphin, Canon of Geneva, aged 80 years ; M. Jannus, Superior of Brens in Chablais; M. Gard, Canon of the Collegiate Church of Our Lady at Annecy ; M. F. Fauvre, who was twenty years valet to the servant of God.

" All the above witnesses certify that the said writings are of the hand and composition of this great Bishop of Geneva, and they even certify that they have heard him preach part of them when he converted the countries of Gex and Chablais."

M. de Castagnery and M. de Blancheville testify that " part was written by the Saint, and that the other part, written by the hand of his secretary, was corrected by him."

From the many other attestations, given by the chief officials, ecclesiastical and civil, of the diocese and county, we select a part of one given by the Rev. Father Louis Rofavier, Chief Secretary to the Commission of Beatification and Canonization.

". . . Amongst other most authentic papers there were found some *cahiers* in folio, written by the Saint's own hand, and others by a foreign hand but noted and corrected by him, which proved to be one of the Treatises of Controversy composed by him during his mission to the Chablais . . . which Treatise was inserted in the Acts, and produced under requisition, that the court of Rome might have due regard to so excellent a work in defence of the Holy Roman Church. The requisition and production having been made it was judged fit to send the original to our Holy Father Pope Alexander VII. . . . I have had the honour of handling it and of inserting it in the Acts, and moreover of having a faithful copy of it made to be hereafter published." The Marquis de Sales speaks of "two or three copies."

The autograph, with the attestations in original, was deposited by the Pope in the archives of the Chigi family to which he belonged; and there we will leave it for the present while we follow the fortunes of the copy which had been made for publication. It was placed in the hands of Léonard of Paris, editor of the Saint's other works, who brought it out in 1672. We have only to endorse M. Hamon's above quoted condemnation of this edition. Léonard himself says: "We have not added or diminished or changed anything in the substance of the matter, and only softened a few of the words." But such an editor puts his own meaning on the expressions he uses. As a fact there is not a single page or half-page which does not contain serious omissions, additions, and faulty alterations of matters more or less substantial. The verbal changes are to be counted by thousands; in fact the nerve is quite taken out of the expression, the terse, vigorous and personal sixteenth century language of the man of genius being buried under the trivial manner of the everyday writer employed by Léonard eighty years later. The style and wording of the original make it a monument of early French literature and the nascent powers of the French tongue.

Léonard, again, has garbled the Saint's quotations, and almost habitually given the wrong references to the Fathers. In the MS. the citations are in almost every case correct as to the sense though free as to the words, and the references are most exact, though too hastily and briefly jotted down to be of much use to a careless and self-sufficient editor.

Finally, Léonard has made most serious mistakes as to order. He has quite failed to grasp the true division of Part II., simple and logical as it is. He has mingled in almost inextricable confusion the sections on the Church, the Councils, the Fathers, miracles, and reason,* he has unnecessarily repeated sections on Scripture and on the Indefectibility of the Church, while saying no word of a second recension of the section on the Pope which contains some important additions to the first. He has dragged out of their proper places parts on the unity of the Church, on miracles, and on the analogy of faith, and thrust them respectively into the sections on the Pope, on the sanctity of the Church, and on the Fathers. In some places he alters the past tense into

---

* For instance, Discours XLVI. is made up of a part on the Fathers, a part on the analogy of faith, and two parts, properly distinct from one another, on the unity of the Church. At each change he puts a note to apologise for the *Saint's* digressions.

the future to suit his changes, instead of letting himself be guided back to the true order, and when he
finds the Saint speaking of the last Part as Part III.
he drops the numeral rather than give up his mistake
in making it Part IV. He says the division into
three parts is the Saint's own. So it is; but Léonard
does not follow it. He makes four parts, dividing
Part II. into two, and then goes on to blame S.
Francis for making a sub-section into a section. He
divides the Treatise into *"discours,"* which is just
what they were not. They *had* been; that is, the
book was worked up from sermons, but the Saint's
very point was to turn these into ordinary writings,
and he always speaks of his own divisions as chapters
and articles.

Such was Léonard's edition of 1672, and we find
no further edition until that of Blaise in 1821, which
is merely a reprint as far as the Saint's own words
go. It has thus almost all the faults of the first
edition, with such deliberate further alterations as
approved themselves to the Gallican editor. Some of
the quotations are verified and references corrected,
the discredit of the mistakes being attributed to the
author instead of the first editor. The notes are the
special feature, the special disgrace, of this edition.
The editor cannot forgive S. Francis for upholding the
full authority of the Pope, and the true principles of
the Church with regard to such matters as miracles
and heresy; and his notes on the chapters treating
of these subjects are full of such expressions as these:
" the saintly author's innumerable negligences ; "
" facts whose falsehood is generally recognised ; "
" this sketch of the life of S. Peter must be corrected

by reference to Fleury and others;" "with what superiority Bossuet treats the question!" "the Saint here"
(speaking of the shameless Marot) "quits his usual
moderation;" "there reigns such an obscurity, such
confusion in his citations;" "he has quoted wrongly
according to his custom;" "this miracle is no better witnessed than most;" "the relation of so many miracles
shows that in his time there was little criticism;"
"here he argues in a vicious circle." Blaise's chief
indignation is reserved for the famous list of papal
titles, on which he permits himself the following
remark, at the end of a note of three pages: "S.
Francis de Sales has collected at hazard fifty titles
accorded to the Apostolic See. It would have been
easy to augment the number without having recourse
to forged records, false decretals, and a modern doctor,
and still that would not be found which is sought for
with so much ardour."

We see how low the credit of the work must have
been brought by a corrupt text and such annotations
as these. It was not till 1833 that the publication
by Blaise, in a supplementary volume, of part of the
section on papal authority began to give an idea of
the way in which the Saint had been misrepresented.
Blaise's naive commendation of this part is the
condemnation of all the rest, which is neither better
nor worse than the section he amended: "this piece
already forms part of our collection of the Works in
the 'Controversies,' but so disfigured that we do not
hesitate to offer it here as unpublished (*inédite*)."
What he did for a part we have done, in an English
version, for the whole. Vivès in 1858 and Migne in
1861 brought out editions in which the new part was

printed and which had the grace to omit the Gallican
notes, but otherwise the text remained the same as
in the previous editions, no serious attempt apparently
being made to follow up Blaise's discovery. Even
the Abbé Baudry, who spent his life in collecting,
throughout France and Northern Italy, materials bearing on the life and works of S. Francis, and who
made researches in the Vatican Library, only got so
far as to have heard that the autograph was in the
Chigi Library. It was brought forward at the Vatican
Council, and made an immense impression upon the
Fathers. But it was reserved for the present publishers and translator to have the singular honour of
resuscitating this glorious work, and of bringing it out
in its true and full beauty.

This autograph, still preserved in the Chigi Library,
is a richly bound volume of foolscap size containing
155 sheets numbered on one side, thus making 310
pages. It is in bold writing, perfectly clear and easy
to read, but with corrections and slips. Nearly every
page has a cross at the top. The arranging and
numbering of the sheets is not the Saint's, and there
is much disorder here. There are some repetitions,
chiefly on the Pope and on Scripture, and slight varia-
tions, as might be expected in a work composed as this
was, the Saint probably making more than one copy
himself. We call it the autograph; two portions of
it, however, are not autograph, but, as the attestations say, written by a secretary, and only noted and
corrected by the Saint;—viz. (1.) sheets 76 to 90,
containing the chief part of the section on Purgatory:
(2.) one of the two recensions of the part on the
Pope, and about half the section on the Church,

sheets 121 to 155. We mention this in order to be strictly accurate, but there is no difference to be made between the autograph and the non-autograph parts. All the sheets were together, the section on Purgatory is taken up by the Saint in the middle of a sentence and completed by himself, the non-autograph part on the Church fits exactly into the autograph part, was analysed by Charles Auguste as the Saint's work within ten years after his death, and contains two chapters which occur again in autograph in Part I. The two recensions of the part on the Pope only differ in order and in a few sentences, those on Scripture are both in the Saint's hand. The non-autograph part on the Church is extremely difficult to read, being badly written in German characters and badly spelt.

With the autograph is a *copy*, of the same date, bound in the same way, and very possibly one of the several copies spoken of by the Marquis De Sales. The writing is like print, large and clear, except in the last part, containing the second recension on the Pope and half the section on the Church, which are written in a cramped hand, and being copied from the difficult German character are full of misspells and grammatical errors. The copy contains 207 sheets, numbered only on one side, forming 414 pages. It is not quite complete, omitting the chief part of the article on Scripture, the first half of that on the Church, and the whole of Tradition. Except that it is not complete this copy is an exact transcript of the original, with which it has been most carefully collated. Our version has been made from this copy, graciously lent to us by Prince Chigi. The translator's brother has transcribed for him the omitted parts.

III.

This Roman MS. is our chief but not our only
source.   There is also an autograph portion of the
work at Annecy, certified by the Vicar General of the
diocese, Poncet, in an attestation given June 11th,
1875, and by the Mother Superior, exactly fitting in
to the other MS.   It contains some further most
important portions on the Pope and on the Church,
and almost all we have on Councils.   This autograph
has been printed for private circulation in the *Pro-
cessus*, of which we have procured a certified copy.

Our first duty was to arrange the Treatise in its
proper order.   Here the autograph and the copy were
different from each other and from the printed text.
The parts misplaced had to be brought back, and the
whole distributed according to the logical plan laid
down by the saintly author in the introduction to Part
II.   The Annecy autograph had to be rightly joined
with the Roman.   Then came the question of omitting repetitions, viz., the parts on scandal, on Scripture,
and on the Pope.   Then had to be studied the many
single sentences and words about which any difficulty
arose.   Such difficulties were not frequent concerning
the autograph part, but in the non-autograph part
they frequently occurred.   The original was hard to
make out, the copy was not of great assistance here,
the printed text was all wrong.   Sometimes the consideration of one word would occupy an hour or more
in Rome or in England.   But success was at last
obtained, except in the three instances mentioned in
the notes,* and scarcely amounting to two lines in

---

* We have forgotten to mention that we took the responsibility of
putting Fisher (p. 154) where the Annecy text spells " Fucher ; " and
(p. 180) of translating fleet (*caravelles*—ships) where the printed French

all. The quotations had to be carefully verified and the true references given : the original was found to be correct in almost every instance. In fine, titles had to be placed to the three parts, and to such articles and chapters as had not received their headings from the Saint. We will now indicate the points which we consider to deserve special notice.

(1.) The General Introduction will be seen to be made up, in the French text, of two parts. The ending of the first appears in the middle of the united parts. As the same words form the end of the whole Introduction (p. 10), we have omitted them on p. 4.*
There is a second copy of that part of the Introduction which treats of scandal, carefully corrected by the Saint. We give it at the end of our Preface.

(2.) The *Discours* which is called the first in the French being repeated in the second and third, we have omitted it, greatly clearing the text. The Saint gives no guide to the divisions here ; we have therefore made our own divisions and titles of the first four chapters.

(3.) The Introduction to Part II. has a second treatment in another part of the MS., but there is no practical difference between the two. This Introduction is important as regulating the number of Parts,

text has *caravanes,* which is certainly wrong. Our MS. copy has *Carvaranée.* The same incident is related in the *Etendard de la Croix* (II. 4) as having taken place in *l'isle Camarane.*

* The following lines, of no substantial importance, have been inadvertently omitted on this p. 4. " You will see in this Treatise good reasons—and which I will prove good—which will make you see clearly as the day that you are out of the way that must be followed for salvation ; and this not by fault of your holy guide, but in punishment of having left her."

and the order of articles and chapters. Three Parts,*
and three Parts only, are mentioned, and this division
is confirmed in the Introduction to the next and
last Part. The eight articles of Part II. are clearly
indicated on p. 86.

(4.) Of the first part of Article I., on Holy Scripture, we have two very similar recensions. The first
editor, who has been followed in subsequent French
editions, adopted the plan of giving first the four
chapters of the one, afterwards the four chapters of
the other, with the effect of burdening his text and
confusing his readers. We have united the chapters
which have the same titles, our table of contents
showing the way in which the chapters have been
blended. We have made an exception as to c. 7
(the matter of which is given again in cc. 5, 8),
because the arguments are put differently and from
a different point of view. In c. 5 the Saint gives the
heretical violation of Scripture as a consequence of
their belief in private inspiration, in the others he
gives them absolutely. In this part, particularly at
the end of Discours xxxiii., the MS. gives many slight
directions for locating the different points treated.
Similar indications appear here and there throughout,
and we need scarcely say that the Saint's intentions
have been religiously observed by us.

(5.) In cc. 9, 11 of this Article I. we have quota-

* We have just discovered in an obscure corner of the MS. a sentence
which belongs to this subject, p. 87, and which is important as giving
the object of Part III. "And because I could not easily prove that we
Catholics have most strictly kept them (the Rules of Faith), without
making too many interruptions and digressions, I will reserve this
proof for Part III., which will also serve as a very solid confirmation
of all this second Part."

tions from Montaigne. The fact of quoting him was made an objection against conferring the Doctorate, on the ground that Montaigne was not only a profane but also an irreligious and immoral writer. The objection is sufficiently answered by Alibrandi's reference to the practice of S. Paul and the Fathers, but there is a much fuller defence than that, both of the Saint and of Montaigne. It is enough here to say that these passages are taken from the grand and most religious essay " On Prayer," near the beginning of which Montaigne speaks as follows of what he calls his *fantaisies informes et irresolues.* " And I submit them to the judgment of those whose it is to regulate not only my actions and my writings but my thoughts likewise. Equally well taken by me will be their condemnation or their approbation, and I hold as impious and absurd anything which by ignorance or inadvertence may be found contained in this rhapsody contrary to the holy decisions and commands of the Catholic, Apostolic, and Roman Church, in which I die and in which I was born. Wherefore, ever submitting myself to the authority of their censure, &c."

(6.) Immediately after Scripture and Tradition we place the article on the Church. The French editions have here put that on the Pope, probably on account, originally, of a marginal note in the MS. at the beginning of that section: "this chapter to be put first for this part." The same note it probably was which led them to make this article the commencement of a Part III. It ought to have been clear that the Saint used the word *part* not for a division of his work but in the sense of *subject.*

We have said that nothing can be more incorrect

and confusing than the order of the French printed texts in this Article III. The first four pages are right, though under a wrong title, but on p. 153 we come to a broken sentence: * "every proposition which stands this test . . ." Léonard quickly finished it off with " is good," and then goes off in the same *Discours* to the subject of Councils. We have been fortunate enough to find the continuation of the sentence and chapter in the Annecy autograph, which we now begin to use for the first time. ". . . I accept as most faithful and sound." It is not necessary to make further mention of the errors of the French editions down to our Chapter IV. Our Chapter II. begins with another section from the Annecy MS. We have brought back the chapter *On the unity of the Church in headship* to its proper place here (c. 3), and relegated the parts on Fathers, and Councils, and the Pope, to their proper places elsewhere. With regard to the exquisite passage on the analogy between the Creed and the Blessed Sacrament, whilst it certainly does not come between the Fathers and the Church where Léonard has thrust it (Discours XLVI.), we cannot be certain that it belongs strictly to Article VIII. (c. 2), where we have placed it, though it treats of the same subject. It exactly occupies sheet 31 of the

---

* We find in a detached note elsewhere an amplification of the sentence immediately preceding this. " As those who look at the neck of a dove see it change into as many various colours as they make changes of their point of view and their distance, so those who observe the Holy Scripture, through which, as through a neck, we receive heavenly nourishment, seem to themselves to see there all sorts of opinions according to the diversity of their passions. Is it not a marvellous thing to see how many kinds of heresies there have been up to now, the source of which their authors all confidently professed to show in the Holy Scriptures?"

Roman autograph, and we are inclined to think that it was a sheet sent round separately. It may have been an abstract of his little printed work, *Considerations on the Creed,* and perhaps may have helped to produce the good effect referred to in a letter to Favre (5), written about the time when it would be going about: "The ministers have confessed that we drew good conclusions from the Holy Scriptures about the mystery of the Holy Sacrament of the Altar."

(7.) Our text now runs on in substantial agreement with the French until the end of the article on the Church, except that we have transferred part of the section on Miracles to its proper place as Article VII., and omitted from cc. 13, 14 what is already given in Part I.

The verbal corrections, however, required in this article are very numerous. After c. 3 the MS. ceases for a time to be autograph, and the German character has puzzled our copyist and much more the French editor. Some examples may be of interest.

"Si fecond" becomes "et tailleurs" in the copy; Léonard removing the difficulty by substituting a safe but irrelevant text. "Frederick Staphyl" is in the copy "Sedenegue Stapsit," afterwards "Seneque Staphul" or "Staphu," Blaise supplying the note—"unknown work of an unknown author." Vivès gives "Tilmann, Heshisme et Oraste;" he also has "Vallenger" for "Bullinger," and "Tesanzaüs" for "Jehan Hus;" both editors have "Tanzuelins" instead of "Zuingliens." There is some excuse for the word "vermeriques," which we have translated "fanatic" (p. 174); it turns out to be "suermericos," a favourite word with Cochlæus, probably from *schwärmer.* "Diego of Alcala"

becomes " Diogenes of Archada," " Judas " is put for
" Donatus ; " " Heshushius," or " Zosime," or " Zuingle,"
for " Ochin." " Treves," " patriarche," " ou moyne,"
become respectively " Thebes," " paterneche," " à
moins." " Cochin " is turned into " Virne." * Chid-
abbe " escapes perversion because it is in autograph
elsewhere, but Blaise, forgetting that the African S.
Augustine is speaking, sagely informs us that " this
mountain is in the environs of Thonon." The note
on p. 191 represents a not unimportant restoration of
the text. The copy had *sapines,* the printed text
besoins; the context easily guided one to the right
word, *psaulmes.*

In Article IV. we return to the Saint's own clear
hand in the MS. and so to greater verbal correctness.
Most of this invaluable section is supplied by the
Annecy MS.

(9.) Article VI., on the Pope, has been fairly well
edited from the Roman MS. We are able to supply
from the Annecy autograph a large and most important addition on the qualities of an *ex cathedrâ*
judgment (pp. 299–311), of which we give the original
French text in an appendix.

Of this Article we find two recensions in the Roman
text, one in autograph, and the other, which lacks the
first two chapters, not. The autograph is much superior
on the whole, but the order of the other recension is
better, and in this we have followed it. From it also
we have introduced into our translation the important

---

* One of Blaise's attacks on the Saint's "criticism" turns on this
word. The statement here attributed to the Bishop of Virne is put
down, in the *Standard of the Cross,* to the Bishop of Cecine. This latter
word only requires the change of the first e into o to make it an
Italianized Cochin.

passage (pp. 276–7) : " And if the wills, &c." to end of paragraph. On the same p. 276 occurs the pregnant statement that the headship of Peter is the *form* of Apostolic unity, that is, that the Apostles formed one body precisely by virtue of their union with Peter. This word *forme* was correctly printed in Blaise's edition of this part in 1833, but Vivès and Migne have altered it into *fermeté*. We have paid particular attention to the important list of Papal titles (pp. 291–2). Blaise had certainly a right to complain of the mistakes in the references here, but they are the fault of the first editor, not of the author, and on careful examination we find that of the fifty-three titles all are correct except perhaps two ; of which one cannot be traced, another attributes to Anacletus a letter which belongs to Siricius. Almost the same list is given in the first chapter of the Fabrian code, Article V.*

(10.) Article VII., on Miracles, now put in its proper place, needs no special remark, except as to the note p. 312. The sentence of Montaigne's there referred to is probably the following, from the twenty-second Essay, " On Custom " : " Miracles are miracles to our ignorance of nature, but not according to the actual powers of nature." Montaigne of course is speaking as the Saint is, of apparent miracles. We have a beautiful expression of Montaigne's faith in real miracles, such for instance as those related by S. Augustine (*de Civ. Dei* xxii.), in Essay 26 :

* In the note to p. 297 allusion is made to the substitution of the word *permanent* for *infaillible*. The Bull of Doctorate says that the discovery of the true reading of this passage led many of the Fathers of the Vatican Council, "as by the hand," to subscribe to the definition of Papal Infallibility.

"Of what shall we accuse him (S. Augustine) and the two holy Bishops, Aurelius and Maximinus, whom he calls to be witnesses with him? Of ignorance, simplicity, facility of belief, or of malice and imposture? Is there any man in our age impudent enough to think himself comparable to them, whether in virtue and piety or in learning, judgment, and competence? Giving no reason they would conquer one by their very authority.* To despise what we cannot comprehend is a dangerous boldness and serious risk, to say nothing of the absurd rashness which it brings in its train. For after you have established, according to your fine understanding, the limits of truth and falsehood, and it turns out that you are forced to believe things which are still more extraordinary than those you deny, you are already obliged to give them up."

(11.) The early sentences of Article VIII. will be seen to be a little unconnected. The first paragraph consists of detached notes from various parts of the M.S. In c. 3 we have inserted the part on the analogy of faith, as in what seemed to be the most suitable place.

We have now said what we think necessary as to the substance of this work and as to our editing. As to its manner we only repeat that to many this volume will be a new revelation of the Saint. The same calm sanctity, the same heavenly wisdom, the same charisma of sweetness, pervade all his works, but as a controversialist, as a champion of the Church, he here puts on that martial bearing, takes up those mighty weapons, proper to inspire confidence into

* Cic. Tusc. Qu. i. 21.

his comrades and to make his enemies quail before him.

It is remarkable that after a sleep of ten generations the Saint should appear first to preach again his true words in a country so similar to that for which they were first preached and providentially written. And though the heresy is more inveterate, yet it is therefore the more excusable, and he comes, as he did not come to the Chablais, first recommended by his moral and devotional teaching. It is providential, too, that he should wait so long, that he should slumber during the fierce Gallican and Jansenist struggles of the seventeenth and eighteenth centuries, that his words on these controverted matters should up to now be so doubtful that neither friend nor foe could safely dare to quote them. He appears like an ancient record, or rather like an ancient Prophet, to witness to the plain and simple belief of the Church in the days before these storms arose ; to prove to us that the Church's exclusive right to teach, the necessity of having Mission from her, the evilness of heresy, the supremacy and infallibility of the Pope are not inventions, not doctrines of to-day or yesterday, but the perpetual and necessary truths of Catholic faith. And this is the particular excellence of S. Francis : he defends the Church from accusations of falseness, but indirectly he still more fully clears her doctrines of the charge of novelty.* It might well be thought that the Controversy of the sixteenth century would be somewhat out of date now. But

---

* We have drawn this out at some length in our pamphlet entitled "Four Essays on the Life and Writings of S. Francis De Sales," pp. 98–114.

this is not true of the present work, not only on account of the intrinsic efficacy of its argument and language, not only on account of the sort of prophetic insight by which he reaches in advance of his time and answers objections that had scarcely yet arisen, but chiefly because there lies behind the strength of his reasons the weight of his authority as a witness, as a Doctor, we had almost said, in these days of rapid movement, as a Father of the Church. And there is no Doctor who better represents the true Catholic supernatural spirit, far removed from rationalism on the one hand, from superstition and fanaticism on the other. Instead of being an extremist, as Gallicans would nickname true believers, he was accused, in his own time, of *lessening* the fulness of Catholic doctrine. He says (p. 2): "It will be seen that I deny a thousand impieties attributed to Catholics: this is not in order to escape from the difficulty, as some have said, but to follow the holy intention of the Church." He preaches the full but simple Catholic truth, and his teaching was at last accepted as such by the 72,000 heretics of the Chablais. They had rejected Catholic doctrine when misunderstood, but when they understood what it was they hesitated indeed, from worldly motives, as to accepting it at all, but then they took it with simplicity as a whole, making no hesitation as to a part, or on the ground of inconsistency of part with part. Modern heretics would make such a distinction, there are even within the Church those who try to do so. For such we add, by way of conclusion to our Preface and of introduction to the Saint's argument, the testimony of an unsuspected witness of his own age :

" What seems to me," says Montaigne, in the Essay we last quoted, " to bring so much disorder into our consciences in these troubles which we are in as to religious matters is this dispensation which Catholics make in their belief. They fancy they act as moderate and enlightened men when they grant their adversaries some article which is in debate. But besides that they do not see what an advantage it is to the man who attacks you to begin to yield to him, and to draw back yourself, and how this encourages him to pursue his advantage,—those articles which they choose as the lightest are sometimes very important. We must entirely submit to the authority of our ecclesiastical tribunal or entirely dispense ourselves from it; it is not for us to determine the amount of obedience we owe to it. Besides,—and I can say it as having tried it, because I formerly used this liberty of choosing for myself and of personal selection, holding in light esteem certain points of observance belonging to our Church, which appear on the face of them somewhat idle or strange ;—when I came to discuss them with learned men I have found that these things have a strong and very solid base, and that it is only folly and ignorance which make us receive them with less reverence than the rest." *

WEOBLEY.

Feast of S. Francis de Sales,
29th January 1886.

* [We append here the Saint's second treatment of the subject of scandal, see. p. 5.] There is nothing of which the Holy Scripture gives more warning, history more testimony, our age more experience, than of the facility with which man is scandalized. It is so great that there is nothing, however good it may be, from which he does not draw some occasion of his ruin ; being unhappy indeed in this that having every-

where opportunities of drawing profit he turns and takes them all to his own disadvantage and misery. We may put so exactly into practice what Plutarch teaches,—to draw benefit even from our enemy— that even sin, our capital enemy and the sovereign evil of the world, can bring us to the knowledge of self, to humility and contrition. And a good man's fall makes him afterwards walk straighter and more circumspectly. So true is the word of S. Paul : *We know that all things work together unto good to them that love God* (Rom. viii. 28).

Not indeed that sin within us helps us, or when no longer in us can work us any good, for sin is bad in every sense, but from it can be derived occasions of great good which it would never of itself produce, imitating the bees which went and made honey within the putrid carcase of the fierce lion which Samson had slain. Is it not then a strange thing that being able to profit by all things, however bad they may be, we should turn all to our harm ? If indeed we only took evil from what is evil it would not be a great wonder, for that is what first offers ; if we drew evil from indifferent and harmless things nature would not be so much outraged, for these are arms which all hands may use :—though our baseness would still be great in that having it in our power to change everything into good by so easy and cheap an alchemy, for which one single spark of charity suffices, we were of so ill a disposition as to remain in our misery and procure our own hurt. But it is a wonderful thing, and passing all wonder, that in good, profitable, holy, divine things, in God himself, the malice of men finds matter to occupy itself with, to feed and to thrive upon ; that in a subject of infinite beauty it finds things to blame ; in this illimitable sea of all goodness it finds evil, and in the sovereign felicity the occasion of its misery.

The great Simeon predicted of Our Lord, having him in his arms and the Holy Ghost in his soul, that the child would be the ruin of many and a sign to be contradicted. Almost the same had Isaias said long before when he called Our Lord a stone of stumbling and of scandal, according to the interpretation of S. Paul. Is there not here reason for lamenting the misery of man who stumbles and falls over the stone which had been placed for his firm support, who founds his perdition on the stone of salvation ? . . . But the necessity there is in this world that scandals should come must not serve as an excuse to him who by his bad life gives it, nor to him who receives it from the hand of the scandalizer, nor to him who of his own malice goes seeking and procuring it for himself. For as to those who give it, they have no other necessity than what lies in the design and resolution which they have themselves made of living wickedly and viciously. They could if they liked, by the grace of God, avoid infecting and poisoning the world with the noisome exhalations of their sins, and be a good odour in Jesus Christ. The world, however, is so filled with sinners that, although many amend and are put back into grace, there always remains an infinite number who give testimony that scandal must needs come. Still, *woe to him by whom scandal cometh.*

And as to those who forge scandals for themselves, tickling themselves to make themselves laugh in their iniquities, who, like their forerunner, Esau, at the slightest difficulty to their understanding in matters of faith, or to their will in the holy commandments, persuade themselves that they will die if they do not alienate the portion which they have in the Church,—since they will have malediction and seek it, no wonder if they are accursed. Both the one and the other, the giver and the taker of scandal, are very wicked, but he who takes it without having it given to him is as much more cruel than the man who gives it as to destroy oneself is a more unnatural crime than to kill another.

In fine, he who takes the scandal which is given, that is, who has some occasion of scandalizing himself and does so, can have no other excuse than Eve had with regard to the serpent, and Adam with regard to Eve, which Our God found unacceptable. And all of them, the scandalizer, the scandalized, and the taker of scandal, are inexcusable and guilty, but unequally. For the scandalized man has more infirmity, the scandalizer more malice, and the taker of scandal goes to the extreme of malice. The first is scandalized, the second is scandalous, the third scandalous and scandalized together. The first is wanting in firmness, the second in kindness towards others, the third in kindness towards himself. . . .

How greatly this third form of scandal has been in use up to this present the universal testimony of ecclesiastical history shows us in a thousand places. We shall scarcely find as many instances of all the other vices as we shall find of this alone. Scandal, whether passive or taken, appears so thickly in the Scriptures that there is scarcely a chapter in which its marks are not seen. It would be pointing out daylight at high noon to take much pains to produce the passages. These will serve for all. Did not those of Capharnaum scandalize themselves in good earnest over Our Lord's words, as S. John relates (vi.), saying : *This is a hard saying, and who can hear it ?* And on what an occasion ! Because Our Lord is so good as to desire to nourish them with his flesh, because he says words of eternal life, do they turn against him. And over what do those labourers scandalize themselves—those (Matt. xx.) who murmured because the lord of the vineyard gave to the last comers as to the first—save over kindness and liberality and benefits ? What ! says the good lord, *is thy eye evil because I am good?* Who sees not, in that holy banquet and supper which was given to Our Lord at Bethany (John xii.), how Judas grows indignant and murmurs when he sees the honour which devout Magdalen does to her Saviour—how the sweetness of the odour of that poured out ointment offends the smell of that hideous reptile? Already then did they stumble over that holy stone. But since then—who could recount all that history tells us of the same? All those who have abandoned the true Church, under what pretext soever, have made themselves [his imitators]. . . .

TABLE OF CONTENTS.

[The Roman numerals refer to the French "Discours."]

Part I.

MISSION.

Part II.

THE RULE OF FAITH.

ARTICLE I.

HOLY SCRIPTURE FIRST RULE OF FAITH.—THAT THE PRE-
TENDED REFORMERS HAVE VIOLATED HOLY SCRIPTURE,
THE FIRST RULE OF OUR FAITH.

ARTICLE II.

THAT THE CHURCH OF THE PRETENDERS HAS VIOLATED THE
APOSTOLIC TRADITIONS, THE SECOND RULE OF OUR FAITH.

ARTICLE III.

THE CHURCH: THIRD RULE OF FAITH. HOW THE MINISTERS
HAVE VIOLATED THE AUTHORITY OF THE CHURCH, THE
THIRD RULE OF OUR FAITH.

ARTICLE IV.

THAT THE MINISTERS HAVE VIOLATED THE AUTHORITY OF COUNCILS, THE FOURTH RULE OF OUR FAITH.

ARTICLE V.

THAT THE MINISTERS HAVE VIOLATED THE AUTHORITY OF THE ANCIENT FATHERS OF THE CHURCH, FIFTH RULE OF OUR FAITH.

ARTICLE VI.

THE AUTHORITY OF THE POPE, THE SIXTH RULE OF OUR FAITH.

ARTICLE VII.

MIRACLES : THE SEVENTH RULE OF FAITH.

ARTICLE VIII.

HARMONY OF FAITH AND REASON : EIGHTH RULE OF FAITH.

Part III.

CHURCH DOCTRINES AND INSTITUTIONS.

ARTICLE I.

OF THE SACRAMENTS.

ARTICLE II.

PURGATORY.

ERRATA IN THE TEXT

Page   15   *Heb.* v:4 (not x).

                     Ps. xcviii:7 (not 6).

      55   *Luke* xi:21-22 (not 22-23).

    169   *Ps.* lxxxvi (not lxxvi).

    188   *Joel* 2:28 or 3:1.

    205   *1 John* ii:19 (not xix).

    286   *Acts* xii:3 (not 6).

    295   *Matt.* xix:27 (not xxvii).

INTRODUCTION

———◆———

In September, 1594, a 27-year-old priest entered the Chablais region, on the south shore of Lake Geneva, to begin a difficult apostolic mission. For a young man ordained less than a year—a young man of refined upbringing and education—its physical and moral hardships must have been daunting.

Although the Catholic Duke of Savoy had regained control of the Chablais a short time earlier, Calvinism had put down roots and anti-Catholic feeling was rife. When, responding to the Duke's plea, the Bishop of Geneva looked about for priests to send and the young man volunteered, his father protested: "I allowed my son to devote himself to the service of the Church to be a confessor, but I cannot give him up to be a martyr."

The young priest prevailed; he went to the Chablais, accompanied by his cousin Louis. Four months later, his personal resources exhausted, Louis left. The priest stayed, wrestling with a problem: How do you evangelize people who slam their doors in your face and will not listen to your sermons?

"He decided to confute their errors by means of leaflets which he wrote between his sermons and scattered to be passed hand to hand, hoping they might reach the heretics." So explains the encyclical *Rerum Omnium* (1923) in which Pope Pius XI, marking the third centenary of the priest's death, designated him the Patron of Writers and Journalists—for the solution which St. Francis de Sales hit upon was to turn to the pen and use the written word to reconcile his separated brethren with the Church.

He kept it up for over two years, writing and printing leaflets and distributing them however he could. (Often, it is said, he slipped them under Calvinist doors in the villages and towns he visited.) While these tracts can scarcely have turned the tide by themselves, there is little doubt they helped. When St. Francis left the region after four years, the restoration of Catholicism in the Chablais was well underway.

Once their immediate purpose had been accomplished, he seems not to have paid these early essays much attention, neither reprinting them nor listing them among his literary works. It was nevertheless to them that he apparently referred when he spoke later to an archbishop of certain "studies" which might yet prove useful as a guide to "a method of converting heretics by holy preaching." Revised copies were found among his papers years after his death. They were brought together in book form in an edition (by all accounts, a highly defective one) which was published in Paris in 1672 under the title *Controversies*. The work has been known under that name, or as *The Catholic Controversy,* from that time until now.

What interest do these essays have for today's reader? In fact, it is of three kinds: religious, literary and exemplary—as expressions of their author's mind and heart.

In religious terms, the essays are exercises in apologetics. Their aim is to explain, defend and render attractive the teaching of the Catholic Church. And, although they deal with controverted questions of the sixteenth and seventeenth centuries, neither the questions nor St. Francis' thoughts on them are of merely antiquarian interest.

On that score, the judgment of Dom Henry Benedict Mackey, O.S.B. (whose attractive nineteenth-century English translation is used in the present edition) remains sound. In these pages, he says, St. Francis

> appears like an ancient record, or rather like an ancient Prophet, to witness to the plain and simple belief of the Church . . . to prove to us that the Church's exclusive right to teach, the necessity of having Mission from her, the evilness of heresy, the supremacy and infallibility of the Pope are not inventions, not doctrines of to-day or yester-day, but the perpetual and necessary truths of Catholic faith.

It hardly needs saying that these matters are as important now as they were in Dom Mackey's time—or, for that matter, in St. Francis'. Declaring him a Doctor of the Church in 1877, Pope Pius IX called this work ''a full and complete demonstration of the Catholic religion.'' And, as his translator remarks, ''there is no Doctor who better represents

the true Catholic supernatural spirit, far removed
from rationalism on the one hand, from superstition and fanaticism on the other,'' than St. Francis
de Sales.

He begins by considering legitimacy and illegitimacy in the preaching of the Gospel, arguing forcefully that, as Pius XI was to say long after, ''in the
Church of Christ, it is not possible even to think
of any authority granted without [a] legitimate mandate.'' That leads to an examination of the attributes of the true Church, after which St. Francis
takes up what he calls the ''Rules of Faith.'' He discerns eight: Scripture, Tradition, the Church, Councils, the Fathers, the Pope, miracles and natural
reason. Ultimately, however, all come down to this
one: ''[T]he sole and true rule of right-believing is
the Word of God preached by the Church of God.''

St. Francis has no patience with the suggestion
that in anything of doctrinal consequence the Catholic Church has wandered from the truth. ''He who
considers how perfectly authentic is the testimony
which God has given of the Church,'' he says, ''will
see that to say the Church errs is to say no less than
that God errs, or else that he is willing and desirous
for us to err; which would be a great blasphemy.''

This is not hollow triumphalism, however, for he
recognizes the faults of the Church's human clay.
In fact, if the Reformers had ''censured vices, proved
the inutility of certain decrees and censures, borrowed some holy counsels from the ethical books
of St. Gregory, and from St. Bernard's *De Consideratione,* brought forward some good plan for removing

the abuses which have crept into the administration
of benefices through the malice of the age and of
men, and had addressed themselves to His Holiness
with humility and gratitude, all good men would
have honoured them and favoured their designs.''
Unfortunately, that is *not* what happened. Instead:
''You listen to your ministers; impose silence upon
them as regards railings, detraction, calumnies
against the Holy See, and you will have your sermons half their length.''

Such spirited prose suggests the work's second
point of interest for the contemporary reader: its
literary quality.

St. Francis de Sales was a man of the Renaissance,
with an excellent classical and ecclesiastical education acquired at the University of Paris in the Jesuit
college of Clermont and at the University of Padua.
Plainly, too, he had outstanding natural gifts. The
literary first fruits of this combination of talent and
training—the essays in this book—exhibit an impres-
sively mature grasp of content and style. The work
has been called a monument of early French literature; already one sees operative in it that blend of
spiritual ardor and literary genius which would in
time produce *The Introduction to the Devout Life, The
Treatise on the Love of God,* and other works.

If this book is a literary monument, however, it
is a living one. Four centuries after they were written,
St. Francis' essays retain much of their original vi-
vacity and charm—qualities, happily, which are also
present in Mackey's older yet still very readable translation.

xlvi   *The Catholic Controversy*

He has a knack for the telling phrase: "Their scandal," he says of those who claim to be scandalized by the Church, "has no other subject than their own malice, which keeps ever tickling them to make them laugh in their iniquities"—but he is no less at home in passages rich in rhetorical artifice. For instance:

> Our Lord had cast the fire of his charity upon the earth, the Apostles blowing on it by their preaching had increased it and spread it throughout the world: you say it has been extinguished by the waters of ignorance and iniquity;—who shall enkindle it again? Blowing is of no use: what is to be done then? Perhaps we must strike again with nails and lance on Jesus Christ the holy living stone, to bring forth a new fire:—or shall it be enough to have Calvin or Luther in the world to relight it?

In this and many places like it, one sees what Pope Paul VI meant when he remarked (in an apostolic letter of 1967 celebrating the fourth centenary of the Saint's birth) that St. Francis de Sales "reinstated sacred eloquence and let it flow like a broad river."

Finally, there is the evidence afforded here of the author's special qualities of character. Biographers never tire of speaking of his kindliness, his amiability; together with the zeal for souls which St. Jane de Chantal considered his outstanding characteristic, it constitutes the distinctive Salesian trait. And, as these essays illustrate, kindliness peeps through along with zeal even when St. Francis turns his hand to controversy.

He can, and does, write with strenuous indignation about those he blames for fracturing Christendom and leading souls away from the true Church. But by the standards of the time, even his polemics are gentle—an exercise in wit and the rhetoric of argumentation rather than a violent verbal assault on his adversaries. Mackey calls this "true controversy, yet unlike all other controversy." Citing his "supreme mildness and benignity," Pope Paul VI says of St. Francis: "He is never violent in dispute, he loves those who err while he corrects errors." One recalls St. Francis' remark to Theodore de Beza, Calvin's successor, with an eye to whose conversion Pope Clement VIII had sent him to Geneva: "Sir, I have not come to dispute with you but to talk with you frankly about the most important business that you can have in the world." It is that spirit which makes this volume not only a valuable record of the Counter-Reformation but a lasting testimonial to a saintly heart, at once ardent and charitable, which has much to say to the ecumenical movement of our times.

Over a century ago, Leigh Hunt captured something of this spirit in a panegyric, "The Gentleman Saint," which praised St. Francis by measuring him by Samuel Johnson: ". . . a man as sensible as Dr. Johnson, with all the piety and patience the Doctor desired to have, all the lowliness and kind fellowship it would have puzzled him to behold in a prelate, and all the delicacy and truth which would have trans-

ported him.'' Today's readers may not refer so readily to Dr. Johnson, but they will find ample evidence
here to support this praise of St. Francis de Sales.

—Russell Shaw

ST. FRANCIS DE SALES
AND THE ORIGIN OF
THE CATHOLIC CONTROVERSY

———◆———

The Catholic Controversy is a remarkable work, a book one would admire as the accomplishment of a middle-aged cleric who had spent years in study and who had a long history of pastoral experience behind him. But the fact is that St. Francis wrote these pages between the ages of 27 and 29, beginning about one year after his ordination to the priesthood. He wrote them during a seemingly hopeless mission to win back to the Faith the 72,000 Calvinists in the Chablais (now eastern France). These people had heard just about nothing of the True Faith since the Church had been virtually obliterated in their area 60 years earlier by violent persecution and heavy fines for worshiping in the old religion (Catholicism). The government had recently returned to Catholic hands in principle, but the Calvinists still held sway and were adamant against a return to the old Faith. Salesian tradition tells us that when St. Francis arrived, only 27 persons out of the 72,000 were still Catholic, but that after four years of his efforts, the figure was exactly reversed, there remaining only 27 Calvinists: seventy-two thousand souls had returned to the True Faith. It is one of the most remarkable conversion stories in all Catholic history.

When St. Francis set out on this assignment on September 14, 1594, he was accompanied by his cousin, Canon Louis de Sales, though Louis returned home shortly because of a critical lack of funds. Entering into the Chablais, St. Francis would be seen as both a religious and a political enemy (although he had been invited in by the Duke), so for the time being he made the garrison of Allinges his home base, though he almost never accepted the offer of an armed escort as he traveled about the region on foot; he made light of the occasional physical attacks he had to face. This high-born young man of the nobility, with two university degrees—one in civil law and one in canon law—spent his first winter tramping around the countryside going door to door searching out Catholics and trying to make a friendly contact here and there among the Protestants. St. Francis' main financial support was supposed to come from his family, but his father, who deeply disapproved of Francis' mission to the Chablais, refused to send him any money. It was left to his mother to send him surreptitiously some items of necessary clothing and a little money.

Sometimes St. Francis would spend the night in a hayloft, and on one occasion, to escape from wolves, he spent the night in a tree after tying himself onto a branch so he would not fall off in his sleep; some peasants found him the next morning and unfastened him, numb with cold. Though St. Francis had a strong constitution, he always suffered from poor circulation, which made the cold winter even more painful for him.

For many months, the results of St. Francis' mission were about nil. He had found a few Catholics, but Calvinists were afraid to listen to him preach, even if they wanted to, for fear of reprisals, and the Saint was often greeted with jeers and stones. The one hopeful sign he could count was the fact that one or two Calvinist leaders had gone out of their way to be friendly to him. Some people "back home" did not approve of St. Francis' work, as they felt he might be stirring up political trouble. Yet in the midst of these struggles, during a month-long break from his arduous mission, St. Francis was to receive a special grace on the Feast of Corpus Christi. During prayer he experienced a sense of closeness to God which made him say, "Hold back, O Lord, this flow of grace. Come not so near me, for I am not strong enough to endure the greatness of Your consoling touch, which forces me to the ground." This was one of the extraordinary graces which St. Francis de Sales received during his life.

As time went on and St. Francis saw his efforts to preach to the Calvinists frustrated, he began to work on another approach: writing pamphlets. In these pamphlets the Apostle of the Chablais could say the things he could not preach to the Calvinists in person. These little tracts in defense of the truths of the Faith would be small enough to be slipped under the doors of those the Saint wished to reach. Soon he was having them printed to be passed out hand to hand and also to be posted in appropriate places.

It was these pamphlets that would be gathered together after St. Francis' death and published as *Controversies*, or *The Catholic Controversy*. They are remarkably to the point, showing a thorough grasp of the Calvinist claims, courage in standing up to them, and a keen intelligence in exposing them. Despite the fact that St. Francis de Sales had only three books with him for reference (the Bible, St. Robert Bellarmine's *Controversies* and St. Peter Canisius' *Catechism*), his learning is obvious, as he confidently quotes the Sacred Scriptures, the Fathers and Doctors of the Church and speaks of the Greek and Hebrew versions of the Bible. Yet these pamphlets were by no means academic; St. Francis was right there in the thick of the religious controversy fray, and he knew exactly what points to go after.

The tracts apparently did their work, enabling the Saint to reach his intended audience, who would not listen to him, and enabling the Calvinists to see that it is the Catholic Church, after all, which is the true religion of Christ, with the mission to teach in His name.

These people who for 60 years—two or three entire generations—had not heard what the Catholic Faith teaches now learned about it again. Centuries later, in declaring St. Francis de Sales a Doctor of the Church (1877), Pope Pius IX stated that this book is "a full and complete demonstration of the Catholic religion." St. Francis begins his argument with an examination of *mission* from God, showing that the Catholic Church possesses this mission and the Protestant sects do not. He also delineates eight

Rules of Faith—Holy Scripture, the Apostolic Traditions, the authority of the Church, the authority
of Councils, the authority of the ancient Fathers of
the Church, the authority of the Pope, miracles, and
the harmony between faith and reason—showing how
all point to the Catholic Faith as the divinely given
religion. He states: "Ultimately, however, the sole
and true Rule of right-believing is the Word of God
preached by the Church of God." But why, he asks,
should anyone bow to the supposed authority of a
Luther or a Calvin?

Our admiration of St. Francis' technique must
not blind us to the fact that his weapons were first
of all spiritual. He had planned to take Geneva by
love—"Love will shake the walls of Geneva." "Ardent prayer must break down the walls of Geneva
and brotherly love charge them . . . Everything gives
way to love. Love is as strong as death, and to him
who loves, nothing is hard. . . ." In speaking of his
hope to win back the Chablais for the Church, St.
Francis said, "But the way to this is the propitiation
of Almighty God by our penances." A huge mural
in the Visitation Monastery of Thonon in the Chablais gives another clue to the Saint's success: It pic-
tures him and his cousin Louis invoking the Guardian
Angel of the diocese as they approached the region
for the first time. And it will be recalled that in his
youth St. Francis had promised Our Lady to pray
the Rosary daily. His apostolic use of intelligence,
perseverance and personal contact were certainly
fueled and directed by much grace.

St. Francis' own beautiful personality played a

large part here, as it would for the rest of his apostolic life. He took time to speak with the peasants, joining in the daily chitchat. To a talkative old woman who loved to converse with him and who one day said she was scandalized by the celibacy of the clergy, St. Francis answered, "But, my dear, you keep on coming to see me. Think of the time it takes to talk to you. How on earth could I manage to help you with all your difficulties if I had a wife and children!"

Slowly the tide began to turn, such that on Christmas day of 1596 St. Francis felt bold enough to offer the first public Mass offered in Thonon in 60 years. (He had made that city his headquarters some time before.) The fact that there was no public disturbance on this occasion was in itself a sign of the great progress made in the preceding two years. The church furnishings were gone, and he had to make do with, as he expressed it, a "badly made, simple wooden altar we put together for Christmas."

Having the Mass gave the Catholics new heart and set many Calvinists to thinking. The following Lent, however, some of the latter created a great disturbance when St. Francis proceeded to restore the old Catholic custom of giving out ashes; in the face of threats of prison and even death, he had to retreat out an open door.

When St. Francis de Sales had been in the area three years, he organized a Forty Hours Adoration—40 hours of continual solemn exposition of the Blessed Sacrament, accompanied by constant prayers. This was then a new devotion which had started in Italy, but was not yet widespread. It was still too risky to hold it in the city of Thonon, but a procession of 500 people began in Thonon and moved 18 miles to the town of Annemasse, where the devotion would be held. Another procession, headed by the Bishop, came up from Annecy. Many more people joined along the way, and in the end something like 30,000, including some curious Calvinists, were present. A year later Forty Hours Devotion was again held, this time in Thonon itself. At this occasion, many Protestants asked to be baptized and confirmed—200 from one parish, 60 from another, etc. Priests and a bishop were busy administering the Sacraments. Another Forty Hours was held two weeks later, attended by officials of Church and State. On this occasion the Papal Legate was present to receive the abjurations of Protestantism from many notable persons; the Vatican Archives has a list of some 2,300.

Around this time there was a stir over a report of a miracle attributed to St. Francis de Sales. A baby, the child of a Protestant mother, had died without Baptism. St. Francis had gone to speak to the mother about Catholic doctrine, and prayed that the child would be restored to life long enough to receive Baptism. His prayer was granted, and the whole family became Catholic.

With souls being won back to God and the Church, St. Francis' task became one of an administrator who had to reopen parishes and obtain the missals, chalices, crosses and other needed items which had disappeared over the years. Around 18 parishes would come back into operation. A priest named Père

Cherubin would largely take charge of these matters, with St. Francis de Sales in the background to help out in difficulties. At this point, St. Francis was still only 31 years old.

Soon after the conversion of the Chablais, political conflicts again arose to test the new converts' faith, but they held firm. This is a testimony to the fact that St. Francis had gone right to the core with his little tracts, dismantling the very heart of the Calvinist position, rather than simply engaging in ostentatious rhetoric. And of course he went beyond tearing down, as he worked to rebuild the edifice of faith that had been possessed by the Catholic ancestors of these peasants of the Chablais three generations before.

When one considers the poor prospects of success St. Francis had faced at the beginning of his mission to the Chablais, the results are rightly seen as truly remarkable. In one of his later sermons St. Francis would assure his hearers that no amount of preaching and exhortation will produce religious vocations, which are something only God can give; he would certainly affirm the same thing with regard to conversions to the Faith. We can be sure that we will never on this earth know the full story behind the remarkable success of St. Francis de Sales' mission to the Chablais.

We are indeed blessed to have, four centuries later, these tracts which were so instrumental in so many conversions. They are still apropos today, as the same objections against the Faith have unfortunately seen a resurgence in recent years. We hope that St. Francis de Sales' pamphlets may still work today to clear away obstacles to the acceptance of the Catholic Faith in minds and hearts and lead many back to that ancient and ever fresh and pure Faith which is the Faith of Peter, the Faith of our Fathers, the Faith left to us by Our Lord Jesus Christ Himself and still taught the world over by the Roman Catholic Church.

—The Publishers
November 28, 1989

AUTHOR'S GENERAL INTRODUCTION.*

by St. Francis de Sales

GENTLEMEN, having prosecuted for some space of time the preaching of the Word of God in your town, without obtaining a hearing from your people save rarely, casually, and stealthily,—wishing to leave nothing undone on my part, I have set myself to put into writing some principal reasons, chosen for the most part from the sermons and instructions which I have hitherto addressed to you by word of mouth, in defence of the faith of the Church. I should indeed have wished to be heard, as the accusers have been ; for words in the mouth are living, on paper dead. " The living voice," says S. Jerome, " has a certain indescribable secret strength, and the heart is far more surely reached by the spoken word than by writing." † This it is which made the glorious Apostle S. Paul say in the Scripture : *How shall they believe him of whom they have not heard ? And how shall they hear without a preacher ? . . . Faith then cometh by hearing, and hearing by the word of Christ.*‡ My best chance, then, would have been to be heard, in lack of which this writing will not be without good results. (1.) It will carry to your houses what you will not receive

* Addressed to the inhabitants of Thonon.   [Tr.]
† Ep. *ad Paulinum.*   ‡ Rom. x.

2 The Catholic Controversy.

at our house, at our meetings. (2.) It will satisfy
those who, as sole answer to the arguments I bring
forward, say that they would like to see them laid
before some minister, and who believe that the mere
presence of the adversary would make them tremble,
grow pale, and faint away, taking from them all
strength; now they can be laid before them. (3.)
Writing can be better handled; it gives more leisure
for consideration than the voice does; it can be
pondered more profoundly. (4.) It will be seen that
I deny a thousand impieties which are attributed to
Catholics; this is not in order to escape from the difficulty, as some have said, but to follow the holy intention of the Church; for I write in everybody's sight,
and under the censorship of superiors, being assured
that, while people will find herein plenty of ignorance,
they will not find, God helping, any irreligion or any
opposition to the doctrines of the Roman Church.

I must, however, protest, for the relief of my conscience, that all these considerations would never have
made me take the resolution of writing. It is a trade
which requires apprenticeship, and belongs to learned
and more cultivated minds. To write well, one must
know extremely well; mediocre wits must content
themselves with speech, wherein gesture, voice, play
of feature, brighten the word. Mine, which is of the
less, or, to say the downright truth, of the lowest
degree of mediocrity, is not made to succeed in this
exercise; and indeed I should not have thought of
it, if a grave and judicious gentleman had not invited
and encouraged me to do it: afterwards several of my
chief friends approved of it, whose opinion I so highly
value that my own has no belief from me save in default

of other. I have then put down here some principal reasons of the Catholic faith, which clearly prove that all are in fault who remain separated from the Catholic, Apostolic, and Roman Church. And I address and offer it to you with good heart, hoping that the causes which keep you from hearing me will not have power to hinder you from reading what I write. Meanwhile, I assure you, that you will never read a writing which shall be given you by any man more devoted to your spiritual service than I am ; and I can truly say that I shall never receive a command with more hearty accept-ance, than I did that which Monseigneur, our most reverend Bishop, gave me, when he ordered me, accord-ing to the holy desire of His Highness, whose letter he put into my hand, to come here and bring you the holy Word of God. Nor did I think that I could ever do you a greater service. And in fact I thought that as you will receive no other law for your belief than that interpretation of the Scripture which seems to you the best, you would hear also the interpretation which I should bring, viz., that given by the Apostolic Roman Church, which hitherto you have not had except perverted and quite disfigured and adulterated by the enemy, who well knew that had you seen it in its purity, never would you have abandoned it. The time is evil; the Gospel of Peace has hard striving to get heard amid so many rumours of war. Still I lose not courage; fruits a little late in coming pre-serve better than the forward ones. I trust that if Our Lord but once cry in your ears his holy *Ephpheta*, this slowness will result in much the greater sureness. Take then, gentlemen, in good part, this present which I make you, and read my reasons attentively. The hand of God is not withered nor shortened, and readily shows its power in feeble and low things. If you have with so much promptitude heard one of the parties, have yet patience to hear the other. Then take, I charge you on the part of God, take time and leisure to calm your understanding, and pray God to assist you with his Holy Spirit in a question of such great importance, in order that he may address you unto salvation. But above all I beg you never to let other passion enter your spirits than the passion of Our Lord and Master Jesus Christ, by which we all have been redeemed and shall be saved, unless we are wanting on our part; since he *desires that all men should be saved and should come to the knowledge of his truth.** I beseech his sacred Majesty that he would deign to help me and you in this affair, as he deigned to regard the glorious Apostle S. Paul [whose] conversion [we celebrate] to-day.

All comes back to the saying of the prophet, *Destruction is thy own, O Israel!*† Our Lord was the true Saviour who came to enlighten every man and to be a light unto the revelation of the Gentiles, and the glory of Israel; whereas Israel takes hereby occasion of ignominy. Is not this a great misfortune ? And when it is said that he is set for the ruin of many, this must be understood as to the actual event, not as to the intention of the divine Majesty. As the Tree of the knowledge of good and evil had no virtue to teach Adam either good or evil, though the event gave it this name, because Adam by taking the fruit experienced the evil which his disobedience caused him. The Son of God came for peace and benediction, and

* 1 Tim. ii. 4. † Osee xiii. 9.

not for evil to men ; unless some madman would dare
to cast up to our Lord his holy Word : *Woe to that
man through whom scandal cometh,** and would condemn
him by his own law to have a millstone tied about
his neck and be cast into the depths of the sea. Let
us then confess that not one of us men is scandalised
save by his own fault. This is what I undertake to
prove by force of argument. O my God, my Saviour,
purify my spirit ; make this your word distil sweetly
into the hearts of my readers, as a sacred dew, to cool
the ardour of the passions which they may have ;
and they shall see how true, in you, and in the Church
your Spouse, is that which you have said.

It was, I think, that great facility which men find
for taking scandal, which made Our Lord say that
scandals needs must come,† or, as S. Matthew says,
Woe to the world because of scandals; ‡ for if men take
occasion of their harm from the sovereign good itself,
how could there not be scandals in a world where
there are so many evils ? §

Now there are three sorts of scandals, and all three
very evil in their nature, but unequally so. There is
a scandal which our learned theologians call *active.*
And this is a bad action which gives to another an
occasion of wrong-doing, and the person who does this
action is justly called scandalous. The two other sorts
of scandal are called *passive* scandals, some of them
passive scandals *ab extrinseco,* others *ab intrinseco.* For
of persons who are scandalised, some are so by the bad
actions of another, and receive the active scandal, letting their wills be affected by the scandal ; but some

---

* Matt. xviii. 7.   † Luke xvii. 1.   ‡ xviii. 7.
§ See, in note to Preface, a fuller treatment of the subject of scandal.

are so by their own malice, and, having otherwise no occasion, build and fabricate them in their own brain, and scandalise themselves with a scandal which is all of their own making. He who scandalises another fails in charity towards his neighbour, he who scandalises himself fails in charity towards himself, and he who is scandalised by another is wanting in strength and firmness. The first is scandalous, the second scandalous and scandalised, the third scandalised only. The first scandal is called *datum*, given, the second *acceptum*, taken, the third *receptum*, received. The first passes the third in evil, and the second so much passes the first that it contains first and second, being active and passive both together, as the murdering and destroying oneself is a cruelty more against nature than the killing another. All these kinds of scandal abound in the world, and one sees nothing so plentiful as scandal: it is the principal trade of the devil; whence Our Lord said, *Woe to the world because of scandals.* But scandal taken without occasion holds the chief place by every right, [being] the most frequent, the most dangerous, and the most injurious.

And it is of this alone that Our Lord is the object in souls which are given up as a prey to iniquity. But a little patience: Our Lord cannot be scandalous, for all in him is sovereignly good; nor scandalised, for he is sovereignly powerful and wise;—how then can it happen that one should be scandalised in him, and that he should be set for the ruin of many? It would be a horrible blasphemy to attribute our evil to his Majesty. *He wishes that every one should be saved and should come to the knowledge of his truth.* He would have no one perish. Our destruction is from ourselves, and our *help* from his divine goodness.* Our Lord then does not scandalise us, nor does his holy Word, but we are scandalised in him, which is the proper way of speaking in this point, as himself teaches, saying: *Blessed is he that shall not be scandalised in me.*† And when it is said that he has been set for the ruin of many, we must find this verified in the event, which was that many were ruined on account of him, not in the intention of the supreme goodness, which had only sent him as a light for the revelation of the Gentiles and for the glory of Israel. But if there are men who would say the contrary, they have nothing left [as I have said] but to curse their Saviour with his own words: *Woe to him by whom scandal cometh.*

I beseech you, let us look in ourselves for the cause of our vices and sins. Our will is the only source of them. Our mother Eve indeed tried to throw the blame on the serpent, and her husband to throw it on her, but the excuse was not valid. They would have done better to say the honest *peccavi*, as David did, whose sin was immediately forgiven.

I have said all this, gentlemen, to make known to you whence comes this great dissension of wills in matter of religion, which we see amongst those who in their mouths make profession of Christianity. This is the principal and sovereign scandal of the world, and, in comparison with the others, it alone deserves the name of scandal, and it seems to be almost exactly the same thing when Our Lord says it is necessary that

* The Saint adds in margin : *This is the will of God, your sanctification.* 1 Thess. iv. 3. [Tr.]
† Matt. xi. 6.

scandals come, and St. Paul says that *there must be heresies;* * for this scandal changes with time, and, like a violent movement, gradually grows weaker in its evilness.   In those Christians who begin the division and this civil war, heresy is a scandal simply *taken,* passive *ab intrinseco,* and there is no evil in the heresiarch save such as is entirely in his own will; no one has part in this but himself.   The scandal of the first whom he seduces already begins to be divided;—but unequally, for the heresiarch has his share therein on account of his solicitation, the seduced have a share as much the greater as they have had less occasion of following him.   Their heresy having taken root, those who are born of heretical parents among the heretics have ever less share in the fault: still neither these nor those come to be without considerable fault of their own, and particularly persons of this age, who are almost all in purely passive scandal.   For the Scripture which they handle, the neighbourhood of true Christians, the marks which they see in the true Church, take from them all proper excuse; so that the Church from whom they are separated can put before them the words of her Lord: *Search the Scriptures, for you think in them to have life everlasting: and the same are they that give testimony of me.*†   *The works that I do in the name of my Father, they give testimony of me.*‡

Now I have said that their scandal is purely or almost purely passive.   For it is well known that the occasion they pretend to have for their division and departure is the error, the ignorance, the idolatry, which they aver to be in the Church they have abandoned, while it is a thing perfectly certain that the

* 1 Cor. xi. 19.   † John v. 39.   ‡ Ib. x. 25.

Church in her general body cannot be scandalous, or scandalised, being like her Lord, who communicates to her by grace and particular assistance what is proper to him by nature: for being her Head he guides her feet in the right way. The Church is his mystical body, and therefore he takes as his own the honour and the dishonour that are given to her; so it cannot be said that she gives, takes, or receives any scandal. Those then who are scandalised in her do all the wrong and have all the fault: their scandal has no other subject than their own malice, which keeps ever tickling them to make them laugh in their iniquities.

See then what I intend to show in this little treatise. I have no other aim than to make you see, gentlemen, that this Susanna is wrongfully accused, and that she is justified in lamenting over all those who have turned aside from her commandments in the words of her Spouse: *They have hated me without cause.**

This I will do in two ways: (1.) by certain general reasons; (2.) by particular examples which I will bring forward of the principal difficulties, by way of illustration. All that so many learned men have written tends and returns to this, but not in a straight line. For each one proposes a particular path to follow. I will try to reduce all the lines of my argument to this point as to the centre as exactly as I can. The first part will serve almost equally for all sorts of heretics: the second will be addressed rather to those whose reunion we have the strongest duty to effect. So many great personages have written in our age, that their posterity have scarcely anything more to say, but have only to consider, learn, imitate, admire. I will there-

* John xv. 25.

fore say nothing new and would not wish to do so.
All is ancient, and there is almost nothing of mine
beyond the needle and thread: the rest I have only
had to unpick and sew again in my own way, with
this warning of Vincent of Lerins: "Teach, however,
what thou hast learnt; that whilst thou sayest things
in a new way thou say not new things." *

This treatise will seem perhaps to some a little too
meagre: this does not come from my stinginess but
from my poverty. My memory has very little stored
up, and is kept going only from day to day; and I
have but very few books here with which I can enrich
myself. But still receive favourably, I beg you,
gentlemen of Thonon, this work, and though you have
seen many better made and richer, still give some little
of your attention to this, which will perhaps be more
adapted to your taste than the others are; for its air
is entirely Savoyard, and one of the most profitable
prescriptions, and the last remedy, is a return to one's
natal air. If this profit you not, you shall try others
more pure and more invigorating, for there are, thank
God, of all sorts in this country. I am about therefore to begin, in the name of God, whom I most
humbly beseech to make his holy Word distil sweetly
as a refreshing dew into your heart. And I beg you,
gentlemen, and those who read this, to remember the
words of S. Paul: *Let all bitterness and anger, and
indignation, and clamour, and blasphemy be taken away
from you, with all malice. Amen.*†

* Comm. 1$^{um.}$ cap. xxxvii.   † Eph. iv. 31.

PART I.

𝕸𝖎𝖘𝖘𝖎𝖔𝖓.

CHAPTER I.

THE LACK OF MISSION IN THE MINISTERS OF THE NEW PRETENDED CHURCH LEAVES BOTH THEM AND THEIR FOLLOWERS WITHOUT EXCUSE.

FIRST, then, your ministers had not the conditions required for the position which they sought to maintain, and the enterprise which they undertook. Wherefore they are inexcusable; and you yourselves also, who knew and still know or ought to know, this defect in them, have done very wrong in receiving them under such colours. The office they claimed was that of ambassadors of Jesus Christ Our Lord; the affair they undertook was to declare a formal divorce between Our Lord and the ancient Church his Spouse; to arrange and conclude by words of present consent, as lawful procurators, a second and new marriage with this young madam, of better grace, said they, and more seemly than the other. For in effect, to stand up as preacher of God's Word and pastor of souls,—what is it but to call oneself ambassador and legate of Our Lord, according to that of the Apostle : * *We are therefore ambassadors for Christ ?* And to say that the whole of Christendom has failed, that the whole Church has erred, and all truth disappeared,—what is this but to say that Our Lord has abandoned his Church, has broken the sacred tie of marriage he had contracted with her ? And to put forward a new Church,—is it not to attempt to thrust upon this sacred and holy Husband a second wife ? This is what the ministers of the pretended church have undertaken ; this is what they boast of having done ; this has been the aim of their discourses, their designs, their writings. But what an injustice have you not committed in believing them ? How did you come to take their word so simply ? How did you so lightly give them credit ?

To be legates and ambassadors they should have been sent, they should have had letters of credit from him whom they boasted of being sent by. The affairs were of the greatest importance, for there was question of disturbing the whole Church. The persons who undertook them were extraordinaries, of mean quality, and private persons ; while the ordinary pastors were men of mark, and of most ancient and acknowledged reputation, who contradicted them and protested that these extraordinaries had no charge nor commandment of the Master. Tell me, what business had you to hear them and believe them without having any assurance of their commission and of the approval of Our Lord, whose legates they called themselves ? In a word, you have no justification for having quitted that ancient Church in which you were baptized, on the

* 2 Cor. v. 20.

faith of preachers who had no legitimate mission from the Master.

Now you cannot be ignorant that they neither had, nor have, in any way at all, this mission. For if Our Lord had sent them, it would have been either mediately or immediately. We say mission is given mediately when we are sent by one who has from God the power of sending, according to the order which he has appointed in his Church; and such was the mission of S. Denis into France by Clement and of Timothy by S. Paul. Immediate mission is when God himself commands and gives a charge, without the interposition of the ordinary authority which he has placed in the prelates and pastors of the Church: as S. Peter and the Apostles were sent, receiving from Our Lord's own mouth this commandment : *Go ye into the whole world, and preach the Gospel to every creature ;* * and as Moses received his mission to Pharao and to the people of Israel. But neither in the one nor in the other way have your ministers any mission. How then have they undertaken to preach ? *How shall they preach,* says the Apostle, *unless they be sent ?* †

CHAPTER II.

THAT THE PRETENDED REFORMERS HAD NO MEDIATE MISSION EITHER FROM THE PEOPLE OR THE BISHOPS.

AND first, as to ordinary and mediate mission, they have none whatever. For what they can put forward is either that they are sent by the people and secular

* Mark xvi. 15.   † Rom. x. 15.

princes, or else that they are sent by the imposition
of the hands of the bishops who made them priests, a
dignity to which at last they must have recourse,
although they despise it altogether and everywhere.

Now, if they say that the secular magistrates and
people have sent them, they will have two proofs to give
which they never can give, the one that the seculars have
done it, the other that they could do it, for we deny
both the fact and the right (*factum et jus faciendi*).

And that they could not do it the reason is absolute.
For (1.) they will never find that the people and
secular magistrates had the power to establish and
institute bishops in the Church.* They will indeed
perhaps find that the people have given testimony and
assisted at ordinations; yea, perhaps, that the choice
has been given to them, like that of the deacons, as
S. Luke tells us (Acts vi.), which the whole body
of the faithful made; but they will never show that
the people or secular princes have authority to give
mission or to appoint pastors. How then do they
allege a mission by people or princes, which has no
foundation in the Scripture? (2.) On the contrary,
we bring forward the express practice of the whole
Church, which from all time has been to ordain the
pastors by the imposition of the hands of the other
pastors and bishops. Thus was Timothy ordained;
and the seven deacons themselves, though proposed
by the Christian people, were ordained by the imposi-

---

* The Saint in a detached note elsewhere draws particular attention
to the necessity of mission shown in the fact that Jeroboam is rebuked
not for dividing the kingdom but for dividing the Church, and making
temples in the high places, *and priests of the lowest of the people, who
were not sons of Levi.* (3 Kings xii. 31.)

tion of the Apostles' hands. Thus have the Apostles
appointed in their Constitutions; and the great Council
of Nice (which methinks one will not despise) and that
of Carthage—the second, and then immediately the
third, and the fourth, at which S. Augustine assisted.
If then they have been sent by the laity, they are not
sent in Apostolic fashion, nor legitimately, and their
mission is null. (3.) In fact, the laity have no mission, and how then shall they give it ? How shall
they communicate the authority which they have not ?
And therefore S. Paul, speaking of the priesthood and
pastoral order, says : *Neither doth any man take the
honour to himself but he that is called by God, as Aaron
was* (Heb. x. 4). Now Aaron was consecrated and
ordained by the hands of Moses, who was a priest
himself, according to the holy word of David (Ps.
xcviii. 7), *Moses and Aaron among his priests and
Samuel among those who call upon his name*; and, as
is indicated in Exodus (xxviii. 1) in this word, *Take
unto thee also Aaron thy brother, with his sons . . . that
they may minister to me in the priest's office;* with
which agree a great army of our Ancients. Whoever
then would assert his mission must not assert it
as being from the people nor from secular princes.
For Aaron was not called in that way, and we cannot
be called otherwise than he was. (4.) Finally, *that
which is less is blessed by the better,* as S. Paul says
(Heb. vii. 7). The people then cannot send the
pastors ; for the pastors are greater than the people,
and mission is not given without blessing.* For after
this magnificent mission the people remain sheep, and

---

* *Amen, Amen, I say to you ; the servant is not greater than his Lord,
neither is an Apostle greater than he that sent him* (John xiii. 16).

the shepherd remains shepherd. (5.) I do not insist
here, as I will prove it hereafter, that the Church is
monarchical, and that therefore the right of sending
belongs to the chief pastor, not to the people. I omit
the disorder which would arise if the people sent; for
they could not send to one another, one people having
no authority over the other;—and what free play would
this give to all sorts of heresies and fancies? It is
necessary then that the sheep should receive the shepherd
from elsewhere, and should not give him to themselves.*

The people therefore were not able to give legitimate mission or commission to these new ambassadors.
But I say further that even if they could they did not.
For this people was of the true Church or not: if
it was of the true Church why did Luther take it
therefrom? Would it really have called him in order
to be taken out of its place and of the Church?
And if it were not of the true Church, how could
it have the right of mission and of vocation?—outside the true Church there cannot be such authority.
If they say this people was not Catholic, what was
it then? It was not Lutheran; for we all know
that when Luther began to preach in Germany there
were no Lutherans, and it was he who was their
origin. Since then such a people did not belong to
the true Church, how could it give mission for true
preaching? They have then no vocation from that
source, unless they have recourse to the invisible
mission received from the principalities and powers of
the world of this darkness, and the spiritual wicked-

* Here may be added a detached note of the Saint's. " Acts xv. 24 :
*Forasmuch as we have heard that some who went out from us have troubled
you with words, to whom we gave no commands.* If they had given
charge, much less would they themselves teach without charge."

nesses against which good Catholics have always waged war. Many therefore of our age, seeing the road cut off on that side, have betaken themselves to the other, and say that the first masters and reformers,—Luther, Bucer, Œcolampadius,—were sent by the bishops who made them priests; then they sent their followers, and so they would go on to blend their rights with those of the Apostles.

In good sooth it is to speak frankly (*parler Français*) and plainly indeed, thus to confess that mission can only have passed to their ministers from the Apostles by the succession of our bishops and the imposition of their hands. Of course the case is really so: one cannot give this mission so high a fall that from the Apostles it should leap into the hands of the preachers of now-a-days without having touched any of our ancients and foregoers: it would have required a very long speaking-tube (*sarbacane*) in the mouth of the first founders of the Church to call Luther and the rest without being overheard by any of those who were between: or else, as Calvin says on another occasion, not much to the point, these must have had very long ears. It must have been kept sound indeed, if these were to find it. We agree then that mission was possessed by our bishops, and particularly by their head, the Roman Bishop. But we formally deny that your ministers have had any communication of it, to preach what they have preached. Because (1.) they preach things contrary to the Church in which they have been ordained priests; therefore either they err or the Church which has sent them errs;—and consequently either their church is false or the one from which they have taken mission.

III.

If it be that from which they have taken mission, their mission is false, for from a false Church there cannot spring a true mission. Whichever way it be, they had no mission to preach what they preached, because, if the Church in which they have been ordained were true, they are heretics for having left it, and for having preached against its belief, and if it were not true it could not give them mission. (2.) Besides, though they had had mission in the Roman Church, they had none to leave it, and withdraw her children from her obedience. Truly the commissioner must not exceed the limits of his commission, or his act is null. (3.) Luther, Œcolampadius, and Calvin were not bishops: how then could they communicate any mission to their successors on the part of the Roman Church, which protests always and everywhere that it is only the bishops who can send, and that this belongs in no way to simple priests? In which even S. Jerome has placed the difference between the simple priest and the bishop, in the *Epistle to Evagrius,* and S. Augustine * and Epiphanius † reckon Aerius with heretics because he held the contrary.

CHAPTER III.

THE PRETENDED REFORMERS HAD NO IMMEDIATE OR EXTRAORDINARY MISSION FROM GOD.

THESE reasons are so strong that the most solid of your party have taken ground elsewhere than in the ordinary mission, and have said that they were sent

* *De Hær.* 53.　　　† *Hæres.* 75.

CHAP. III.]   *Mission.*   19

extraordinarily by God because the ordinary mission had been ruined and abolished, with the true Church itself, under the tyranny of Antichrist. This is their most safe refuge, which, since it is common to all sorts of heretics, is worth attacking in good earnest and overthrowing completely. Let us then place our argument in order, to see if we can force this their last barricade.

First, I say then that no one should allege an extraordinary mission unless he prove it by miracles: for, I pray you, where should we be if this pretext of extraordinary mission was to be accepted without proof? Would it not be a cloak for all sorts of reveries? Arius, Marcion, Montanus, Messalius—could they not be received into this dignity of reformers, by swearing the same oath?

Never was any one extraordinarily sent unless he brought this letter of credit from the divine Majesty. Moses was sent immediately by God to govern the people of Israel. He wished to know his name who sent him; when he had learnt the admirable name of God, he asked for signs and patents of his commission: God so far found this request good that he gave him the grace of three sorts of prodigies and marvels, which were, so to speak, three attestations in three different languages, of the charge which he gave him, in order that any one who did not understand one might understand another. If then they allege extraordinary mission, let them show us some extraordinary works, otherwise we are not obliged to believe them. In truth Moses clearly shows the necessity of this proof for him who would speak extraordinarily: for having to beg from God the gift of eloquence, he only asks it after having the power of miracles; showing that it is more necessary to have authority to speak than to have readiness in speaking.

The mission of S. John Baptist, though it was not altogether extraordinary,—was it not authenticated by his conception, his nativity, and even by that miraculous life of his, to which our Lord gave such excellent testimony? But as to the Apostles,—who does not know the miracles they did and the great number of them? Their handkerchiefs, their shadow, served for the prompt healing of the sick and driving away of the devils: *by the hands of the apostles many signs and wonders were done amongst the people* (Acts xix. v.); and that this was in confirmation of their preaching S. Mark declares quite explicitly in the last words of his Gospel, and S. Paul to the Hebrews (ii. 4). How then shall those who in our age would allege an extraordinary mission excuse and relieve themselves of this proof of their mission? What privilege have they greater than an Apostolic, a Mosaic? What shall I say more. If our sovereign Master, consubstantial with the Father, having a mission so authentic that it comprises the communication of the same essence, if he himself, I say, who is the living source of all Ecclesiastical mission, has not chosen to dispense himself from this proof of miracles, what reason is there that these new ministers should be believed on their mere word? Our Lord very often alleges his mission to give credit to his words:—*As my Father hath sent me I also send you* (John xx. 21); *My doctrine is not mine, but of him that sent me* (ibid. vii. 16); *You both know me, and you know whence I am; and I am not come of myself* (ibid. 28). But also, to give authority to his mission, he brings forward his miracles, and attests that if he had not done among the Jews works which no other man had done, they would not have sinned in not believing him. And elsewhere he says to them : *Do you not believe that I am in the Father and the Father in me ?   Otherwise believe for the works themselves* (ibid. xiv. 11, 12).   He then who would be so rash as to boast of extraordinary mission without immediately producing miracles, deserves to be taken for an impostor. Now it is a fact that neither the first nor the last ministers have worked a single miracle : therefore they have no extraordinary mission. Let us proceed.

I say, in the second place, that never must an extraordinary mission be received when disowned by the ordinary authority which is in the Church of Our Lord. For, (1.) we are obliged to obey our ordinary pastors under pain of being heathens and publicans (Matt. xviii. 17) :—how then can we place ourselves under other discipline than theirs ?   Extraordinaries would come in vain, since we should be obliged to refuse to listen to them, in the case that they were, as I have said, disowned by the ordinaries.   (2.) God is not the author of *dissension, but of union and peace* (1 Cor. xiv. 33), principally amongst his disciples and Church ministers; as Our Lord clearly shows in the holy prayer he made to his Father in the last days of his mortal life (John xvii.)

How then should he authorise two sorts of pastors, the one extraordinary, the other ordinary ?   As to the ordinary—it certainly is authorised, and as to the extraordinary we are supposing it to be ; there would then be two different churches, which is contrary to

the most pure word of Our Lord, who has but one
sole spouse, one sole dove, one sole perfect one (Cant.
vi.) And how could that be a united flock which
should be led by two shepherds, unknown to each
other, into different pastures, with different calls
and folds, and each of them expecting to have the
whole. Thus would it be with the Church under a
variety of pastors ordinary and extraordinary, dragged
hither and thither into various sects. Or *is* Our Lord
divided (1 Cor. i. 13), either in himself or in his
body, which is the Church?—no, in good truth. On
the contrary, there is but one Lord, who has composed
his mystic body with a goodly variety of members, a
body *compacted and fitly joined together by what every
joint supplieth, according to the operation in the measure
of every part* (Eph. iv. 16). Therefore to try to make in
the Church this division of ordinary and extraordinary
members is to ruin and destroy it. We must then
return to what we said, that an extraordinary vocation
is never legitimate where it is disapproved of by the
ordinary. (3.) And in effect where will you ever show
me a legitimate extraordinary vocation which has not
been received by the ordinary authority. S. Paul was
extraordinarily called,—but was he not approved and
authorised by the ordinary once and again? (Acts ix.
xiii.) And the mission received from the ordinary
authority is called a mission by the Holy Spirit (ibid.
xiii. 4). The mission of S. John Baptist cannot properly be called extraordinary, because he taught nothing
contrary to the Mosaic Church, and because he was
of the priestly race. All the same, his doctrine being
unusual was approved by the ordinary teaching office
of the Jewish Church in the high embassy which was

sent to him by the priests and Levites (John i. 19), the tenor of which implies the great esteem and reputation in which he was with them; and the very Pharisees who were seated on the chair of Moses,— did they not come to communicate in his baptism quite openly and unhesitatingly? This truly was to receive his mission in good earnest. Did not Our Lord, who was the Master, will to be received by Simeon, who was a priest, as appears from his blessing Our Lady and Joseph; by Zachary the priest; and by S. John? And for his passion, which was the principal fulfilment of his mission,—did he not will to have the prophetic testimony of him who was High Priest at that time. And this is what S. Paul teaches when he will have no man to *take the* pastoral *honour to himself, but he that is called by God, as Aaron was* (Heb. v. 4). For the vocation of Aaron was made by the ordinary, Moses, so that it was not God who placed his holy word in the mouth of Aaron immediately, but Moses, whom God commanded to do it: *Speak to him, and put my words in his mouth; and I will be in thy mouth, and in his mouth* (Ex. iv. 15). And if we consider the words of S. Paul, we shall further learn that the vocation of pastors and Church rulers must be made visibly; and so with Our Lord and Master;—who, being sovereign pontiff, and pastor of all the ages, *did not glorify himself*, that is, did not *take to himself the honour* of his holy priesthood, as S. Paul had previously said, *but he who said to him: Thou art my Son, this day have I begotten thee;* and, *Thou art a priest for ever according to the order of Melchisedech.* I beg you to ponder this expression—Jesus Christ is *a high priest according to the order of Melchise-*

dech. Was he inducted and thrust into this honour by himself? No, he was called thereto. Who called him? His eternal Father. And how? Immediately and at the same time mediately: immediately at his Baptism and his Transfiguration, by this voice: *This is my beloved Son, in whom I am well pleased, hear ye him;* mediately by the Prophets, and above all by David in the places which S. Paul cites to this effect from the Psalms: *Thou art my Son, this day have I begotten thee: Thou art a priest for ever according to the order of Melchisedech.* And everywhere the vocation is externally perceptible: the word in the cloud was heard, and in David heard and read; but S. Paul when proving the vocation of Our Lord quotes only the passage from David, in which he says Our Lord had been glorified by his Father; thus contenting himself with bringing forward the testimony which was perceptible, and given by means of the ordinary Scriptures and the received Prophets.

I say, thirdly, that the authority of the extraordinary mission never destroys the ordinary, and is never given to overthrow it. Witness all the Prophets, who never set up altar against altar, never overthrew the priesthood of Aaron, never abolished the constitutions of the Synagogue. Witness Our Lord, who declares that *every kingdom divided against itself shall be brought to desolation, and a house upon a house shall fall* (Luke xi. 17). Witness the respect which he paid to the chair of Moses, the doctrine of which he would have to be observed. And indeed if the extraordinary ought to abolish the ordinary, how should we know when, and how, and to whom, to give our obedience. No, no; the ordinary is immortal for such time as the Church is here below in the world.   The pastors and teachers whom he has once given to the Church are to have a perpetual succession *for the perfection of the saints . . . till we all meet in the unity of faith, and of the knowledge of the Son of God, unto a perfect man, unto the measure of the age of the fulness of Christ. That we may not now be children, tossed to and fro, and carried about with every wind of doctrine, in the wickedness of men and in their craftiness* (Eph. iv.)   Such is the strong argument which S. Paul uses to prove that if the ordinary pastors and doctors had not perpetual succession, and were liable to have their authority abrogated by the extraordinary, we should also have but an irregular faith and discipline, interrupted at every step ; we should be liable to be seduced by men, who on every occasion would boast of having an extraordinary vocation.   Thus, *like the Gentiles we should walk* (as he infers afterwards) *in the vanity of* our *mind* (ibid. 17), each one persuading himself that he felt the movement of the Holy Ghost ; of which our age furnishes so many examples that this is one of the strongest proofs that can be brought forward in this connection. For if the extraordinary may take away the ordinary ministration, to which shall we give the guardianship of it—to Calvin or to Luther, to Luther or to Paciomontanus, to Paciomontanus or to Brandratus, to Brandratus or to Brentius, to Brentius or to the Queen of England ?—for each will draw to his or her side this pretext of extraordinary mission.

But the word of Our Lord frees us from all these difficulties, who has built his Church on so good a foundation and in such wise proportions that the gates of hell shall never prevail against it.   And if they have never prevailed nor shall prevail, then the extraordinary vocation is not necessary to abolish it, for *God hateth nothing of those things which he has made* (Wis. xi. 25). How then did they abolish the ordinary Church, to make an extraordinary one, since it is he who has built the ordinary one, and cemented it with his own blood?

CHAPTER IV.

AN ANSWER TO THE TWO OBJECTIONS WHICH ARE MADE BY THE SUPPORTERS OF THE THEORY OF IMMEDIATE MISSION.

I HAVE not been able hitherto to find but two objections amongst your masters to this reasoning which I have just made, one of which is taken from the example of Our Lord and the Apostles, the other from the example of the Prophets.

And as to the first—tell me, I pray, do you think it right to place in comparison the vocation of these new ministers and that of Our Lord? Had not Our Lord been prophesied as the Messias?—had not his time been determined by Daniel?—did he do a single action which had not been described almost exactly in the books of the Prophets, and prefigured in the Patriarchs? He changed the Mosaic law from good into better;—but had not this change been predicted? He consequently changed the Aaronic priesthood into that of Melchisedech, far better: is not all this according to the ancient testimonies? Your ministers have not been prophesied as preachers of the word of God, nor the time of their coming, nor a single one of their actions. They have made a revolution in the Church much greater and bolder than Our Lord made in the synagogue; for they have taken all away, only putting back certain shadows : but testimonies to this effect have they none. At any rate they should not elude their obligation of bringing forward miracles in support of such a change, whatever pretext you may draw from the Scriptures, since our Lord dispensed not himself from this, as I have shown above. But whence will they show me that the Church was ever to receive another form, or a like reformation to the one which our Lord made ?

And as to the Prophets, I see many persons under a delusion. It is supposed that all the vocations of the Prophets were extraordinary and immediate. A false idea : for there were colleges and congregations of the Prophets approved by the Synagogue, as may be gathered from many passages of the Scriptures. There were such in Ramatha, in Bethel, in Jericho where Eliseus dwelt, on Mount Ephraim, in Samaria ; Eliseus himself was anointed by Heli; the vocation of Samuel was recognised and approved by the High Priest; and with Samuel the Lord began to appear again in Silo, as says the Scripture : [*] whence the Jews regard Samuel as the founder of the congregations of Prophets.

It is supposed that all those who prophesied exercised the office of preaching;—which is not true, as appears from what occurred with the officers of Saul and with Saul himself : [†] in such sort that the vocation

* 1 Kings iii. 21.   † Ibid. xix.

of the Prophets has no bearing on that of heretics or
schismatics. For (1.) it was either ordinary, as we
have shown above, or else approved by the remainder
of the Synagogue, as is easy to see in their being
immediately recognised, and in their being highly
esteemed everywhere amongst the Jews, who called
them "men of God:" and he who will attentively
examine the history of that ancient Synagogue will
see that the office of priests was as common among
them as that of preachers amongst us. (2.) Never
can be pointed out Prophet who wished to overthrow
the ordinary power; on the contrary, all followed it,
and spoke nothing contrary to the doctrine of those
who sat upon the chair of Moses and of Aaron; indeed,
some of them were of the priestly race, as Jeremias
son of Helcias, and Ezechiel son of Buzi. They have
always spoken with honour of the priests and the
sacerdotal succession, though they have reprehended
their lives. Isaias, when about to write in a great
book which was shown him, took Urias the priest,
though the things were yet to come, and Zacharias the
prophet as witnesses,* as if he were taking the testimony of all the Priests and Prophets. And does not
Malachy bear witness † that *the lips of the priest shall
keep knowledge, and they shall seek the law at his mouth*:
because he is the Angel of the Lord of hosts?—so far
were they from ever having withdrawn the Jews from
the communion of the Ordinary. (3). How many
miracles did the Prophets work in confirmation of the
prophetic vocation? I should never end if I were to
enter upon the computation of these: but at such
times as they did a thing which had an appearance of

* Isa. viii. 1, 2. † ii. 7.

extraordinary power, immediately miracles followed.
Witness Elias, who, setting up an altar on Mount
Carmel according to the instinct which the Holy
Spirit had given him, and offering sacrifice, showed by
miracle that he did it to the honour of God and of the
Jewish religion. (4.) And finally, it would well become your ministers to usurp the power of the
Prophets—they who have never had either their gift
or their light! It should rather be for us to do so;—
for us, who could bring forward an infinity of Prophets
on our side. For instance, S. Gregory Thaumaturgus,
on the authority of S. Basil; S. Anthony, on the testimony of Athanasius; the Abbot John, on the testimony
of S. Augustine; S. Benedict, S. Bernard, S. Francis,
and a thousand others. If, then, there is question
between us of the prophetic authority, this is on our
side, be it ordinary or be it extraordinary, since we
have the reality; not with your ministers, who have
never given the shadow of a proof of its possession;—
unless they would call a prophecy Zwingle's vision in
the book called *Subsidium de Eucharistiâ,* and the
book entitled *Querela Lutherii,* or the prediction he
made in the twenty-fifth year of this century that if
he preached two years more there would remain no
Pope, nor priests, nor monks, nor belfries, nor mass.
Truly there is but one defect in this prophecy—just
want of truth. For he preached nigh twenty-two
years longer, and yet there are still found priests and
belfries, and in the chair of Peter sits a lawful Pope.

Your first ministers then, gentlemen, are of the
prophets whom God forbade to be heard, in Jeremias:*
Hearken not to the words of the prophets that prophesy

* xxiii.

*to you and deceive you: they speak a vision of their
own heart and not out of the mouth of the Lord. . . .
I did not send prophets, yet they ran: I have not spoken
to them, yet they prophesied. . . . I have heard what the
prophets said, that prophecy lies in my name, and say,
I have dreamed, I have dreamed.* Does it not seem
to you that it is Zwingle and Luther, with their prophecies and visions? that it is Carlostadt, with his
revelation which he pretended to have had about
the Lord's Supper, and which gave occasion to Luther
to write his book *Contra scelestos prophetas.* At any
rate they certainly possess this property of not having
been sent; it is they *who use their tongues, and say,
The Lord saith it.* For they can never prove any right
to the office which they usurp; they can never produce
any legitimate vocation. And how then shall they
preach? One cannot enrol oneself under any captain
without the approval of one's prince: how then were
you so ready to engage yourselves under the command
of these first ministers, without the permission of your
ordinary pastors, and so far as to leave the state in
which you were born and bred, which is the Catholic
Church? They are guilty of having made this disturbance by their own authority, and you of having
followed them, in which you are inexcusable. The
good little Samuel, humble, gentle, and holy, having
been called thrice by God, thought all the time that
it was Heli who was calling him, and only at the
fourth time addressed himself to God as to the one
calling him. It has seemed to your ministers that
God has thrice called them, (1.) by peoples and magistrates; (2.) by our bishops; (3.) by his extraordinary
voice. No, no! Let them not bring this forward,

that Samuel was called thrice by God, and in his
humility thought it was a call by man, until, instructed
by Heli, he knew that it was the divine voice. Your
ministers, gentlemen, allege three vocations of God,
by secular magistrates, by the bishops, and by his extraordinary voice. They think that it is God who has
called them in those three ways: but you do not find
that when they are instructed by the Church they acknowledge that theirs is a vocation of man, and that
their ears have tingled to the old Adam; by no means
do they submit the question to him who, as Heli did,
now presides in the Church.

Such then is the first reason which makes your
ministers and you also inexcusable, though unequally
so, before God and men in having left the Church.

On the contrary, gentlemen, the Church, who contradicted and opposed your first ministers, and still
opposes those of the present day, is so clearly marked
on all sides that no one, blind as he may be, can pretend that his is a case of ignorance of the duty which
all good Christians owe her, or that she is not the true,
sole, inseparable, and dearest Spouse of the heavenly
King, which makes the separation from her all the
more inexcusable. For, to leave the Church and dis-
regard her commands is evermore to become a heathen
and a publican, let it be at the persuasion of an
angel or a seraph. But, at the persuasion of men
who were sinners on the largest scale against other
private persons, who were without authority, without
approval, without any quality required in preachers
or prophets save the mere knowledge of certain
sciences, to break all the ties of the most religious
obligation of obedience which is in the world, namely,

that which is owing to the Church as Spouse of our Lord!—this is a fault which cannot be covered save by a great repentance and penitence—to which I invite you on the part of the living God.

CHAPTER V.

THAT THE INVISIBLE CHURCH FROM WHICH THE INNO-
VATORS PRETEND TO DERIVE THEIR MISSION IS A
FIGMENT; AND THAT THE TRUE CHURCH OF CHRIST
IS VISIBLE.

OUR adversaries, clearly perceiving that by this touch-stone their doctrine would be recognised as of base gold, try by all means to turn us from that invincible proof which we find in the marks of the true Church. And therefore they would maintain that the Church is invisible and unperceivable. I consider that this is the extreme of absurdity, and that immediately beyond this abide frenzy and madness. I speak of the militant Church of which the Scripture has left us testimony, not of that which men put forward. Now, in all the Scripture it will never be found that the Church is taken for an invisible assembly. Here are our reasons.

(1.) Our Lord and Master sends us to the Church in our difficulties and variances (Matt. xviii. 16, 17). S. Paul teaches how we ought *to behave in* it (1 Tim. iii. 15); *he called* together *the ancients of the Church* militant (Acts xx. 17); he shows them that they are *placed* by *the Holy Ghost* (ibid. 28); he is *sent* by *the*

Church, with S. Barnabas (ibid. xiii. 1, 3); he is *received by the Church* (ibid. xv. 4); *he confirmed the Churches* (ibid. 41); *he ordained for them priests in every Church* (ibid. xiv. 22); *he assembled the Church* (ibid. 26); *he saluted the Church* at Cæsarea (ibid. xviii. 22); *he persecuted the Church* (Gal. i. 13). How can all this be understood of an invisible Church? Where should one seek it to lay complaints before it, to converse in it, to rule it? When it sent S. Paul, and received him, when he confirmed it, ordained priests in it, assembled it, saluted it, persecuted it—was this in figure or in faith only, and in spirit? I am sure that everybody must see that these were visible and perceptible acts on both sides. And when he wrote to it, did he address himself to some invisible chimera?

(2.) What will be said about the Prophets, who represent the Church to us as not only visible, but quite distinct, illustrious, manifest, magnificent? They depict it as a queen *in golden borders clothed round about with varieties* (Ps. xliv. 14, 15); as a *mountain* (Isa. ii. 2); as a *sun* (Ps. lxxxviii.); as a full *moon;* as the rainbow, *a faithful* and certain *witness* of the favour of God towards men, who are all of the posterity of Noe: such is the signification of this Psalm in our version: *Et thronus ejus sicut sol in conspectu meo, et sicut luna perfecta in æternum et testis in cœlo fidelis.*

(3.) The Scripture everywhere testifies that she can be seen and known, yea, that she is known. Solomon, in the Canticle of Canticles (vi.), speaking of the Church,—does he not say that *the daughters saw her and declared her most blessed?* and then introducing the daughters, full of admiration he makes them say:

*Who is she that cometh forth as the morning rising,
fair as the moon, bright as the sun, terrible as an army
set in array?* Is this not to declare her visible?
And when he makes them call upon her thus: *Return,
return, O Sulamitess ; return, return, that we may
behold thee ;* and makes her answer: *What shalt thou
see in the Sulamitess but the companies of camps ?*—is
not this again to declare her visible ? If one regard
those admirable Canticles and pastoral representations
of the loves of the celestial Bridegroom with the
Church, one will see that she is throughout most
visible and prominent. Isaias speaks of her thus
(xxxv. 8): *This shall be unto you a straight way, so
that fools shall not err therein ;*—must she not be dis-
played and easy to see, since even the simplest shall
be able to guide themselves by her without fail ?

(4.) The pastors and doctors of the Church are
visible, therefore the Church is visible. For, I ask
you, are not the pastors of the Church a part of the
Church, and must not pastor and sheep know each
other, must not the sheep hear the shepherd's voice
and follow him, must not the good shepherd go seek
his sheep that is lost, and recognise his enclosure and
fold ? They would indeed be a fine sort of shepherd,
who could not know or see his flock. I know not
whether I am to prove that the pastors of the Church
are visible ; things as evident are denied. S. Peter
was a pastor, I suppose, since Our Lord said to him,
Feed my sheep ; so were the Apostles, and they were
seen. I suppose that those to whom S. Paul said,
*Take heed to yourselves and to all the flock, over which
the Holy Ghost hath placed you, to rule the Church of
God ;*—I suppose, say I, that they saw him ; and

when like good children they fell upon the neck of this good shepherd, bathing his face with their tears, I presume that he touched, and felt, and saw them; and what makes me still more sure of it is that they were chiefly *grieved* at his departure *for the word which he had said that they should see his face no more.* And then, Zwingle, Œcolampadius, Luther, Calvin, Beza and Musculus are visible; and as to the two last many of you have seen them, and yet they are called pastors by their disciples. The pastors then are seen, and consequently the sheep also.

(5.) It is the property of the Church to carry on the true preaching of the Word of God, the true administration of the Sacraments,—and is not all this visible? How then would you have their subject invisible?

(6.) Do we not know that the twelve patriarchs, the children of the good Jacob, were the living spring of the Church of Israel? And when their father had assembled them to bless them, they were seen and saw one another. Why do I delay on this? All sacred history testifies that the ancient synagogue was visible, and why not the Catholic Church?

(7.) As the patriarchs, fathers of the synagogue of Israel, *of whom was Christ according to the flesh* (Rom. ix. 5), formed the visible Church, so the Apostles with their disciples, children of the synagogue according to the flesh and spirit, gave beginning to the Catholic Church visibly, as the Psalmist says (xliv. 17): *Instead of thy father, sons are born to thee; thou shalt make them princes over all the earth.*

For twelve patriarchs are born to thee twelve Apostles, says Arnobius.* Those Apostles being

* Arnobii (Junioris), *Comm. in Ps. xliv.*

gathered together in Jerusalem with the little company of the disciples and the most glorious Mother of
the Saviour formed the true Church,—and of what
kind ?   Visible without doubt, yea so visible that the
Holy Spirit came to water these holy plants and seed-
plots of Christianity.

(8.) How did the ancient Jews begin their course
as the people of God ?   By circumcision, a visible
sign ;—and we by baptism, a visible sign.   By whom
were those of old governed ?   By the priests of the
race of Aaron, visible men ;—we by the bishops,
visible men.   By whom were the ancients taught ?
By the prophets and doctors, visibly ;—we by our
pastors and preachers, visibly.   What religious and
sacred food had the ancients to eat ?   The paschal
lamb, the manna, it is all visible ;—we have the most
holy Sacrament of the Eucharist, a visible sign though
of an invisible thing.   By whom was the synagogue
persecuted ?   By the Egyptians, Babylonians, Madianites, Philistines, all visible nations :—the Church by
the Pagans, Turks, Moors, Saracens, heretics ;—all is
visible.   Goodness of God !—and we are still to ask
whether the Church is visible !   But what is the
Church ?   An assembly of men who have flesh and
bones ;—and are we to say that it is but a spirit
or phantom, which seems to be visible and is so only
by illusion ?   No, no ; *Why are you troubled, and
why do thoughts arise in your hearts ?   See* her *hands* ;
behold her ministers, officers, and governors : *see* her
feet ; look at her preachers how they carry her east
and west, north and south.   All are flesh and bones.
Feel her ; come as humble children to throw yourselves
into the bosom of this sweet mother.   Consider her

throughout her whole body, entirely beautiful as she
is, and you will see that she is visible; for a spiritual
and invisible thing *hath not flesh and bones, as you see*
her *to have* (Luke *ult.*)

CHAPTER VI.

ANSWER TO THE OBJECTIONS MADE AGAINST THE VISIBILITY OF THE CHURCH.

Such are our reasons, sound under every test. But
they have some counter-reasons, which, as they fancy,
they draw from the Scriptures, but which are very
easy of refutation to any one who will consider what
follows.

(1.) Our Lord had in his humanity two parts, body
and soul; so the Church his spouse has two parts,
the one interior, which is as her soul, invisible—Faith,
Hope, Charity, Grace,—the other exterior, as her body,
and visible—the Confession of Faith, Praises and
Canticles, Preaching, Sacraments, Sacrifices. Yea, all
that is done in the Church has its exterior and interior. Prayer is interior and exterior; Faith fills the
heart with assurance and the mouth with confession;
Preaching is made exteriorly by men, but the secret
light of the Heavenly Father is required in it, for we
must always hear him and learn from him before
coming to the Son; and as to the Sacraments, the
sign is exterior but the grace is interior, as every one
knows. Thus then we have the interior of the Church
and the exterior. Its greatest beauty is within, the

outside is not so excellent, as says the Spouse in the
Canticles (iv.) : *Thy eyes are doves' eyes besides what is
hid within. . . . Honey and milk are under thy tongue,*
that is, in thy heart ;—behold the interior. *And the
smell of thy garments as the odour of frankincense ;—*
behold the exterior service. And the Psalmist (xliv.) :
All the glory of the King's daughter is within ;—there
is the interior. *Clothed round in golden borders with
varieties ;*—there is the exterior.

(2.) We must consider that as well the interior as
the exterior of the Church may be called spiritual,
but differently. For the interior is spiritual purely
and of its own nature ; the exterior of its own nature
is corporal, but because it has a reference and tendency
to the spiritual, the interior, we call it spiritual, as S.
Paul calls those who made the flesh subject to the
spirit, although they were corporeal ; and although each
person be particular, of his own nature, still when he
serves the public he is called a public man. Now, if
one say that the Evangelical law was given on
the hearts interiorly, not on tables of stone exteriorly,
as Jeremias says (xxxi. 33), the answer is ; that in the
interior of the Church and in its heart is all the chief
of its glory, but this fails not to shine out over the
exterior, by which it is known and recognised. So
when it is said in the Gospel (John iv. 23) that *the
hour cometh, and now is, when the true adorer shall adore
the Father in spirit and in truth ;*—we are taught that
the interior is the chief thing, and that the exterior
is vain if it do not tend and flow towards the interior
to spiritualise itself therein. In the same way, when
S. Peter calls the Church a *spiritual house* (1 Pet. ii. 5),
it is because all that proceeds from the Church tends

to the spiritual life, and because its greatest glory is interior; or again because it is not a house made with
lime and sand, but a mystical house of living stones,
to which charity serves as cement.   The holy Word
says (Luke xvii. 20), *The kingdom of God cometh not
with observation:* but the kingdom of God is the
Church, therefore the Church is not visible;—answer:
the kingdom of God in this place is Our Lord with
his grace, or, if you will, the company of Our Lord
while he was in this world; whence it continues: for
behold the kingdom of God is within you; and this
kingdom did not come with the surroundings and
glory of a worldly magnificence, as the Jews expected;
besides, as we have said, the fairest jewel of this
King's daughter is hidden within, and cannot be seen.
As to what S. Paul says to the Hebrews (xii. 18),
that *we are not come to the mountain that might be
handled,* like Mount Sina, but *to the heavenly Jerusalem*
—he is not proposing to show that the Church is
invisible: for S. Paul shows in this place that the
Church is more magnificent and richly endowed than
the Synagogue, and that she is not a natural mountain like that of Sina, but a mystical; from which it
does not follow that it is in any way invisible.   Indeed, it may reasonably be said that he is actually
speaking of the heavenly Jerusalem, that is, the
triumphant Church; wherefore he adds *the company of
angels,* as if to say that in the Old Law God was
seen on the mountain after a terrible manner, and
that the New leads us to see him in his glory there
in Paradise above.

   Finally, here is the argument which everybody
loudly asserts to be the strongest,—*I believe in the*

Holy Catholic Church: if I believe in it, I do not see it, therefore it is invisible. Is there anything feebler in the world than this phantom of a reason? Did the Apostles not believe that Our Lord was risen again, and did they not see him? *Because thou hast seen me,* he says himself to S. Thomas (John xx. 27): *thou hast believed;* and to make him believing he says to him, *See my hands, and bring hither thy hand, and put it into my side, and be not faithless but believing.* See how sight hinders not faith but produces it. Now Thomas saw one thing and believed another; he saw the body and he believed the spirit and the divinity; for it was not his seeing which led him to say, *My Lord and my God!*—but his faith. So do we believe one Baptism for the remission of sins; we see the Baptism, but not the remission of sins. Similarly, we see the Church, but not its interior sanctity; we see its eyes as of a dove, but we believe what is hidden within: we see its richly broidered garments, in beautiful variety, with golden borders, but the brightest splendour of its glory is within, which we believe. In this royal Spouse there is wherewith to feed the interior and the exterior eye, faith and sense, and all for the greater glory of her Spouse.

———————

CHAPTER VII.

THAT IN THE CHURCH THERE ARE GOOD AND BAD, PREDESTINATE AND REPROBATE.

To prove the invisibility of the Church each one brings forward his reason ; but the most feeble of all is that derived from eternal predestination. Certainly it is with no little artfulness that they turn the spiritual eyes of the militant Church upon eternal predestination, in order that, dazzled by the lightnings of this inscrutable mystery, we may not perceive what lies before us. They say that there are two Churches, one visible and imperfect, the other invisible and perfect, and that the visible can err and can be blown away by the wind of errors and idolatries, the invisible not. And if one ask what is the visible Church, they answer that it is the assemblage of those persons who profess the same faith and sacraments, which contains bad and good, and is a Church only in name ; and that the invisible Church is that which contains only the elect, who are not in the knowledge of men, but are only recognised and seen by God.

But we will clearly show that the true Church contains the good and the bad, the reprobate and the elect ; —and here are the proofs.

(1.) Was not that the true Church which S. Paul called *the pillar and ground of truth* and *the house of the living God* (1 Tim. iii. 15) ? Certainly ;—for to be a pillar of truth cannot appertain to an erring and straying Church. Now the Apostle witnesses of this true Church, the house of God, that there are in it

vessels unto honour and unto dishonour (2 Tim. ii. 20,)
that is, good and bad.

(2.) Is not that Church against which *the gates of
hell shall not prevail* (Matt. xvi. 18) the true Church?
Nevertheless there are therein men who have to be
loosed from their sins, and others whose sins have to
be retained, as Our Lord shows us in the promise and
the power he gave to S. Peter in this matter. Those
whose sins are retained—are they not wicked and
reprobate? Indeed, the reprobate are precisely those
whose sins are retained, and by the elect we ordinarily
mean those whose sins are pardoned. Now, that those
whose sins S. Peter had power to forgive or to retain
were in the Church is evident; for *them that are outside*
the Church only *God will judge* (1 Cor. v. 13). Those
therefore of whom S. Peter was to judge were not
outside the Church but within, though amongst them
there were some reprobate.

(3.) And does not Our Lord teach us that when we
are offended by some one of our brethren, after having
reprehended and corrected him twice, in two different
fashions, we should take him to the Church? *Tell the
Church ; and if he will not hear the Church let him be
to thee as the heathen and the publican* (Matt. xviii. 17).
Here one cannot escape—the consequence is inevitable. There is question of one of our brethren who
is neither heathen nor publican, but under the discipline and correction of the Church, and consequently
member of the Church, and yet there is no inconsistency in his being reprobate, perverse, and obstinate.
Not only then do the good belong to the true Church,
but the wicked also, until such time as they are cast out
from it, unless one would say that the Church to which

Our Lord sends us is an erring, sinful, and antichristian Church. This would be too open a blasphemy.

(4.) When Our Lord says,* *The servant abideth not in the house for ever; but the Son abideth for ever* (John viii. 35);—is it not the same as if he said that in the house of the Church the elect and the reprobate are for a time? Who can this servant be who abideth not in the house for ever except the one who *shall be cast into exterior darkness.* And in fact Christ clearly shows that he so understands it when he says immediately before, *Whosoever committeth sin is the servant of sin.* Now this man, though he abide not for ever, yet abideth during such time as he is required for service. S. Paul writes to *the Church of God which* was *at Corinth* (1 Cor. i. 2), and yet he wishes them to drive out a certain incestuous man (ibid. v.) If he be driven out he was there, and if he were there and the Church were the assemblage of the elect, how could they drive him out? The elect cannot be reprobate.

But why may we not lay down that the reprobate and wicked are of the true Church, when they can even be pastors and bishops therein? That is certain: is not Judas reprobate? And yet he was

* In a detached note elsewhere the Saint draws special attention to the force of this text. "From this," he says, "it is conclusively shown that there are sinners in the Church." And he proceeds to give an argument from the utility of their presence. "Those passages of the Psalm (cxviii.), *Thou hast made me wise over my enemies,* then, *over all my teachers,* then, *over ancients,* &c., prove that we can gain excellent knowledge and profit from our enemies. For, by *over* (*super*), in the expression *over my enemies,* may be understood, says Genebrard, *by occasion of my enemies, from* or *out of my enemies.* And since the being made wise by means of enemies is put before the being made wise by means of elders or teachers, it rightly follows that we have richer sources of knowledge in the school of enemies than in that of teachers," &c.

Apostle and bishop; according to the Psalmist (cviii. 8), and according to S. Peter (Acts i. 17), who says that *he had obtained part of* the *ministry* of the apostolate, and according to the whole Gospel, which ever places him in the number of the college of the Apostles. Was not Nicholas of Antioch a deacon like S. Stephen? —and yet many ancient Fathers make no difficulty on that account of considering him an heresiarch; witness, amongst others, Epiphanius, Philostratus, Jerome. And in fact the Nicolaites took occasion from him to recommend their abominations, of whom S. John makes mention in the Apocalypse (ii. 6), as of real heretics. S. Paul declares to the priests of Ephesus that the Holy Ghost had made them *bishops to rule the Church of God* (Acts xx. 28), but he assures them also that some *of* their *own selves would rise up speaking perverse things, to draw away disciples after* them. He speaks to all when he says that the Holy Spirit has made them bishops, and speaks of those very same persons when he says that from amongst them shall schismatics arise. But when should I have finished if I would here heap up the names of all those bishops and prelates who, after having been lawfully placed in this office and dignity, have fallen from their first grace and have died heretics. Who, for a simple priest, ever said anything so holy, so wise, so chaste, so charitable as Origen? No one could read what is written of him by Vincent of Lerins, one of the most judicious and learned of Church writers, no one could ponder over his accursed old age, after a life so admirable and holy, without being filled with compassion, to see this grand and brave pilot,—after so many storms weathered, after so many and such lucrative voyages to Hebrews, Arabs, Chaldæans, Greeks, and Latins,—on his return, full of honour and of spiritual riches, suffer shipwreck and perish in port, on the edge of the tomb! Who would dare to say that he had not been of the true Church, he who had always fought for the Church, and whom the whole Church honoured and held as one of its grandest Doctors? And yet behold him at last a heretic, excommunicate outside the Ark, perishing in the deluge of his own conceit! All this corresponds with the holy word of Our Lord (Matt. xxiii. 2), who considered the Scribes and Pharisees as the true pastors of the true Church of that time, since he commands that they should be obeyed, and yet considered them not as elect but rather as reprobate. Now what an absurdity would it be, I ask you, if the elect alone were of the Church? That would follow which is said of the Donatists, that we could not know our prelates, and consequently could not pay them obedience. For how should we know whether those who were called prelates and pastors were of the Church, since we cannot know who of the living is predestinate and who is not, as will be said elsewhere?—and if they are not of the Church, how can they hold the place of elect there? It would indeed be one of the strangest monsters that could be seen—if the head of the Church were not of the Church. Not only then can one who is reprobate be of the Church but even pastor in the Church. The Church then cannot be called invisible on the ground that it is composed of the predestinate alone.

I conclude all this discourse by the Gospel comparisons which show this truth clearly and completely.

S. John likens the Church to the threshing-floor of

a farm, on which is not only *the wheat* for the barn,
but also *the chaff* to be burnt *with unquenchable fire*
(Matt. iii. 12); are these not the elect and the reprobate? Our Lord compares it to *a net cast into the sea,
and gathering together of all kind of fishes,* good and
bad (ibid. xiii. 47); to *ten virgins, five of them foolish
and five wise* (ibid. xxv. 2); to three *servants,* one of
whom is *slothful,* and therefore *cast into the exterior
darkness* (ibid. 14); finally, to a marriage-feast, unto
which have entered both good and bad, and the bad,
not having on the nuptial garment, are cast into
exterior darkness (ibid. xxii.) Are not all these as
many sufficient proofs that not only the elect but also
the reprobate are in the Church? We must therefore
close the door of our judgment to all sorts of notions
of this kind, and to this one amongst them, by means
of that never-enough-pondered proposition: *Many are
called, but few are chosen* (ibid.) All those who are
in the Church are called, but all who are therein are
not elect; and indeed Church does not mean election
but convocation.

CHAPTER VIII.

ANSWER TO THE OBJECTIONS OF THOSE WHO WOULD
HAVE THE CHURCH TO CONSIST OF THE PREDES-
TINATE ALONE.

WHERE will they find the Scripture passage which
can furnish them any excuse for so many absurdities, and against proofs so clear as those we have
given? Yet counter-reasons are not wanting in this

matter : never does obstinacy leave its followers without them.

Will they then bring forward what is written in the Canticles (iv.) concerning the Spouse ; how she is *a garden enclosed, a fountain* or spring *sealed up, a well of living waters,* how she is *all fair* and *there is not a spot* in her; or, as the Apostle says, how she is *glorious, not having spot or wrinkle, holy, without blemish* (Eph. v. 27) ? I earnestly beg them to consider the conclusion they wish to draw, namely, that there can be in the Church none but saints, immaculate, faultless, glorious. I will, with the same passages, show them that in the Church there are neither elect nor reprobate. For is it not the humble but truthful saying, as the great Council of Trent declares, of all the just and elect, *Forgive us our trespasses, as we forgive them that trespass against us.* I suppose S. James was elect, and yet he confesses (iii. 2), *In many things we all offend.* S. John closes our mouth and the mouth of all the elect, so that no one may boast of being without sin ; on the contrary, he will have each one know and confess that he sins (1 John i.) I believe that David in his rapture and ecstasy knew what the elect are, and yet he considered *every man* to be a *liar* (Ps. cxv. 11). If then these holy qualities given to the Spouse, the Church, are to be taken precisely, and if there is to be no spot or wrinkle anywhere in it, we must go out of this world to find the verification of these fair titles, the elect of this world will not be able to claim them. Let us then make the truth clear.

(1.) The Church as a whole is entirely fair, holy, glorious, both as to morals and as to doctrine. Morals depend on the will, doctrine on the understanding. Into the understanding of the Church there never entered falseness, nor wickedness into her will. By the grace of her Spouse she can say with him, *Which of you*, O sworn enemies, *shall convince me of sin?* (John viii. 46.) And yet it does not follow that in the Church there are no sinners. Remember what I have said to you elsewhere: the Spouse has hair, and nails, which are not living though she is living; the senate is sovereign, but not each senator; the army is victorious, but not each soldier—it wins the battle while many of its soldiers are killed. In this way is the militant Church always glorious, ever victorious over the gates and powers of hell, although many of her members, either straying and thrown into disorder like yourselves, are cut to pieces and destroyed, or by other mishaps are wounded and die within her. Take then one after another the grand praises of the Church which are scattered throughout the Scriptures and make her a crown out of them, for they are richly due to her; just as maledictions are due to those who being in so excellent a way are lost. She is an *army set in array* (Cant. vi. 9), though some fall out of her ranks.

(2.) But who knows not how often that is attributed to a whole body which belongs only to one of the parts? The Spouse calls her beloved *white and ruddy;* but immediately she says *his locks* are *black* (ibid. v. 10, 11). S. Matthew says (xxvii. 44) that *the thieves who were crucified with* Our Saviour blasphemed him, whereas it was only one of them who did so, as S. Luke relates (xxiii. 39). We say that lilies are white, but there are yellow and there are green. He who speaks the language of love readily uses such expressions, and the Canticles are the chaste expressions of love. All these qualities then are justly attributed to the Church on account of the many holy souls therein who most exactly observe the holy Commandments of God, and are perfect—with the perfection that may be had in this pilgrimage, not with that which we hope for in our blessed fatherland.

(3.) Moreover, though there were no other reason for thus describing the Church than the hope she has of ascending, all pure, all beautiful, to heaven above, the fact that this is the sole term towards which she aspires and runs, would suffice to let her be called glorious and perfect, especially while she has so many fair pledges of this holy hope.

He would never end who should take notice of all the trifles which they stay examining here, and on which they raise a thousand false alarms amongst the poor common people. They bring forward that of S. John (x.); *I know my sheep, and no one shall snatch them out of my hand:* and they say that those sheep are the predestinate, who alone belong to the fold of the Lord. They bring forward what S. Paul says to Timothy (2 Tim. ii. 19): *The Lord knows who are his;* and what S. John has said to apostates: *they went out from us, but they were not of us* (1 John ii. 19). But what difficulty is there in all this ? We admit that the predestinate sheep hear the voice of their pastor, and have sooner or later all the qualities which are described in S. John; but he also maintains that in the Church, which is the fold of Our Lord, there are not only sheep but also goats. Otherwise, why should it be said that at the end of the world, in the Judgment, the sheep shall be separated, unless because, until the

III.

Judgment, whilst the Church is in this world, she has within herself goats with the sheep? Certainly if they had never been together they would never be separated. And in the last instance, if the predestinate are called sheep, so also are the reprobate. Witness David: *Why is thy wrath enkindled against the sheep of thy pasture?* (Ps. lxxiii. 1). *I have gone astray like a sheep that is lost* (cxviii. *ult.*). And elsewhere, where he says: *Give ear, O thou that rulest Israel; thou that leadest Joseph like a sheep* (lxxix. 1): —when he says *Joseph,* he means those of Joseph, and the Israelitish people, because to Joseph was given the primogeniture, and the eldest gives the name to the race. But who knows not that among the people of Israel every one was not predestinate or elect, and yet they are called sheep, and all are together under one shepherd. We confess then that there are sheep saved and predestinated, of whom it is spoken in S. John: there are others damned, of whom it is spoken elsewhere, and all are in the same flock.

Isaias (liii. 6) compares all men, both the reprobate and the elect, to sheep: *All we like sheep have gone astray;* and in verse 7 he similarly compares Our Saviour: *He shall be led as a sheep to the slaughter.* And so throughout the whole of c. xxxiv. of Ezechiel, where there is no doubt but that the whole people of Israel are called sheep, over which David has to reign (v. 23).

And in the same way,—who denies that Our Lord knows those who are his? He knew certainly what would become of Judas, yet Judas was not therefore not one of his Apostles. He knew what would become of those *disciples* who *went back* (John vi. 67) on account of the doctrine of the real eating of his flesh, and yet he received them as disciples. It is a quite different thing to belong to God according to the eternal fore-knowledge, as regards the Church Triumphant, and to belong to God according to the present communion of Saints for the Church Militant. The first are known only to God, the latter are known to God and to men. "According to the eternal foreknowledge," says S. Augustine,* "how many wolves are within; how many sheep without!" Our Lord then knows those who are his for his Triumphant Church, but besides these there are many others in the Militant Church whose end will be perdition, as the same Apostle shows when he says that *in a great house there are* all sorts of *vessels* and utensils, *some indeed unto honour, but some unto dishonour* (2 Tim. ii. 20).

So, what S. John says: *They have gone out from amongst us, but they were not of us,* is nothing to the purpose. For I will say, as S. Augustine said: They were with us *numero,* but they were not with us *merito:* that is, as the same Doctor says,† "they were with us and were ours by the Communion of the Sacraments, but according to their own individual vices they were not so." They were already heretics in their soul and will, though they were not so after the external appearance. And this is not to say that the good are not with the bad in the Church: on the contrary indeed, how could they go out of the company of the Church if they were not in it? They were doubtless in it actually, but in will they were already without.

Finally, here is an argument which seems to be complete in form and in figure. "He has not God

* In J. lxv.   † Ib. lxi.

for Father who has not the Church for mother;" *
that is certain: similarly he who has not God for
Father has not the Church for mother; most certainly: now the reprobate have not God for Father,
therefore they have not the Church for mother; and
consequently the reprobate are not in the Church.
But the answer is this. We accept the first foundation of this reason; but the second—that the reprobate are not children of God—requires to be well-
sifted. All the faithful baptized can be called sons
of God, so long as they are faithful, unless one would
take away from Baptism the name of regeneration or
spiritual nativity which Our Lord has given it. If
thus understood there are many of the reprobate who
are children of God, for how many persons are there,
faithful and baptized, who will be damned, men *who,*
as the Truth says, *believe for a while, and in time of
temptation fall away* (Luke viii. 13). So that we
totally deny this second proposition, that the reprobate are not children of God.† For being in the
Church they can be called children of God by Creation, Redemption, Regeneration, Doctrine, Profession
of faith; although our Lord laments over them in
this sort by Isaias (i. 2): *I have brought up children
. . . . and they have despised me.* But if one say
that the reprobate have not God for their Father
because they will not be heirs, according to the word
of the Apostle, *if a son an heir also* (Gal. iv. 7)—we
shall deny the consequence: for not only are the
children within the Church, but so are the servants

* Cyp. *de unit. Eccl.* v.
† Gal. iii. 26. *For you are all the children of God by faith in Christ
Jesus;*—and yet he calls them *senseless* (iii. 1), and *removed,* &c. (i. 6).

too, with this difference, that the children will abide there for ever as heirs; the servants shall not, but shall be turned out when it seems good to the master. Witness the Master himself in S. John (viii. 35), and the penitent son who knew well and acknowledged that many hired servants in his father's house abounded in bread, while he, true and lawful son, was amongst the swine, perishing with hunger, a proof of the Catholic faith in this point. O how many *princes* are *walking on the ground as servants* (Eccles. x. 7)! How many unclean animals and ravens in the Ark of the Church! O how many fair and sweet-smelling apples are on the tree cankered within yet attached to the tree, and drawing good sap from the trunk! He who had eyes clear-seeing enough to see the issue of the career of men, would see in the Church reason indeed to cry: *many are called and few are chosen;* that is, many are in the Militant Church who will never be in the Triumphant. How many are within who shall be without;—as S. Anthony foresaw of Arius, and S. Fulbert of Berengarius. It is then a certain thing that not only the elect but also the reprobate can be and are of the Church. And he who to make it invisible would place only the elect therein, acts like the wicked scholar who excused himself for not going to the assistance of his master, on the ground that he had learnt nothing about his body but only about his soul.

CHAPTER IX.

THAT THE CHURCH CANNOT PERISH.

I SHALL be more brief here, because what I shall say in the following chapter forms a strong proof for this belief in the immortality of the Church and its perpetuity. It is said then, to escape the yoke of the holy submission which is owing to the Church, that it perished eighty odd years ago ; that it is dead and buried, and the holy light of the true faith extinguished. All this is open blasphemy against the Passion of our Lord, against his Providence, against his goodness, against his truth.

Do we not know the word of our Lord himself : *And I, if I be lifted up from the earth, will draw all things to myself* (John xii. 32) ? Was he not lifted up on the cross ? did He not suffer ?—and how then having drawn to himself the Church, should he let it escape so utterly from him ? how should he let go this prize which had cost him so dear ? Had the prince of the world, the devil, been driven out with the stick of the cross for a time of three or four hundred years, to return and reign a thousand years ? Would you make so absolutely vain the might of the cross ? Is your faithfulness in judgment of such a sort that you would thus iniquitously divide our Lord, and henceforward place a certain comparison between the divine goodness and diabolical malice ? No, no : *When a strong man armed keepeth his court, those things which he possesseth are in peace : but if a stronger than he come upon him, and overcome him, he will take*

away all his armour and will distribute his spoils
(Luke xi. 22, 23). Are you ignorant that Our Lord
has purchased the Church with His own Blood ?—
and who can take it from him ? Think you that he
is weaker than his adversary ? Ah ! I pray you,
speak honourably of this captain. And who then
shall snatch his Church out of his hands ? Perhaps
you will say he is one who can keep it, but who will
not. It is then his Providence, his goodness, his truth
that you attack. The goodness of God has given gifts
to men as he ascends to heaven . . . apostles, prophets,
evangelists, pastors, doctors—*for the perfection of the
saints in the work of the ministry, unto the edification
of the body of Christ* (Eph. iv. 12). Was the perfection of the saints already accomplished eleven or
twelve hundred years ago ? Had the edification of
the mystical body of our Lord, that is, the Church,
been completed ? Either cease to call yourselves
edifiers or answer no :—and if it has not been completed, as in fact it has not, even yet, why wrong you
thus the goodness of God, saying that he has taken
back and carried away from men what he had given
them ? It is one of the qualities of the goodness of
God that, as S. Paul says (Rom. xi. 29) his *gifts are
without repentance* : that is to say, he does not give in
order to take away.

His divine Providence, as soon as it had created
man, the heavens, the earth, and the things that are
in heaven and on earth, preserved them and perpetually preserves them, in such a way that the species
(*generation*) of each tiniest bird is not yet extinct.
What then shall we say of the Church ? All this
world cost him at the dearest but a simple word : *he*

spoke and all were made (Ps. cxlviii. 5); and he preserves it with a perpetual and infallible Providence.
How, I ask you, should he have abandoned the Church,
which cost him all his blood, so many toils and travails ?
He has drawn Israel out of Egypt, out of the desert,
out of the Red Sea, out of so many calamities and
captivities;—and we are to believe that he has let
Christianity be engulfed in infidelity ! He has had
such care of his Agar, and he will despise Sara ! He
has so highly favoured the servant who was to be
driven out of the house, and he will hold the legitimate wife in no esteem ! He shall so greatly have
honoured the shadow, and will abandon the substance !
Oh ! how utterly vain and good for nothing would be
the promises on promises which he has made of the
perpetuity of this Church.

It is of the Church that the Psalmist sings: *God
hath founded it for ever* (xlvii. 9); *In his days shall
justice spring up, and abundance of peace, till the moon
be taken away* for ever (lxxi. 7). What peace, what
justice, except in the Church ? His throne (he is
speaking in the person of the eternal Father, of the
Church, which is the throne of the Messiah, David's
son) *shall be as the sun before me, and as the moon
perfect for ever, and a faithful witness in heaven*
(lxxxviii. 38). And: *I will make his seed to endure
for evermore; and his throne as the days of heaven*
(30);—that is, as long as heaven shall endure. Daniel
(ii. 44) calls it: *A kingdom which shall not be destroyed for ever.* The angel says to Our Lady that *of
his kingdom there shall be no end* (Luke i. 33), and he
is speaking of the Church, as we prove elsewhere.
Did not Isaias prophesy thus of Our Lord (liii. 10):

If he shall lay down his life for sin, he shall see a long-lived seed, that is, of long duration: and elsewhere (lxi. 8): *I will make a perpetual covenant with them;* and: *all that see them* (he speaks of the visible Church) *shall know them?*

Now, I ask you, who has given Luther and Calvin a commission to revoke so many holy and solemn promises of perpetuity which Our Lord has made to his Church? Is it not Our Lord who, speaking of his Church, says that the gates of hell shall not prevail against it? How shall this promise be verified if the Church has been abolished a thousand years or more? How shall we understand that sweet adieu our Lord made to his Apostles: *Behold I am with you all days, even to the consummation of the world* (Matt. *ult.*), if we say that the Church can perish? Or do we really wish to violate the sound rule of Gamaliel, who speaking of the rising Church used this argument: *If this design or work be of men, it will fall to nothing; but if it be of God, you are not able to destroy it* (Acts v. 38, 39)? Is not the Church the work of God?—and how then shall we say that it has come to nothing?

If this fair tree of the Church had been planted by man's hand I would easily acknowledge that it could be rooted up, but having been planted by so good a hand as is that of our Lord, I could not offer better counsel to those who hear people crying at every turn that the Church had perished than what our Lord said: Let these blind people alone, for *every plant which God hath not planted shall be rooted* up (Matt. xv. 13, 14).

S. Paul says that *all shall be made alive; but each one in his own order: the first-fruits Christ, then they*

that are of Christ, . . . afterwards the end (1 Cor. xv.
22, 23, 24). Between Christ and those that are of
Christ, that is, the Church, there is no interval, for
ascending up to heaven he has left them on earth;
between the Church and the end there is no interval,
since it was to last unto the end. How! was not our
Lord to reign in the midst of his enemies, until he had
put under his feet and subjected all who were opposed
to him (Ps. cix. 2)?—and how shall these authorities
be fulfilled, if the Church, the kingdom of our Lord,
has been ruined and destroyed? How should he reign
without a kingdom, and how should he reign among
his enemies unless he reigned in this world below?

But, I pray you, if this Spouse had died, who first
drew life from the side of her Bridegroom asleep on
the cross, if, I say, she had died, who would have
raised her from the dead? Do we not know that the
resurrection of the dead is not a less miracle than
creation, and much greater than continuation or preservation? Do we not know that the re-formation of
man is a much deeper mystery than the formation?
In the formation God spake, and man was made, he
breathed into him the living soul, and had no sooner
breathed it into him than this man began himself to
breathe: but in his re-formation God employed thirty-
three years, sweated blood and water, yea, he died over
this re-formation. Whoever then is rash enough to
say that this Church is dead, calls in question the
goodness, the diligence and the wisdom of this great
Reformer. And he who thinks himself to be the
reformer or resuscitator thereof, attributes to himself
the honour due to Jesus Christ alone, and makes himself greater than the Apostles. The Apostles have

not brought the Church back to life, but have preserved its life by their ministry, after our Lord had
instituted it.   He then who says that having found
the Church dead he has raised it to life—does he not
in your opinion deserve to be seated on the throne of
audacity ?   Our Lord had cast the fire of his charity
upon the earth, the Apostles blowing on it by their
preaching had increased it and spread it throughout
the world : you say it has been extinguished by the
waters of ignorance and iniquity ;—who shall enkindle
it again ? *   Blowing is of no use : what is to be done
then ?   Perhaps we must strike again with nails and
lance on Jesus Christ the holy living stone, to bring
forth a new fire :—or shall it be enough to have Calvin
or Luther in the world to relight it ?   This would
indeed be to be third Eliases, for neither Elias nor S.
John Baptist did ever as much.   This would be leaving
all the Apostles far far behind, who did indeed carry
this fire throughout the world, but did not enkindle it.
" O impudent cry ! " says S. Augustine against the
Donatists,† " the Church is not, because you are not
in it ! "   " No, no," says S. Bernard,† " *the floods came,
and the winds blew, and they beat upon that house, and
it fell not ; for it was founded upon a rock* (Matt. vii.
25), *and the rock was Christ* (1 Cor. x. 4)."

And to say the Church has failed—what else is it
but to say that all our predecessors are damned.   Yes,
truly ; for outside the true Church there is no salvation, out of this Ark every one is lost.   Oh what a
return we make to those good Fathers who have
suffered so much to preserve to us the inheritance of
the Gospel : and now so arrogant are their children

* In Ps. ci., S. 2.   † S. 79 *in Cant.*

that they scorn them, and hold them as silly fools and madmen.

I will conclude this proof with S. Augustine,* and say to your ministers: "What do you bring us new? Shall it be necessary to sow again the good seed, whereas from the time of its sowing it is to grow till the harvest? If you say that what the Apostles sowed has everywhere perished, we answer to you: read this to us from the Holy Scriptures: this you shall never do without having first shown us that this is false which is written, saying, that the seed which was sown in the beginning should grow till the time of the harvest. The good seed is the children of the kingdom, the cockle is the wicked, the harvest is the end of the world (Matt. xiii.). Say not then that the good seed is destroyed or choked, for it grows even to the consummation of the world."

CHAPTER X.

THE COUNTER-ARGUMENTS OF OUR ADVERSARIES, AND THE ANSWERS THERETO.

(1.) Was not the Church everywhere destroyed when Adam and Eve sinned? Answer: Adam and Eve were not the Church, but the commencement of the Church. And it is not true that the Church was ruined then, or yet that it had been, because they did not sin in doctrine or belief but in act.

(2.) Did not Aaron the High Priest adore the golden

* *De Unit. Eccl.* xvii.

calf with all his people ?   Answer: Aaron was not
as yet High Priest, nor head of the people, but became
so afterwards.   And it is not true that all the people
worshipped idols:—for were not the children of Levi
men of God, who joined themselves to Moses ?

(3.) Elias lamented that he was alone in Israel
(3 K. xix. 14).   Answer: Elias was not the only
good man in Israel, for there were seven thousand
men who had not given themselves up to idolatry, and
what the Prophet says here is only to express better
the justice of his complaint.   It is not true again that
if all Israel had failed, the Church would have thereby ceased to exist, for Israel was not the whole Church.
Indeed it was already separated therefrom by the
schism of Jeroboam ; and the kingdom of Juda was
the better and principal part; and it is Israel, not
Juda, of which Azarias predicted (II Par. xv. 3), that
it should be without priest and sacrifice.

(4.) Isaias says (i. 6) that from head to foot *there
is no soundness.*   Answer: these are forms of speaking, and of vehemently detesting the vice of a people.
And although the Prophets, pastors and preachers use
these general modes of expression, we are not to understand them of each particular person, but only of a
large porportion ; as appears by the example of Elias
who complained that he was alone, notwithstanding
that there were yet seven thousand faithful.   S. Paul
complains to the Philippians (ii. 21) that *all seek their
own* interest and advantage; still at the end of the
Epistle he acknowledges that there were many good
people with him and with them.   Who knows not
the complaint of David (Ps. xiii. 3), that *there is none
that doth good, no, not one ?*—and who knows not on the

other hand that there were many good people in his day ? These forms of speech are frequent, but we must not draw a particular conclusion about each individual. Further,—such things do not prove that faith had failed in the Church, nor that the Church was dead: for it does not follow that if a body is everywhere diseased it is therefore dead. Thus, without doubt, are to be understood all similar things which are found in the threats and rebukes of the Prophets.

(4.) Jeremias tells us (vii. 4) *not to trust in lying words, saying: the Temple of the Lord, the Temple of the Lord.* Answer: who maintains that under pretence of the Church we are to trust to a lie ? Yea, on the contrary, he who rests on the judgment of the Church rests on the pillar and ground of truth; he who trusts to the infallibility of the Church trusts to no lie, unless that is a lie which is written : *the gates of hell shall not prevail against it.* We place our trust then in the Holy Word, which promises perpetuity to the Church.

(5.) Is it not written that *the revolt* and separation must *come* (2 Thess. ii. 3), and that the sacrifice shall cease (Dan. xii. 11), and that the Son of Man shall hardly find faith on earth at his second visible return (Luke xviii. 8), when he will come to judge ? Answer: all these passages are understood of the affliction which antichrist will cause in the Church, during the three and a half years that he shall reign mightily; but in spite of this the Church during even these three years shall not fail, and shall be fed and preserved amid the deserts and solitudes whither it shall retire, as the Scripture says (Apoc. xii.).

CHAPTER XI.

THAT THE CHURCH HAS NEVER BEEN DISPERSED NOR HIDDEN.

THE ancients had wisely said that to distinguish
correctly the different times referred to in the Scriptures is a good rule for interpreting them aright;
for lack of which distinction the Jews continually err,
attributing to the first coming of the Messias what
is properly said of the second: and the adversaries of
the Church err yet more grossly, when they would
make the Church such from the time of S. Gregory
to this age as it is to be in the time of antichrist.
They wrest to this sense that which is written in the
Apocalypse (xii. 6), that *the woman fled into solitude;*
and draw the consequence that the Church has been
hidden and secret, trembling at the tyranny of the
Pope, this thousand years, until she has come forward
in Luther and his adherents. But who sees not that
all this passage refers to the end of the world, and the
persecution of antichrist, the time three years and a
half being expressly determined therein; and in Daniel
also (xii. 7)? And he who would by some gloss
extend this time which the Scripture has limited would
openly contradict Our Lord, who says (Matt. xxiv. 22)
that *for the sake of the elect those days shall be shortened.*
How then do they dare to transfer this Scripture to
an interpretation so foreign to the intention of the
author, and so contrary to its own circumstances,
refusing to look at so many other holy words which
prove and certify, loudly and clearly, that the Church

shall never be in the desert thus hidden until that extremity, and for that short time; that she will be seen to flee thither and be seen thence to come forth? I will not again bring forward the numerous passages previously cited, in which the Church is said to be like to the sun, the moon, the rainbow, a queen, a mountain as great as the world,—and a multitude of others. I will content myself with putting before your consideration two great captains of the ancient Church, two of the most valiant that ever were, S. Augustine and S. Jerome. David had said (Ps. xlvii. 1): *The Lord is great and exceedingly to be praised, in the city of our God in his holy mountain.* "This is the city," says S. Augustine,* "*set on a mountain,* that cannot be hid. This is *the light* which cannot be concealed, nor *put under a bushel,* which is known to all, famous to all:" for it follows: *With the joy of the whole earth is Mount Sion founded.* And in fact how would Our Lord, who said that *men do not light a candle and put it under a bushel* (Matt. v. 15), have placed so many lights in the Church to go and hide them in certain unknown corners? S. Augustine continues:† "This is the mountain which covers the whole face of the earth: this is the city of which it is said: *A city set on a mountain cannot be hid.* The Donatists (the Calvinists) come up to the mountain, and when we say to them, ascend;—it is not a mountain, say they, and they rather strike their heads against it than establish their dwelling on it. Isaias, whom we read yesterday, —cried out (ii. 2): *In the last days the mountain of the house of the Lord shall be prepared on the top of*

* In Ps. xlvii.
† In Ep. 1ᵃᵐ Joan. Tr. i. The order is slightly changed [Tr.].

mountains, and all nations shall flow into it. What is there so visible as a mountain?—Yet there are mountains unknown because they are situated in a corner of the earth. Who amongst you knows Olympus? No one, I am sure, any more or any less than its inhabitants know our Mount Giddaba. These mountains are in parts of the earth: but that mount not so; for it has filled the whole face of the earth. The stone cut from the mountain, without any new operation (Dan. ii.), is it not Jesus Christ, springing from the race of the Jews without operation of marriage? And did not this stone break in pieces all the kingdoms of the earth, that is, all the dominations of idols and demons?—did it not increase until it filled the whole earth? It is then of this mountain that is said the word, *prepared on the top of mountains;* it is a mountain elevated above the heads of all mountains, and all nations shall flow into it. Who can get lost, or can miss this mountain? Who knocks against and breaks his head against this? Who fails to see the city set on a mountain? Yet no; be not astonished that it is unknown to those who hate the brethren, who hate the Church. For by this they walk in darkness, and know not where they go. They are separated from the rest of the universe, they are blind with anger." Such are the words of S. Augustine against the Donatists, but the present Church so perfectly resembles the first Church, and the heretics of our age those of old, that by merely changing the names the ancient reasons press the Calvinists as closely home as they did those ancient Donatists.

S. Jerome * enters into the fray from another side,

* *Contra Lucif.* 14, 15.

III.

which is just as dangerous to you as the former; for
he makes it clearly evident that this pretended dispersion, this retreat and hiddenness, destroy the glory
of the cross of Our Lord.   For, speaking to a schismatic who had rejoined the Church, he says: " I
rejoice with thee, and give thanks to Jesus Christ my
God, in that thou hast turned back in good earnest
from the heat of falsehood to that which is the sweetness and savour of the whole world.   And say not
like some do: *Save me, O Lord, for there is now no
saint* (Ps. xi. 1); whose impious voice makes vain
the cross of Christ, subjects the Son of God to the
devil, and understands that grief which the Saviour
has poured out over sinners to be expressed concerning all men.   But let it never be that God should
die for nothing, the mighty one is bound and despoiled
of all, the word of God is accomplished: *ask of me,
and I will give thee the Gentiles for thy inheritance, and
the utmost parts of the earth for thy possession* (Ps. ii. 8).
Where, I pray you, are those too religious, yea, rather
too profane persons, who declare there are more
synagogues than churches ?   How shall the cities of
the devil be destroyed, and at last, that is, at the
consummation of the world, how shall the idols be
thrown down, if Our Lord has had no Church, or has
had it only in Sardinia ?   Certainly he is become
too indigent."   Yes, indeed, if Satan possess at the
same time England, France, the East, the Indies,
barbarous nations and every place,—how would the
trophies of the cross be collected and squeezed into
one corner of the world.   And what would this great
man say of those who not only deny that it has been
general and universal, but say that it was only in

certain unknown persons, and will not specify one
single little village where it was eighty years ago?
Is not this greatly to bring down the glorious trophies
of Our Lord? The heavenly Father, for the great
humiliation and annihilation which Our Lord had
undergone on the tree of the cross, had made his
name so glorious that all knees were to bow and bend
in reverence of him; but these people do not thus
value the cross or the actions of the Crucified, taking
from this account all the generations of a thousand
years. The Father had given him as his inheritance
many nations, because he had *delivered his soul to
death* (Isa. liii. 12), and had been reputed with male-
factors and robbers; but these people make his inheritance narrow indeed, and so cut away his portion
that hardly during a thousand years shall he have a few
secret followers, yea, shall have had none at all! For
I address myself to you, O predecessors, who bear the
name of Christian, and who have been in the true
Church. Either you had the true faith or you had it
not. If you had it not, O unhappy ones, you are
damned; and if you had it why did you conceal it
from others, why did you leave no memorials of it,
why did you not set yourselves against impiety, idolatry? In no wise were you ignorant that God has
recommended to each one his neighbour. Certainly
with the heart we believe unto justice; but for *salvation*
we must make *confession* of our faith (Rom. x. 10),
and how could you say : *I have believed, therefore have
I spoken* (Ps. cxv. 1)? O miserable again for having
so excellent a talent and hiding it in the earth. If
the case is so ye are in the exterior darkness; but if,
on the contrary, O Luther, O Calvin, the true faith

has always been published and continually preached by all our predecessors, yourselves are miserable who have a quite opposite one, and who, to find some excuse for your wills and your fancies, accuse all the Fathers either of impiety if they have believed ill, or of treachery if they have kept silence.

CHAPTER XII.

THE CHURCH CANNOT ERR.

ONCE when Absalom wished to form a faction and division against his good father David, he sat in the way near the gate, and said to each person that went by : *There is no man appointed by the king to hear thee . . . O that they would make me judge over the land, that all that have business might come to me, that I might do them justice.** Thus did he seduce the loyalty of the Israelites. O how many Absaloms have there been in our age, who, to seduce and distort the people of Our Lord from obedience to the Church and her pastors, and to lead away Christian lealty into rebellion and revolt, have cried up and down the ways of Germany and of France : there is no one appointed by God to hear doubts concerning the faith and to answer them ; the Church itself, the rulers of the Church, have no power to determine what we are to hold as to the faith and what we are not ; we must seek other judges than the prelates, the Church can err in its decrees and rules. But what more hurtful

* 2 Kings xv.

and audacious proposition could they make to Christianity than that? If then the Church can err, O
Calvin, O Luther, to whom shall I have recourse in
my difficulties? To the Scripture, say they. But
what shall I, poor man, do, for it is precisely about
the Scripture that my difficulty lies. I am not in
doubt whether I must believe the Scripture or not; for
who knows not that it is the Word of Truth? What
keeps me in anxiety is the understanding of this
Scripture, is the conclusions to be drawn from it,
which are innumerable and diverse and opposite on
the same subject; and everybody takes his view, one
this, another that, though out of all there is but one
which is sound :—Ah! who will give me to know
the good among so many bad? who will tell me the
real verity through so many specious and masked
vanities. Everybody would embark on the ship of
the Holy Spirit; there is but one, and only that one
shall reach the port, all the rest are on their way to
shipwreck. Ah! what danger am I in of erring!
All shout out their claims with equal assurance and
thus deceive the greater part, for all boast that theirs
is the ship. Whoever says that our Master has not
left us guides in so dangerous and difficult a way,
says that he wishes us to perish. Whoever says that
he has put us aboard at the mercy of wind and tide,
without giving us a skilful pilot able to use properly
his compass and chart, says that the Saviour is wanting in foresight. Whoever says that this good Father
has sent us into this school of the Church, knowing
that error was taught there, says that he intended to
foster our vice and our ignorance. Who has ever heard
of an academy in which everybody taught, and nobody

was a scholar?—such would be the Christian commonwealth if the Church can err.   For if the Church herself err, who shall not err? and if each one in it err,
or can err, to whom shall I betake myself for instruction?—to Calvin? but why to him rather than to
Luther, or Brentius, or Pacimontanus?   Truly, if I
must take my chance of being damned for error, I will
be so for my own not for another's, and will let these
wits of mine scatter freely about, and maybe they will
find the truth as quickly as anybody else.   We should
not know then whither to turn in our difficulties if the
Church erred.   But he who shall consider how perfectly authentic is the testimony which God has given
of the Church, will see that to say the Church errs is
to say no less than that God errs, or else that he is
willing and desirous for us to err; which would be a
great blasphemy.   For is it not Our Lord who says:
*If thy brother shall offend thee . . . tell the Church, and
if he will not hear the Church, let him be to thee as the
heathen and the publican* (Matt. xviii.)   Do you see
how Our Lord sends us to the Church in our differences, whatever they may be?   How much more
in more serious offences and differences!   Certainly
if by the order of fraternal correction I am obliged to
go to the Church to effect the amendment of some evil
person who has offended me, how much more shall I
be obliged to denounce him who calls the whole Church
Babylon, adulterous, idolatrous, perjured?   And so
much the more because with this evil-mindedness of his
he can seduce and infect a whole province;—the vice
of heresy being so contagious that *it spreadeth like a
cancer* (2 Tim. ii. 17) for a time.   When, therefore, I
see some one who says that all our fathers, grand-

fathers, and great-grandfathers have fallen into idolatry, have corrupted the Gospel, and committed all the iniquities which follow upon the fall of religion, I will address myself to the Church, whose judgment every one must submit to. But if she can err then it is no longer I, or man, who will keep error in the world: it will be our God himself who will authorise it and give it credit, since he commands us to go to this tribunal to hear and receive justice. Either he does not know what is done there, or he wishes to deceive us, or true justice is really done there; and the judgments are irrevocable. The Church has condemned Berengarius; if any one would further discuss this matter, I hold him as a heathen and a publican, in order to obey my Saviour, who leaves me no choice herein, but gives me this order: *Let him be to thee as a heathen and a publican.* It is the same as S. Paul teaches when he calls the Church *the pillar and ground of truth* (1 Tim. iii. 15). Is not this to say that truth is solidly upheld in the Church? Elsewhere truth is only maintained at intervals, it falls often, but in the Church it is without vicissitude, unmovable, unshaken, in a word steadfast and perpetual. To answer that S. Paul's meaning is that Scripture has been put under the guardianship of the Church, and no more, is to weaken the proposed similitude too much. For to uphold the truth is a very different thing from guarding the Scripture. The Jews guard a part of the Scriptures, and so do many heretics; but they are not on that account a column and ground of truth. The bark of the letter is neither truth nor falsehood, but according to the sense that we give it is it true or false. The truth consists in the sense, which is, as it were, the marrow. And therefore if the Church were guardian of the truth, the sense of the Scripture would have been entrusted to her care, and it would be necessary to seek it with her, and not in the brain of Luther or Calvin or any private person. Therefore she cannot err, ever having the sense of the Scriptures. And in fact to place with this sacred depository the letter without the sense, would be to place therein the purse without the gold, the shell without the kernel, the scabbard without the sword, the box without the ointment, the leaves without the fruit, the shadow without the body. But tell me, if the Church has the care of the Scriptures, why did Luther take them and carry them away from her? And why do you not receive at her hands the Machabees, Ecclesiasticus, and the rest, as much as the Epistle to the Hebrews? For she protests that she has just as jealous a care of those as of these. In short, the words of S. Paul cannot suffer this sense that you would give them: he speaks of the visible Church,— for where would he direct his Timothy to *behave himself?* He calls it the house of Our Saviour; therefore it is well founded, well ordered, well sheltered against all storms and tempest of error. It is *the pillar and ground of truth*; truth then is in it, it abides there, it dwells there; who seeks it elsewhere loses it. It is so thoroughly safe and firm that all the gates of hell, that is, all the forces of the enemy, cannot make themselves masters of it. And would not the place be taken by the enemy if error entered it, with regard to the things which are for the honour and service of the Master? Our Lord is the head of the Church,—are you not ashamed to say that the body of so holy a head is adulterous, profane, corrupt ?   And say not that he is head of an invisible Church, for, since there is only a visible Church (as I have shown above) our Lord is the head of that; as S. Paul says: *And he hath made him head over all the Church* (Eph. i 22); not over one Church out of two, as you imagine, but over the whole Church.   Where two or three are gathered together in the name of the Lord, he is in the midst of them (Matt. xviii. 20).   Ah ! who shall say that the assembly of the universal Church of all time has been abandoned to the mercy of error and impiety ?   I conclude then that when we see that the universal Church has been and is in the belief of some article,—whether we see it expressly in the Scripture, whether it is drawn therefrom by some deduction, or again by tradition,—we must in no way judge, nor dispute, nor doubt concerning it, but show obedience and homage to this heavenly Queen, as Christ commands, and regulate our faith by this standard: And if it would have been impious in the Apostles to contest with their Master, so will it be in him who contests with the Church.   For if the Father has said of the Son : *Hear ye him*, the Son has said of the Church : *If any one will not hear the Church, let him be to thee as a heathen and a publican.*

CHAPTER XIII.

THE MINISTERS HAVE VIOLATED THE AUTHORITY OF THE CHURCH.

I AM not now concerned to show how your ministers have degraded the holiness and majesty of the Spouse of Jesus Christ. They cry out loud and clear that she has remained eight hundred years adulterous and anti-christian, from S. Gregory to Wicliffe—whom Beza considers the first restorer of Christianity. Calvin indeed would shield himself under a distinction, saying that the Church can err in things unnecessary for salvation, not in others. But Beza openly confesses that she has so far erred that she is no longer the Church. And is this not to err in things necessary for salvation, although he avows that outside the Church there is no salvation? It follows then from what he says—let him turn and turn about as he likes—that the Church has erred in things necessary for salvation. For if outside the Church there is no salvation, and the Church has so gravely erred that she is no more the Church, certainly in her there is no salvation. Now she can only lose salvation by giving up the things necessary for salvation; she has therefore erred in things necessary for salvation; other-wise, having what is necessary for salvation, she would be the true Church, or else men can be saved outside the true Church, which is impossible. And Beza says that he learnt this way of speaking from those who instructed him in his pretended religion, that is, from Calvin. Indeed if Calvin thought that the Church of

Rome had not erred in things necessary for salvation
he would have done wrong to separate himself from it,
for being able to secure his salvation in it, and true
Christianity residing in it, he would have been obliged
to stay therein for his salvation, which could not be in
two different places.

Perhaps I may be told that Beza says indeed that
the Roman Church, as it is now, errs in things necessary for salvation, and that therefore he left it; but
that he does not say the true Church has ever erred.
He cannot, however, escape in that direction; for what
Church was there in the world two, three, four, five
hundred years ago, save the Church Catholic and
Roman, just exactly as it is at present? There was
certainly no other, therefore it was the true Church—
and yet it erred; or there was no Church in the world
—and in that case again he is constrained to confess
that this disappearance of the Church arose from in-
tolerable error, and error in things necessary for salvation. For as to that dispersion of the faithful, and
that secret Church that he fancies he can bring
forward, I have already sufficiently exposed the vain-
ness of it. Besides the fact that when they confess
the visible Church can err, they dishonour the Church
to which Our Lord directs us in our difficulties, and
which S. Paul calls the pillar and ground of truth.
For it is only of the visible Church that these testimonies are understood, unless we would say that Our
Lord had sent us to speak to an invisible and unperceivable thing, a thing utterly unknown, or that S.
Paul instructed his Timothy to converse in a society
of which he had no knowledge.

But is it not to violate all the respect and reverence

due to this Queen, this spouse of the heavenly King, to
have brought back into the realm almost all the rout
which with such cost of blood, of sweat, and of
travails, she had by solemn penal sentence banished
and driven from these her confines, as rebels and as
sworn enemies of her crown ?   I mean this setting
up so many heresies and false opinions which the
Church had condemned, infringing thereby the sove-
reignty of the Church, absolving those she had condemned, condemning those whom she has absolved.
Examples follow.

Simon Magus said that God was the cause of sin,
says Vincent of Lerins (*Com.* 1um c. 34).   But
Calvin and Beza say no less; the former in the
treatise on eternal predestination, the latter in his
answer to Sebastian Castalio :*   though they deny the
word, they follow the things and substance of this
heresy,—if heresy it is to be called, and not atheism.
But of this so many learned men convict them by
their own words that I will not stay upon it.

Judas, says S. Jerome (in Matt. xxvi. 48), thought
that the miracles he saw worked by the hand of Our
Lord were diabolical operations and illusions.†   I know
not whether your ministers think of what they are saying, but when we bring forward miracles, what do they
say but that they are sorceries ?   The glorious miracles
which Our Lord does, O men of this world, instead of
opening your eyes, how do you speak of them ? ‡

---

* See Claude de Sainctes on *Atheism ;* Francis Feuardent in his
Dialogues ; Bellarmine *Controv.* Tom. iv. Lib. ii. c. 6 [where find quotations from Calvin and Beza. Tr.] ; Hay in his *Questions and Answers.*

† Porphyry and Eunomius did the same.   See Jerome *adv. Vig.* (10).

‡ See Calvin in Pref. to *Instit. ;* the Centuriators ; Peter Martyr
(c. viii. Ind. de Hær. c. 27).

The Pepusians, says S. Augustine * (or Montanists and Phrygians, as the Code calls them), admitted women to the dignity of the priesthood. Who is ignorant that the English brethren hold their Queen Elizabeth to be head of their Church ?

The Manicheans, says S. Jerome, † denied free-will : Luther has composed a book against free-will, which he calls *de servo arbitrio* : for Calvin I appeal to yourselves.‡

The Donatists believed that the Church was de-stroyed throughout the world and remained only with them (Aug. *de Hær.* 69): your ministers say the same. Again, they believe that a bad man cannot baptize (Ib. *contra Pet.* i. 7); Wicliff said just as much, whom I bring forward in mockery, because Beza holds him for a glorious reformer. As to their lives, their virtues were such as these : they gave the most precious Sacrament to the dogs, they cast the holy Chrism upon the ground, they overthrew the altars, broke the chalices and sold them, they shaved the heads of the priests to take the sacred unction from them, they took and tore away the veil from nuns to reform them.§

Jovinian, as S. Augustine testifies, ‖would have any kind of meat eaten at any time and against every prohibition ; he said that fasting was not meritorious before God, that the saved were equal in glory, that

---

* *De Hær.* 27.   † Præf. in *Dial. c. Pelag.*

‡ The Saint adds in marginal note : Amb. Ep. 83 (Migne Ep. xxiii.) : " We rightly condemn the Manicheans on account of their Sunday fasts."

§ See Optatus *de sch. Don.* ii. 17, vi. 1.

‖ *De Hær.* 82 : and see Jerome *cont. Jov.*

virginity was no better than marriage, and that all sins were equal. Your masters teach the same.

Vigilantius, as S. Jerome says,* denied that the relics of the Saints are to be honoured, that the prayers of the Saints are profitable, that priests should live in celibacy; [he rejected] voluntary poverty. And what of all those things do you not deny? †

About the year 324, Eustathius despised the ordinary fasts of the Church, ecclesiastical traditions, the shrines of the holy Martyrs, and places dedicated to their honour. The account is given by the Council of Gangra (*in præf.*) in which for these reasons he was anathematized and condemned. See how long your reformers have been condemned.

Eunomius would not yield to plurality, dignity, antiquity, as S. Basil testifies.‡ He said that faith alone was sufficient for salvation, and justified (Aug. *hær.* 54). As to the first point, see Beza in his treatise on the marks of the Church; as to the second, does it not agree with that celebrated sentence of Luther's,§ whom Beza holds to be a most glorious reformer: " You see how rich is the Christian, that is, the baptized man, who even if he wishes is not able to lose his salvation by any sins whatever, unless he refuses to believe" ?

Aerius, according to S. Augustine (H. 53), denied prayer for the dead, ordinary fasts, and the superiority of a bishop over a simple priest. Your masters deny all this.

* *Cont. Vig. ;* and Ep. ii. adv. eundem.

† For this and preceding paragraph the Saint refers to Luther (de Nat. B.M. ; in 1 Pet. Ep. ; and *Epithal.*) ; and Calvin (*in Antid.* S. vi.).

‡ *Contra Eun.* i.   § *de Cap. Bab.* i.

Lucifer called his Church alone the true Church and said that the ancient Church had become, instead of a Church, a house of ill-fame : * and what do your ministers cry out all the day ?

The Pelagians considered themselves assured and certain of their justice, promised salvation to the children of the faithful who died without Baptism, held that all sins were mortal.† As to the first, this is your ordinary language, and that of Calvin (*in Antidoto*, p. vi.). The second and third points are too ordinary with you to have anything said about them.

The Manicheans rejected the sacrifices of the Church, and images,‡ as your people also do.

The Messalians despised Sacred Orders, Churches, Altars, as says S. Damascene (Hæres. 80) ; and S. Ignatius says :§ They do not admit the Eucharist and the oblations, because they do not acknowledge the Eucharist to be the flesh of our Saviour, Jesus Christ, which suffered for our sins, which the Father mercifully raised up. Against whom S. Martial has written.‖

Berengarius taught the same, long afterwards, and was condemned by three Councils, in the two last of which he abjured his heresy.

Julian the Apostate despised the sign of the cross. Xenaias did the same,¶ the Mahometans treat it no worse.** But he who would see this at full length, let him look at Sanders (viii. 57) and Bellarmine in

---

* Jer. *contra Lucif.*
† Jerome *adv. Pel.* ii. and iii. ; S. Aug. *contra Jul.* vi.
‡ S. Aug. *contra Faustum* xx.
§ Apud Theodoret. Dial. 3, called *Impatibilis.*
‖ Epist. ad Burdigalenses (apocryphal Tr.).
¶ Niceph. xvi. 27.   ** Damas. 100.

his *Notes of the Church.* Do you see the mould on which your ministers lay and form their reformation ?

Now, ought not this agreement of opinions, or, to speak more rightly, this close parentage and consanguinity which your first masters had with the most cruel, inveterate, and sworn enemies of the Church,— ought not this alone to dissuade you from following them, and to bring you under the right banner ? I have not cited one heresy which was not held as such by that Church which Calvin and Beza confess to have been the true Church,—that is, in the first five hundred years of Christianity. Ah ! I pray you, is it not to trample the majesty of the Church under foot thus to produce as reformations, and necessary and holy reparations, what she has so greatly abominated when she was in her purest years, and which she had crushed down as impiety, as the ruin and corruption of true doctrine ? The delicate stomach of this heavenly Spouse had scarcely been able to bear the violence of these poisons, and had rejected them with such energy that many veins of her martyrs had burst with the effort, and now you offer them to her again as a precious medicine ! The Fathers whom I have quoted would never have placed them on the list of heretics if they had not seen the body of the Church hold them as such. These Fathers being in the highest rank of orthodoxy, and closely united with all the other Catholic bishops and doctors of their time, we see that what they held to be heretical was so in reality. Picture to yourselves this venerable antiquity in heaven round about the Master, who regards your reformers and their works. Those have gained their crown combatting the opinions which the ministers adore ; they have held as heretics those whose steps you follow. Do you think that what they have judged to be error, heresy, blasphemy, in the Arians, the Manichæans, Judas, they now judge to be sanctity, reformation, restoration ? Who sees not that this is the greatest contempt for the majesty of the Church that can be shown ? If you would be in the succession of the true and holy Church of those first centuries, do not then oppose what it has so solemnly established and instituted. Nobody can be partly heir and partly not. Accept the inheritance courageously ; the charges are not so great but that a little humility will give a good account of them—to say good-bye to your passions, and to give up the difference which you have with the Church : the honours are infinite—the being heirs of God, co-heirs of Jesus Christ in the happy society of all the Blessed !

PART II.

The Rule of Faith.

INTRODUCTION.

If the advice which St. John * gives to Christians, *not to believe every spirit,* was ever necessary, it is so now more than ever, when so many different and contrary spirits in Christendom demand belief, on the strength of the Word of God; in whose name we have seen so many nations run astray in every direction, each one after its humour. As the common sort admire comets and wandering fires, and believe that they are true stars and bright planets, while better-informed people know well that they are only airy flames which float over some vapour as long as there is anything to feed them, which always leave some ill effect behind them, and which have nothing in common with the incorruptible stars save the coarse light which makes them visible; so the miserable people of our age, seeing in certain foolish men the glitter of human subtlety and a false gleam of the Word of God, have believed that here were heavenly truths, and have given heed to them;

* 1 Ep. iv. 1.

although men of worth and judgment testified that they were only earthly inventions, which would in time disappear, nor leave other memorial of them than the sense of the many miseries which follow. O how men ought to have abstained from giving themselves up to these spirits, and before following them to have tried whether they were of God or no! Ah! there is not wanting a touchstone to distinguish the base metal of their counterfeits. For he who caused us to be told that we must *prove the spirits*, would not have done so unless he knew that we had infallible rules to tell the holy from the false spirit. We have such rules, and nobody denies it. But these deceivers produce rules which they can falsify and adapt to their pretensions, in order that, having rules in their hands, they may gain the credit of being masters in their craft by a visible sign under pretext of which they can form a faith and a religion such as they have imagined. It is then of the most extreme importance to know what are the true rules of our belief, for thereby we can easily discern heresy from the true religion: and this is what I intend to make clear in this Second Part. My plan is as follows.

The Christian faith is grounded on the Word of God. This is what places it in the sovereign degree of certainty, as having the warrant of that eternal and infallible Truth. Faith which rests on anything else is not Christian. Therefore, the Word of God is the true rule of right-believing, as ground and rule are in this case one and the same thing.

Since this rule does not regulate our faith save when it is applied, proposed and declared, and since this may be done well or ill,—therefore it is not enough to know that the Word of God is the true and infallible rule of right-believing, unless I know what Word is God's, where it is, who has to propose, apply, and declare it. It is useless for me to know that the Word of God is infallible, and for all this knowledge I shall not believe that Jesus is the Christ, Son of the living God, unless I am certified that this Word is revealed by the heavenly Eather: and even when I come to know this I shall not be out of doubt if I do not know how this is to be understood, —whether of an adoptive filiation in the Arian sense, or a natural filiation in the Catholic.

There is need, then, besides this first and fundamental rule the Word of God, of another, a second rule, by which the first may be rightly and duly proposed, applied, and declared. And in order that we may not be subject to hesitation and uncertainty, it is necessary not only that the first rule, namely, the Word of God, but also the second, which proposes and applies this rule, be absolutely infallible ; otherwise we shall always remain in suspense and in doubt as to whether we are not being badly directed and supported in our faith and belief, not now by any defect in the first rule, but by error and defect in the proposition and application thereof. Certainly the danger is equal,—either of getting out of rule for want of a right rule, or getting out of rule for want of a regular and right application of the rule itself. But this infallibility which is required as well in the rule as in its proper application, can have its source only in God, the living and original fountain of all truth. Let us proceed.

Now as God revealed his Word, and spoke, or preached, by the mouth of the Fathers and Prophets, and at last by his own Son, then by the Apostles and Evangelists, whose tongues were but as the pens of scribes writing rapidly, God thus employing men to speak to men; so to propose, apply, and declare this his Word, he employs his visible Spouse as his mouthpiece and the interpreter of his intentions. It is God then who rules over Christian belief, but with two instruments, in a double way : (1) by his Word as by a formal rule ; (2) by his Church as by the hand of the measurer and rule-user. Let us put it thus : God is the painter, our faith the picture, the colours are the Word of God, the brush is the Church. Here then are two ordinary and infallible rules of our belief : the Word of God, which is the fundamental and formal rule ; the Church of God, which is the rule of application and explanation.

I consider in this second part both the one and the other, but to make my exposition of them more clear and more easy to handle, I have divided these two rules into several, as follows.

The Word of God, the formal rule of our faith, is either in Scripture or in Tradition. I treat first of Scripture, then of Tradition.

The Church, the rule of application, expresses herself either in her universal body by a general belief of all Christians, or in her principal and nobler parts by a consent of her pastors and doctors ; and in this latter way it is either in her pastors assembled in one place and at one time, as in a general council, or in her pastors divided as to place and time, but assembled in union and correspondence of faith ; or, in fine, this same Church expresses herself and speaks by her head-minister.* And these are four explaining and apply-ing rules of our faith;—the Church as a whole, the General Council, the consent of the Fathers, the Pope.

Other rules than these we are not to seek; these are enough to steady the most inconstant. But God, who takes pleasure in the abundance of his favours, wishing to come to the help of the weakness of men, goes so far as to add sometimes to these ordinary rules (I refer to the establishment and founding of the Church) an extraordinary rule, most certain and of great importance,—namely, miracles—an extraordinary testimony of the true application of the Divine Word.

Lastly, natural reason may also be called a rule of right-believing, but negatively and not affirmatively. For if any one should speak thus: such a proposition is an article of faith, therefore it is according to natural reason:—this affirmative consequence would be badly drawn, since almost all our faith is outside of and above our reason. But if he were to say: this is an article of faith, therefore it cannot be against natural reason:—the consequence is good. For natural reason and faith, being supported on the same prin-ciples, and starting from one same author, cannot be contrary to each other.

Here then are eight rules of faith: Scripture, Tradi-tion, the Church, Councils, the Fathers, the Pope, miracles, natural reason. The two first are only a formal rule, the four following are only a rule of appli-cation, the seventh is extraordinary, and the eighth negative. Or, he who would reduce all these rules to

* *Chef ministeriel.* That is, ruler of the Church, but ruling as prime minister of Christ. [Tr.]

a single one, would say that the sole and true rule of right-believing is the Word of God preached by the Church of God.

Now I undertake here to show, as clearly as the light of day, that your reformers have violated and forced all these rules (and it would be enough to show that they have violated one of them, since they are so closely connected that he who violates one violates all the others); in order that, as you have seen in the first part, that they have taken you out of the bosom of the true Church by schism, so you may know in this second part, that they have deprived you of the light of the true faith by heresy, to drag you after their illusions. And I keep ever in the same position : for I prove firstly that the rules which I bring forward are most certain and infallible, then I prove, so closely that you can touch it with your hand, that your doctors have violated them. Here now I appeal to you in the name of the Almighty God, and summon you on his part, to judge justly.

ARTICLE I.

HOLY SCRIPTURE: FIRST RULE OF FAITH.

THAT THE PRETENDED REFORMERS HAVE VIOLATED
HOLY SCRIPTURE, THE FIRST RULE OF OUR FAITH.

CHAPTER I.

THE SCRIPTURE IS A TRUE RULE OF CHRISTIAN FAITH.

I WELL know, thank God, that Tradition was before all Scripture, since a good part of Scripture itself is

only Tradition reduced to writing, with an infallible
assistance of the Holy Spirit. But, since the authority
of Scripture is more easily received by the reformers
than that of Tradition, I begin with the former in
order to get a better entrance for my argument.

Holy Scripture is in such sort the rule of the Christian faith that we are obliged by every kind of obligation to believe most exactly all that it contains, and
not to believe anything which may be ever so little
contrary to it: for if Our Lord himself has sent the
Jews to it * to strengthen their faith, it must be a
most safe standard. The Sadducees erred because
they did not understand the Scriptures; † they would
have done better to attend to them, *as to a light
shining in a dark place*, according to the advice of
S. Peter,‡ who having himself heard the voice of the
Father in the Transfiguration of the Son, bases himself
more firmly on the testimony of the Prophets than on
this experience. When God says to Josue: *Let not
the book of this law depart from thy mouth,*§ he shows
clearly that he willed him to have it always in his
mind, and to let no persuasion enter which should be
contrary to it. But I am losing time; this disputa-
tion would be needful against free-thinkers (*les Liber-
tins*); we are agreed on this point, and those who are
so mad as to contradict it, can only rest their contradiction on the Scripture itself, contradicting themselves
before contradicting the Scripture, using it in the very
protestation which they make that they will not
use it.

* John v. 39. † Mark xii. 24. ‡ Ep. 2, i. 19. § Jos. i. 8.

CHAPTER II.

HOW JEALOUS WE SHOULD BE OF THEIR INTEGRITY.

On this point, again, I will scarcely delay. The Holy Scripture is called the Book of the Old and of the New *Testament.* When a notary has drawn a contract or other deed, when a testament is confirmed by the death of the testator, there must not be added, withdrawn, or altered, one single word under penalty of falsification. Are not the Holy Scriptures the true testament of the eternal God, drawn by the notaries deputed for this purpose, duly sealed and signed with his blood, confirmed by death? Being such, how can we alter even the smallest point without impiety? " A testament," says the great Ulpian, " is a just expression of our will as to what we would have done after our death." * Our Lord by the Holy Scriptures shows us what we must believe, hope for, love, and do, and this by a true expression of his will; if we add, take away, or change, it will no longer be the true expression of God's will. For our Lord having duly expressed in Scripture his will, if we add anything of our own we shall make the statement go beyond the will of the testator, if we take anything away we shall make it fall short, if we make changes in it we shall set it awry, and it will no longer correspond to the will of the author, nor be a correct statement. When two things exactly correspond, he who changes the one destroys the equality and the correspondence between them. If it be a true statement, whatever right have

---

* Test. i. ff. *Qui test. facere possunt.*

we to alter it?   Our Lord puts a value on the iotas,
yea, the mere little points and accents of his holy
words.   How jealous then is he of their integrity, and
what punishment shall they not deserve who violate
this integrity!   *Brethren,* says S. Paul * (*I speak after
the manner of man*), *yet a man's testament, if it be confirmed, no man despiseth, nor addeth to it.*   And to
show how important it is to learn the Scripture in its
exactness he gives an example.   *To Abraham were the
promises made, and to his seed.   He says not and to his
seeds as of many, but as of one ; and to thy seed, who is
Christ.*   See, I beg you, how the change from singular
to plural would have spoilt the mysterious meaning of
this word.

The Ephrathites [Ephraimites] said *Sibolleth,* not
forgetting a single letter, but because they did not
pronounce it thickly enough, the Galaadites slew them
at the fords of Jordan.†   The simple difference of
pronunciation in speaking, and in writing the mere
transposition of one single point on the letter *scin*
caused the ambiguity, and changing the *janin* into
semol, instead of an ear of wheat expressed a weight
or a burden.   Whosoever alters or adds the slightest
accent in the Scripture is a sacrilegious man, and
deserves the death of him who dares to mingle the
profane with the sacred.

The Arians, as S. Augustine tells us,‡ corrupted this
sentence of S. John i. 1 : *In principio erat verbum, et
verbum erat apud Deum, et Deus erat verbum.   Hoc
erat in principio apud Deum :* by simply changing a
point.   For they read it thus : *Et verbum erat apud*

* Gal. iii. 15, 16.   † Judges xii. 6.
‡ *De doc. Chris.* iii. 2.

Deum et Deus erat.   Verbum hoc, &c.: instead of:
Deus erat verbum.   Hoc erat in principio apud Deum:
They placed the full stop after the *erat,* instead of
after the *verbum.*   They so acted for fear of having to
grant that the Word was God; so little is required to
change the sense of God's Word.   When one is handling glass beads, if two or three are lost, it is a small
matter, but if they were oriental pearls the loss would
be great.   The better the wine the more it suffers from
the mixture of a foreign flavour, and the exquisite sym-
metry of a great picture will not bear the admixture
of new colours.   Such is the conscientiousness with
which we ought to regard and handle the sacred
deposit of the Scriptures.

CHAPTER III.

WHAT ARE THE SACRED BOOKS OF THE WORD OF GOD.

THE Council of Trent gives these books as sacred,
divine and canonical: Genesis, Exodus, Leviticus,
Numbers, Deuteronomy, Josue, Judges, Ruth, the four
Books of Kings, two of Paralipomenon, two of Esdras
(a first, and a second which is called of Nehemias),
Tobias, Judith, Esther, Job, one hundred and fifty
Psalms of David, Proverbs, Fcclesiastes, the Canticle
of Canticles, Wisdom, Ecclesiasticus, Isaias, Jeremias
with Baruch, Ezechiel, Daniel, Osee, Joel, Amos,
Abdias, Jonas, Micheas, Nahum, Habacuc, Sophonias,
Aggeus, Zacharias, Malachy, two of Machabees, first
and second: of the New Testament, four Gospels,—S.

Matthew, S. Mark, S. Luke, S. John,—the Acts of the
Apostles by S. Luke, fourteen Epistles of S. Paul,—to
the Romans, two to the Corinthians, to the Galatians,
to the Ephesians, to the Philippians, to the Colossians,
two to the Thessalonians, two to Timothy, to Titus, to
Philemon, to the Hebrews,—two of S. Peter, three of
S. John, one of S. James, one of S. Jude, and the
Apocalypse. The same books were received at the
Council of Florence, and long before that, at the third
Council of Carthage about twelve hundred years ago.

These books are divided into two ranks. For of
some, both of the Old and of the New Testament, it
was never doubted but that they were sacred and
canonical: others there are about whose authority the
ancient Fathers doubted for a time, but afterwards
they were placed with those of the first rank.

Those of the first rank in the Old Testament are:
the five of Moses, Josue, Judges, Ruth, four of Kings,
two of Paralipomenon, two of Esdras and Nehemias,
Job, one hundred and fifty Psalms, Proverbs, Ecclesiastes, Canticles, the four greater Prophets, the twelve
lesser Prophets. These were formed into the canon
by the great synod at which Esdras was present, and
to which he was scribe; and no one ever doubted of
their authority without being at once considered a
heretic, as our learned Genebrard fully proves in his
Chronology.* The second rank contains the following:
Esther, Baruch, a part of Daniel (the history of Susanna,
the Canticle of the Three Children, and the history of
the death of the dragon in the fourteenth chapter),
Tobias, Judith, Wisdom, Ecclesiasticus, Machabees 1
and 2. And as to these there is a great probability

* Ad ann. 3638.

in the opinion of the same Doctor Genebrard * that in the meeting which was held at Jerusalem to send the seventy-two interpreters into Egypt, these books, which were not in existence when Esdras made the first canon, were placed on the canon, at least tacitly, because they were sent with the others to be translated, except the Machabees, which were received in another meeting afterwards, wherein the preceding were again approved. But however the case may be, as the second canon was not made so authentically as the first, this placing on the canon could not procure them an entire and unquestionable authority among the Jews, nor make them equal with the books of the first rank.

Coming to the books of the New Testament, I say that in the same way there are some of the first rank, which have always been acknowledged and received as sacred and canonical. These are the four Gospels, S. Matthew, S. Mark, S. Luke, S. John, all the Epistles of S. Paul except that to the Hebrews, one of S. Peter, one of S. John. Those of the second rank are the Epistle to the Hebrews, that of S. James, the second of S. Peter, the second and third of S. John, that of S. Jude, the 16th chapter of S. Mark, as S. Jerome says, and S. Luke's history of the bloody sweat of Our Lord in the garden of Olives, according to the same S. Jerome; in the eighth chapter of S. John there has been a doubt concerning the history of the woman taken in adultery, or at least some suspect that it has been doubted, and concerning verse seven of the last chapter of S.

* Ib. seqq. et ad ann. 3860. He quotes S. Epiph., *de mens. et pond.*, and Josephus, *contra App.* ii. S. Epiph. speaks only of Baruch.

John's First Epistle. These are, as far as we know, the books and parts of books concerning which it appears there was anciently some doubt. And these were not of undoubted authority in the Church at first, but as time went on they were at length recognised as the sacred work of the Holy Spirit, and not all at once but at different times. And first, besides those of the first rank, whether of the new or of the Old Testament, about the year 364 there were received at the Council of Laodicea * (which was afterwards approved in the sixth general Council †), the book of Esther, the Epistle of S. James, the Second of S. Peter, the Second and Third of S. John, that of S. Jude, and the Epistle to the Hebrews as the fourteenth of S. Paul. Then some time afterwards at the third Council of Carthage ‡ (at which S. Augustine assisted, and which was confirmed in the sixth general Council *in Trullo*), besides those of the second rank just mentioned, there were received into the canon, as of full authority, Tobias, Judith, First and Second Machabees, Wisdom, Ecclesiasticus, and the Apocalypse. But of all those of the second rank, the book of Judith was first received and acknowledged as divine, in the first General Council of Nice, as S. Jerome witnesses in his preface to this book. Such is the

---

* Can. lx.

† *i.e.* in Canon ii. of the Council *in Trullo* (or Quinisext), which is called by the Greeks the sixth General Council, as being a continuation or supplement of it. Such canons of this Council as were not opposed to previous decrees were approved by Rome. See Hefele Conc. Bk. xvii. The Saint's words are well defended by Alibrandi in the *processus*. Respons. pp. 80, 81. [Tr.]

‡ *i.e.* in Canon xxxvi. of the Council of Hippo, approved in third Council of Carthage. [Tr.]

way in which the two ranks were brought together into one, and ever made of equal authority in the Church of God, but progressively and with succession, as a beautiful morning rising, which little by little lights up our hemisphere.

Thus was drawn up in the Council of Carthage, that same ancient list of the canonical books which has ever since been in the Catholic Church, and which was confirmed in the sixth general Council, at the great Council of Florence 160 years ago for the union of the Armenians by the whole Church both Greek and Latin, in our age by the Council of Trent, and which was followed by S. Augustine.* Before the Council of Carthage they were not all received as canonical by any decree of the general Church. I had almost forgotten to say that you must not therefore make a difficulty against what I have just laid down because Baruch is not quoted by name in the Council of Carthage. For since Baruch was secretary of Jeremias, the book of Baruch was reckoned by the ancients as an accessory or appendix of Jeremias, being comprised under this; as that excellent theologian Bellarmine proves in his *Controversies.* But it is enough for me to have said thus: my brief outline is not obliged to dwell on every particular. In a word, all these books, whether of first or second rank, with all the parts, are equally certain, sacred and canonical, and are received in the Catholic Church.

* *De doc. Chr.* ii. 8.

CHAPTER IV.

FIRST VIOLATION OF THE HOLY SCRIPTURES MADE BY
THE REFORMERS : BY CUTTING OFF SOME OF ITS
PARTS.

SUCH are the sacred and canonical books which the
Church has unanimously received and acknowledged
during twelve hundred years. And by what authority
have these new reformers dared to wipe out at one
stroke so many noble parts of the Bible ? They have
erased a part of Esther, and Baruch, Tobias, Judith,
Wisdom, Ecclesiasticus, Machabees. Who has told
them that these books are not legitimate, and not to
be received ? Why do they thus dismember this
sacred body of the Scriptures ?

Here are their principal reasons, as far as I have
been able to gather them from the old preface to the
books which they pretend to be apocryphal, printed
at Neufchastel, in the translation of Peter Robert,
otherwise Olivetanus, a relation and friend of Calvin,
and again from the newer preface placed to the same
books by the professors and pretended pastors of the
Church of Geneva, 1588.

(1.) They are not found either in Hebrew or
Chaldaic, in which languages they (except perhaps the
Book of Wisdom) were originally written : therefore it
would be very difficult to restore them. (2.) They are
not received as legitimate by the Jews. (3.) Nor by
the whole Church. (4). S. Jerome says that they are
not considered proper for corroborating the authority
of Ecclesiastical doctrines. (5.) Canon Law condemns

them; (6.) as does also the Gloss, which says they are read, but not generally, as if to say that they are not approved generally everywhere. (7.) They have been corrupted and falsified, as Eusebius says ; * (8.) notably the Machabees, (9.) and particularly the Second of Machabees, which S. Jerome says he did not find in Hebrew. Such are the reasons of Olivetanus. (10.) "There are in them many false things," says the new preface. Let us now see what these fine researches are worth.

(1.) And as to the first,—are you unwilling to receive these books because they are not in Hebrew or Chaldaic ? Receive Tobias then, for S. Jerome attests that he translates it from Chaldaic into Latin, in the Epistle which you yourselves quote,† which makes me think you are hardly in good faith. And why not Judith, which was also written in Chaldaic, as the same S. Jerome says in the prologue ? And if S. Jerome says he was not able to find the second of Machabees in the Hebrew,—what has that to do with the first ? This then receive as it deserves; we will treat of the second afterwards. I say the same to you about Ecclesiasticus, which S. Jerome had and found in Hebrew, as he says in his preface on the books of Solomon. Since, then, you reject these books written in Hebrew or Chaldaic equally with the others which are not written in one of those languages, you will have to find another pretext than that which you have alleged for striking out these books from the canon. When you say that you reject them because they are not written in Hebrew or Chaldaic, this is not your real reason ; for you would not reject on this

* *Hist. Eccl.* iv. 22. † *Ep. ad Chrom. et Heliod.*

III.

ground Tobias, Judith, the first of Machabees, Ecclesiasticus, which are written either in Hebrew or Chaldaic.
But let us now speak in defence of the other books,
which are written in a language other than that which
you would have. Where do you find that the rule
for rightly receiving the Holy Scriptures is that they
should be written in these languages rather than in
Greek or Latin? You say that nothing must be
received in matter of religion but what is written;
and you bring forward in your grand preface the saying of jurisconsults: "We blush to speak without a
law." Do you not consider that the controversy
about the validity or invalidity of the Scriptures is
one of the most important in the sphere of religion?
Well then, either remain confounded, or else produce
the Holy Scripture for the negative which you maintain. The Holy Spirit certainly declares himself as
well in Greek as in Chaldaic. There would be, you
say, great difficulty in restoring them, since we do not
possess them in their original language, and it is this
which troubles you. But, for God's sake, tell me who
told you that they were lost, corrupted or altered, so
as to need restoration? You take for granted, perhaps,
that those who have translated them from the originals
have translated badly, and you would have the original
to compare them and judge them. Make your meaning clear then, and say that they are therefore apocryphal because you cannot yourselves be the translators
of them from the original, and cannot trust the judgment of the translator. So there is to be nothing
certain except what you have had the control of.
Show me this rule of certitude in the Scripture.
Further, are you fully assured that you have the

Hebrew texts of the books of the first rank, as pure and exact as they were in the time of the Apostles and of the Seventy ? Beware of errors. You certainly do not always follow them, and you could not, with good conscience. Show me this again in the Holy Scripture. Here, therefore, is your first reason most wanting in reason.

(2.) As to your saying that these books which you call apocryphal are not received by the Jews, you say nothing new or important. S. Augustine loudly exclaims : * "It is the Catholic Church which holds the Books of Machabees as canonical, not the Jews." Thank God, we are not Jews, we are Catholics. Show me from Scripture that the Christian Church has not as much power to give authority to the sacred books as the Mosaic may have had. There is not in this either Scripture or reason to show for it.

(3.) Yes, but the whole of the Church itself does not receive them, you say. Of what Church are you speaking ? Unquestionably the Catholic, which is the true Church, receives them, as S. Augustine has just now borne witness to you, and he repeats it, citing the Council of Carthage.† The Council *in Trullo* the 6th General, that of Florence, and a hundred ancient authors are [witnesses] thereto. I name S. Jerome, who witnesses for the book of Judith that it was received in the first Council [of Nice]. Perhaps you would say that of old time some Catholics doubted of their authority. This is clear from the division which I have made above. But does their doubt then make

* *De civ. Dei.* xviii. 36.

† The necessary references and explanations are given in notes to preceding chapter. [Tr.]

it impossible for their successors to come to a conclusion ? Are we to say that if one cannot decide at
the very first glance one must always remain wavering,
uncertain, and irresolute ? Was there not for some
time an uncertainty about the Apocalypse and Esther?
You would not dare to deny it: my witnesses for
Esther are too sound,—S. Athanasius * and S. Gregory
Nazianzen : † for the Apocalypse, the Council of
Laodicea :—and yet you receive them. Either receive
them all, since they are in equal position, or receive
none, on the same ground. But in God's name what
humour takes you that you here bring forward the
Church, whose authority you hold to be a hundred
times more uncertain than these books themselves,
and which you say to have been erring, inconstant,—
yea apocryphal, if apocryphal means hidden ? You
only prize it to despise it, and to make it appear inconstant, now recognising, now rejecting these books.
But there is a great difference between doubting
whether a thing is to be accepted and rejecting it.
Doubt does not hinder a subsequent resolution, indeed
it is its preliminary stage. To reject presupposes a
decision. Inconstancy does not consist in changing a
doubt into resolution, but in changing from resolution
to doubt. It is not instability to become settled after
wavering, but to waver after being settled. The
Church then, having for a time left these books in
doubt, at length has received them with authentic
decision, and you wish that from this resolution she
should return into doubt. It belongs to heresy and
not to the Church thus to advance from bad to worse.
But of this elsewhere.

* In *Synopsi.*   † In carm. *de lib. sac.*

(4.) As for S. Jerome whom you allege, this is not to the purpose, since in his time the Church had not yet come to the resolution which she has come to since, as to the placing of these books on the canon, except that of Judith.

(5.) And the canon *Sancta Romana,* which is of Gelasius I.—I think you have taken it by guess, for it is entirely against you; because, while censuring the apocryphal books, it does not name one of those which we receive, but on the contrary witnesses that Tobias and the Machabees were publicly received in the Church.

(6.) And the poor Gloss does not deserve to be thus glossed, since it clearly says that these books are read, though not perhaps generally. This " perhaps " guards it from stating what is false, and you have forgotten it. And if it reckon the books in question as apocryphal, this is because it considered that apocryphal meant the having no certain author, and therefore it includes as apocryphal the Book of Judges: and its statements are not so authentic that they must pass as decisive judgment; after all it is but a Gloss.

(7.) And these falsifications which you allege are not in any way sufficient to abolish the authority of these books, because they have been justified and have been purified from all corruption before the Church received them. Truly, all the books of Holy Scripture have been corrupted by the ancient enemies of the Church, but by the providence of God they have remained free and pure in the Church's hands, as a sacred deposit; and they have never been able to spoil so many copies as that there should not remain enough to restore the others.

(8.) But you would have the Machabees, at any rate, fall from our hands, when you say that they have been corrupted; but since you only advance a simple assertion I will return your pass by a simple negation.

(9.) S. Jerome, you say, could not find the Second in Hebrew; and although it is true that it is only as it were a letter which [those of] Israel sent to their Jewish brethren who were then out of Judea, and although it is written in the best known and most general language of those times, does it thence follow that it is not worthy to be received? The Egyptians used the Greek language much more than the Hebrew, as Ptolemy clearly showed when he procured the version of the Seventy. This is why this second book of Machabees, which was like an epistle or commentary sent for the consolation of the Jews who were in Egypt, was written in Greek rather than in Hebrew.

(10.) It remains for the new preachers to point out those falsehoods of which they accuse these books; which they will in truth never do. But I see them coming, bringing forward the intercession of Saints, prayer for the dead, free-will, the honouring of relics, and similar points, which are expressly confirmed in the Books of Machabees, in Ecclesiasticus, and in other books which they pretend to be apocryphal. For God's sake take care that your judgment does not deceive you. Why, I pray you, do you call false, things which the whole of antiquity has held as articles of faith? Why do you not rather censure your fancies which will not embrace the doctrine of these books, than censure these books which have been received for so long a time because they do not jump with your humour? Because you will not believe what the books teach, you condemn it;—why do you not rather condemn your presumption which is incredulous to their teaching ?

Here now, I think, are all your reasons scattered to the winds, and you can bring no more. But we may well say : if it be thus lawful indifferently to reject or make doubtful the authority of those Scriptures, about which there was formerly a doubt, though the Church has now decided, it will be necessary to reject or to doubt of a great part of the Old and the New Testament. It is then no little gain to the enemy of Christianity, to have at one stroke scratched out of the Holy Scripture so many noble parts. Let us proceed.

CHAPTER V.

SECOND VIOLATION OF THE SCRIPTURES : BY THE RULE WHICH THESE REFORMERS BRING FORWARD TO DISTINGUISH THE SACRED BOOKS FROM THE OTHERS : AND OF SOME SMALLER PARTS THEY CUT OFF FROM THEM ACCORDING TO THIS RULE.

THE crafty merchant keeps out the worst articles of his stock to offer first to buyers, to try if he can get rid of them and sell them to some simpleton. The reasons which these reformers have advanced in the preceding chapter are but tricks, as we have seen, which are used only as it were for amusement, to try whether some simple and weak brain will be content with them ; and, in reality, when one comes to the grapple, they confess that not the authority of the

Church, nor of S. Jerome, nor of the Gloss, nor of the
Hebrew, is cause sufficient to receive or reject any
Scripture. The following is their protestation of faith
presented to the King of France by the French pretended reformers. After having placed on the list, in
the third article, the books they are willing to receive,
they write thus in the fourth article: "We know
these books to be canonical and a most safe rule of
our faith, not so much by the common accord and consent of the Church, as by the testimony and interior
persuasion of the Holy Spirit, which gives us to discern them from the other ecclesiastical books." Quitting then the field of the reasons preceding, and
making for cover, they throw themselves into the
interior, secret, and invisible persuasion which they
consider to be produced in them by the Holy Spirit.

Now in truth it is judicious in them not to choose
to rely in this point on the conmon accord and consent
of the Church; for this common accord has placed on
the canon Ecclesiasticus and the Machabees, as much as
and as early as the Apocalypse, and yet they choose to
receive this and to reject those. Judith, made authoritative by the grand and irreproachable Council of
Nice, is blotted out by these reformers. They have
reason then to confess that in the reception of canonical books, they do not accept the accord and consent
of the Church, which was never greater or more solemn
than in that first Council.

But for God's sake notice the trick. "We know,"
say they, "these books to be canonical, *not so much* by
the common consent and accord of the Church." To
hear them speak, would you not say that at least to
some extent they let themselves be guided by the

Church ?   Their speech is not sincere : it seems as if
they did not altogether refuse credit to the common
accord of Christians, but only did not receive it as on
the same level with their interior persuasion :—in
reality, however, they hold it in no account at all :
they are thus cautious in their language in order not to
appear altogether arrogant and unreasonable.   For, I
ask you, if they deferred as little as you please to
ecclesiastical authority, why would they receive the
Apocalypse rather than Judith or the Machabees ?   S.
Augustine and S. Jerome are faithful witnesses to us
that these have been unanimously received by the
whole Catholic Church ; and the Councils of Carthage,
in Trullo, Florence, assure us thereof.   Why then do
they say that they do receive these sacred books *not
so much* by the common accord of the Church or by
interior persuasion, since the common accord of the
Church has neither value nor place in the matter ?
It is their custom when they would bring forward
some strange opinion not to speak clearly and frankly,
in order to give the reader a better impression.

And now let us look at the rule they have for
distinguishing the canonical books from the other
Ecclesiastical ones.   " The testimony," they say, " and
interior persuasion of the Holy Spirit."   Good heavens !
what obscurity, what dense fog, what shades of night !
Are we not now fully enlightened in so important
and grave a difference !   The question is how one
can tell these canonical books ; we wish to have some
rule to distinguish them ;—and they offer us something that passes in the interior of the soul, which
no one sees, nobody knows save the soul itself and its
Creator !

(1.) Show me clearly that when you tell me that such and such an inspiration exists in your conscience, you are not telling a lie. You say that you feel this persuasion within you. But why am I bound to believe you ? Is your word so powerful that I am forced under its authority to believe that you think and feel what you say. I am willing to hold you as good people enough, but when there is question of the foundations of my faith, as of receiving or rejecting the Ecclesiastical Scriptures, I find neither your ideas nor your words steady enough to serve me as a base.

(2.) Show me clearly that these inspirations and persuasions that you pretend to have are of the Holy Spirit. Who knows not that the spirit of darkness very often appears in clothing of light ?

(3.) Does this spirit grant his persuasions indifferently to every one, or only to some particular persons ? If to every one, how does it happen that so many millions of Catholics have never perceived them, nor so many women, working-people, and others among yourselves ? If it is to some in particular, show them me, I beg you,—and why to these rather than to others ? What mark will you give me to know them and to pick them out from the crowd of the rest of men ? Must I believe in the first who shall say : here you are ? This would be to put ourselves too much at a venture and at the mercy of deceivers. Show me then some infallible rule to recognise these inspired ones, these persuaded ones, or else permit me to credit none of them.

(4.) But, in conscience, do you think that the interior persuasion is a sufficient means to distinguish the Holy Scriptures, and put the nations out of doubt ?

How comes it then that Luther throws off the Epistle
of S. James, which Calvin receives? Try to harmonise,
I pray you, this spirit and his persuasions, who persuades the one to reject what he persuades the other
to receive. You will say, perhaps, that Luther is
mistaken. He will say as much of you. Which is
to be believed? Luther ridicules Ecclesiastes, he
considers Job a fable. Will you oppose him your
persuasion? he will oppose you his. So this spirit,
divided against himself, will leave you no other conclusion except to grow thoroughly obstinate, each in
his own opinion.

(5.) Then what reason is there that the Holy Spirit
should give inspirations as to what every one must
believe to nobodies, to Luther, to Calvin,—they having
abandoned without any such inspiration the Councils
and the entire Church. We do not deny, to speak
clearly, but that the knowledge of the true sacred
books is a gift of the Holy Spirit, but we say that
the Holy Spirit gives it to private individuals through
the medium of the Church. Indeed if God had a
thousand times revealed a thing to a private person we
should not be obliged to believe it unless he stamped
it so clearly that we could no longer call its validity
in question. But we see nothing of this among your
reformers. In a word, it is to the Church General
that the Holy Spirit immediately addresses his inspirations and persuasions, then, by the preaching of
the Church, he communicates them to private persons.
It is the Spouse in whom the milk is produced, then
the children suck it from her breasts. But you
would have it, on the contrary, that God inspires
private persons, and by these means the Church, that the

children receive the milk and the mother is nourished at their breasts ;—an absurdity.

Now if the Scripture is not violated and its majesty offended by the setting up of these interior and private inspirations, it never was nor will be violated. For by this means the door is open to every one to receive or reject of the Scriptures what shall seem good to him.   Why shall one allow Calvin to cut off Wisdom or the Machabees, and not Luther to remove the Epistle of S. James or the Apocalypse, or Castalio the Canticle of Canticles, or the Anabaptists the Gospel of S. Mark, or another person Genesis and Exodus ?   If all protest that they have interior revelation why shall we believe one rather than another, so that this rule supposed to be sacred on account of the Holy Spirit, will be violated by the audacity of every deceiver.

Recognise, I pray you, the stratagem.   They have taken away all authority from Tradition, the Church, the Councils,—what more remains ?   The Scripture. The enemy is crafty : if he would take all away at one stroke he would cause alarm.   He starts a certain and infallible method of getting rid of it bit by bit, and very gradually : that is, this idea of interior inspiration, by which everybody can receive or reject what seems good to him.   And in fact consider a little how the process works itself out.   Calvin removes and erases from the canon Baruch, Tobias, Judith, Wisdom, Ecclesiasticus, Machabees ; Luther takes away the Epistle of S. James, of S. Jude, the Second of S. Peter, the Second and Third of S. John, the Epistle to the Hebrews ; he ridicules Ecclesiastes, and holds Job a fable.   In Daniel, Calvin has erased the Canticle of the Three Children, the history of Susanna and that of the dragon of Bel; also a great part of Esther. In Exodus, at Geneva and elsewhere among these reformers, they have cut out the twenty-second verse of the second chapter, which is of such weight that neither the Seventy nor the other translators would ever have written it if it had not been in the original. Beza casts a doubt over the history of the adulteress in the Gospel of S. John (S. Augustine warns us that already the enemies of Christianity had erased it from their books; but not from all, as S. Jerome says). In the mysterious words of the Eucharist, do they not try to overthrow the authority of those words: *Which shall be shed for you,* because the Greek text * clearly shows that what was in the chalice was not wine, but the blood of Our Saviour? As if one were to say in French: *Ceci est la coupe du nouveau Testament en mon sang, laquelle sera respandüe pour vous.* For in this way of speaking that which is in the cup must be the true blood, not the wine; since the wine has not been shed for us but the blood, and the cup cannot be poured out except by reason of what it contains. What is the knife with which one has made so many amputations? This tenet of private inspiration. What is it that makes you reformers so bold to cut away one this piece, another that, and the other something else? The pretext of these interior persuasions of the Spirit, which makes them supreme each

---

* Not $\tau\hat{\varphi}$ in the Dative, agreeing with $a'\mu a\tau\iota$, but $\tau\hat{o}$ in the Nominative, agreeing with $\pi o\tau\eta\rho\iota o\nu$. The Saint represents this in French by the change of gender. It is not clearly expressed in the Latin, and our English translation would seem to favour the wrong meaning. *Shall be poured out* is more correct, but still ambiguous. [Tr.]

in his own idea, in judging as to the validity or invalidity of the Scriptures.   On the contrary, gentlemen, S. Augustine protests : * " For my part, I would not believe the Gospel unless the authority of the Catholic Church moved me thereto."   And elsewhere : † " We receive the New and the Old Testament in that number of books which the authority of the Catholic Church determines."   The Holy Spirit can give his inspirations as he likes, but as to the establishment of the public and general belief of the faithful, he only directs us to the Church.   It is hers to propose which are the true Scriptures and which are not.

CHAPTER VI.

ANSWER TO AN OBJECTION.

BUT here is the difficulty.   If these books were not from the beginning of undoubted authority in the Church, who can give them this authority ?   In truth the Church cannot give truth or certitude to the Scripture, or make a book canonical if it were not so, but the Church can make a book known as canonical, and make us certain of its certitude, and is fully able to declare that a book is canonical which is not held as such by every one, and thus to give it credit in Christendom ; not changing the substance of the book which of itself was canonical, but changing the persuasion of Christians, making it quite assured where previously it had not been so.

* *Contra Ep. Fund.* v.   † *Serm. de Temp.* cxci.

But how can the Church herself define that a book is canonical ?—for she is no longer guided by new revelations but by the old Apostolic ones, of which she has infallibility of interpretation. And if the Ancients have not had the revelation of the authority of a book, how then can she know it ? She considers the testimony of antiquity, the conformity which this book has with the others which are received, and the general relish which the Christian people find in it. For as we can know what is a proper and wholesome food for animals when we see them fond of it and feed on it with advantage, so, when the Church sees that the Christian people heartily relishes a book as canonical and gains good from it, she may know that it is a fit and wholesome meat for Christian souls ; and as when we would know whether one wine is of the same vintage as another we compare them, observing whether the colour, the smell and the taste are alike in the two, so when the Church has properly decided that a book has a taste, colour and smell— holiness of style, doctrine and mysteries—like to the other canonical books, and besides has the testimony of many good and irreproachable witnesses of antiquity, she can declare the book to be true brother of the other canonical ones. And we must not doubt that the Holy Spirit assists the Church in this judgment : for your ministers themselves confess that God has given the Holy Scriptures into her charge, and say that it is on this account S. Paul calls her the *pillar and ground of the truth.** And how would she guard them if she could not know and separate them from the mixture of other books ? And how important is

* 1 Tim. iii. 15.

it for the Church that she should be able to know
in proper time and season which Scriptures is holy
and which not: for if she received such and such
Scripture as holy and it was not, she would lead us
into superstition; and if she refused the honour and
belief which befit God's Word to a holy Scripture,
it would be an impiety. If ever then Our Lord
defends his Church against the gates of hell, if ever
the Holy Spirit assisted her so closely that she could
say: It *hath seemed good to the Holy Spirit and to us,*[*]
—we must firmly believe that he inspires her on
occasions of such great consequences as these; for it
would indeed be to abandon her at her need if he left
her at this juncture, on which depends not only an
article or two of our faith, but the substance of our
religion. When, therefore, the Church has declared
that a book is canonical, we must never doubt but
that it is so. We [are] here in the same position.
For Calvin and the very bibles of Geneva, and the
Lutherans, receive several books as holy, sacred, and
canonical which have not been acknowledged by all
the Ancients as such, and about which there has been a
doubt. If there has been a doubt formerly, what
reason can they have to make them assured and
certain nowadays, except that which S. Augustine had
[as we said above]: "I would not believe the Gospel
unless the authority of the Catholic Church moved
me;" and "We receive the New and the Old Testament in that number of books which the authority
of the Holy Catholic Church determines." Truly
we should be very ill assured if we were to rest
our faith on these particular interior inspirations, of

* Acts xv. 28.

which we only know that they exist or ever did exist,
by the testimony of some private persons.   And
granted that they are or have been, we do not know
whether they are from the false or of the true spirit;
and supposing they are of the true spirit, we do not
know whether they who relate them, relate them faithfully or not, since they have no mark of infallibility
whatever.   We should deserve to be wrecked if we
were to cast ourselves out of the ship of the public
judgment of the Church, to sail in the miserable skiff
of these new discordant private inspirations.   Our
faith would not be Catholic, but private.

But before I quit this subject, I pray you, reformers,
tell me whence you have taken the canon of the
Scriptures which you follow?   You have not taken it
from the Jews, for the books of the Gospels would
not be there; nor from the Council of Laodicea, for
the Apocalypse would not be in it; nor from the
Councils of Carthage or of Florence, for Ecclesiasticus
and the Machabees would be there.   Whence, then,
have you taken it?   In good sooth, like canon was
never spoken of before your time.   The Church never
saw canon of the Scriptures in which there was not
either more or less than in yours.   What likelihood
is there that the Holy Spirit has hidden himself from
all antiquity, and that after 1500 years he has disclosed
to certain private persons the list of the true Scriptures?   For our part we follow exactly the list of the
Council of Laodicea, with the addition made at the
Councils of Carthage and Florence.   Never will a man
of judgment leave these Councils to follow the
persuasions of private individuals.   Here, then, is the
fountain and source of all the violations which have

III.

been made of this holy rule; namely, when people have taken up the fancy of not receiving it save by the measure and rule of the inspirations which each one believes and thinks he feels.

CHAPTER VII.*

HOW GREATLY THE REFORMERS HAVE VIOLATED THE INTEGRITY OF THE SCRIPTURES.

Now, how can an honest soul refrain from giving the rein to the ardour of a holy zeal, and from entering into a Christian anger, without sin, considering with what presumption those who do nothing but cry, Scripture, Scripture, have despised, degraded, and profaned this divine Testament of the eternal Father, as they have falsified this sacred contract of so glorious an alliance! O ministers of Calvinism, how do you dare to cut away so many noble parts of the sacred body of the Bibles? You take away Baruch, Tobias, Judith, Wisdom, Ecclesiasticus, the Machabees:—why do you thus dismember the Holy Scripture? Who has told you that they are not sacred? There was some doubt about them in the ancient Church; but was there not doubt in the ancient Church about Esther, the Epistle to the Hebrews, those of S. James and S. Jude, the Second of S. Peter, the two last of

---

* Passages in this chapter coincide with passages in the chapters immediately preceding and following, but we have thought it better, for reasons explained in the Preface, to print it as it stands. It seems to be a fragment of a more extended treatment of this part. [Tr.]

S. John, and especially of the Apocalypse ? Why do you not also erase these as you have done those ? Acknowledge honestly that what you have done in this has only been in order to contradict the Church. You were angry at seeing in the Machabees the intercession of Saints and prayers for the departed : Ecclesiasticus stung you in that it bore witness to free-will and the honour of relics. Rather than do violence to your notions, adjusting them to the Scriptures, you have violated the Scriptures to accommodate them to your notions : you have cut off the holy Word to avoid cutting off your fancies : how will you ever cleanse yourselves from this sacrilege ? Have you degraded the Machabees, Ecclesiasticus, Tobias, and the rest, because some of the Ancients have doubted of their authority ? Why then do you receive the other books, about which there has been as much doubt as about these ? What can you oppose to them except that their doctrine is hard for you to accept ? Open your heart to faith, and you will easily receive that which your unbelief shuts out from you. Because you do not will to believe what they teach, you condemn them : rather condemn your presumption, and receive the Scripture. I would chiefly lay stress on the authority of those books which exercise you the most. Clement of Alexandria (*Strom.* v. 5, &c.), Cyprian (*Ep.* lxv.), Ambrose (*de fide* iv.), Augustine (*Ep. ad Oros. contra Prisc.*), and the rest of the Fathers consider Ecclesiasticus canonical. S. Cyprian (*Serm. de op et Eleem.*), S. Ambrose (*lib. de Tobiâ,* i.), S. Basil (*de avar.*), honour Tobias as Holy Scripture. S. Cyprian again (*de exhort. mar.*), S. Gregory Nazianzen (*orat. de Mach.*), S. Ambrose (*de Jacob et vit beat.*

x. xi.), believed the same of the Machabees. S. Augustine protests that : "it is the Catholic Church which holds the Books of Machabees as canonical, not the Jews." What will you say to this ?—that the Jews had them not in their catalogues ? S. Augustine acknowledges it ; but are you Jews, or Christians ? If you would be called Christians, be satisfied that the Christian Church receives them. Is the light of the Holy Spirit extinguished with the synagogue ? Had not our Lord and the Apostles as much power as the synagogue ? Although the Church has not taken authority for her books from the mouth of the Scribes and Pharisees, will it not suffice that she has taken it from the testimony of the Apostles ? Now we must not think that the ancient Church and these most ancient doctors would have had the boldness to rank these books as canonical, if they had not had some direction by the tradition of the Apostles and their disciples who could know in what rank the Master himself held them :—unless, to excuse our imaginations, we are to accuse of profanation, and of sacrilege, such holy and grave doctors as these, and the whole ancient Church. I say the ancient Church, because the Council of Carthage, Gelasius in the decree *de libris canonicis,* Innocent I. in the epistle to Exuperius, and S. Augustine, lived before S. Gregory, before whose time Calvin confesses that the Church was still in its purity, and yet these bear witness that all the books which we held to be canonical when Luther appeared were already so in their time. If you would destroy the credit of those holy books, why did you not destroy that of the Apocalypse, about which there has been so much doubt, and that of the

Epistle to the Hebrews? But I return to you, gentlemen of Thonon, who have hitherto given ear to such
men; I beseech you, let us say in conscience, is there
any likelihood that Calvin knows better what grounds
they had who anciently doubted of these books, and
what grounds they who doubted not, than the Bishops
and Councils of these days? And still, all things
well considered, antiquity received them;—what do we
allege to the contrary? Oh! if it were lawful for men,
in order to raise their opinions on horseback, to use
the Scripture as stirrups, to lengthen and shorten
them, each one to his own size, where, I beg you,
should we be? Do you not perceive the stratagem?
All authority is taken away from Tradition, the Church,
the Councils, the Pastors: what further remains? The
Scripture. The enemy is crafty. If he would tear it all
away at once he would cause an alarm; he takes away
a great part of it in the very beginning, then first one
piece, then the other, at last he will have you stripped
entirely, without Scripture and without Word of God.

Calvin takes away seven books of the Scripture : *
Baruch, Tobias, Judith, Wisdom, Ecclesiasticus, and
the Machabees; Luther has removed the Epistle of S.
James, that of S. Jude, the 2nd of S. Peter, the 2nd
and 3rd of S. John, the Epistle to the Hebrews; he ridi-
cules Ecclesiastes, he holds Job as a fable. Reconcile,
I pray you, this false spirit, who takes away from
Luther's brain what he puts back in that of Calvin.
Does this seem to you a trifling discord between these
two evangelists? You will say you do not hold
Luther's intelligence in great account; his party think
no better of that of Calvin. But see the progress of

* *In prologis Bib. et horum lib.*

your fine church, how she ever pushes on further.
Calvin had removed seven books, she has further
thrown out the 8th, that of Esther : * in Daniel she
cuts off the canticle of the Three Children (c. iii.),
the history of Susanna (c. xiii.), and that of the dragon
slain by Daniel (xiv). In the Gospel of S. John is
there not doubt among you of the history of the
woman taken in adultery ? S. Augustine had indeed
said formerly that the enemies of the faith had erased
it from their books, but not from all, as S. Jerome
says. Do they not wish to take away these words of
S. Luke (xxii. 20), *which shall be shed for you,* because
the Greek text (το ὑπερ ὑμῶν ἐκχυνόμενον) clearly
shows that what was in the chalice was not wine, but
the true blood of our Lord ?——as if one were to say in
French : *Cecy est la coupe du Nouveau Testament, en
mon sang, laquelle sera respandue pour vous* : *this is the
chalice, the New Testament in my blood, which* (chalice)
shall be shed for you? For in this way of speaking
one sees clearly that what is in the cup must be the
blood, not wine, since the wine has not been shed for
us, but the blood. In the Epistle of S. John, have
they not taken away these noble words : *every spirit
who dissolveth Jesus is not of God* (iv. 3) ? What say
you, gentlemen ? If your church continues in this
liberty of conscience, making no scruple to take away
what she pleases, soon the Scripture will fail you, and
you will have to be satisfied with the *Institutes* of Calvin, which must indeed have I know not what excellence, since they censure the Scriptures themselves !

---

* At this time the so-called reformers did not decidedly accept the
book of Esther as canonical. It is now accepted by their followers up
to chap. x. v. 4. [Tr.]

CHAPTER VIII.

HOW THE MAJESTY OF THE SCRIPTURES HAS BEEN VIOLATED IN THE INTERPRETATIONS AND VERSIONS OF THE HERETICS.

SHALL I say further this word? Your fine church has not contented itself with cutting off from the Scripture entire books, chapters, sentences and words, but what it has not dared to cut off altogether it has corrupted and violated by its translations. In order that the sectaries of this age may altogether pervert this first and most holy rule of our faith, they have not been satisfied with shortening it or with getting rid of so many beautiful parts, but they have turned and turned it about, each one as he chose, and instead of adjusting their ideas by this rule they have adopted it to the square of their own greater or less sufficiency. The Church had universally received (more than a thousand years ago) the Latin version which the Catholic Church proposes; S. Jerome, that most learned man, was the author, or corrector of it; when, in our age, behold arise a thick mist created by *the spirit of giddiness,** which has so led astray these refurbishers of old opinions formerly current, that everybody has wanted to drag, one to this side, one to that, and always according to the inclination of his own judgment, this holy and sacred Scripture of God. Herein who sees not the profanation of this sacred vase of the holy letter, in which was preserved the precious balm of the Evangelical doctrine? For would it not have been a profanation of the Ark of the

* Isa. xix. 14.

Covenant to maintain that everybody might seize it, carry it home, take it all to pieces, and then give it what form he liked provided that it had some semblance of an ark ? And what but this is it to maintain that one may take the Scriptures and turn and adjust them according to one's own sense ? And in just the same way, as soon as we are assured that the ordinary edition of the church is so out of shape that it must be built up again new, and that a private man is to set his hand to it and begin the process, the door is open to presumption. For if Luther dares to do it, —why not Erasmus ? And if Erasmus, why not Calvin or Melancthon, why not Henricus Mercerus, Sebastian Castalio, Beza, and the rest of the world, provided that they know some verses of Pindar and four or five words of Hebrew, and have close by some good *Thesaurus* of the one or other language ? And how can so many translations be made by brains so different, without the complete overthrow of the sincerity of the Scripture ? What say you ? that the ordinary version is corrupt ? We allow that transcribers and printers have let certain ambiguities of very slight importance slip in (if, however, anything in the Scripture can be called of slight importance). The Council of Trent commanded that these should be taken out, and that for the future care should be taken to print as correctly as possible. For the rest, there is nothing in it which is not most conformable to the meaning of the Holy Spirit who is its author, as has been shown by so many learned men of our Church,* opposing the presumption of these new re-

* Genebrard *in præf. Psalt. ;* Titelman, Toletus, *in apol.* Bellarminus et alii.

formers of religion, that it would be losing time to
try to speak more of it ; besides that it would be folly
in me to wish to speak of the correctness of translations, who never well knew how to read with the
points in one of the languages necessary for this
knowledge, and am hardly more learned in the other.
But how have you improved matters ? Everybody
has held to his own views, everybody has despised
his neighbour's ; they have turned it about as they
liked, but no one speaks of his comrade's version.
What is this but to overthrow the majesty of the
Scripture, and to bring it into contempt with the
people, who think that this diversity of editions
comes rather from the uncertainty of the Scriptures
than from the variety of the translators, a variety
which alone ought to put us in assurance concerning the ancient translation, which, as the Council
says, the Church has so long, so constantly, and so
unanimously approved.

An example or two will suffice. In the Acts,*
where there is : *Thou shalt not leave my soul in hell*
(*animam in inferno*), they make it : Thou shalt not
leave my corpse in the tomb (*cadaver in sepulchro*).
Whoever saw such versions ? Instead of soul (and it
is Our Lord who is spoken of) to say carrion, and
instead of hell to say sepulchre ! Peter Martyr (*in
def. de Euch.* p. 3ᵃ, p. 392) cites I Cor. x. 3, *and
they all eat the same spiritual food as we (nobiscum) :*
he inserts this *nobiscum* to prove his point. I have
seen in several bibles in this country a very subtle
falsehood, in the mysterious words of the institution of
the most Holy Sacrament : instead of *hoc est corpus*

* ii. 27.

meum, cecy est mon corps; they had put: *c'est cy mon corps.** Who does not perceive the deceit?

You see something then of the violence and profanation your ministers do and offer to the Scriptures: what think you of their ways? What will become of us if everybody takes leave, as soon as he knows two words of Greek, and the letters in Hebrew, thus to turn everything topsy turvy? I have therefore shown you what I promised,—that this first rule of our faith has been and still is most sadly violated in your pretended church; and that you may know it to be a property of heresy thus to dismember the Scriptures, I will close this part of my subject with what Tertullian says,† speaking of the sects of his time. "This heresy" [of the Gnostics], says he, "does not receive some of the Scriptures; and if it receives some it does not receive them whole . . . and what it receives in a certain sense whole, it still perverts, devising various interpretations."

CHAPTER IX.

OF THE PROFANATIONS CONTAINED IN THE VERSIONS MADE INTO THE VULGAR TONGUE.

BUT if the case be thus with the Latin versions, how great are the contempt and profanation shown in the French, German, Polish, and other languages! And yet here is one of the most successful artifices adopted

---

* Here is my body, instead of *This is my body.* [Tr.]
† de Prœscr. xvii.

by the enemy of Christianity and of unity in our age, to attract the people. He knew the curiosity of men, and how much one esteems one's own judgment; and therefore he has induced his sectaries to translate the Holy Scriptures, every one into the tongue of the province where he finds himself placed, and to maintain this unheard-of opinion, that every one is capable of understanding the Scriptures, that all should read them, and that the public offices should be celebrated and sung in the vulgar tongue of each district.

But who sees not the artifice? There is nothing in the world which, passing through many hands, does not change and lose it first lustre: wine which has been often poured out and poured back loses its freshness and strength, wax when handled changes its colour, coins lose their stamp. Be sure also that Holy Scripture, passing through so many translators, in so many versions and re-versions, cannot but be altered. And if in the Latin versions there is such a variety of opinion among these turners of Scripture, how much more in their vernacular and mother-tongue editions, which not every one is able to check or to criticise? It gives a very great license to translators to know that they will only be tested by those of their own province. Every district has not such clear seeing eyes as France and Germany. "Are we sure," says a learned profane writer,* "that in the Basque provinces and in Brittany there are persons of sufficient judgment to give authority to this translation made into their tongue; the universal Church has no more arduous decision to give;" it is Satan's plan for corrupting the integrity of this holy Testament. He well knows

* Montaigne. Essaies 1. 56. See Preface.

the result of disturbing and poisoning the source; it is at once to spoil all that comes after.

But let us be frank. Do we not know that the Apostles spoke all tongues? How is it then that their gospels and their epistles are only in *Hebrew*, as S. Jerome witnesses * of the Gospel of S. Matthew; in *Latin*, as some think concerning that of S. Mark; † and in *Greek*, as is held concerning the other Gospels? which were the three languages chosen at Our Lord's very cross for the preaching of the Crucified. Did they not carry the Gospel throughout the world? and in the world were there no other languages but these three? Truly there were, and yet they did not judge it expedient to vary their writings in so many languages. Who then shall despise the custom of our Church, which has for its warrant the imitation of the Apostles? ‡ Now for this, besides the great weight

* Prol. in Matt.

† In Pontificali Damasi. The Saint mentions the opinion, but he himself held the now universal sentiment of Doctors that S. Mark wrote in Greek. [Tr.]

‡ Of this we have a notable trace and evidence in the Gospel: for the day Our Lord entered into Jerusalem, the crowds kept crying out: *Hosanna to the Son of David; blessed is he that cometh in the name of the Lord: hosanna in the highest* (Matt. xxi. 9.) And this word, *hosanna*, has been left in its integrity in the Greek text of S. Mark and S. John, to signify that it was the very word of the people. Now *hosanna*, or *hosianna* (for one is the same as the other in this language, the learned tell us) is a Hebrew, not a Syriac word, taken, with the rest of that praise which was given to Our Lord, from the 117th Psalm. · These people then were accustomed to recite the Psalms in Hebrew; yet the Hebrew was no longer their vulgar tongue;—as one may see by several words said in the Gospel by Our Lord, which were Syriac and which the Evangelists have retained: as *Abba, Haceldama, Golgotha, Pascha*, and others. Learned men tell us that these were not Hebrew but Syraic, though they may be called Hebrew as being of the vernacular tongue of the Hebrews after the captivity of Babylon.

it should have to put down all our curious questionings, there is a reason which I hold to be most sound: it is that these other languages are not fixed, they change between town and town; in accents, in phrases, and in words, they are altered, and vary from season to season and from age to age. Take up the *Memoires* of the Sire de Joinville, or of Philip de Comines, and you will see that time has entirely altered their language; and yet these historians must have been among the most polished of their age, both having been brought up at Court. If then we were to have (particularly for the public services) bibles each in our own tongue, every fifty years it would be necessary to have a revolution, and in every case with adding to, or taking away from, or altering, much of the holy exactness of the Scripture, which could not be done without a great loss. In short, it is more than reasonable that so holy a rule as is the holy Word of God should be kept in fixed languages, since it could not be maintained in this perfect integrity within bastard and unstable languages.

But I inform you that the holy Council of Trent does not reject translations in the vulgar tongue printed by the authority of the Ordinaries; only it commands * that we should not begin to read them without leave of superiors. This is a very reasonable precaution against putting this sharp and *two-edged sword* † into the hands of one who might kill himself therewith. But of this we will speak by and by.

The Church, then, does not approve that everybody who can read, without further assurance of his capacity than that which he persuades himself of in his

* Reg. iv. Indicis.   † Heb. iv. 12.

own presumption, should handle this sacred memorial, nor truly is it right that she should so approve.

I remember to have read in an Essay of the Sieur de Montaigne's (see above), " It is certainly wrong that there should be seen tossing about in everybody's hands, in parlour and in kitchen, the holy book of the sacred mysteries of our belief. . . . It is not casually or hurriedly that we are to prosecute so serious and venerable a study; it should be a reflective and steady act, to which should always be added that preface of our office : *sursum corda,* and for which the body itself should be brought into a haviour which may betoken a particular attention and reverence . . . and I more-over believe that liberty for everybody to translate it, and by this means to dissipate words so religious and important into all sorts of languages, has much more danger than profit."

The Council also commands* that the public services of the Church shall not be celebrated in the vulgar tongue, but in a fixed language, each one according to the ancient formularies approved by the Church. This decree takes its reasons from what I have already said; for if it is not expedient thus to translate, at every turn, province by province, the venerable text of the Scripture, the greatest part, and we may say all, that is in the offices being taken from the Holy Scripture, it is also not becoming to give these in French. Indeed, is there not a greater danger in reciting the Holy Scripture in the vulgar tongue at public services, on this account that not only the old but little children, not only the wise but the foolish, not only men but women, in short both he who knows

* Sess. ii.

and he who knows not how to read, may all take
occasion of erring, each one as he likes? Read the
passages of David where he seems to murmur against
God concerning the prosperity of the wicked; you
will see the unwise people justify themselves by this
in their impatience. Read where he seems to demand
vengeance against his enemies, and the spirit of
vengeance will cloak itself under this. Let them see
those heavenly and entirely divine loves in the
Canticle of Canticles; from not knowing how to spiri-
tualize them these will only profit them unto evil.
And that word of Osee : * *Vade et fac tibi filios forni-
cationes*, and those acts of the ancient Patriarchs,—
would they not give license to fools? But pray give
us some little reason why we should have the Scriptures and Divine Services in the vulgar tongue. To
learn doctrine thereby? But surely the doctrine
cannot be therein found unless we open the bark of
the letter, in which is contained the intelligence:
I will show this directly in its place. What is useful
for this purpose is not the reciting of the service
but preaching, in which the Word of God is not only
pronounced but expounded by the pastor. And who
is he, however well furnished at all points (*tant
houppé soit il et ferré*), who can understand without
study the prophecies of Ezechiel, and others, and the
Psalms? What, then, will the people do with them
when they hear them except profane them and cast a
doubt on them.

At any rate we who are Catholics must in no wise
bring down our sacred offices into vernacular languages;
but rather, as our Church is universal in time and in

* i. 2.

place, it ought also to celebrate public offices in a
language which is universal in time and in place, as is
Latin in the West, Greek in the East; otherwise our
priests could not say Mass nor others understand them
outside their own countries.   The unity and the great
extension of our brethren require that we should say
our public prayers in a language which shall be common to all peoples.   In this way our prayers are
universal, by means of the number of persons who in
each province can understand Latin, and it seems to
me, in conscience, that this reason alone should suffice;
for if we consider rightly, our prayers are heard no less
in Latin than in French.   Let us divide the body of
a commonwealth into three parts, according to the
ancient French division, or, according to the new, into
four; there are four sets of persons: the clergy, the
nobility, they of the long robe, and the people or third
estate.   The three first understand Latin or should
understand it, if they do not rather make it their own
language; there remains the lowest rank, of which,
again, a part understand; and truly as for the rest, if
one do not speak the jargon of their country, it is only
with great difficulty that they could understand the
simple narrative of the Scripture.   That most excellent
theologian, Robert Bellarmine,* relates, having heard
it from a most trustworthy source, that a good dame
in England having heard a minister read the twenty-
fifth chapter of Ecclesiasticus (though they only hold
it to be an ancient book, not a canonical one), because
it there speaks of the wickedness of women, rose up,
saying: What!—is this the Word of God?—of the
devil rather.   He quotes from Theodoret † an excellent

* On this question.   * Hist. i.

and true word of S. Basil the Great. The chief of the
Emperor's kitchen wishing to play the sage, began to
bring forward certain passages of the Scripture : " It
is yours [said the Saint] to mind your dishes, not to
cook divine dogmata: " as if he had said : Occupy
yourself with tasting your sauces, not with devouring
the divine Word.

CHAPTER X.

OF THE PROFANATION OF THE SCRIPTURES THROUGH THE
FACILITY THEY PRETEND THERE IS IN UNDERSTAND-
ING SCRIPTURE.

THE imagination must have great power over Huguenot
understandings, since it persuades them so absolutely
of this grand absurdity, that the Scriptures are easy
to everybody, and that everybody can understand them.
It is true that to bring forth vulgar translations with
honour it was necessary to speak in this manner; but
tell me the truth, do you think that the case really
runs so ? Do you find them so easy, do you understand them so well ? If you think you do, I admire
your credulity, which goes not only beyond experience, but is contrary to what you see and feel. If it
is true that the Scripture is so easy to understand,
what is the use of so many commentaries made by
your ministers, what is the object of so many har-
monies, what is the good of so many schools of Theology ? There is need of no more, say you, than the
doctrine of the pure word of God in the Church. But
where is this word of God ? In the Scripture ? And

III.

Scripture—is it some secret thing? No—you say not to the faithful. Why, then, these interpreters and these preachers? If you are faithful, you will understand the Scriptures as well as they do; send them off to unbelievers, and simply keep some deacons to give you the morsel of bread and pour out the wine of your supper. If you can feed yourselves in the field of the Scripture, what do you want with pastors? Some young innocent, some mere child who is able to read, will do just as well. But whence comes this continual and irreconcilable discord which there is among you, brethren in Luther, over these words, *This is my body*, and on Justification? Certainly S. Peter is not of your thinking, who assures us in his 2nd Epistle* that in the letters of S. Paul there are certain points *hard to be understood, which the unlearned and unstable wrest, as also the other Scriptures, to their own perdition.* The eunuch who was treasurer-general of Ethiopia was certainly faithful, † since he came to adore in the Temple of Jerusalem; he was reading Isaias; he quite understood the words, since he asked of what prophet that which he had read was to be understood; yet still he had not the understanding nor the spirit of them, as he himself confessed: *How can I, unless some one shows me?* Not only does he not understand, but he confesses that he has not the power unless he is taught. And we shall see some washerwoman boast of understanding the Scripture as well as S. Bernard did! Do you not know the spirit of discord? It is necessary to convince oneself that the Scripture is easy in order that everybody may drag it about, some one way, some another, that each

* iii. 16.   † Acts viii.

one may be a master in it, and that it may serve
everybody's opinions and fancies. Certainly David
held it to be far from easy when he said: * *Give me
understanding, that I may learn thy commandments.*
If they have left you the Epistle of S. Jerome to
Paulinus in the preface of your bibles, read it, for it
treats this point expressly. S. Augustine speaks of it
in a thousand places, but particularly in his Confessions. In the 119th Epistle he confesses that there
is much more in the Scripture of which he is ignorant
than there is of what he knows. Origen and S.
Jerome, the former in his preface on the Canticles,
the latter in his on Ezechiel, say that it was not permitted to the Jews before the age of thirty to read
the three first chapters of Genesis, the commencement
and the end of Ezechiel, or the Canticle of Canticles,
on account of the depth of the difficulties therein, in
which few persons can swim without being submerged.
And now, everybody talks of them, everybody criticises
them, everybody knows all about them.

And how great the profanation of the Scriptures is
in this way nobody could sufficiently believe who had
not seen it. As for me, I will say what I know, and I
lie not. I have seen a person in good society who, when
one objected to an expression of hers the sentence of
Our Lord †— *To him that striketh thee on the one cheek
offer also the other*,—immediately explained it in this
sense : that as to encourage a child who studies well
we lay our hand lightly with little pats upon his cheek
to excite him to do better, so Our Lord meant to say :
be so grateful to one who may find you doing right
and who may caress you for it that he may take

* Ps. cxviii. 73.   † Luke vi. 29.

occasion another time to treat you still better and to caress or fondle you on both sides. Is not that a fine meaning and a precious? But the reason was even better,—that to understand this text otherwise would be against nature, and that while we must interpret Scripture by Scripture, we find in Scripture that Our Lord did not do so when the servant struck him: this is the fruit of your translated theology. An honest man, and one who in my opinion would not lie, has related to me that he heard a minister of this country, treating of the Nativity of Our Lord, assert that he was not born in a crib, and expound the text (which is express on the other side) figuratively, saying: Our Lord also says that he is the vine, yet for all that he is not one; in the same way, although it is said that he is born in a crib, yet born there he is not, but in some honourable place which in comparison with his greatness might be called a crib. The character of this interpretation leads me still more to believe the man who told me, for being simple and unable to read he could hardly have made it up. It is a most curious thing to see how this pretended enlightenment causes the Holy Scripture to be profaned. Is it not doing what God says in Ezechiel: * *Was it not enough for you to feed upon good pastures ; but you must also tread down with your feet the residue of the pastures ?*

* xxxiv. 18.

CHAPTER XI.

ON THE PROFANATION OF THE SCRIPTURES IN THE VERSIFIED PSALMS USED BY THE PRETENDED REFORMERS.

BUT amongst all profanations it seems to me that this comes out above the rest, that in the temples publicly, and everywhere, in the fields, in the shops, they sing the rhymes of Marot as Psalms of David. The mere incompetence of the author, who was utterly ignorant; his licentiousness, which he testifies by his writings; his most profane life, which had nothing whatever of the Christian about it, caused him to be refused the communion of the Church. And yet his name and his psalms are, as it were, sacred in your churches; they are recited among you as if they were David's,—whereas who sees not how the sacred word is violated ? The measure and restrictions of verse make it impossible that the sacred meaning of the Scripture words should be followed; he mixes in his own to make sense, and it becomes necessary for this ignorant rhymester to choose one sense in places where there might be several. What! is it not an extreme violation and profanation to have left to such an empty-headed witling a judgment of such great consequence, and then in the public prayers to follow as closely this buffoon's selection as one ever did formerly the interpretation of the Seventy, who were so particularly assisted by the Holy Spirit ? How many words and how many sentences has he secreted therein which were never in the Scriptures ?

This is a very different thing from ill-pronouncing
*Scibboleth.** At the same time it is well known that
there is nothing which has so delighted busybodies,
and above all women, as this authorisation to sing in
the church and at the meetings. Certainly we forbid
no one to sing devoutly, modestly, and becomingly ;
but it seems more proper that Ecclesiastics and their
deputies should sing as a general rule, as was done in
the Dedication of Solomon's Temple. O how delightful
to get one's voice heard in the church ! But do they
not betray you in the songs they make you utter ?
I have not leisure or convenience for going into the
matter further. When you shout these verses of the
8th Psalm :—*Thou hast made him such that no more
remains to him except to be God ; but as to all else thou
hast,* &c.—how delighted you are to be able to chant
and sing these French rhymes *Marotées.* It would
be much better to keep to the Latin than to blaspheme
in French. Accept this warning. When you sing
this verse, whom do you suppose you speak of ? You
speak of Our Lord, unless, to excuse the audacity of
Marot and of your church, you also erase the Epistle
to the Hebrews from the holy Bible: for S. Paul
clearly there (ii. 6, 7, 8) expounds this verse of Our
Lord. And if you speak of Our Lord, why do you
say he is such that no more now remains for him
except to be God ? Questionless if anything now
remains to him to be God he will never be it. What
say you, poor people ?—that it " remains " for Jesus
Christ to be God ? See how those men make you
swallow the poisoned morsel of Arianism, in singing
these sorry rhymes. I am no longer astonished that

* Judges xii. 6.   *i.e.* of Marot. [Tr.]

Calvin confessed to Valentine Gentilis, that the Name of God by excellence belongs only to the Father. Behold the splendid eversions of the Scripture with which you are well pleased; behold the blasphemies which your Church sings in a body, and which she makes you repeat so often.

And as to this fashion of having the Psalms sung indifferently in all places and during all occupations, who sees not that it is a contempt of religion? Is it not to offend His Divine Majesty to say to him words as excellent as those of the Psalms, without any reverence or attention? To say prayers after the manner of common talking, is this not a mocking of him to whom we speak? When we see at Geneva or elsewhere a shop-boy laughing during the singing of the Psalms, and breaking the thread of a most beautiful prayer, to say: What will you buy, sir?— do we not clearly see that he is making an accessary of the principal, and that it is only for pastime that he was singing this divine song, which he at the same time believes to be of the Holy Spirit? Is it not good to hear cooks singing the penitential Psalms of David, and asking at each verse for the bacon, the capon, the partridge! "That voice," says De Montaigne, "is too divine to have no other use than to exercise the lungs and please the ears." * I allow that all places are good to pray in privately, and the same holds good of every occupation which is not sin, provided that we pray in spirit, because God sees the interior wherein lies the chief and substantial part of prayer. But I consider that he who prays in public ought to make exterior demonstration of the

* Same Essay.

reverence which the very words he is uttering demand :
otherwise he scandalises his neighbour, who is not
bound to think there is religion in the interior when
he sees the contempt in the exterior.   I hold, then, that
both in singing as divine Psalms what is very often
an imagination of Marot's, and in singing them irrever-
ently and without respect, they very often sin in that
reformed church of yours against that word : *God is a*
spirit, and those who adore him must adore him in
spirit and in truth.*   For besides that in these
Psalms you very often attribute to the Holy Ghost
the conceptions of Marot contrary to *the truth*, the
mouth also cries in streets and kitchens : *O Lord !*
O Lord ! when the heart and *the spirit* are not there
but in traffic and gain, as Isaias says : † You *draw*
near God *with* your *mouth, and with* your *lips glorify*
him, *but* your *heart is far from* him, *and* you *have*
feared him *according to the commandment and doctrines*
of men.   It is quite true that this impropriety of
praying without devotion occurs very often among
Catholics, but it is not with the advertence of the
Church : and I am not now blaming particular
members of your party, but your body in general,
which by its versions and liberties bring into profane
use what should be treated with the greatest reverence. ‡   In chapter 14 of the 1st of Corinthians, the
Let women keep silence in the churches seems to be
understood of hymns (*cantiques*) as much as of the
rest : our nuns are *in oratorio non in ecclesiâ.*

---

* John iv. 23.   † xxix. 13.
‡ The following sentence is in the autograph placed between bars,
and seems meant to be amplified. [Tr.]

CHAPTER XII.

ANSWER TO OBJECTIONS; AND CONCLUSION OF THIS FIRST ARTICLE.

Now follows what you allege in your defence. S. Paul seems * to want to have the service performed in a language intelligible to the Corinthians; you will see that at the same time he does not wish the service to be diversified with all sorts of languages, but only that the exhortations and hymns which were uttered by means of the gift of tongues should be interpreted, in order that the Church where any one might be should know what was said: *And therefore he that speaketh by a tongue, let him pray that he may interpret.* He intends, then, that the praises which were made at Corinth should be made in Greek: for as they were made not now as ordinary services, but as the extraordinary hymns of those who had this gift, for the gladdening of the people, it was reasonable that they should be made in intelligible language, or be at once interpreted. This he seems to show when he says lower down: *If, therefore, the whole church come together into one place, and all speak with tongues, and there come in unlearned persons or infidels, will they not say that you are mad?* And further on: *If any speak with a tongue, let it be by two, or at the most by three, and in course, and let one interpret. But if there be no interpreter, let him hold his peace in the church, and speak to himself and to God.* Who sees not that he is not speak-

* Cor. xiv.

ing of the solemn offices in the Church, which were only
performed by the pastor, but of the hymns which were
made through the gift of tongues, which he wished to
be understood? for in truth if they were not, it dis-
tracted the assembly, and was of no benefit.   Several
ancient Fathers speak of these hymns, and amongst
others Tertullian, who, treating of the holiness of the
agapes or *love feasts* of the ancients, says : * " After the
washing of hands and the lamps, each one is pressed
to sing publicly to God as he is able, out of the Holy
Scriptures or his own heart."

This people glorify me with their lips, but their heart,
&c.†   This is meant of those who, singing and praying
in any language whatever, speak of God mechanically,
without reverence and devotion; not of those who
speak a language unknown to them but known to the
Church, and who, moreover, have their heart rapt
unto God.

In the Acts of the Apostles they praised God in all
tongues.   So they should do; but in universal and
Catholic offices there is need of a universal and
Catholic language.   Except for this, every tongue
confesses that Jesus Christ is at the right hand of
God the Father.‡

In Deuteronomy,§ it is said that the commandments
of God are not secret or sealed up; and does not the
Psalmist say : *The commandment of the Lord is light-
some : thy word is a lamp to my feet?* ‖   That is all
very true, but it means when preached and explained,
and properly understood.   *How shall they believe with-*

---

* *Apol.* xxxix. See the notes of Messire Æmar Ennequin, bishop
of Rennes, on Book vi. c. 2 of S. Augustine's *Confessions.*
† Is. xxix. 13.   ‡ Phil. ii. 11.   § xxx.   ‖ xviii. cxviii.

out a preacher! * And all that the great Prophet David has said is not to be understood of everybody.

But you object to me: in any case, ought I not to seek the meat of my soul and of my salvation? Poor man, who denies it? But if everybody goes to pasture like the old ewes, what is the need of shepherds? Seek the pastures, but with your pastor. Should we not laugh at the sick man who would find his health in Hippocrates without the help of the doctor, or at him who would seek out his rights in Justinian without betaking himself to the judge? Seek, one would say to him, your health by means of doctors; seek your right and gain it, but by the hands of the magistrate. "What man of moderately sound mind does not understand that the exposition of the Scriptures is to be sought from those who are doctors in them?" says S. Augustine.† But if no one can find his salvation except the one who can read the Scriptures, what will become of so many poor ignorant people? Surely they find and seek their salvation quite satisfactorily when they learn from the mouth of the pastor the substance of what they must believe, hope for, love, do, and ask of God. Believe that also according to the spirit that is true which the Wise Man says: *Better is the poor man walking in his simplicity than the rich in crooked ways* (Prov. xxviii. 6); and elsewhere: *The simplicity of the just shall guide them* (xi. 3); and: *He that walketh sincerely walketh confidently* (x. 9), where I do not mean to say that we must not take the trouble to understand, but only that we must not expect to find our salvation and our pasturage of ourselves, without the guidance of those whom God has

* Rom. x. 14.   † *De Moribus Eccl.*

appointed unto this end, according to the same Wise Man : *Lean not upon thy prudence, and be not wise in thy own conceit* (iii. 5, 7). Which they do not practice who think that of their own wisdom they know all sorts of mysteries ; not observing the order which God has established ; who has made amongst us some doctors and pastors,—not all, and not each one for himself. Indeed, S. Augustine found that S. Anthony, an unlearned man, failed not to know the way of Paradise ; and he with all his doctrine was very far therefrom, at that time amid the errors of the Manichæans.*

But I have some testimonies of antiquity, and some signal examples, which I would leave you at the end of this article as its conclusion.

S. Augustine † " Your charity was to be admonished that confession (*confessionem*) is not always the voice of a sinner ; for as soon as this word of the Lector sounded, there followed the sound of your striking your breast ; that is, as soon as you heard that the Lord said : *I confess to thee, Father,* immediately the word *I confess* sounded, you struck your breasts ; now to strike the breast, what is it but to signify what lies in the breast, and with a visible stroke to chastise an unseen sin ? Why did you do this but because you heard *I confess to thee, Father* ? You heard *I confess,* but you did not take notice who was confessing. Now therefore take notice." Do you see how the people heard the public reading of the Gospel, and did not understand it, except this word : *I confess to thee, Father,* which they understood by custom, because it was said just at the beginning of the Mass as

* *Confess.* viii. 8.   † *De Verbis Domini.* Serm. viii.

we say it now. It was, no doubt, because the reading was in Latin, which was not their vulgar tongue.

But he who would see the esteem in which Catholics hold the holy Scripture, and the respect they bear it, should regard the great Cardinal Borromeo, who never studied in the Holy Scriptures save on his knees, it seeming to him that he heard God speaking in them, and that such reverence was due to so divine a hearing. Never was a people better instructed, considering the malice of the age, than the people of Milan under the Cardinal Borromeo ; but the instruction of the people does not come by force of hurrying over the holy Bible, or often reading the mere letter of this divine Scripture, nor by singing snatches of the Psalms as the fancy takes one; but by using them, by reading, hearing, singing, praying to God, with a lively apprehension of the majesty of God to whom we speak, whose Word we read, evermore with that Preface of the ancient Church : *sursum corda.*

That great servant of God, S. Francis, of whose glorious and most holy memory the Feast was celebrated yesterday * throughout the whole world, showed us a beautiful example of the attention and reverence with which we ought to pray to God. This is what the holy and fervent Doctor of the Church, S. Bonoventure, tells of it.† "The holy man was accustomed to recite the Canonical Hours not less reverently than devoutly ; for although he was labouring under an infirmity of the eyes, the stomach, the spleen, and the liver, he would not lean against wall or other support while he was singing, but recited the hours always standing and bare-headed, not with wandering eyes,

* Written probably Oct. 5, 1595.   † *In Vitâ Fr.*

nor with any shortening of verse or word; if sometimes he were on a journey he then made a fixed
arrangement of time, not omitting this reverent and
holy custom on account of pouring rain: for he used
to say: If the body eat quietly its food which, with
itself, is to be food of worms, how great should be the
peace and tranquillity with which the soul should take
the food of life?"

ARTICLE II.

*THAT THE CHURCH OF THE PRETENDERS HAS
VIOLATED THE APOSTOLIC TRADITIONS, THE
SECOND RULE OF OUR FAITH.*

CHAPTER I.

WHAT IS UNDERSTOOD BY APOSTOLIC TRADITIONS.

HERE are the words of the holy Council of Trent,*
speaking of Christian and Evangelical truth: " (The
holy Synod), considering that this truth and discipline
are contained in written books, and in unwritten
Traditions which, being received by the Apostles from
the mouth of Christ himself, or from the same Apostles
at the dictation of the Holy Spirit, and being delivered
as it were from hand to hand, have come down to us,
following the examples of the orthodox Fathers, receives and honours with an equal affectionate piety
and reverence, all the books as well of the Old as of
the New Testament, since the one God is the author
of both, and also these Traditions, as it were orally

* Sess. iv.

dictated by Christ or the Holy Ghost, and preserved in the Catholic Church by perpetual succession." This is truly a decree worthy of an assembly which could say : *It hath seemed good to the Holy Ghost, and to us ;* for there is scarcely a word of it which does not strike home against our adversaries, and which does not take their weapons from their grasp. For what does it henceforth serve them to exclaim : *In vain do they serve me, teaching doctrines and commandments of men* (Matt. xv. 9) ; *You have made void the commandment of God for your tradition.* (ibid. 6). *Not attending to Jewish fables* (Tit. i. 14) ; *Zealous for the traditions of my fathers* (Gal. i. 14) ; *Beware lest any man impose upon you by philosophy and vain fallacy, according to the tradition of men* (Col. ii. 8); *Redeemed from your vain conversation of the tradition of your fathers* (1 Pet. i. 18) ? All this is not to the purpose, since the Council clearly protests that the traditions it receives are neither traditions nor commandments of men, but those " which, being received by the Apostle from the mouth of Christ himself, or from the same Apostles, at the dictation of the Holy Spirit, and being delivered as it were from hand to hand, have come down to us. They are then the word of God, and the doctrine of the Holy Spirit, not of men ; and here you will see almost all your ministers stick, making mighty harangues to show that human tradition is not to be put in comparison with the Scriptures. But of what use is all this save to beguile the poor hearers ?—for we never said it was.

In a similar way they bring against us what S. Paul said to his good Timothy: * *All Scripture divinely*

* 2 Tim. iii. 16, 17.

inspired is profitable to teach, to reprove, to correct, to instruct in justice, that the man of God may be perfect, furnished unto every good work. Whom are they angry with ? This is to force a quarrel.* Who denies the most excellent profitableness of the Scriptures, except the Huguenots who take away as good for nothing some of its finest pieces ? The Scriptures are indeed most useful, and it is no little favour which God has done us to preserve them for us through so many persecutions ; but the utility of Scripture does not make holy Traditions useless, any more than the use of one eye, of one leg, of one ear, of one hand, makes the other useless. The Council says : it " receives and honours with an equal affectionate piety and reverence all the books as well of the Old as of the New Testament, and also these Traditions." It would be a fine way of reasoning—faith profits, therefore works are good for nothing ! Similarly,—*Many other things also did Jesus, which are not written in this book. But these are written that you may believe that Jesus is the Son of God, and that believing you may have life in his name* (John xx. 30, 31) : therefore there is nothing to believe except this !—excellent consequence ! We well know that *whatever is written is written for our edification* (Rom. xv. 4), but shall this hinder the Apostles from preaching ? *These things are written that you may believe that Jesus is the Son of God :* but that is not enough ; for *how shall they believe without a preacher* (ibid. x. 14) ? The Scriptures are given for our salvation, but not the Scriptures alone ; Traditions also have their place. Birds have a right wing to fly with ; is the left wing therefore of no use ?

* *Querelle d'Allemand.*

The one does not move without the other. I leave on one side the exact answers: for S. John is speaking only of the miracles which he had to record, of which he considers he has given enough to prove the divinity of the Son of God.

When they adduce these words :— *You shall not add to the word that I speak to you, neither shall you take away from it* (Deut. iv. 2); *But though we or an angel from heaven preach a gospel to you beside that which we have preached to you, let him be anathema* (Gal. i. 8): they say nothing against the Council, which expressly declares that this Gospel teaching consists not only in the Scriptures, but also in Traditions; the Scripture then is the Gospel, but it is not the whole Gospel, for Traditions form the other part. He then who shall teach against what the Apostles have taught, let him be accursed; but the Apostles have taught by writing and by Tradition, and the whole is the Gospel.

And if you closely consider how the Council compares Traditions with the Scriptures you will see that it does not receive a Tradition contrary to Scripture: for it receives Tradition and Scripture with equal honour, because both the one and the other are most sweet and pure streams, which spring from one same mouth of our Lord, as from a living fountain of wisdom, and therefore cannot be contrary, but are of the same taste and quality; and uniting together happily water this tree of Christianity which shall give its fruit in due season.

We call then Apostolic Tradition the doctrine, whether it regard faith or morals, which our Lord has taught with his own mouth or by the mouth of the Apostles, which without having been written in the

III.

Canonical books have been preserved till our time,
passing from hand to hand by continual succession of
the Church.   In a word, it is the Word of the living
God, witnessed not on paper but on the heart.*   And
there is not merely Tradition of ceremonies and of a
certain exterior order which is arbitrary and of mere
propriety, but as the holy Council says, of doctrine,
which belongs to faith itself and to morals;—though
as regards Traditions of morals there are some which
lay us under a most strict obligation, and others which
are only proposed to us by way of counsel and
becomingness; and the non-observance of these latter
does not make us guilty, provided that they are
approved and esteemed as holy, and are not despised.

CHAPTER II.

THAT THERE ARE APOSTOLIC TRADITIONS IN THE CHURCH.

WE confess that the Holy Scripture is a most excellent
and profitable doctrine.   It is written in order that
we may believe; everything that is contrary to it is
falsehood and impiety: but to establish these truths
it is not necessary to reject this which is also a truth,
that Traditions are most profitable, given in order that
we may believe; everything that is contrary to them
is impiety and falsehood.   For to establish one truth

* The learned Antony Possevin, *contra Chytræum*, remarks that the
Christian doctrine is not called *Eugraphium* [good writings], but
Evangelium [good tidings].

we are never to destroy another. The Scripture is useful to teach; learn then from the Scripture itself that we must receive with honour and faith holy Traditions. If we are to add nothing to what our Lord has commanded,—where has he commanded that we should condemn Apostolic Traditions? Why do you add this to his words? Where has our Lord ever taught it? Indeed so far is he from having ever commanded the contempt of Apostolic Traditions that he never despised any Tradition of the least Prophet in the world. Run through all the Gospel, and you will see nothing censured there except Traditions which are human and contrary to the Scripture. But if neither our Lord has written it nor his Apostles, why would you evangelise unto us these things? On the contrary, it is forbidden to take anything away from the Scripture; why then would you take away the Traditions which are so expressly authorised therein?

Is it not the Holy Scripture of S. Paul which says: *Therefore, brethren, hold fast the Traditions which you have received, whether by word or by our epistle*"? (2 Thess. ii. 14). "Hence it is evident that the Apostles did not deliver everything by Epistle, but many things also without letters. They are, however, worthy of the same faith, these as much as those," are the words of S. Chrysostom in his commentary on this place.

This S. John likewise confirms: *Having more things to write to you*, I would not by paper and ink: for I hope that I shall be with you and speak face to face (Epp. 2, 3). They were things worthy of being written, yet he has not done it, but has said them, and instead of Scripture has made Tradition.

Hold the form of sound words, which thou hast heard from me . . . Keep the good deposited, said S. Paul to his Timothy (2 Ep. i. 14). Was not this recommending to him the unwritten Apostolic word? and that is Tradition. And lower down: *And the things which thou hast heard from me before many witnesses, the same commend to faithful men, who shall be fit to teach others also* (ii. 2). What is there more clear for Tradition? Behold the method; the Apostle speaks, the witnesses relate, S. Timothy is to teach it to others, and these to others yet. Do we not see here a holy substitution and spiritual trusteeship?

Does not the same Apostle praise the Corinthians for the observances of Tradition? If this were written in the 2nd of Corinthians, one might say that by his *ordinances* he understands those of the 1st, though the sense of the passage would be forced (but to him who does not want to move every shadow is an excuse); but this is written in the 1st (xi. 2). He speaks not of any gospel, for he would not call it my ordinances. What was it then but an unwritten Apostolic doctrine?—this we call Tradition. And when he says to them at the end: *The rest I will set in order when I come,* he lets us see that he had taught them many very important things, and yet we have no writing about them elsewhere. Will what he said, then, be lost to the Church? certainly not; but it has come down by Tradition. Otherwise the Apostle would not have delivered it to posterity, and would have written it.

And Our Lord says: *Many things I have to say to you, but you cannot bear them now* (John xvi. 12). I ask you, when did he say these things which he had to say ? Certainly it was either after his Resurrection, during the forty days he was with them, or by the coming of the Holy Spirit. But what do we know of what he comprehended under the word:—*I have many things, &c.*—if all is written ? It is said indeed that he was forty days with them teaching them of the Kingdom of God ; but we have neither all his apparitions nor what he told them therein.

ARTICLE III.

THE CHURCH: THIRD RULE OF FAITH. HOW THE MINISTERS HAVE VIOLATED THE AUTHORITY OF THE CHURCH, THE THIRD RULE OF OUR FAITH.

CHAPTER I.

THAT WE NEED SOME OTHER RULE BESIDES THE WORD OF GOD.

ONCE when Absalom * wished to form a faction against his good father, he sat in the way near the gate, and said to all who went by : *There is no man appointed by the king to hear thee . . . O that they would make me judge over the land, that all that have business might come to me, and I might do them justice.* Thus did he undermine the loyalty of the Israelites. But how many Absaloms have there been in our age, who, to seduce and distract the people from obedience to the Church, and to lead Christians into revolt, have cried

* 2 Kings xv. The Saint has used the same illustration, almost in the same words, in Part I. c. xii. [Tr.]

up and down the ways of Germany and of France:
There is no one appointed by the Lord to hear and
resolve differences concerning faith and religion; the
Church has no power in this matter! If you consider
well, Christians, you will see that whoever holds this
language wishes to be judge himself, though he does
not openly say so, more cunning than Absalom. I
have seen one of the most recent books of Theodore
Beza, entitled: *Of the true, essential and visible marks
of the true Catholic Church;* he seems to me to aim at
making himself, with his colleagues, judge of all the
differences which are between us; he says that the
conclusion of all his argument is that "the true Christ
is the only true and perpetual mark of the Catholic
Church,"—understanding by true Christ, he says,
Christ as he has most perfectly declared himself from
the beginning, whether in the Prophetic or Apostolic
writings, in what belongs to our salvation. Further on
he says: "This was what I had to say on the true,
sole, and essential mark of the true Church, which is
the written Word, Prophetic and Apostolic, well and
rightly ministered." Higher up he had admitted that
there were great difficulties in the Holy Scriptures,
but not in things which touch faith. In the margin
he places this warning, which he has put almost everywhere in the text: "The interpretation of Scripture
must not be drawn elsewhere than from the Scripture
itself, by comparing passages one with another, and
adapting them to the analogy of the faith." And in
the *Epistle to the King of France:* "We ask that the
appeal be made to the holy canonical Scriptures, and
that, if there be any doubt as to the interpretation of
them, the correspondence and relation which should

exist among these passages of Scripture and the articles
of faith, be the judge." He there receives the Fathers
as of authority just as far as they should find their
foundation in the Scriptures. He continues : " As to
the point of doctrine we cannot appeal to any irreproachable judge save the Lord himself, who has
declared all his counsel concerning our salvation by
the Apostles and the Prophets." He says again that
" his party are not such as would disavow a single
Council worthy of the name, general or particular,
ancient or later, (take note)—" provided," says he,
" that the touchstone, which is the word of God, be
used to try it." That, in one word, is what all these
reformers want—to take Scripture as judge. And to
this we answer *Amen* : but we say that our difference
is not there ; it is here, that in the disagreements we
shall have over the interpretation, and which will
occur at every two words, we shall need a judge.
They answer that we must decide the interpretation
of Scripture by collating passage with passage and the
whole with the Symbol of faith. *Amen, Amen,* we
say : but we do not ask how we ought to interpret the
Scripture, but—who shall be the judge ? For after
having compared passages with passages, and the whole
with the Symbol of the faith, we find by this passage :
*Thou art Peter, and upon this rock I will build my
Church, and the gates of hell shall not prevail against it,
and I will give to thee the keys of the kingdom of heaven*
(Matt. xvi.), that S. Peter has been chief minister and
supreme steward in the Church of God : you say, on
your side that this passage : *The kings of the nations
lord it over them . . . but you not so* (Luke xxii.), or
this other (for they are all so weak that I know not

what may be your main authority): *No one can lay
another foundation*, &c. (1 Cor. iii. 11), compared with
the other passages and the analogy of the faith makes
you detest a chief minister. The two of us follow
one same way in our enquiry concerning the truth in
this question—namely, whether there is in the Church
a Vicar General of Our Lord—and yet I have arrived
at the affirmative, and you, you have ended in the
negative; who now shall judge of our difference ?
Here lies the essential point as between you and me.

I quite admit, be it said in passing, that he who
shall enquire of Theodore Beza will say that you have
reasoned better than I, but on what does he rely for
this judgment except on what seems good to himself,
according to the pre-judgment he has formed of the
matter long ago ?—and he may say what he likes, for
who has made him judge between you and me ?

Recognise, Christians, the spirit of division : your
people send you to the Scriptures ;—we are there before you came into the world, and what we believe, we
find there clear and plain. But,—it must be properly
understood, adapting passage to passage, the whole
to the Creed ;—we are at this now fifteen hundred
years and more. You are mistaken, answers Luther.
Who told you so ? Scripture. What Scripture ?
Such and such, collated so, and fitted to the Creed.
On the contrary, say I, it is you, Luther, who are mistaken : the Scripture tells me so, in such and such a
passage, nicely joined and adjusted to such and such
a Scripture, and to the articles of the faith. I am not
in doubt, as to whether we must give belief to the
holy Word ;—who knows not that it is in the supreme
degree of certitude ? What exercises me is the under-

standing of this Scripture—the consequences and conclusions drawn from it, which being different beyond
number and very often contradictory on the same
point, so that each one chooses his own, one here the
other there—who shall make me see truth through so
many vanities ?   Who shall give me to see this Scripture in its native colour ?   For the neck of this dove
changes its appearance as often as those who look
upon it change position and distance.   The Scripture
is a most holy and infallible touchstone; every proposition, which stands this test * I accept as most
faithful and sound.   But what am I to do, when I
have in my hands this proposition : the natural body
of our Lord is really, substantially and actually in the
Holy Sacrament of the Altar.   I have it touched at
every angle and on every side, by the express and
purest word of God, and by the Apostles' Creed.
There is no place when I do not rub it a hundred
times, if you like.   And the more I examine it the
finer gold and purer metal do I recognise it to be
made of.   You say that having done the same you
find base metal in it.   What do you want me to do ?
All these masters have handled it already, and all
have come to the same decision as I, and with such
assurance, that in general assemblies of the craft, they
have turned out all who said differently.   Good heavens !
who shall resolve our doubts ?   We must not speak
again of the touchstone or it will be said : *The wicked
walk round about (in circuitu)* (Ps. xi. 9).   We must
have some one to take it up, and to test the piece
himself; then he must give judgment, and we must
submit, both of us, and argue no more.   Otherwise

* See Preface.

each one will believe what he likes. Let us take care
lest with regard to these words we be drawing the
Scripture after our notions, instead of following it. *If
the salt hath lost its savour, with what shall it be salted*
(Matt. v. 13)? If the Scripture be the subject of our
disagreement, who shall decide?

Ah! whoever says that Our Lord has placed us in
the bark of his Church, at the mercy of the winds
and of the tide, instead of giving us a skilful pilot
perfectly at home, by nautical art, with chart and compass, such a one says that he wishes our destruction.
Let him have placed therein the most excellent compass and the most correct chart in the world, what
use are these if no one knows how to gain from them
some infallible rule for directing the ship? Of what
use is the best of rudders if there is no steersman to
move it as the ship's course requires? But if every
one is allowed to turn it in the direction he thinks
good, who sees not that we are lost?

It is not the Scripture which requires a foreign
light or rule, as Beza thinks we believe; it is our
glosses, our conclusions, understandings, interpretations, conjectures, additions, and other such workings
of man's brain, which, being unable to be quiet, is
ever busied about new inventions. Certainly we do
not want a judge to decide between us and God, as
he seems to infer in his *Letter.* It is between a man
such as Calvin, Luther, Beza, and another such as
Eckius, Fisher, More; for we do not ask whether
God understands the Scripture better than we do, but
whether Calvin understands it better than S. Augustine or S. Cyprian. S. Hilary says excellently: *

* Lib. 2 *de Trin.* xviii.

" Heresy is in the understanding, not in the Scripture, and the fault is in the meaning, not in the words." and S. Augustine:* " Heresies arise simply from this, that good Scriptures are ill-understood, and what is ill-understood in them is also rashly and presumptuously given forth." It is a true Michol's game; it is to cover a statue, made expressly, with the clothes of David (1 Kings xix.) He who looks at it thinks he has seen David, but he is deceived, David is not there. Heresy covers up, in the bed of its brain, the statue of its own opinion in the clothes of Holy Scripture. He who sees this doctrine thinks he has seen the Holy Word of God, but he is mistaken; it is not there. The words are there, but not the meaning. " The Scriptures," says S. Jerome, † " consist not in the reading but in the understanding: " that is, faith is not in the knowing the words but the sense. And it is here that I think I have thoroughly proved that we have need of another rule for our faith, besides the rule of Holy Scripture. " If the world last long (said Luther once by good hap‡) it will be again necessary, on account of the different interpretations of Scripture which now exist, that to preserve the unity of the faith we should receive the Councils and decrees and fly to them for refuge." He acknowledges that formerly they were received, and that afterwards they will have to be.

I have dwelt on this at length, but when it is well understood, we have no small means of determining a most holy deliberation.

I say as much of Traditions; for if each one will

* In Joan. Tr. xviii, 1.   † Adv. Lucif. 28.
‡ Contr. Zuing. et Œcol.

bring forward Traditions, and we have no judge on earth to make in the last resort the difference between those which are to be received and those which are not, where, I pray you, shall we be ? We have clear examples. Calvin finds that the Apocalypse is to be received, Luther denies it; the same with the Epistle of S. James. Who shall reform these opinions of the reformers ? Either the one or the other is ill formed, who shall put it right ? Here is a second necessity which we have of another rule besides the Word of God.

There is, however, a very great difference between the first rules and this one. For the first rule, which is the Word of God, is a rule infallible in itself, and most sufficient to regulate all the understandings in the world. The second is not properly a rule of itself, but only in so far as it applies the first and proposes to us the right doctrine contained in the Holy Word. In the same way the laws are said to be a rule in civil causes. The judge is not so of himself, since his judging is conditioned by the ruling of the law; yet he is, and may well be called, a rule, because the application of the laws being subject to variety, when he has once made it we must conform to it.

The Holy Word then is the first law of our faith; there remains the application of this rule, which being able to receive as many forms as there are brains in the world, in spite of all the analogies of the faith, there is need further of a second rule to regulate this application. There must be doctrine and there must be some one to propose it. The doctrine is in the Holy Word, but who shall propose it ? The way in which one deduces an article of faith is this: the

Word of God is infallible; the Word of God declares
that Baptism is necessary for salvation; therefore
Baptism is necessary for salvation. The 1st Proposition cannot be gainsayed, we are at variance with
Calvin about the 2nd;—who shall reconcile us?
Who shall resolve our doubt? If he who has
authority to propose can err in his proposition all has
to be done over again. There must therefore be some
infallible authority in whose propounding we are
obliged to acquiesce. The Word of God cannot err,
He who proposes it cannot err; thus shall all be
perfectly assured.

CHAPTER II.

THAT THE CHURCH IS AN INFALLIBLE GUIDE FOR OUR FAITH. THAT THE TRUE CHURCH IS VISIBLE. DEFINITION OF THE CHURCH.

Now is it not reasonable that no private individual
should attribute to himself this infallible judgment on
the interpretation or explanation of the Holy Word?
—otherwise, where should we be? Who would be
willing to submit to the yoke of a private individual?
Why of one rather than of another? Let him talk as
much as he will of analogy, of enthusiasm, of the
Lord, of the Spirit,—all this shall never so bind my
understanding as that, if I must sail at hazard, I will
not jump into the vessel of my own judgment, rather
than that of another, let him talk Greek, Hebrew,
Latin, Tartar, Moorish, and whatever you like. If we
are to run the risk of erring, who would not choose to

run it rather by following his own fancy, than by slavishly following that of Calvin or Luther? Everybody shall give liberty to his wits to run promiscuously about amongst opinions the most diverse possible; and, indeed, he will perhaps light on truth as soon as another will. But it is impious to believe that Our Lord has not left us some supreme judge on earth to whom we can address ourselves in our difficulties, and who is so infallible in his judgments that we cannot err.

I maintain that this judge is no other than the Church Catholic, which can in no way err in the interpretations and conclusions she makes with regard to the Holy Scripture, nor in the decisions she gives concerning the difficulties which are found therein. For who has ever heard this doubted of?

All that our adversaries can say is that this infallibility is only true of the invisible Church.* But they arrive at this their opinion of the invisibility of the Church by two roads; for some say it is invisible because it consists only of persons elect and predestinate: the others attribute this invisibility to the rareness and scattering of the believers and faithful. Of these the first consider the Church to be invisible at all times, the others say that this invisibility has lasted about a thousand years, more or less; that is, from S. Gregory to Luther, during which time the papal authority was peaceably established among Christians: for they say that during this time there were some true Christians in secret, who did not manifest their intentions, and were satisfied with thus serving God in concealment. This theology is imagination and guesswork; so that others have preferred to say, that during

* See Preface.

those thousand years the Church was neither visible
nor invisible, but altogether effaced and suffocated by
impiety and idolatry.   Permit me, I beseech you, to
say the truth freely ; all these words are the incoher-
encies of fever, they are but dreams had while awake,
and not worth the dream Nabuchodonosor had while
asleep.   And they are entirely contrary to it if we
believe Daniel's interpretation ; * for Nabuchodonosor
saw a stone cut out of a mountain without hands, which
went rolling till it overthrew the great statue, and so
increased that having become a mountain it filled the
whole earth: this Daniel understood of the Kingdom of Our Lord, which shall last for ever.   If it be
as a mountain, and a mountain so large as to fill the
whole earth, how shall it be invisible or secret ?   And
if it last for ever, how shall it have failed a thousand
years ?   And it is certainly of the Kingdom of the
Church militant that this passage is to be understood ;
for that of the triumphant will fill heaven, not earth
only, and will not arise during the time of the other
Kingdoms, as Daniel's interpretation says, but after
the consummation of the world.   Add to this that to
be cut from the mountain without hands, belongs to
the temporal generation of Our Lord, according to
which he has been conceived in the womb of the
Virgin, and engendered of her own substance without
work of man, by the sole benediction of the Holy
Ghost.   Either then Daniel has badly prophesied, or
the adversaries of the Catholic Church have done so
when they have said the Church was invisible, hidden
and destroyed.   In God's name have patience ; we
will go in order and briefly, while showing the vanity

* Daniel ii.

of those opinions. But we must, before all things, say what the Church is.

Church comes from the Greek word meaning *to call*. Church then signifies an assembly, or company of persons called. Synagogue means a flock, to speak properly. The assembly of the Jews was called Synagogue, that of Christians is called Church : because the Jews were as a flock of animals, assembled and herded by fear; Christians are brought together by the Word of God, called together in the union of charity, by the preaching of the Apostles and their successors. Wherefore S. Augustine has said * that the Church is named from convocation, the synagogue from flock, because to be convoked belongs more to men, to be driven together refers rather to cattle. Now it is with good reason that we call the Christian people the Church, or convocation, because the first benefit God does to a man whom he is about to receive into grace is to call him to the Church. *Those whom he predestinated them he also called*, said S. Paul to the Romans (viii. 30);—that is the first effect of his predestination:—and to the Colossians (iii. 15): *Let the peace of Christ rejoice in your hearts, wherein also you are called in one body*. To be called in one body is to be called in the Church, and in those comparisons which Our Lord makes, in S. Matthew (xx. xxii.), of the vineyard and the banquet to the Church, the workmen in the vineyard and the guests at the banquet, he names the called and invited ones: *Many*, says he, *are called, but few are chosen*. The Athenians called the assemblage of the citizens the church, an assemblage of strangers was called by another name—

* In Ps. lxxxi.

Διακλήσις. Whence the word Church belongs properly to Christians, who are *no more strangers and
foreigners, but fellow-citizens of the saints and domestics
of God* (Eph. ii. 19). You see whence is taken the
word Church, and here is its definition : * The Church
is a holy university or general company of men united
and collected together in the profession of one same
Christian faith; in the participation of the same
Sacraments and Sacrifice; and in obedience to one
same Vicar and Lieutenant-general on earth of Our
Lord Jesus Christ, and successor of S. Peter; under
the charge of lawful Bishops.

CHAPTER III.

THE CATHOLIC CHURCH IS ONE.   MARK THE FIRST.   IT
IS UNDER ONE VISIBLE HEAD; THAT OF THE PRO-
TESTANTS IS NOT.

I will not dwell long on this point. You know that
all we Catholics acknowledge the Pope as Vicar of
Our Lord. The universal Church acknowledged him
lately at Trent, when she addressed herself to him for
confirmation of what she had resolved, and when she
received his deputies as the ordinary and legitimate
presiding body of the Council. I should lose time
also [to prove that] you have no visible head; you
admit it. You have a supreme Consistory, like those
of Berne, Geneva, Zurich and the rest, which depend

* From Ephes. v. 27 ; John xi. 52 ; S. Cyprian *de unit Eccl.* ;
Ephes. iv. 4 ; Matt. xvi. ; Heb. vii. 11 ; Ephes. iv. 11, 12.
    III.

on no other. You are so far from consenting to
recognise a universal head, that you have not even a
provincial head. Your ministers are one as good as
another, and have no prerogative in the Consistory,
yea, are inferior in knowledge and in vote to the president who is no minister. As for your bishops or
superintendents, you are not satisfied with lowering
them to the rank of ministers, but have made them
inferior, so as to leave nothing in its proper place.

The English hold their queen as head of their
church, contrary to the pure Word of God. Not that
they are mad enough, so far as I know, to consider her
head of the Catholic Church, but only of those unhappy countries.

In short, there is no one head over all others in
spiritual things, either amongst you or amongst the rest
of those who make profession of opposing the Pope.

How many times and in how many places is the
Church, as well militant as triumphant, both in Old
and New Testament, called house and family! It
would seem to me lost time to search this out, since it
is so common in the Scriptures that he who has read
them will never question it, and he who has not read
them will find, as soon as he reads them, this form of
speech in a manner everywhere. It is of the Church
that S. Paul says to his dear Timothy (1 iii. 15):
*That thou mayest know how thou oughtest to behave
thyself in the house of God, which is the Church, . .
the pillar and ground of the truth.* It is of her that
David says: *Blessed are they who dwell in thy house,
O Lord* (Ps. lxxxiii. 5). It is of her that the angel
said: *He shall reign in the house of Jacob for ever*
(Luke i. 32). It is of her that Our Lord said: *In*

my Father's house there are many mansions (John xiv. 2). *The kingdom of heaven is like to a master of a family,* in Matthew, chapter 20, and in a hundred thousand other places.

Now the Church being a house and a family, the Master thereof can doubtless be but one, Jesus Christ: and so is it called house of God. But this Master and householder ascending to the right hand of God, having left many servants in his house, would leave one of them who should be servant-in-chief, and to whom the others should be responsible; wherefore Christ said: *Who (thinkest thou) is a faithful and wise servant, whom his lord hath set over his family* (Matt. xxiv. 45). In truth, if there were not a foreman in a shop, think how the business would be done—or if there were not a king in a kingdom, a captain in a ship, a father in a family—in fact it would no longer be a family. But hear Our Lord in S. Matthew (xii.): *Every city or house divided against itself shall not stand.* Never can a province be well governed by itself, above all if it be large. I ask you, gentlemen so wise, who will have no head in the Church, can you give me an example of any government of importance in which all the particular governments are not reduced to one? We may pass over the Macedonians, Babylonians, Jews, Medes, Persians, Arabians, Syrians, French, Spaniards, English, and a vast number of eminent states, in regard to which the matter is evident; but let us come to republics. Tell me, where have you ever seen any great province which has governed itself? Nowhere. The chief part of the world was at one time in the Roman Republic, but a single Rome governed; a single Athens, Carthage, and so of the other ancient republics; a single Venice, a single Genoa, a single Lucerne, Fribourg and the rest. You will never find that the single parts of some notable and great province have set to work to govern themselves. But it was, is, and will be necessary that one man alone, or one single body of men residing in one place, or one single town, or some small portion of a province, has governed the province if the rest of the province were large. You, gentlemen, who delight in history, I am assured of your suffrages; you will not let me be contradicted. But supposing (which is most false) that some particular province was self-governed, how can this be said of the Christian Church, which is so universal that it comprehends all the world? How could it be one if it governed itself? And if not, there would be need to have a council of all the bishoprics always standing—and who would convoke it? It would be necessary for all the bishops to be absent;—and how could that be? And if all the bishops were equal, who would call them together? And how great a difficulty would it be, if there were some doubt in a matter of faith, to assemble a council! It cannot then possibly be that the whole Church and each part thereof should govern itself, without dependence of one part on the other.

Now, since I have sufficiently proved that one part should depend on another, I ask which part it is on which the dependence should be, whether a province, or a city, or an assembly, or a single person? If a province, where is it? It is not England, for when it was Catholic [it did not claim this right]. Where is it? and why this one rather than that? Besides no province has ever claimed this privilege. If it be a city, it must be one of the Patriarchal ones : now of the Patriarchal cities there are but five, Rome, Antioch, Alexandria, Constantinople and Jerusalem. Which of the five ?—all are pagan except Rome. If then it must be a city, it is Rome ; if an assembly, it is that at Rome. But no; it is not a province, not a town, not a simple and perpetual assembly ; it is a single man, established head over all the Church : *A faithful and prudent servant whom the Lord hath* appointed. Let us conclude then that Our Lord, when leaving this world, in order to leave all his Church united, left one single governor and lieutenant-general, to whom we are to have recourse in all our necessities.

Which being so, I say to you that this servant general, this dispenser and governor, this chief steward of the house of Our Lord is S. Peter, who on this account can truly say : *O Lord, for I am thy servant* (Ps. cxv. 16), and not only servant but doubly so : *I am thy servant,* because *they who rule well* are *worthy of double honour* (1 Tim. v. 17). And not only *thy servant,* but also *son of thy handmaid.* When there is some servant of the family kin he is trusted the more, and the keys of the house are willingly entrusted to him. It is therefore not without cause that I introduce S. Peter saying : *O Lord, for I am thy servant,* &c. For he is a good and faithful servant, to whom, as to a servant of the same kin, the Master has given the keys : *To thee I will give the keys of the kingdom of heaven.*

S. Luke shows us clearly that S. Peter is this servant ; for after having related that Our Lord had said by way of warning to his disciples (Luke xii.) : *Blessed are those servants whom the Lord when he cometh shall find watching: Amen I say to you, that he will gird himself, and make them sit down to meat, and passing will minister to them:*—S. Peter alone asked Our Lord: *Dost thou speak this parable to us, or likewise to all?* Our Lord answering S. Peter does not say: Who (thinkest thou) are the faithful servants? —as he had said: *Blessed are those servants,*—but: *Who (thinkest thou) is the faithful and wise steward whom his Lord setteth over his family to give them their measure of wheat in due season?* And in fact Theophylact here says that S. Peter asked this question as having the supreme charge of the Church, and S. Ambrose in the 7th book on S. Luke, says that the first words, *blessed,* &c. refer to all, but the second, *who, thinkest thou,* refer to the bishops, and much more properly to the supreme bishop. Our Lord, then, answers S. Peter as meaning to say: what I have said in general applies to all, but to thee particularly: for whom dost thou think to be the prudent and faithful servant?

And truly, if we sift this parable a little, who can be the servant who is to distribute the bread except S. Peter, to whom the charge of feeding the others has been given:—*feed my sheep?* When the master of the house goes out he gives the keys to the chief steward and procurator; and, is it not to S. Peter that Our Lord said: *I will give to thee the keys of the kingdom of heaven?* Everything has reference to the governor, and the rest of the officers depend on him for their authority, as all the building does upon the foundation; thus S. Peter is called the stone on which the Church is founded: *Thou art Cephas, and upon this rock,* &c. Now Cephas means a stone in Syriac as well as in Hebrew; but the Latin translator has

said *Petrus*, because in Greek there is πέτρος, which also means stone, like *petra*. And Our Lord in S. Matthew, chapter vii., says that the wise man builds and founds his house on the rock, *supra petram.**
Whereof the devil, the father of lies, the ape of Our Lord, has wished to make a sort of imitation, founding his miserable heresy principally in a diocese of S. Peter,† and in a *Rochelle.*‡

Further, Our Lord requires that this servant should be prudent and faithful. And St. Peter truly has these two qualities; for how could prudence be wanting to him, since neither flesh nor blood directs him but the heavenly Father? And how could fidelity fail him, since Our Lord said: *I have prayed for thee that thy faith fail not* (Luke xxii. 32)?—and he, we must believe, *was heard* for his reverence (Heb. v. 7). And that he was heard he gives an excellent testimony when he adds: *And thou being converted, confirm thy brethren.* As if he would say: I have prayed for thee, and therefore be the confirmer of the others, because for the others I have only prayed that they may have a secure refuge in thee. Let us then conclude that as Our Lord was one day to quit his Church as regards his corporal and visible being, he left a visible lieutenant and vicar general, namely S. Peter, who could therefore rightly say: *O Lord, for I am thy servant.*

You will say to me: Our Lord is not dead, and moreover is always with his Church, why then do you give him a vicar? I answer you that not being dead he has no successor but only a vicar; and moreover

---

* Note the pronoun *hanc.*   † Geneva. [Tr.]

‡ Little rock. [Tr.]

that he truly assists his Church in all things and
everywhere by his invisible favour, but, in order not
to make a visible body without a visible head, he has
willed further to assist it in the person of a visible
lieutenant, by means of whom, besides invisible favours,
he perpetually administers his Church, and in a manner suitable to the sweetness of his providence.   You
will tell me, again, that there is no other foundation
than Our Lord in the Church : *No one can lay another
foundation than that which is laid, which is Christ
Jesus* (1 Cor. iii. 11).   I grant you that as well the
Church militant as the triumphant is supported and
founded on Our Lord, as on the principal foundation :
but Isaias has foretold to us that in the Church there
were to be two foundations.   In chapter xxviii. : *Behold I will lay a stone in the foundations of Sion, a
tried stone, a corner stone, a precious stone, founded in
the foundation.*   I know how a great personage explains
it, but it seems to me that that passage of Isaias
ought certainly to be interpreted without going outside
chapter xvi. of St. Matthew, in the Gospel of to-day.*
There then Isaias, complaining of the Jews and of their
prophets, in the person of Our Lord, because they
would not believe :—*Command, command again ; expect,
expect again,* and what follows,—adds : *Therefore thus
saith the Lord :* and hence it was the Lord who said :
Behold I will lay a stone in the foundations of Sion.
He says *in the foundations,* because although the other
Apostles were foundations of the Church : (*And the
wall of the city,* says the Apocalypse (xxi. 14), *had
twelve foundations,* and in them the *twelve names of
the twelve apostles of the Lamb :*—and elsewhere : *Built*

* Probably S. Peter's Chair, Jan. or Feb. 1596. [Tr.]

*upon the foundation of the prophets and apostles, Jesus
Christ himself being the chief corner-stone* (Eph. ii. 20):
—and the Psalmist (lxxvi.): *The foundations thereof
are in the holy mountains*). Yet, amongst all, there is
one who by excellence and in the highest sense is
called stone and foundation, and it is he to whom Our
Lord said: *Thou art Cephas,* that is, stone, *tried stone.*
Listen to St. Matthew: he declares that Our Lord
will lay a tried stone;—what trying would you have
other than this: *whom do men say that the Son of man
is?* A hard question, which St. Peter, explaining the
secret and difficult mystery of the communication of
idioms, answers so much to the point that more could
not be, and gives proof that he is truly a stone, saying:
Thou art Christ, the Son of the living God. Isaias
continues and says: *a precious stone;* hear the esteem
in which Our Lord holds St. Peter: *Blessed art thou,
Simon Barjona:—corner stone;* Our Lord does not say
that he will build only a wall of the church, but the
whole,—*My Church;* he is then a corner-stone:—
founded in the foundation; he shall be a foundation,
but not first: for there will be another foundation—
Christ himself being the chief corner-stone. See how
Isaias explains St. Matthew, and St. Matthew Isaias.

I should never end if I would say all that comes
to my mind when I have this subject before me.
Now let us see the conclusion of it all. The true
Church ought to have a visible head in its government
and administration; yours has none, therefore it is not
the true church. On the other hand, there is in the
world one true Church and lawful, which has a visible
head: no one has [but ours], therefore ours is the true
Church. Let us pass on.

CHAPTER IV.

UNITY OF THE CHURCH (*continued*).   OF THE UNITY OF
THE CHURCH IN DOCTRINE AND BELIEF.   THE TRUE
CHURCH MUST BE ONE IN ITS DOCTRINE.   THE
CATHOLIC CHURCH IS UNITED IN BELIEF, THE SO-
CALLED REFORMED CHURCH IS NOT.

Is Jesus Christ divided? No, surely, for he is the
God of peace, not of dissension, as S. Paul taught
throughout the Church. It cannot then be that the
true Church should be in dissension or division of
belief and opinion, for God would no longer be its
Author or Spouse, and, like a kingdom divided
against itself, it would be brought to desolation. As
soon as God takes a people to himself, as he has done
the Church, he gives it unity of heart and of path:
the Church is but one body, of which all the faithful
are members, compacted and united together by all
its joints; there is but one spirit animating this
body: *God is in his holy place: who maketh men of
one manner to dwell in a house* (Ps. lxvii. 7); therefore the true Church of God must be united, fastened
and joined together in one same doctrine and belief.

It is necessary, says S. Irenæus (iii. 3) that all the
faithful should come together and unite themselves to
the Roman Church [on account of] its superior ruling
power. She is the mother of their sacerdotal dignity,
says Julius I. (*ad Euseb.*) "She is the commencement of the unity of the priesthood, she is the bond of
unity," says S. Cyprian (Ep. 55). Again: "We are
not ignorant that there is but one God, one Christ and

Lord, whom we have confessed, one Holy Spirit, one
pastoral office (*episcopatus*) in the Catholic Church"
(*de un. Ec.* iv.).   The good Optatus also said to the
Donatists (ii. 2, 3): "Thou canst not deny that
thou knowest that in the city of Rome the chief
chair has been first granted to S. Peter, in which sat
the chief of the Apostles, S. Peter, whence he was
called Cephas; the chair in which the unity of the
whole was preserved, in order that the other Apostles
might not seek to put forward and maintain each his
own, and that henceforward he might be a schismatic
who would set up another chair against this one
chair.   Therefore in this one chair, which is the first
of its prerogatives, was first seated S. Peter."   These
are almost the words of this ancient and holy doctor;
and every Catholic of this age is of the same convic-
tion.   We hold the Roman Church to be our refuge
in all our difficulties; we all are her humble children,
and receive our food from the milk of her breasts; we
are all branches of this most fruitful stock, and draw
no sap of doctrine save from this root.   This is what
clothes us all with the same livery of belief; for
knowing that there is one chief and lieutenant general
in the Church, what he decides and determines with
the other prelates of the Church when he is seated in
the chair of Peter to teach Christendom, serves as law
and measure to our belief.   Let there be error everywhere throughout the world, yet you will see the
same faith in Catholics.   And if there be any difference of opinion, either it will not be in things belonging to the faith, or else, as soon as ever a General
Council or the Roman See shall have determined it, you
will see every one submit to their decision.   Our under-

standings do not stray away from one another in their belief, but keep most closely united and linked together by the bond of the superior authority of the Church, to which each one gives in with all humility, steadying his faith thereon, as upon the pillar and ground of truth. Our Catholic Church has but one language and one same form of words throughout the whole earth.

On the contrary, gentlemen, your first ministers had no sooner got on their feet, they had no sooner begun to build a tower of doctrine and science which was visibly to reach the heavens, and to acquire them the great and magnificent reputation of reformers, than God, wishing to traverse this ambitious design, permitted amongst them such a diversity of language and belief, that they began to contradict one another so violently that all their undertaking became a miserable Babel and confusion. What contradictions has not Luther's reformation produced! I should never end if I would put them all on this paper. He who would see them should read that little book of Frederick Staphyl's *de concordiâ discordi,* and Sanders, Book 7 of his *Visible Monarchy,* and Gabriel de Preau, in the *Lives of Heretics:* I will only say what you cannot be ignorant of, and what I now see before my eyes.

You have not one same canon of the Scriptures: Luther will not have the Epistle of S. James, which you receive. Calvin holds it to be contrary to the Scripture that there is a head in the Church; the English hold the reverse: the French Huguenots hold that according to the Word of God priests are not less than bishops; the English have bishops who govern priests, and amongst them two archbishops, one of whom is called *primate*, a name which Calvin so greatly detests : the Puritans in England hold as an article of faith that it is not lawful to preach, baptize, pray, in the Churches which were formerly Catholic, but they are not so squeamish in these parts. And note my saying that they make it an article of faith, for they suffer both prison and banishment rather than give it up. Is it not well known that at Geneva they consider it a superstition to keep any saint's day ?—yet in Switzerland some are kept ; and you keep one of Our Lady. The point is not that some keep them and others do not, for this would be no contradiction in religious belief, but that what you and some of the Swiss observe the others condemn as contrary to the purity of religion. Are you not aware that one of your greatest ministers teaches that the body of our Lord is as far from the Lord's Supper as heaven is from earth, and are you not likewise aware that this is held to be false by many others ? Has not one of your ministers lately confessed the reality of Christ's body in the Supper, and do not the rest deny it ? Can you deny me that as regards Justification you are as much divided against one another as you are against us:—witness that anonymous controversialist. In a word, each man has his own language, and out of as many Huguenots as I have spoken to I have never found two of the same belief.

But the worst is, you are not able to come to an agreement :—for where will you find a trusted arbitrator ? You have no head upon earth to address yourselves to in your difficulties ; you believe that the very Church can err herself and lead others into error : you would not put your soul into such unsafe

hands; indeed, you hold her in small account. The
Scripture cannot be your arbiter, for it is concerning
the Scripture that you are in litigation, some of you
being determined to have it understood in one way,
some in another. Your discords and your disputes
are interminable, unless you give in to the authority
of the Church. Witness the Colloquies of Lune-
bourg, of Malbron, of Montbeliard, and that of Berne
recently. Witness Titman, Heshusius and Erastus,
to whom I add Brenz and Bullinger. Take the great
division there is amongst you about the number of the
Sacraments. Now, and ordinarily amongst you, only
two are taught; Calvin made three, adding to Baptism
and the Supper, Order; Luther here puts Penance for
the third, then says there is but one: in the end, the
Protestants, at the Colloquy of Ratisbonne, at which
Calvin assisted, as Beza testifies in his life, confessed
that there were seven Sacraments. How is it you are
divided about the article of the almightiness of God?
—one party denying that a body can by the divine
power be in two places, others denying absolute
almightiness; others make no such denials. But if I
would show you the great contradictions amongst those
whom Beza acknowledges to be glorious reformers of
the Church, namely, Jerome of Prague, John Hus,
Wicliff, Luther, Bucer, Œcolampadius, Zuingle, Pomer-
anius and the rest, I should never come to an end:
Luther can sufficiently inform you as to the good
harmony there is amongst them, in the lamentation
which he makes against the Zuinglians and Sacramentarians, whom he calls Absaloms and Judases, and
fanatic spirits (in the year 1527).

His deceased Highness of most happy memory,

Emmanuel [of Savoy], related to the learned Anthony Possevin, that at the Colloquy of Cormasse when the Protestants were asked for their profession of faith, they all one after the other departed from the assembly, as being unable to agree together. That great prince, most worthy of trust, relates this as having been present there. All this division has its foundation in the contempt which you have for a visible head on earth, because, not being bound as to the interpretation of God's Word by any superior authority, each one takes the side which seems good to him. This is what the wise man says, that *among the proud there are always contentions,** which is a true mark of heresy. Those who are divided into several parties cannot be called by the name of Church, because, as S. Chrysostom says, the name of Christ is a name of agreement and concord. But as for us, we all have the same canon of the Scriptures, one same head, one like rule for interpreting them ; you have a diversity of canon, and in the understanding you have as many heads and rules as you are persons. We all sound the trumpet of one single Gideon, and have all one same spirit of faith in the Lord, and in his Vicar, the sword of the decisions of God and the Church, according to the words of the Apostles : *It hath seemed good to the Holy Ghost and to us.†* This unity of language amongst us is a true sign that we are the army of the Lord, and you can but be acknowledged as Madianites, whose opinions are only cries and shouts : each in your own fashion you slash at one another, cutting one another's throats, and cutting your own throats by your dissensions, as God says by Isaias ‡ : *The*

* Prov xiii. 10.   † Acts xv. 28.   ‡ Isa. xix.

Egyptians shall fight against the Egyptians . . . and the spirit of Egypt shall be broken. And S. Augustine says that as Donatus had tried to divide Christ, so he himself was by a daily separation of his party divided within himself.

This mark [of unity] alone ought to make you quit your pretended church, for he who is not with God is against God. God is not in your church, for he only inhabits a place of peace, and in your church there is neither peace nor concord.

CHAPTER V.

OF THE SANCTITY OF THE CHURCH: SECOND MARK.

THE Church of Our Lord is holy; this is an article of faith. Our Lord has given himself for it, that he may sanctify it. It is *a holy nation,* says St. Peter (1. ii. 9). The bridegroom is holy, and the bride holy. She is holy as being dedicated to God, as the Elders under the ancient synagogue were called holy on this account alone; she is holy again because the Spirit who informs her is holy, and because she is the mystical body of a head who is called most holy; she is holy, moreover, because all her actions, interior and exterior, are holy; she neither believes nor hopes nor loves but holily; in her prayers, sermons, sacraments, sacrifices, she is holy. But this Church has her interior sanctity, according to the word of David (Ps. xliv. 14): *All the glory of the King's daughter is within;* she has also her exterior sanctity *in golden borders clothed about* *with varieties* (Ib.)   The interior sanctity cannot be seen; the exterior cannot serve as a mark, because all the sects vaunt it, and because it is hard to recognise the true prayer, preaching and administration of the Sacraments; but beyond this there are signs by which God makes his Church known, which are as it were perfumes and odours; as the Spouse says in the Canticles (iv. 11): *The smell of thy garments as the smell of frankincense.*   Thus can we by the scent of these odours and perfumes run after and find the true Church and the trace of the *son of the unicorn.**

CHAPTER VI.

SECOND MARK (*continued*).   THE TRUE CHURCH OUGHT
TO BE RESPLENDENT IN MIRACLES.

THE Church then has milk and honey under her tongue and in her heart, which is interior sanctity, and which we cannot see: she is richly dight with a fair robe, beautifully bordered with varieties, which are her exterior sanctities, which can be seen.   But because the sects and heresies disguise their clothing, and by false stuffs make them look like hers, she has, besides that, perfumes and odours which are her own, and these are certain signs and shinings of her sanctity, which are so peculiarly hers, that no other society can boast of having them, particularly in our age.

For, first, she shines in miracles, which are a most sweet odour and perfume, and are express signs of the

* Referring probably to Psalm xxviii. 6. [Tr.]

III.

presence of the immortal God with her, as S. Augustine styles them. And, indeed, when Our Lord quitted this world he promised that the Church should be filled with miracles: *These signs*, he said, *shall follow them that believe : in my name they shall cast out devils, they shall speak with new tongues : they shall take up serpents*, poison shall not hurt them, and by the imposition of hands they shall heal the sick.*

Consider, I pray you, these words closely. (1) He does not say that the Apostles only would work these miracles, but simply, *those who believe*: (2) he does not say that every believer in particular would work miracles, but that those who believe will be followed by these signs: (3) he does not say it was only for them—ten or twenty years—but simply that miracles will follow them that believe. Our Lord, then, speaks to the Apostles only, but not for the Apostles only ; he speaks of the faithful ; of the body and general congregation † of the Church; he speaks absolutely, without limitation of time; let us take his holy words in the extent which Our Lord has given them. The believers are in the Church, the believers are followed by miracles, therefore in the Church there are miracles : there are believers in all times, the believers are followed by miracles, therefore in all times there are miracles.

But let us examine a little why the power of miracles was left in the Church. There is no doubt it was to confirm the Gospel preaching; for S. Mark so testifies, and S. Paul, who says that God gave testimony by miracles to the faith which they an-

---

* Mark *ult.*

† Six words in the MS. here cannot be distinctly ascertained, but their sense is obvious. [Tr.]

nounced.* God placed these instruments in the hand
of Moses, that he might be believed : wherefore Our
Lord said that if he had not done miracles the Jews
would not have been obliged to believe him. Well
now, must not the Church ever fight with infidelity ?
—and why then would you take away from her this
good stick which God has put into her hand ? I am
well aware that she has not so much need of it as at
the beginning ; now that the holy plant of the faith
has taken firm and good root, one need not water it
so often ; but, all the same, to wish to have the effect
altogether taken away, the necessity and cause remaining intact, is poor philosophy.

Besides, I beg you to show me at what period the
visible Church may have been without miracles, from
the time that it began until this present ? In the time
of the Apostles there were miracles beyond number;
you know that well. After that time, who knows not
the miracles, related by Marcus Aurelius Antoninus,
worked by the prayers of the legion of Christian
soldiers who were in his army, which on this account
was called *thundering ?* Who knows not the miracles
of S. Gregory Thaumaturgus, S. Martin, S. Anthony,
S. Nicholas, S. Hilarion, and the wonders concerning
Theodosius and Constantine, for which we have authors
of irreproachable authority — Eusebius, Rufinus, S.
Jerome, Basil, Sulpicius, Athanasius ? Who knows not
again what happened at the Invention of the Holy
Cross, and in the time of Julian the Apostate ? In
the time of SS. Chrysostom, Ambrose, Augustine, many
miracles were seen, which they themselves relate :
why then would you have the same Church now cease

* 1 Cor. ii. 4.

from miracles ? What reason would there be ? In truth, what we have always seen, in all varieties of times, accompanying the Church, we cannot do otherwise than call a property of the Church.

The true Church then makes her sanctity appear by miracles. And if God made so admirable the Propitiatory, and his Sinai, and his Burning Bush, because he wished to speak with men, why shall he not have made miraculous this his Church in which he wills to dwell for ever ?

CHAPTER VII.

SANCTITY OF THE CHURCH (*continued*). THE CATHOLIC CHURCH IS ACCOMPANIED WITH MIRACLES, THE PRETENDED IS NOT.

HERE now I desire that you show yourselves reasonable, free from quibbling and from obstinacy. It is found on informations duly and authentically taken that about the commencement of this century S. Francis of Paula was renowned for undoubted miracles, such as are the raising of the dead to life. We find the same as to S. Diego of Alcala. These are not uncertain rumours, but proved, signed informations, taken in regular process of law.

Would you dare to deny the apparition of the cross granted to the valiant captain Albukerque, and to all those in his fleet, which so many historians describe,* and so many persons had part in ?

* See Raynald, ad an. 1513. [Tr.]

The devout Gaspar Berzée, in the Indies, healed the sick by simply praying to God for them in the Mass, and so suddenly that other than God's hand could not have done it.

The Blessed Francis Xavier has healed the paralysed, the deaf, the dumb, the blind, and raised a dead man to life; his body has had power to remain entire though buried with lime, as those have testified who saw it entire fifteen years after his death; and these two died within the last forty-five years.

In Meliapor has been found a cross cut on a stone, which is considered to have been buried by the Christians in the time of S. Thomas. A wonderful but true thing!—almost every year, about the feast of this glorious Apostle, that cross sweats a quantity of blood, or liquid like blood, and changes colour, becoming white, pale, then black, and sometimes blue, brilliant and then of softer hue, and at last it returns to its natural colour: this many people have seen, and the Bishop of Cochin sent a public attestation of it to the holy Council of Trent. Miracles, therefore, are worked in the Indies, where the faith is not yet established, a whole world of which I leave on one side, in order to observe due brevity.

The good Father Louis of Granada, in his *Introduction on the Creed,* narrates many recent and unquestionable miracles. Amongst others he brings forward the cures which the Catholic kings of France have worked in our age, even in incurable cases of king's evil, by saying no more than these words : May God heal you; —and the king touches the person, no other disposition being required than Confession and Communion on that day.

I have read the history of the miraculous cure of James, son of Claude Andrew, of Belmont, in the bailiwick of Baulme in Burgundy. He had been helpless during eight years; after making his devotions in the Church of S. Claude, on the very day of the feast, 8th June 1588, he found himself immediately cured. Do you not call that a miracle? I am speaking of things in the neighbourhood; I have read the public act, I have spoken to the notary who took it and sent it, rightly and duly signed—Vion. Witnesses were not wanting, for there were people in crowds. But why do I stay to bring forward the miracles of our age? S. Malachy, S. Bernard, and S. Francis—were they not of our Church? You cannot deny it. Those who have written their lives are most holy and learned men, for S. Bernard himself has written that of S. Malachy, and S. Bonaventure that of S. Francis, men who lacked neither knowledge nor conscientiousness, and still many miracles are related therein. But, above all, the wonders which take place now, at our gates, in the sight of our princes and of our whole Savoy, near Mondovi, ought to close the door against all obstinacy.

Now, what will you say to this? Will you say that Antichrist will do miracles? S. Paul testifies that they will be false,[*] and the greatest S. John mentions is that he will make fire descend from heaven; Satan can work miracles, indeed has done so, no doubt, but God will leave a prompt remedy with his Church; for, to those false miracles, the servants of God, Elias and Enoch, as the Apocalypse and interpreters witness, will oppose other miracles of very different make. For not only will they employ fire to punish

* 1 Thess. ii. 9.

their enemies miraculously, but will have power to shut the heavens so that there may be no rain, to change and convert the waters into blood, and to strike the earth with what chastisements they like for three days and a half: after their death they shall rise again and ascend to heaven ; the earth shall tremble at their ascension.   Then, therefore, by the opposition of the true miracles, the illusions of Antichrist will be discovered ; and as Moses at last made the magicians of Pharaoh confess : *The finger of God is here,* so Elias and Enoch will effect that their enemies shall give glory to the God of heaven : Elias will do at that time some of those holy prophet's deeds of his, which he did of old to put down the impiety of the Baalites and other professors of false religions.

I wish then to say : (1) that the miracles of Antichrist are not such as those we bring forward for the Church ; and therefore it does not follow that if those are not marks of the Church these likewise are not so. The former will be proved false and be overcome by greater and more solid ones, the latter are solid, and no one can oppose to them more certain ones : (2) the wonders of Antichrist will be simply an illusion of three years and a half; but the miracles of the Church are so properly hers, that since her foundation she has always shone in miracles.   The miracles of Antichrist will be unnatural, and will not endure ; but in the Church they are grafted as it were naturally on her supernatural nature, and therefore they ever accompany her, to verify these words : *These signs shall follow them that believe.*

You will be ready to say that the Donatists worked miracles, according to S. Augustine : but they were only certain visions and revelations of which they themselves boasted, without any public testimony. Certainly the Church cannot be proved true by these private revelations; on the contrary, these visions themselves cannot be proved or held as true save by the testimony of the Church, says the same S. Augustine. And if Vespasian healed a blind and a lame man, the doctors themselves, according to Tacitus, decided that it was a blindness and an infirmity which were not incurable: it is no marvel then if the devil was able to heal them. A Jew having been baptized went and presented himself to Paulus, a Novatian bishop, to be rebaptized, says Socrates; * the water of the font immediately disappeared. This wonder was not to confirm the truth of Novatianism, but of holy Baptism, which it was not right to repeat. In the same manner were some wonders done amongst the Pagans, says S. Augustine, not in proof of Paganism, but of innocence, virginity, fidelity, which, wherever they are, are loved and valued by God who is the author thereof. Further, these wonders are done but rarely, and from them no conclusion can be drawn: the clouds sometimes give forth light, but it is only the sun which has for its mark and property the giving of light. Let us then conclude this subject: the Church has always been accompanied by miracles, solid and certain as those of her Spouse; therefore she is the true Church: for, to use the argument of the good Nicodemus (John iii. 2) in like case, I will say: *No* society *can do these miracles which* this does, so glorious and so continual, *unless God was with* it. And what did our Lord say to the disciples of S.

* vii. 17.

John (Matt. xi. 5): *Say, the blind see, the lame walk, the deaf hear*, to show that he was the Messias. Hearing that in the Church are done such grand miracles, we must conclude that *the Lord is indeed in this place* (Gen. xxviii. 16). But as regards your pretended Church, I can say nothing more to it than : *If it can believe, all things are possible to him that believes* (Mark ix. 22) : if it were the true Church it would be followed by miracles. You acknowledge to me that it is not your province to work miracles, nor to drive out devils ; once it turned out ill with one of your great masters who wanted to try it,—so says Berzée. " Those raised up the living from the dead," says Tertullian,* " these make dead men out of the living." A rumour is current that one of yours has once cured a demoniac ; it is however not stated when or how the person was cured, nor what witnesses there were. It is easy for apprentices to a trade to make a mistake in their first trial. Certain reports are often started amongst you to keep the simple people going, but having no author they must be without authority. Besides this, in driving out the devil we must not so much regard what is done as we must consider the manner and the form in which it is done ; if it is by the rightful prayers, and invocations of the name of Jesus Christ. Again, one swallow does not make the summer ; it is the perpetual and ordinary succession of miracles which is the mark of the true Church, not something accidental. But it would be fighting with a shadow and with air to refute this rumour, which is so timid and so feeble that nobody ventures to say from which side it came.

* De Præsc. xxx.

The total answer that I have got from you in this extreme necessity is that people do you a wrong when they ask miracles from you. And so they do, I agree with you; it would be turning you into ridicule, like asking a blacksmith to make an emerald or a diamond. Nor do I ask any from you: only I request you to confess frankly that you have not made your apprenticeship with the Apostles, Disciples, Martyrs and Confessors, who have been masters of the craft.

But when you say you have no need of miracles, because you do not want to establish a new faith, tell me then again whether S. Augustine, S. Jerome, S. Gregory, S. Ambrose and the rest preached a new doctrine. And why then were there done miracles so great and so numerous as theirs? Certainly the Gospel was better received in the world than it is at present; there were then pastors more excellent; many martyrs and miracles had gone before; but the Church was still not wanting in that gift of miracles, for the greater glory of most holy religion. Or if miracles were to cease in the Church, it would have been in the time of Constantine the Great, after the Empire had become Christian, the persecutions had ceased and Christianity been quite secured; but so far were they from ceasing then that they were multiplied on all sides.

Moreover, the doctrine which you preach has never been proclaimed, either in general or in detail; your heretical predecessors have preached it, with each of whom you agree on some points, and with all on none, as I will make clear afterwards. Where was your church eighty years ago? It has only just begun, and you call it old. Ah! you say, we have made no new Church, we have rubbed up and

cleaned the old money, which, having long lain in
decayed buildings, had become discoloured, and
encrusted with dirt and mould. Say that no more, I
beg you, that you have the metal and the mould.
Are not the faith, the Sacraments, necessary ingredi-
ents in the composition of the Church?—and
you have changed everything both in the one and
the other. You are then false coiners, if you do not
show the power which you claim to put false stamps
on the King's coin. But let us not delay on this.
Have you purified this Church, have you cleaned this
money? Show us then the characters which it had
when you say that it fell on the ground and began to
get rusty. It fell, you say, in the time of S. Gregory,
or a little after. You may say what you like, but at
that time it had the character of miracles;—show it
to us now? For if you do not show us most unmis-
takably the inscription of the King on your money,
we will show it you on ours; ours will pass as royal
and good, yours, as being light and clipped, will be
sent back to the melting-pot. If you would represent
to us the Church as it was in the time of S. Augustine,
show it to us not only speaking well but doing well,
in miracles and holy operations, as it was then. If
you would say that then it was nearer than it is now,
I answer that so notable an interruption as that which
you pretend of nine hundred or a thousand years,
makes this money so strange that unless we see on it,
in large letters, the ordinary characters, the inscription and the image, we will never receive it. No,
no: the ancient Church was powerful in all seasons,
in adversity and prosperity, in work and in word, like
her Spouse; yours has nought but talk, whether in

prosperity or in adversity.   At least let it now show
some vestiges of the ancient mark : otherwise it will
never be received as the true Church, nor as daughter
of that ancient mother.   If it would boast further, it
must have silence imposed upon it with these holy
words : * *If you are the children of Abraham, do the
works of Abraham.*   The true Church of believers is
to be ever accompanied by miracles; there is no
Church of our age which can show them save ours;
therefore ours alone is the true Church.

CHAPTER VIII.

SANCTITY OF THE CHURCH (*continued*).   THE SPIRIT OF
  PROPHECY OUGHT TO BE IN THE TRUE CHURCH.
  THE CATHOLIC CHURCH HAS THE SPIRIT OF PRO-
  PHECY ; THE PRETENDED HAS IT NOT.

PROPHECY is a very great miracle, which consists in
the certain knowledge which the human understanding
has of things, without any experience or any natural
reasoning, by supernatural inspiration ; and therefore
all that I have said of miracles in general ought to be
predicated of this.   The prophet Joel foretold (ii.) that
in the last days, that is, in the time of the Gospel
Church, as S. Peter interprets (Acts ii.), *Our Lord*
would *pour out* his holy *Spirit* upon his servants,
and that they should *prophesy ;* as Our Lord had said :
These signs shall follow them that believe.   Prophecy

* John viii. 39.

then is to be ever in the Church, where the servants of
God are, and where he ever pours out his Holy Spirit.

The Angel says in the Apocalypse (xix. 10) that
the testimony of Jesus is the spirit of prophecy: now
this testimony of the assurance of Our Lord is not
only given for unbelievers, but principally for believers,
St. Paul says (1 Cor. xiv. 22); how then do you say
that Our Lord having given it once to the Church has
taken it away afterwards? The chief reason for which
it was granted remaining still, the concession therefore
also remains. Add, as I said of miracles, that at all
times the Church has had prophets; we cannot therefore say that this is not one of her qualities and properties, and a good portion of her dowry.

Jesus Christ, ascending on high, led captivity captive,
he gave gifts to men . . . And some indeed he gave to
be apostles, and some prophets, and others evangelists, and
others pastors and teachers (Eph. iv.): the apostolic,
evangelic, pastoral and teaching spirit is always in the
Church, and why shall the spirit of prophecy also not
be left in her? It is a perfume of the garments of
this Spouse.

There have been scarcely any saints in the Church
who have not prophesied. I will only name these
more recent ones: S. Bernard, S. Francis, S. Dominic,
S. Anthony of Padua, S. Bridget, S. Catherine of
Siena, who were most sound Catholics. The saints
of whom I spoke above are of the number, and in our
age Gaspar Berzée and Francis Xavier. You would
find no one of the older generation who did not repeat
with full belief some prophecy of Jean Bourg; many
of them had seen and heard him: *The testimony of*
Jesus is the spirit of prophecy.

And now bring forward some one of yours who has prophesied in your church.   We know that the sybils were in some sort the prophetesses of the Gentiles, and almost all the Ancients speak of them.   Balaam also prophesied, but it was for the true Church, and hence their prophecies did not give credit to the church in which they were made, but to the Church for whom they were made:—though I deny not that there was among the Gentiles a true Church, consisting of a few persons, maintaining by divine grace faith in a true God and the observance of the natural commandents.   Witness Job, in the Old Testament, and the good Cornelius with seven other soldiers fearing God, in the New.   Now where are your prophets? And if you have none be sure that you are not of that body for the edification of which the Son of God has left [them], according to the word of S. Paul (Eph. iv.). *The testimony of Jesus is the spirit of prophecy.*   Calvin has tried, apparently, to prophesy in the preface to his Catechism of Geneva; but his prediction is so favourable to the Catholic Church that when we get its fulfilment we will be content to consider him as something of a prophet.

- - -

CHAPTER IX.

SANCTITY OF THE CHURCH (*continued*).   THE TRUE CHURCH MUST PRACTISE THE PERFECTION OF THE CHRISTIAN LIFE.

HERE are the sublimer instructions of Our Lord and the Apostles.   A rich young man was protesting that he had observed the commandments of God from his tender youth.   Our Lord, who sees everything, looking upon him loved him, a sign that he was such as he had said he was, and still he gave him this counsel (Matt. xix. Mark, x.): *If thou wouldst be perfect, go sell all that thou hast, and thou shalt have treasure in heaven, and come, follow me.*   S. Peter invites us by his example and that of his companions (Matt. xix.): *Behold we have left all things and have followed thee.*   Our Lord returns this solemn promise: *You who have followed me . . . shall sit upon twelve seats, judging the twelve tribes of Israel.   And every one that shall have left house, or brethren, or sisters, or father, or mother, or wife, or children, or lands for my name's sake, shall receive an hundred-fold, and shall possess life everlasting.*   You see the words, now behold the example: *The Son of man hath not where to lay his head* (Luke ix. 58): he was entirely poor to make us rich; he lived on alms, says S. Luke—*certain women ministered to him of their substance* (viii. 3).   In two Psalms * which properly regard his person, as S. Peter and S. Paul interpret, he is called a beggar.   When he sent his Apostles to preach he taught them that they should carry nothing on their journey save a staff only, that they should take neither scrip, nor bread, nor money in their purse, that they should be shod with sandals and not be furnished with two coats.   I know that these instructions are not absolute commands, though the last was commanded for a time; nor do I mean to say that they were more than most wholesome counsels and advice.

---

* Namely, Psalms cviii. and xxxix.; the one referred to by S. Peter in Acts ii., the other by S. Paul in Heb. x. [Tr.]

Here are others similar on another subject (Matt. xix.): *There are eunuchs who were born so from their mother's womb: and there are eunuchs who have made themselves eunuchs for the kingdom of heaven's sake.   He that can receive it, let him receive it.*

It is precisely that which had been foretold by Isaias (lvi.): *Let not the eunuch say: behold I am a dry tree.   For thus saith the Lord to the eunuchs: They that shall keep my Sabbaths, and shall choose the things that please me, and shall hold fast my covenant, I will give them in my house and within my walls a place and a name better than sons and daughters: I will give them an everlasting name which shall never perish.* Who sees not here that the Gospel exactly comes to fit in with prophecy ? And in the Apocalypse xiv. those who sang a new canticle which no other than they could utter were those *who are not defiled with women, for they are virgins: these follow the Lamb whithersoever he goeth.* To this refer the exhortations of S. Paul (1 Cor. vii.): *It is good for a man not to touch a woman: . . . now, I say to the unmarried and to the widows: it is good for them if they so continue, even as I. . . . Concerning virgins I have no commandment, but I give counsel, as having received mercy of the Lord to be faithful.* And here is the reason: *He that is without a wife is solicitous for the things that belong to the Lord, how he may please God.   But he that is with a wife is solicitous for the things of the world, how he may please his wife, and he is divided.   And the unmarried woman and the virgin thinketh on the things of the Lord that she may be holy both in body and in spirit; but she that is married thinketh on the things of the world, how she may please her husband.   And this I speak for your profit : not to cast a snare upon you, but for that which is decent, and which may give you power to attend upon the Lord without impediment . . . He that giveth his virgin in marriage doth well, and he that giveth her not doth better.* Then speaking of the widow: *Let her marry to whom she will, only in the Lord. But more blessed shall she be, if she so remain, according to my counsel ; and I think that I also have the Spirit of God.* Behold the instructions of Our Lord and his Apostles, having the authority of the example of Our Lord, of Our Lady, of S. John Baptist, of S. Paul, S. John, S. James, who have all lived in virginity ; and in the Old Testament, Elias and Eliseus, as the Ancients have pointed out.

Lastly, the most humble obedience of Our Lord, which is so particularly signified in the Evangelists, not only to his Father, to which he was obliged, but to S. Joseph, to his Mother, to Cæsar (to whom he paid tribute), and to all creatures in his Passion :— for the love of us, *He humbled himself, becoming obedient unto death, even the death of the cross* (Phil. ii. 8) :—the humility which he shows in having come to teach us, when he said (Matt. xx., Luke xxii.) : *The Son of man is not come to be ministered unto but to minister. . . . I am amongst you as he that serveth*—are not these perpetual repetitions and expositions of that most sweet lesson (Matt. xi.) : *Learn of me, because I am meek and humble of heart,* and that other (Luke ix.) : *If any man will come after me, let him deny himself, and take up his cross daily and follow me ?* He who keeps the commandments denies himself sufficiently for salvation ; to humble oneself in order to be exalted is quite enough : but still there remains another obedience, humility and

III.

self-abnegnation, to which the examples and instructions of Our Lord invite us.   He would have us learn
humility from him, and he humbles himself, not only
to those whose inferior he was, in so far as he was
wearing the form of a servant, but also to his actual
inferiors.   He desires then, that as he abased himself,
never indeed against his duty but beyond duty, we
also should voluntarily obey all creatures for love of
him : he would have us renounce ourselves, after his
example, but he has renounced his own will so deci-
sively that he has submitted to the cross itself, and
has served his disciples and servants—witness he who
finding it extraordinary said (John xiii.): *Thou shalt
not wash my feet for ever.*   What remains then save
that we should recognise in his words a sweet invita-
tion to a voluntary submission and obedience towards
those to whom otherwise we have no obligation, not
resting, however lightly, on our own will and judgment, according to the advice of the Wise Man
(Prov. iii.), but making ourselves subjects and enslaved
to God, and to men for the love of the same God.   So
the Rechabites are magnificently praised in Jeremias
xxxv., because they obeyed their father Jonadab in
things very hard and extraordinary, in which he had
no authority to oblige them, such as were not to drink
wine, neither they nor any of theirs, not to sow, not to
plant, not to have vineyards, not to build.   Fathers
certainly may not so tightly fasten the hands of their
posterity, unless they voluntarily consent thereto.   The
Rechabites, however, are praised and blessed by God
in approval of this voluntary obedience, by which they
had renounced themselves with an extraordinary and
more perfect renunciation.

Well now, let us return to our road. Such signal examples and instructions as these, in poverty, chastity, and abnegation of self,—to whom have they been left? To the Church. But why? Our Lord tells us: *He who can receive, let him receive.* And who can receive them? He who has the gift of God; and no one has the gift of God but he who asks for it;—but, *how shall they call on him in whom they have not believed. . . . How shall they believe . . . without a preacher! And how can they preach unless they be sent* (Rom. x.)? Now, there is no mission outside the Church, therefore the *he who can receive let him receive,* is addressed immediately only to the Church, or for those who are in the Church, since outside the Church it cannot be put in practice. S. Paul shows it more clearly: *I speak this,* he says, *for your profit,* not to make snares and nets for you, but to persuade you to *that which is decent, and which may give you power* and facility *to attend upon the Lord,* and to honour him *without impediment.* And, in fact, the Scriptures and the examples that are therein are only for our utility and instruction; the Church then ought to use, and put into practice, these most holy counsels of her Spouse: otherwise they would have been vainly and uselessly left, and proposed to her: indeed she has well known how to take them for herself, and to profit by them:— and see how.

Our Lord had no sooner ascended into heaven than every one amongst the first Christians sold his goods and brought the price to the feet of the Apostles. And S. Peter, putting in practice the first rule, said: *Gold and silver have I none* (Acts iii.) S. Philip had four daughters, virgins, whom Eusebius testifies to

have always remained such.   S. Paul kept virginity
or celibacy ; so did S. John and S. James ; and when
S. Paul (1 Tim. v.) reproves, as having damnation,
certain young widows who, *after they have grown
wanton in Christ will marry, having damnation because
they have left their first faith,*—the fourth Council of
Carthage (at which S. Augustine assisted) S. Epiphanius,
S. Jerome, with all the rest of antiquity, understand
it of widows who, being vowed to God and to the
observance of chastity, broke their vows, entering into
the ties of marriage against the faith which previously
they had given to the heavenly Spouse.   From that
time, then, the counsel of [being] eunuchs, and the other
which S. Paul gives, were practised in the Church.

Eusebius of Cæsarea records that the Apostles instituted two lives ; the one according to commandment,
the other according to counsel.   And that so it was,
evidently appears ; for, on the model of the perfection
of life followed and counselled by the Apostles, a
countless number of Christians have so closely formed
theirs, that history is full of it.   Who does not know
how admirable are the accounts given by Philo the
Jew of the life of the first Christians at Alexandria,
in the book entitled *Of the Life of the Beseechers,**
wherein he treats of S. Mark and his disciples, as
Eusebius, Nicephorus, S. Jerome, bear witness ; and
amongst the rest, Epiphanius,† who assures us that
Philo, when writing of the Jessenes, was speaking of
the Christians under this name, who for some time
after the Ascension of Our Lord, whilst S. Mark was
preaching in Egypt, were so called, either on account

---

* *De vitâ Contemplativa sive supplicium virtutibus.*
† Hær. xxix. cc. 4, 5.

of the name of Jesse, from whose race Our Lord sprang, or on account of the name of Jesus, their Master's name, which they ever had in their mouth. Now he who will look at the books of Philo, will see in these Jessenes or Therapeuts (healers or servers) a most perfect renunciation of oneself, of one's flesh, of one's goods.

S. Martial, a disciple of Our Lord, in an Epistle which he wrote to the Tolosians, relates that at his preaching the blessed Valeria, wife of an earthly king, had vowed the virginity of her body and of her spirit to the celestial King. S. Denis, in his *Ecclesiastical Hierarchy*, says that the Apostles, his masters, called the religious of his time Therapeuts, that is, servers or adorers, on account of the special service and worship they paid to God, or monks,* on account of the union with God, in which they made progress. Behold the perfection of the Evangelic life excellently practised in this first time of the Apostles and their disciples, who, having traced this path thus straight to heaven, and ascended by it, have been followed, one after another, by many excellent Christians. S. Cyprian observed continency, and gave all his goods to the poor, as Pontius the Deacon records. The same did S. Paul, the first Hermit, S. Anthony and S. Hilarion, witness S. Athanasius and S. Jerome. S. Paulinus, Bishop of Nola—S. Ambrose is our authority—of an illustrious family in Guienne, gave all his goods to the poor, and, as if discharged from a weighty burden, said farewell to his father and his family, to serve his God more devotedly. By his example it was that S. Martin quitted all, and excited others to the same perfection.

---

* Μονάχοι from μόνος, one or single. [Tr.]

George, Patriarch of Alexandria, relates that S. Chrysostom gave up all and became a monk. Politian, an African gentleman, returning to the Emperor's court, related to S. Augustin, that in Egypt there were a great number of monasteries and religious, who manifested a great sweetness and simplicity in their manners, and that there was a monastery at Milan, outside the town, furnished with a good number of religious, living in great union and brotherhood, to whom S. Ambrose, bishop of the place, was as Abbot. He told them also that near the town of Treves, there was a monastery of good religious, in which two courtiers of the Emperor had become monks; and that two young ladies who were betrothed to these two courtiers, having heard the resolution of their spouses, similarly vowed their virginity to God, and retired from the world to live in religion, poverty, and chastity. S. Augustin himself tells all this. Possidius relates the same, and says that he had instituted a monastery; which S. Augustine himself relates in one of his Epistles. These great Fathers have been followed by S. Gregory, Damascene, Bruno, Romuald, Bernard, Dominic, Francis, Louis, Anthony, Vincent, Thomas, Bonaventure, who having all renounced and said an eternal adieu to the world and its pomps, have presented themselves as a perfect holocaust to the living God.

Now let us conclude. These consequences seem to me inevitable. Our Lord has had these instructions and counsels of chastity, poverty, and obedience laid down in his Scriptures: he has practised them, and has had them practised in his early Church: all the Scripture and all the life of Our Lord were but an instruction for the Church which was to make profit

by them, and it was then to be one of the institutions
of the Church, this chastity, poverty, obedience or
self-renunciation.   Moreover, the Church has always
put in practice these things at all times and in every
season; this then is one of her properties : and what
would be the use of so many exhortations if they
were not to be put in practice ?   The true Church
therefore ought to shine in the perfection of the
Christian life; not so that everybody in the Church
is bound to follow it; it is enough that it be found
in some notable members and parts, in order that
nothing may be written or counselled in vain, and
that the Church may make use of all the parts of
Holy Scripture.

CHAPTER X.

SANCTITY OF THE CHURCH (*continued*).   THE PERFECTION
OF THE EVANGELIC LIFE IS PRACTISED IN OUR
CHURCH ; IN THE PRETENDED, IT IS DESPISED
AND GIVEN UP.

THE Church which is now, following the voice of her
Pastor and Saviour, and the track beaten by her
ancestors, praises, approves, and greatly esteems the
resolution of those who give themselves up to the
practice of the Evangelical counsels, of whom she has
a very great number.   I have no doubt that if you
had frequented the assemblies of the Chartreux,
Camaldolese, Celestines, Minims, Capuchins, Jesuits,
Theatines and numberless others, amongst whom

religious discipline flourishes, you would be uncertain
whether you should call them earthly angels or
heavenly men, and that you would not know which
to admire the more, whether in such blooming youth
so perfect a chastity, or in such great knowledge so
profound a humility, or in so much diversity so close
a fraternity: and all, like heavenly bees, work in and
compose, with the rest of Christianity, the honey of
the Gospel, these by preachings, these by writings,
these by meditations and prayers, these by teaching
and disputations, these by the care of the sick, these
by the administration of the Sacraments, under the
authority of the pastors. Who should ever detract
from the glory of so many religious of all orders, and
of so many secular priests, who, leaving their country,
or, to say it better, their own world, have exposed
themselves to the mercy of wind and tide, to get to the
nations of the New World, in order to lead them to
the true faith, and to enlighten them with the light
of the Gospel; who, without other equipment than
a lively confidence in the Providence of God, without
other expectation than of labours, miseries and martyr-
dom, without other aim than the honour of God and
the salvation of souls, here hastened amongst the
Cannibals, Canarians, Negroes, Brazilians, Malays,
Japanese, and other foreign nations, and made themselves prisoners there, banishing themselves from their
own earthly country in order that these poor people
might not be banished from the heavenly Paradise?
I know that some Ministers have been thither, but
they went having their means of support from men,
and when these failed they returned and did no more,
because an ape is always an ape, but ours remained

there, in perpetual continency to fertilise the Church with these new plants, in extreme poverty to enrich these people with the Gospel, and died in bondage to place that world in Christian liberty.

But if, instead of making your profit of these examples, and refreshing your minds with the sweetness of so holy a perfume, you turn your eyes towards certain places where monastic discipline is altogether ruined, and where there remains nothing sound but the habit;—you will force me to say that you are looking for the sewers and dung heaps, not the gardens and orchards. All good Catholics regret the ill-behaviour of these people, and blame the negligence of the pastors and the uncontrollable ambition of certain persons who, being determined to have power and authority, hinder legitimate elections, and the order of discipline, in order to make the temporal goods of the Church their own. What can we do ? The master has sown good seed, but the enemy has oversown cockle. The Church, at the Council of Trent, had looked to the good ordering of these things, but its ordinances are despised by those who ought to put them into execution ; and so far are Catholic doctors from consenting to this evil that they consider it a great sin to enter into such disorderly monasteries as these. Judas prevented not the honour of the Apostolic order, nor Lucifer of the angelic, nor Nicholas of the diaconate ; and in the same way these abominable men ought not to tarnish the righteousness of so many devout monasteries, which the Catholic Church has preserved amidst all the dissolution of this age of iron, in order that not one word of her Spouse should be in vain or fail to be put in practice.

On the contrary, gentlemen, your pretended church despises and contradicts all this as much as she can. Calvin in the 4th Book of his *Institutions* aims only at the abolition of the observance of the Evangelical counsels, and you cannot show me any effort or good will amongst your party, in which every one down to the ministers marries, every one labours to gather together riches, nobody acknowledges any other superior than force makes him submit to—an evident sign that this pretended church is not the one for which Our Lord has preached and draw the picture of so many excellent examples. For if everybody marries, what will become of the advice of S. Paul (1 Cor. vii.): *It is good for a man not to* touch a woman? If everybody runs after money and possessions, to whom will that word of Our Lord (Matt. vi.) be addressed: *Lay not up for yourselves treasures on earth,* or that other (Ib. xix): *Go, sell* all, *give to the poor?* If every one will govern in his turn, where shall be found the practice of that most solemn sentence (Luke ix): *He who will come after me let him deny himself?* If then your Church puts itself in comparison with ours, ours will be the true Spouse, who puts in practice all the words of her Beloved, and leaves not one talent of the Scripture idle; yours will be false, who hears not the voice of the Beloved, yea, despises it. For it is not reasonable that to keep yours in credit we should make vain the least syllable of the Scriptures, which being addressed only to the true Church, would be vain and useless if in the true Church all these parts are not made use of.

CHAPTER XI.

OF THE UNIVERSALITY OR CATHOLICITY OF THE CHURCH: THIRD MARK.

THAT great Father, Vincent of Lerins, in his most useful *Memorial*, says that he must before all things have a great care to believe "that which has been believed by all [always and everywhere]" . . .* such as the jugglers and tinkers; for the rest of the world call us Catholic; and if we add Roman, it is only to inform people of the See of that Bishop who is general and visible Pastor of the Church. And already in the time of S. Ambrose to be Roman in communion was the same thing as to be Catholic.

But as for your church, it is called everywhere Huguenot, Calvinist, Heretical, Pretended, Protestant, New, or Sacramentarian. Your church was not before these names, and these names were not before your church, because they are proper to it. Nobody calls you Catholics, you scarcely dare to do so yourselves. I am well aware that amongst you your churches call themselves Reformed, but just as much right to that name have the Lutherans, and the Ubiquitarians, Anabaptists, Trinitarians, and other offshoots of Luther, and they will never yield it to you. The name of religion is common to the Church of the Jews and of the Christians, in the Old Law and in the New; the name of Catholic is proper to the Church of Our Lord;

---

* There is an *hiatus* in the MS. here. In the earlier part of the broken sentence the saint has apparently been saying that Catholics are called Romans by the lower orders. [Tr.]

the name of Reformed is a blasphemy against Our Lord,
who has so perfectly formed and sanctified his Church
in his blood, that it must never take other form than
of his all lovely Spouse, of pillar and ground of truth.
One may reform the nations in particular, but not the
Church or religion.   She was rightly formed, change
of formation is called heresy or irreligion.   The tint
of Our Saviour's blood is too fair and too bright to require new colours.

Your church, then, calling itself Reformed, gives up
its part in the form which the Saviour had established.
But I cannot refrain from telling you what Beza,
Luther, and Peter Martyr think on this.   Peter
Martyr calls you Lutherans, and says you are brothers
to them; you are then Lutherans; Luther calls you
Zwinglians * and Sacramentarians; Beza calls the
Lutherans Consubstantiators and Chymists, and yet he
puts them in the number of Reformed churches.   See
then the new names which the reformers acknowledge
for one another.   Your church, therefore, not having
even the name of Catholic, you cannot with a good
conscience say the Apostles' Creed; if you do, you
judge yourselves, who, confessing the Church Catholic
and universal, obstinately keep to your own, which
most certainly is not such.   If S. Augustine were
living now, he would remain in our Church, which
from immemorial time is in possession of the name of
Catholic.

* This word and one or two other names in this sentence cannot be
certainly made out.   The argument is not affected.   [Tr.]

CHAPTER XII.

CATHOLICITY OF THE CHURCH (*continued*).   THE TRUE
CHURCH MUST BE ANCIENT.   THE CATHOLIC CHURCH
IS MOST ANCIENT, THE PRETENDED QUITE NEW.

THE Church to be Catholic must be universal in
time, and to be universal in time it must be ancient;
antiquity then is a property of the Church.   And in
relation to heresies it must be more ancient than any
of them, and must precede all, because, as Tertullian
excellently says : *   "Error is a corruption of truth,
truth then must precede."   The good seed is sown
first, the enemy who oversows cockle comes afterwards.
Moses was before Abiron, Dathan, and Core; the
Angels were before the devils; Lucifer stood in the
light before he fell into the eternal darkness; the privation must follow the form.   S. John says of heretics
(1 Ep. xix. 19): *They went out from us;* they were
then within before they went out; the going out is
heresy, the being within is fidelity; the Church then
precedes heresy.   So the coat of Our Lord was whole
before it was divided.   And although Ismael was
before Isaac, that does not signify that error was before
truth, but that the true shadow, Judaism, was before
the body, Christianity, as S. Paul says (Gal. iv.)

Tell us now, I pray you,—quote the time and the
place when and where our Church first appeared after the
Gospel ?—the author and doctor who called it together.
I will use the very words of a doctor and martyr of
our age,† and they are worthy of close attention.

* De Præsc. xxix.   † Campion, *Decem Rationes,* 7.

"You own to us, and would not dare to do otherwise, that for a time the Roman Church was holy, Catholic, Apostolic. Certainly then, when it deserved those holy praises of the Apostle (Rom. i. xv. xvi.): *Your faith is spoken of in the whole world. . . . I make a commemoration of you always. . . . I know that when I come to you I shall come in the abundance of the blessing of the gospel of Christ. . . . All the Churches of Christ salute you. . . . For your obedience is published in every place;* then, when S. Paul, in prison free, sowed the Gospel; when S. Peter was governing the Church assembled in Babylon; when Clement, so highly praised by the Apostle, was stationed at the rudder; when the profane Cæsars, like Nero, Domitian, Trajan, Antoninus, were massacring the Bishops of Rome; yea and then also when Damasus, Siricius, Anastasius, and Innocent were holding the Apostolic helm: this on the testimony of Calvin himself, for he freely confesses that at that time they had not yet strayed from the Evangelic doctrine. Well then, when was it that Rome lost this widely renowned faith? When did it cease to be what it had been?—at what time?—under what bishop?—by what means?—by what force?— by what steps did the strange religion take possession of the City and of the whole world?—what protest, what troubles, what lamentations did it evoke? How! —was everybody asleep throughout the whole world, while Rome, Rome I say, was forging new Sacraments, new Sacrifices, and new doctrines? Is there not to be found one single historian, either Greek or Latin, friend or stranger, to publish or leave behind some traces of his commentaries and memoirs on so great a matter?"

And, in good truth, it would be a strange hap if historians, who have been so curious to note the most trifling changes in cities and peoples had forgotten the most noteworthy of all those which can occur, that is, the change of religion in the most important city and province of the world, which are Rome and Italy.

I ask you, gentlemen, whether you know when our Church began the pretended error. Tell us frankly; for it is certain that, as S. Jerome says,* "to have reduced heresy to its origin is to have refuted it." Let us trace back the course of history up to the foot of the cross; let us look on this side and on that, we shall never see that this Catholic Church has at any time changed its aspect—it is ever itself, in doctrine and in Sacraments.

We have no need against you, on this important point, of other witnesses than the eyes of our fathers and grandfathers to say when your pretended Church began. In the year 1517 Luther commenced his Tragedy: in '34 and '35 they composed an act in these parts; Zwingle and Calvin were the chief players in it. Would you have me detail by list with what fortune and deeds, by what force and violence, this reformation gained possession of Berne, Geneva, Lausanne, and other towns—what troubles and woes it brought forth? You will not find pleasure in this account; we see it, we feel it. In a word, your Church is not yet eighty years old; its author is Calvin; its result the misery of our age. Or if you would make it older, tell us where it was before that time. Beware of saying that it existed but was invisible;—for if it were not seen who can say that it

* Adv. Lucif. 28.

existed ?   Besides, Luther contradicts you, who confesses that in the beginning he was quite alone.

Now, if Tertullian already in his time bears witness
that Catholics refuted the errors of heretics by their
posteriority and novelty, when the Church was only
in her youth—" We are wont," says he,* " to pre-
scribe against heretics, for brevity's sake, on the argument of posteriority "—how much more right have
we now ?   And if one of the Churches must be the
true, this title falls to ours which is most ancient ;
and to your novelty the infamous name of heresy.

CHAPTER XIII.

CATHOLICITY OF THE CHURCH (*continued.*)   THE TRUE
CHURCH MUST BE PERPETUAL.   OURS IS PERPE-
TUAL, THE PRETENDED IS NOT.

ALTHOUGH the Church might be ancient, yet it would
not be universal in time if it had failed at any period.
The heresy of the Nicolaites is ancient but not universal, for it only lasted a very little while.   And as
a whirlwind which seems ready to displace the sea
then suddenly is lost in itself, or as a mushroom,
which is born of some noxious vapour in a night,
appears and in a day is gone,—so every heresy,
ancient as it may be, has at last disappeared, but the
Church endures perpetually.†

* De Præsc. xxx. *seqq.*

† Here occurs a passage on the perpetuity of the Church, which has
already appeared, in somewhat fuller form, in Part I. chaps. ix., x.
The reader is referred to these chapters and to the Preface.   [Tr.]

I will say to you, as I have said above : show me
a decade of years since Our Lord ascended into heaven
in which decade our Church has not existed. The
reason why you find yourselves unable to say when
our Church began is that it has always existed. And
if you would care to make yourselves honestly clear
about this, Sanders in his *Visible Monarchy,* and
Gilbert Genebrard in his *Chronology* would furnish
you light enough, and particularly the learned Cæsar
Baronius in his *Annals.* But if you are not willing
all at once to abandon the books of your masters, and
have not your eyes blinded with too excessive a passion, you will, if you look closely into the *Centuries*
of Magdebourg, see everywhere nothing but the actions
of Catholics ; for, says very well a learned man of our
age, if they had not collected these there they would
have left one thousand five hundred years without history. I will say something on this point afterwards.

Now, as to your Church,—let us suppose its lie to
be truth, that it was in the time of the Apostles ; it
will not on that account be the Catholic Church, for
the Catholic Church must be universal in time : she
must then always continue. But, tell me, where was
your Church a hundred, two hundred, three hundred
years ago ? Point it out you cannot, for it did not
exist : therefore it is not the true Church. It existed,
some one will perhaps say to me, but unknown.
Goodness of God! who cannot say the same?—Adamite,
Anabaptist, everybody will take up this argument. I
have already shown that the Church militant is not
invisible ; I have shown that she is universal in time ;
I will show you that she cannot be unknown.

III.

CHAPTER XIV.

CATHOLICITY OF THE CHURCH (*continued*). THE TRUE
CHURCH OUGHT TO BE UNIVERSAL IN PLACES
AND PERSONS.* THE CATHOLIC CHURCH IS THUS
UNIVERSAL, THE PRETENDED IS NOT.

THE universality of the Church does not require that
all provinces or missions receive the Gospel at once, it
is enough that they do so one after another; in such
sort, however, that the Church is always seen, and is
always known as that which has existed throughout
the whole world or the greater part thereof; so that
one may be able to say: *Come let us go up into the
mountain of the Lord* (Is. ii. 3). For the Church shall
be as the sun, says the Psalm, and the sun is not
always shining equally in all countries : enough if by
the end of the year *there is no one who can hide from
its heat* (Ps. xviii.) So will it suffice that by the end
of the world Our Lord's prediction be fulfilled, that *it
behoves that penance and remission of sins should be
preached in his name among all nations, beginning at
Jerusalem* (Luke *ult.*).

Now the Church in the time of the Apostles everywhere spread forth its branches, covered with the fruits
of the Gospel, as S. Paul testifies (Rom. i.) S. Irenæus
says the same of his time,† speaking of the Roman or
papal Church, to which he will have all the rest of the
Church subject on account of its superior authority.

Prosper speaks of our Church, not of yours, when

* This passage on the universality of the Church is the same as
Part I. c. xi.; see previous note. [Tr.]
† iii. 3.

he says : * " In the pastoral honour, Rome, see of S. Peter, is head of the universe, which she has not reduced to her dominion by war and arms, but has acquired by religion." You see clearly that he speaks of the Church, that he acknowledged the Pope of Rome as its head. In the time of S. Gregory there were Catholics everywhere, as may be seen by the Epistles which he wrote to bishops of almost all nations. In the time of Gratian, Valentinian and Justinian, there were everywhere Roman Catholics, as may be seen by their laws. S. Bernard says the same of his time; and you know well that it was so in the time of Godfrey de Bouillon. Since then, the same Church has come to our age, ever Roman and papal. So that even if our Church now were much less than it is, it would not cease to be most Catholic, because it is the same Roman Church which has been, and which has possessed all the provinces of the nations, and peoples without number:—but, it is still now extended over the whole world; in Transylvania, Poland, Hungary, Bohemia, and throughout all Germany; in France, in Italy, in Sclavonia, in Candia, in Spain, Portugal, Sicily, Malta, Corsica, in Greece, in Armenia, in Syria, and everywhere.

Shall I add to the list the Eastern and Western Indies ? He who would have a compendium of these must attend a general Chapter or assembly of the Religious of S. Francis, called Observantines. He would see Religious arrive from every quarter of the world, Old and New, under the obedience of a simple, lowly, insignificant man : so that these alone would seem enough for the Church to fulfil that part of the

* *De Ingratis.* 40.

prophecy of Malachy (i.): *In every place there is sacri-fice . . . to my name.*

On the contrary, gentlemen, the pretenders pass not the Alps on our side, nor the Pyrenees on the side of Spain; Greece knows you not; the other three parts of the world do not know who you are, and have never heard of Christians without sacrifice, without altar, without head, without cross, as you are; in Germany your comrades the Lutherans, Brentians, Anabaptists, Trinitarians, eat into your portion; in England the Puritans, in France the Libertines;—how then can you be so obstinate, and continue thus apart from the rest of the world, as did the Luciferians and Donatists? I will say to you, as S. Augustine said to one of your fellows: * "Be good enough, I beseech you, to enlighten us on this point;—how it can be that Our Lord has lost his Church throughout the world, and has began to have none save in you alone." Surely you reduce Our Lord to too great a poverty, says S. Jerome.† But if you say your church was already Catholic, in the time of the Apostle, show us that it existed at that time, for all the sects will say the same. How will you graft this little scion of pretended religion on that holy and ancient stock? Make your church touch by a perpetual continuation the primitive Church, for if they touch not, how can the one draw sap from the other. But this you will never do, unless you submit to the obedience of the Catholic [Church], you will never be, I say, with those who shall sing (Apoc. v. 9): *Thou hast redeemed us in thy blood, from every tribe and tongue, and people and nation, and hast made us a kingdom to our God.*

* *Contra Don.* † *Contra Lucif.*

CHAPTER XV.

CATHOLICITY OF THE CHURCH (*continued*).   THE TRUE
CHURCH MUST BE FRUITFUL.   THE CATHOLIC CHURCH
IS FRUITFUL, THE PRETENDED BARREN.

PERHAPS you will say, at last, that after a time your
church will spread its wings, and will become Catholic
by process of time; but this is talking in the air.
For if an Augustine, a Chrysostom, an Ambrose, a
Cyprian, a Gregory, and that great multitude of excellent pastors, have not been able to manage well enough
to prevent the Church from tumbling over soon after
their time, how [shall] Calvin, Luther, and the rest
[do so]? What likelihood is there that it should grow
stronger now, under the charge of your ministers, who
neither in sanctity nor in doctrine are comparable with
those? If the Church in its spring, summer, and
autumn has not been fruitful, how would you have one
gather fruits from it in winter? If in its youth it
has made no progress, how far would you have it run
in its old age?

But I say further; your church is not only not
Catholic, but never has been, not having the power nor
the faculty of producing children, but only of stealing
the offspring of others, as the partridge does. And
yet it is certainly one of the properties of the Church
to be fertile; it is for that, amongst other reasons, that
she is called *Dove.* And if her Spouse, when he would
bless a man, makes his wife fruitful, *like a fruitful
vine on the sides of his house* (Ps. cxxvii.), and *makes the
barren woman to dwell in a house, the joyful mother of*

many children (Ps. cxii.), ought he not himself to have
a bride who should be fruitful, yea, according to the
holy Word (Is. liv.), this desolate one should have
many children, this new Jerusalem should be most
populous, and have a great generation. *The Gentiles
shall walk in thy light,* says the Prophet (Ib. lx.),
*and kings in the glory of thy rising. Lift up thy eyes
round about and see ; all these are gathered together, they
are come to thee : thy sons shall come from afar, and thy
daughters shall rise up at thy side :* and (liii.) : *because
his soul hath laboured . . . therefore will I distribute to
him very many.* Now this fertility and these great
nations of the Church come principally by preaching,
as S. Paul says (1 Cor. iv. 15): *In the Gospel I have
begotten you.* The preaching, then, of the Church ought
to be as a flame: *Thy word is fiery, O Lord* (Ps.
cxviii. 140). And what is more active, lively, pene-
trating, and more quick to alter and give its form to
other matters than fire ?

Such was the preaching of S. Augustine in England,
of S. Boniface in Germany, of S. Patrick in Ireland,
of Willibrord in Frisia, of Cyril in Bohemia, of Adalbert
in Poland, of Stephen in Hungary, of S. Vincent Ferrer
and John Capistran; such the preaching of * . . . .
Francis Xavier, and a thousand others, who have over-
turned idolatry by holy preaching ; and all were Roman
Catholics.

On the contrary, your ministers have not yet converted any province from paganism, nor any country.
To divide Christendom, to create factions there, to tear

---

* There are four or five words here in the MS. which we fail to make
out. There is some indication of the names of (S.) Louis Bertrand,
and Anchieta, the others appear to be Henrye and Lorier. [Tr.]

in pieces the robe of Our Lord, is the effect of their preachings. Christian doctrine is as a gentle rain, which makes unfruitful soil to bring forth: theirs rather resembles hail, which beats down and destroys the harvests, and makes barren the most fertile lands. Take notice of what S. Jude says: *Woe to them who . . . have perished in the gainsaying of Core* (Core was a schismatic); *these are spots in their banquets, feasting together without fear, feeding themselves, clouds without water which are carried about by the wind :*—they have the exterior of the Scriptures, but they have not the interior moisture of the Spirit :—*unfruitful trees of the autumn,*—which have not the leaves of the letter nor the fruit of the inner meaning; *twice dead,*—dead to charity by schism, and to faith by heresy; *plucked up by the roots,* unable any more to bear fruit ;—*raging waves of the sea, foaming out their own confusion*—of disputes, contests and violent changes ;—*wandering stars,*—which can serve as guides to no one, and have no firmness of faith but change about in every direction. What wonder then that your preaching is sterile? You have but the bark without the sap, and how would you have it germinate? You have only the sheath without the sword, the letter without the meaning; no wonder you cannot uproot idolatry. So S. Paul,* speaking of those who separate from the Church, protests that *they shall advance no further.* If then your Church can in no way style itself Catholic up to this present, still less can you hope it may do so afterwards, since its preaching is so feeble, and its preachers have never undertaken, as Tertullian says,† the business or commission " of converting heathens, but only

* 2 Tim. iii. 9.   † *De Præsc.* xlii.

of perverting our own." Oh what a Church, then, which is neither one, nor holy, nor Catholic, and, which is worse, can have no reasonable hope whatever that it will ever become so.

———

CHAPTER XVI.

THAT THE CHURCH IS APOSTOLIC: FOURTH MARK.

[THIS title is at the top of a blank sheet, but the Saint has implicitly treated the subject in what has gone before. He has proved, on the one hand, that the Catholic Church takes her mission and her doctrine from the Apostles, on the other hand that the founders of the pretended church disclaim Apostolic mission and succession, reject the Sacrament of Orders, despise that priestly Sacrifice for which Orders are chiefly necessary, and not only contradict specific Apostolic utterances but reject the principle of Apostolic authority. Tr.]

———

ARTICLE IV.

THAT THE MINISTERS HAVE VIOLATED THE AUTHORITY OF COUNCILS, THE FOURTH RULE OF OUR FAITH.

CHAPTER I.

OF THE QUALITIES OF A TRUE COUNCIL.

WE will begin with the words of S. Leo:* ("Although the definition of the Apostolic See in matters of faith is certain and irrefragable), still what Our Lord had first decided by our ministry he irrefragably confirmed by the assent of the whole brotherhood; so that he might show that that truly proceeded from him which, having been defined by the first of all the Sees, had been received by the judgment of the whole Christian world, the members in this also agreeing with their head. . . . And truth itself appears more clearly and is held more firmly when examination afterwards confirms what faith had first taught, (so that he would indeed be an impious and sacrilegious man who should leave anything to be decided by his own opinion after the sentence of so many priests.")

One could not better trace out a true and holy Council than on the pattern of that which the Apostles held in Jerusalem.

Now let us see (1.) who convoked it; and we shall find that it was assembled by authority itself, by the pastors: *The Apostles and ancients came together to consider of this matter.*† And in truth it is the pastors

---

* Ep. 63.   We do not find the parts placed in brackets.   [Tr.]
† Acts. xv.

who are charged to instruct the people and to provide for their salvation by resolving the doubts which arise touching Christian doctrine. Emperors and princes ought to be zealous about it, but according to their office, which is after the manner of justice, of police, and of *the sword* which they *bear not in vain.** Those therefore who will have that the Emperor possessed this authority find no foundation either in Scripture or in reason. For what are the principal causes why General Councils are assembled, save to put down and cast out the heretic, the schismatic, the scandalizer, as wolves from the sheep-fold ?—as that first Assembly was held in Jerusalem to resist those who belonged to the heresy of the Pharisees. And who has the charge of driving away the wolf ? And who is shepherd save he to whom Our Lord said : *Feed my sheep ?* Find that a similar charge was given to Tiberius. He who has the authority for feeding the sheep has the authority for calling the shepherds together to learn what pasturage and what waters are wholesome for the flock. This is properly to assemble the pastors in the name of Jesus Christ,† that is, by the authority of Our Lord. For what else is it to assemble the estates in the name of the prince but to convoke them by the authority of the prince ? And who has received this authority except him who as lieutenant has received the Keys of the Kingdom of Heaven ? This made the good Father, Bishop Lucentius, legate of the holy Apostolic See, say that Dioscorus had done greatly wrong in having assembled a council without Apostolic authority. "Having dared," said he, "to convoke a synod without the

* Rom. xiii. 4.   † Matt. xviii. 20.

authority of the Apostolic See, a thing which had never been nor could be lawfully done: " and he said these words in the full assembly of the great Council of Chalcedon.

Still it is necessary that if the town where the meeting is held be subject to the Emperor or to some prince, and a public collection has to be made for the expenses of a Council, the prince in whose territory they meet should have permitted and authorised the meeting, and the collections must be authorised by the princes in whose States they are made. And when the Emperor wishes to assemble a Council [he may do so], provided that the Holy See, consenting thereto, makes the convocation legitimate. Such have been the convocations of some most authentic Councils, and such was that which Herod ordered at Jerusalem to know when the Christ should be born, the priests and scribes consenting. But to go on thence to attribute to princes the right to command the convocation of a Council would be as unreasonable as to draw an argument from his cruelty to S. John the Baptist, or his massacre of the infants.

We next (2.) come to examine in this first Christian Council which was held by the Apostles, who they were that were called : *The Apostles and ancients*, says the text, *came together to consider of this matter*. The Apostles and the priests—in a word, Churchmen. So reason required, for the old proverb ever holds good :—the cobbler not beyond his last; as does the word recorded by S. Athanasius,* which the good Father Hosius wrote to the Emperor Constantius : " To thee God has committed the Empire, to us what

* *Ep. ad Solit.*

belongs to the Church." It is then for Ecclesiastics to be called, although princes, the Emperor, kings and others find a place as protectors of the Church.

(3.) Who is to be judge? Now we do not see that any one gave judgment except four of the Apostles,—S. Peter, S. Paul, S. Barnabas and S. James, in whose sentence every one acquiesced. Whilst they were deliberating, the elders or priests spoke, as appears probable from these words: "*And when there was much disputing*," which shows that the question was most earnestly discussed. But when it came to resolving and passing sentence, we do not find that any one speaks who is not an Apostle; as we find in the ancient and canonical Councils that none but Bishops have subscribed and defined. *Take heed*, says S. Paul,* *to yourselves and to all the flock;* but who is thus to take heed to themselves and to the general body?—*in which the Holy Ghost has placed you Bishops to rule the Church of God?* It belongs to the pastors to provide wholesome doctrine for the sheep, and this was the reason why the Fathers of the Council of Chalcedon, when they saw monks and laymen enter, cried out repeatedly: "Cast out those who are not members; it is a Council of Bishops."

(4.) If we consider who presided, we shall find that it was S. Peter, who first gives sentence and is then followed by the rest, as S. Jerome says.† And indeed he had the chief pastoral charge: *Feed my sheep*,—and he was the grand steward over the rest: *To thee I will give the keys of the kingdom;* further, he was the confirmer of the brethren, an office which properly belongs to the president or superintendent.

* Acts xx. 28.   † *ad Aug.*

From that time, therefore, the successor of S. Peter, the Bishop of Rome, has always presided at Councils by his legates. At the Council of Nice the first who subscribed are Hosius, Bishop, Vitus, and Modestus, priests, envoys of the Holy See.* And, in truth, how could these two priests have come to subscribe before the Patriarchs except because they were holding the place of the Supreme Patriarch? As for S. Athanasius, so far from his having presided, he did not even sit, nor subscribe, being at that time only a deacon. And the great Constantine not only did not preside, but sat below the Bishops, and would not be there as pastor but as a sheep.†

In the Council of Constantinople though he was not there nor any legate for him,—because he was treating the same matter with the Western Bishops at Rome which was being treated at Constantinople by the Easterns, who were thus able to join them only in spirit and deliberation,—still by letters which were mutually exchanged between the Fathers, Damasus, Bishop of Rome, was acknowledged as lawful head and president.‡

In the Council of Ephesus S. Cyril presided as legate and lieutenant of Pope Celestine. Here are the words of S. Prosper of Aquitaine : § "By this man" (he is speaking of Pope Celestine) "the Eastern Churches also were purged of a double pestilence when he helped Cyril of Alexandria, your Bishop, a most glorious defender of the Catholic faith, to cut off with the Apostolic sword the Nestorian impiety." Which the same Prosper says again in the Chronicle :

* *Præf. Conc. Sard.*   † *Theod.* i. 7.   *Rufin.* x. 2.
‡ *Theod.* v. 8, 10.   § *Contra Coll.*

"The Nestorian impiety is opposed by the signal energy of Cyril, Bishop of Alexandria, and the authority of Pope Celestine."

Throughout the Council of Chalcedon everything proclaims that the legates of the Holy See, Paschasinus and Lucentius, presided. One has but to read the acts.

Here then you have Scripture, reason, and the practice of the four most legitimate Councils that ever were, presided over by S. Peter and his successors when they were present. I could show the same of all the others which have been received in the universal Church as legitimate. But this will quite suffice.

(5.) There remain the approval, acceptance, and execution of the decrees of the Council, which were made, as they ought still now to be made, by all those who assisted. Whence it was said: *Then it pleased the Apostles and ancients with the whole Church to choose men,* &c. But as to the authority in virtue of which the decree of that Council was promulgated it was only that of ecclesiastics: *The Apostles and ancients . . . to those . . . that are at Antioch and in Syria and Cilicia.* The authority of the sheep is not there appealed to, but only that of the shepherds. There may indeed be lay persons present at the Council if it be expedient, but not sitting as judges therein.

CHAPTER II.

HOW HOLY AND SACRED IS THE AUTHORITY OF UNIVERSAL COUNCILS.

WE are speaking then here of a Council such as that, in which there is the authority of S. Peter, both in the beginning and in the conclusion, and of the other Apostles and pastors who may choose to assist, or if not of all at least of a notable part; in which discussion is free, that is, in which any one who chooses may declare his mind with regard to the question under discussion; in which the pastors have the judicial voice. Such, in fact, as those four first were of which S. Gregory made so great account that he made this protestation concerning them: "I declare that like the four books of the Holy Gospel do I receive and venerate the four Councils.* Let us then consider a little how strong their authority should be over the understanding of Christians. And see how the Apostles speak of them: *It has seemed good to the Holy Ghost and to us.* Therefore the authority of councils ought to be revered as resting on the action of the Holy Ghost. For if against that Pharisaic heresy the Holy Ghost, doctor and guide of his Church, assisted the assembly, we must also believe that on all like occasions he will still assist the meetings of pastors, to regulate by their mouth both our actions and our beliefs. It is the same Church, as dear to the heavenly Spouse as she was then, in greater need than she was then,—what reason therefore can there be why he should not give her the same assistance as he

* *Epist.* 24.

gave her then on like occasion? Consider, I beg you, the importance of the Gospel words: *And if he will not hear the Church, let him be to thee as the heathen and the publican.** And when can we hear the Church more distinctly than by the voice of a general Council, where the heads of the Church come together to state and resolve difficulties? The body speaks not by its legs, nor by its hands, but only by its head, and so, how can the Church better pronounce sentence than by its heads? But Our Lord explains himself: *Again I say to you, that if two of you shall agree on earth concerning anything whatsoever they shall ask, it shall be done for them by my Father who is in heaven. . . . For where there are two or three gathered together in my name, there am I in the midst of them.* If two or three being gathered together in the name of Our Lord, when need is, have so particular an assistance from him that he is in the midst of them as a general in the midst of his army, as a doctor and regent among his disciples, if the Father infallibly gives them a gracious hearing concerning what they ask, how would he refuse his Holy Spirit to the general assembly of the pastors of the Church?

Again, if the legitimate assembly of the pastors and heads of the Church could once be surprised by error, how would the word of the Master be verified: *The gates of hell shall not prevail against it?*† How could error and hellish strength more triumphantly seize upon the Church than by having subdued doctors, pastors, and captains, with the general? And this word: *I am with you all days even to the consummation of the world:*‡—what would become of it? And how

* Matt. xviii.   † Ib. xvi. 18.   ‡ Ib. xxviii. *ult.*

would the Church be *the pillar and ground of truth,*[*]
if its bases and foundations support error and falsehood?   Doctors and pastors are the visible foundations of the Church, on whose ministry the rest is
supported.

Finally, what stricter command have we than to
take our food from the hand of our pastors?   Does
not S. Paul say that *the Holy Ghost has placed* them
over the flock to rule us,[†] and that Our Lord has given
them to us *that we may not be tossed to and fro, and
carried about with every wind of doctrine!*[‡]   What
respect then must we not pay to the ordinances and
canons which emanate from their general assembly?
It is true that taken separately their teachings are
subject to correction, but when they are together and
when all the ecclesiastical authority is collected into
one, who shall dispute the sentence which comes
forth?   If the salt lose its savour, wherewith shall it
be preserved?   If the chiefs are blind, who shall lead
the others?   If the pillars are falling, who shall hold
them up?   In a word, what has the Church more grand,
more certain, more solid, for the overthrow of heresy,
than the judgment of General Councils?   The Scripture,—Beza will say.   But I have already shown that
"heresy is of the understanding not of the Scripture,
the fault lies in the meaning, not in the words."[§]
Who knows not how many passages the Arian brought
forward?   What was there to be said against him
except that he understood them wrongly?   But he is
quite right to believe that it is you who interpret
wrongly, not he, you that are mistaken, not he; that

* 1 Tim. iii. 15.   † Acts xx. 28.   ‡ Eph. iv. 14.
§ Hilar. *de Trin.* ii.

III.

his appeal to the analogy of the faith is more sound than yours, so long as they are but private individuals who oppose his novelties. Yes, if one deprive the Councils of supreme authority in decision and declarations necessary for the understanding of the Holy Word, this Holy Word will be as much profaned as texts of Aristotle, and our articles of religion will be subject to never-ending revision, and from being safe and steady Christians we shall become wretched academics.

Athanasius says * that "the word of the Lord by the Ecumenical Council of Nice remains for ever." S. Gregory Nazianzen, speaking of the Apollinarists who boasted of having been recognised by a Catholic council:—"If either now," says he,† "or formerly, they have been received, let them prove it and we will agree, for it will be clear that they assent to the right doctrine, and it cannot be otherwise." S. Augustine says ‡ that the celebrated question about Baptism pressed by the Donatists made some Bishops doubt, "until the whole world in plenary council formulated beyond all doubt what was most wholesomely believed." "The decision of the priestly Council (of Nice)," says Rufinus (i.), " is conveyed to Constantine. He venerates it as settled by God, in such sense that if any one were to oppose it he would be working his own destruction, as opposing himself to God." But if any one supposes that because he can produce analogies, texts of Scripture, Greek and Hebrew words, he is therefore allowed to make doubtful again what has already been determined by General Councils, he must bring patents from heaven duly signed and sealed, or else he must

---

* *ad Episc. Afric.* 　† *ad Chelid.* 　‡ *de Bap. Contra Don.* i.

admit that anybody else may do as he does, that everything is at the mercy of our rash speculations, that everything is uncertain and subject to the variety of the judgments and considerations of men. The Wise Man gives us other counsel: * *The words of the wise are as goads, and as nails deeply fastened in, which by the counsel of masters are given from one shepherd. More than these, my son, require not.*

———

CHAPTER III.

HOW THE MINISTERS HAVE DESPISED AND VIOLATED THE AUTHORITY OF COUNCILS.

Now, will you remain asleep during this shock which your masters have given to the Church? Consider with yourselves, I pray you. Luther in the book which he has composed on the Councils is not content with tearing down the stones that are visible, but goes so far as to sap the very foundations of the Church. Who would credit this of Luther, that great and glorious reformer, as Beza calls him? How does he treat the great Council of Nice? Because the Council forbids those who have mutilated themselves to be received into the clerical ministry, and presently again forbids ecclesiastics to keep in their houses other women besides their mothers or their sisters:—
"Pressed on this point," says Luther, "I do not allow [the presence of] the Holy Spirit in this Council. And

* Eccles. xii. 11, 12.

why ?   An debebit episcopus aut concionator illum
intolerabilem ardorem et æstum amoris illiciti sustinere,
et neque conjugio neque castratione se ab his periculis
liberare ?   Is there no other work for the Holy Spirit
to do in Councils than to bind and burden his ministers
by making impossible, dangerous, unnecessary laws ? "
He makes exception for no Council, but seriously
holds that the *Curé* alone can do as much as a Council.
Such is the opinion of this great reformer.

But what need have I to go far ?   Beza says in the
Epistle to the King of France, that your reform will
refuse the authority of no Council; so far he speaks
well, but what follows spoils all : " provided," says he,
" that the Word of God test it."

But, for God's sake, when will they cease darkening
the question !   The Councils, after the fullest consul-
tation, when the test has been made by the holy
touchstone of the Word of God, decide and define
some article.   If after all this another test has to be
tried before their determination is received, will not
another also be wanted ?   Who will not want to
apply his test, and whenever will the matter be settled?
After the test has been applied by the Council, Beza
and his disciples want to try again ?   And who shall
stop another from asking as much, in order to see if
the Council's test has been properly tried ?   And why
not a third to know if the second is faithful ?—and
then a fourth, to test the third ?   Everything must be
done over again, and posterity will never trust antiquity but will go ever turning upside down the
holiest articles of the faith in the wheel of their
understandings.

We are not hesitating as to whether we should

receive a doctrine at haphazard, or should test it by the application of God's Word. But what we say is that when a Council has applied this test, our brains have not now to revise but to believe. Once let the canons of Councils be submitted to the test of private individuals,—as many persons, so many tastes, so many opinions.

The article of the real presence of Our Lord in the most Holy Sacrament had been received under the test of many Councils. Luther wished to make another trial, Zwingle another trial on that of Luther, Brentius another on these, Calvin another,—as many tests so many opinions. But, I beseech you, if the test as applied by a General Council be not enough to settle the minds of men, how shall the authority of some nobody be able to do it? That is too great an ambition.

Some of the most learned ministers of Lausanne, these late years, Scripture and analogy of faith in hand, oppose the doctrine of Calvin concerning justification. To bear the attack of their arguments no new reasons appear, though some wretched little tracts, insipid and void of doctrine, are set a-going. How are these men treated? They are persecuted, driven away, threatened. Why is this? "Because they teach a doctrine contrary to the profession of faith of our Church." Gracious heavens! the doctrine of the Council of Nice, after an approbation of thirteen hundred years, is to be submitted to the tests of Luther, Calvin, and Beza, and there shall be no trial made of the Calvinistic doctrine, quite new, entirely doubtful, patched up and inconsistent! Why, at least, may not each one try it for himself? If that of Nice has not been able to quiet your brains, why would you, by your statements, impose quiet on the brains of your companions, who are as good as you, as wise and as consistent? Behold the iniquitousness of these judges; to give liberty to their own opinions they lower the ancient Councils, while with their own opinions they would bridle those of others. They seek their own glory, be sure of that; and just as much as they take away from the Ancients do they attribute to themselves.

Beza in the *Epistle to the King of France* and in the fore-mentioned Treatise, says that the Council of Nice was a true Council if ever there was one. He says the truth, never did good Christian doubt about it, nor about the other first three; but if it be such, why does Calvin call that sentence in the Symbol of the Council—*Deum de Deo lumen de lumine*—hard? And how is it that that word ὁμοούσιον (*consubstantialem*) was so offensive to Luther—" My soul hates this word *homoousion;*" a word, however, which so entirely approved itself to that great Council? How is it you do not maintain the reality of the body of Our Lord in the holy Sacrament, that you call superstition the most holy sacrifice of the same precious body of Our Saviour which is offered by the priests, and that you will make no difference between the bishop and the priest,—since all this is so expressly not defined but presupposed, there, as perfectly well known in the Church? Never would Luther, or Peter Martyr, or Ochin have been ministers of yours, if they had remembered the acts of the great Council of Chalcedon; for it is most expressly forbidden there for religious men and women to marry.

Oh how good it would have been to see the round

of this your lake if this Council of Chalcedon had been held in reverence! Oh how often would your ministers have kept silence, and most rightfully,—for there is there an express command to laymen by no means to lay hands upon the goods of Ecclesiastics, to everybody to join in no revolt against the bishop, and neither to act nor to speak contumeliously against the ministers of the Church. The Council of Constantinople attributes the primacy to the Pope of Rome, and presupposes this as a thing of universal knowledge; so does that of Chalcedon. But is there any article in which we differ from you, which has not been several times condemned either in holy General Councils, or in particular ones received generally? And yet your ministers have resuscitated them, without shame, without scruple, not otherwise than though they were certain holy deposits and treasures hidden to Antiquity, or by Antiquity most curiously locked up in order that we might have the benefit of them in this age.

I am well aware that in the Councils there are articles concerning Ecclesiastical order and discipline, which can be changed and are but temporary. But it is not for private persons to interfere with them; the same authority which drew them up is required for abrogating them; if anybody else tries to do so it is in vain, and the authority is not the same unless it is a Council, or the general Head, or the custom of the whole Church. As to decrees on doctrines of faith they are invariable; what is once true is so unto eternity; and the Councils call *canons* (that is, rules) what they determine in this, because they are inviolable rules for our faith.

But all this is to be understood of true Councils, either general or provincial, approved by General Councils or the Apostolic See. Such as was not that of the four hundred prophets assembled by Achab : * for it was neither general, since those of Juda were not called to it, nor duly assembled, for it had no priestly authority. And those prophets were not legitimate or acknowledged as such by Josaphat, King of Juda, when he said : *Is there not here some prophet of the Lord that we may inquire by him ?*—as if he would say that the others were not prophets of the Lord. Such, again, was not the assembly of the priests against Our Lord; which was so far from having warrant in Scripture for the assistance of the Holy Spirit, that on the contrary it had been declared a private one by the Prophets; and truly right reason required that when the King was present his lieutenants should lose authority, and that the High Priest being present the dignity of the vicar should be reduced to the condition of the rest. Besides, it had not the form of a Council; it was a tumultuous meeting, wanting in the requisite order, without authority from the supreme head of the Church, who was Our Lord, there present with a visible presence, whom they were bound to acknowledge. In truth, when the great sacrificer is visibly present, the vicar cannot be called chief; when the governor of a fortress is present, it is for him, not for his lieutenant, to give the word. Besides all this, the synagogue was to be changed and transferred at that time, and this its crime had been predicted. But the Catholic Church is never to be transferred, so long as the world shall

* 3 Kings xxii. 6.

be world ; we are not waiting for any third legislator, nor any other priesthood ; but she is to be eternal. And yet Our Lord did this honour to the sacrificial dignity of Aaron that in spite of all the bad intention of those who held it the High Priest prophesied and uttered a most certain judgment (*that it is expedient one man should die for the people, and the whole nation perish not*)*, which *he spoke not of himself* and by chance, but *he prophesied,* says the Evangelist, *being the High Priest of that year.*

Thus Our Lord would conduct the Synagogue and the priestly authority with singular honour to its tomb, when he made it give place to the Catholic Church and the Evangelic priesthood: and then when the Synagogue came to an end (which was in the resolution to put Our Lord to death), the Church was founded in that very death : *I have finished the work which thou gavest me to do,*† said Our Lord after the Supper. And in the Supper Our Lord had instituted the New Testament; so that the Old, with its cere- monies and its priesthood, lost its force and its privi- leges, though the confirmation of the New was only made by the death of the testator, as S. Paul says.‡ We must then no longer take account of the privileges of the Synagogue, as they were founded on a Testa- ment which became old, and was abrogated when they said these cruel words : *Crucify him,* or those others, blaspheming : *What further need have we of witnesses ?* For this was that very dashing against the stumbling- stone, according to the ancient predictions.

My intention has been to destroy the force of the two objections which are raised against the infallible

---

* John xi. 50, 51. † John xvii. 4. ‡ Heb. ix.

authority of Councils and of the Church, the others will be answered in our treatment of particular points of Catholic doctrine. There is nothing so certain but that it can meet with opposition, but truth remains firm and is glorified by the assaults of what is contrary to it.

ARTICLE V.

THAT THE MINISTERS HAVE VIOLATED THE AUTHORITY OF THE ANCIENT FATHERS OF THE CHURCH, FIFTH RULE OF OUR FAITH.

CHAPTER I.

THE AUTHORITY OF THE ANCIENT FATHERS IS VENERABLE.

THEODOSIUS the Elder found no better way of putting down the disputes of his time concerning religious matters than to follow the counsel of Sisinnius,—to bring together the chiefs of the sects, and ask them if they held the ancient Fathers, who had had charge of the Church before all these disputes began, to be honest, holy, good, Catholic and Apostolic men. To which the sectaries answering, yes; he replied: Let us then examine your doctrine by theirs; if yours is conformable to it let us retain it, otherwise let us give it up.* There is no better plan in the world. Since Calvin and Beza own that the Church continued pure for the first six hundred years, let us see whether your Church is in the same faith and the same doctrine.

---

* Sozom. vii. 12. The Saint, in a marginal note, says that this passage is to be put at the beginning of the following chapter; but as, unfortunately, no following chapter is extant, we retain the passage here. [Tr.]

And who can better witness to us the faith which the
Church followed in those ancient times, than they
who then lived with her, at her table ?   Who can
better describe to us the manners of this heavenly
Spouse, in the flower of her age, than those who have
had the honour of holding the principal offices about
her ?   And in this aspect the Fathers deserve that we
yield them our faith, not on account of the exquisite
doctrine with which they were furnished, but for the
uprightness of their consciences, and the fidelity with
which they acted in their charges.

One does not so much require knowledge in witnesses as honesty and good faith.   We do not want
them here as authors of our faith, but as witnesses of
the belief in which the Church of their time lived.
No one can give more conclusive evidence than those
who ruled it : they are beyond reproach in every
respect.   He who would know what path the Church
followed at that time, let him ask those who have
most faithfully accompanied her.   *The wise man will
seek out the wisdom of all the ancients, and will be occu-
pied in the prophets. He will keep the sayings of
renowned men* (Ecclus. xxxix. 1, 2).   Hear what Jeremias says (vi. 16): *Thus saith the Lord : stand ye on
the ways and see, and ask for the old paths, which is
the good way, and walk ye in it ; and you shall find
refreshment for your souls.*   And the Wise Man (Ecclus. viii. 11): *Let not the discourse of the ancients
escape thee, for they have learned of their fathers.*   And
we must not only honour their testimonies as most
assured and irreproachable ; but also give great credit
to their doctrine, beyond all our inventions and curious
searchings.   We are not in any doubt as to whether

the ancient Fathers should be held as authors of our faith; we know, better than all your ministers do, that they are not. Nor are we disputing whether we must receive as certain, that which one or two of the Fathers may have held as opinions. Our difference is in this: You say you have reformed your church on the pattern of the ancient Church; we deny it, and take to witness those who have seen it, who have guarded it, who have governed it:—is not this a straightforward proof, and one clear of all quibbling? Here we are only maintaining the integrity and good faith of the witnesses. Besides this you say that your Church has been cut,* and reformed according to the true understanding of the Scriptures; we deny it, and say that the ancient Fathers had more competence and learning than you, and yet judged that the meaning of the Scriptures was not such as you make out. Is not this a most certain proof? You say that according to the Scriptures the Mass ought to be abolished; all the ancient Fathers deny it. Whom shall we believe—this troop of ancient Bishops and Martyrs, or this band of new-comers? That is where we stand. Now who does not see at first sight, that it is an unbearable impudence to refuse belief to these myriad Martyrs, Confessors, Doctors, who have preceded us? And if the faith of that ancient Church ought to serve as a rule of right-believing, we cannot better find this rule than in the writings and depositions of these our most holy and distinguished ancestors. . .

.   .   .   .   .   .

* Here follows a passage marked as if to be left out: "by the rule and compass of the Scripture; we deny it, and say that you have shortened, narrowed, and bent this rule, as formerly did those of Lesbos, to accommodate it to your notions. And . . ." [Tr.]

ARTICLE VI.

THE AUTHORITY OF THE POPE, THE SIXTH RULE OF OUR FAITH.

CHAPTER I.

FIRST AND SECOND PROOFS.   OF THE FIRST PROMISE
MADE TO S. PETER: UPON THIS ROCK I WILL
BUILD MY CHURCH.

WHEN Our Lord imposes a name upon men he always
bestows some particular grace according to the name
which he gives them. If he changes the name of that
great father of believers, and of Abram makes him
Abraham, also of *a high father* he makes him *father of
many*, giving the reason at the same time: *Thou shalt
be called Abraham; because I have made thee the father
of many nations.** And changing that of Sarai into Sara,
of *lady* that she was in Abraham's house, he makes her
lady of the nations and peoples who were to be born
of her. If he changes Jacob into Israel, the reason is
immediately given: *For if thou hast been powerful
against God, how much more shalt thou prevail against
men.*† So that God by the names which he imposes
not only marks the things named, but teaches us
something of their qualities and conditions. Witness
the angels, who have names only according to their
offices, and S. John Baptist, who has the grace in his
name which he announced in his preaching; as is
customary in that holy language of the Israelites.
The imposition of the name in the case of S. Peter is

---

* Gen. xvii. 5.   † Ib. xxxii. 28.

no small argument of the particular excellence of his charge, according to the very reason which Our Lord appended: *Thou art Peter*, &c.

But what name does he give him? A name full of majesty, not common, not trivial, but one expressive of superiority and authority, like unto that of Abraham himself. For if Abraham was thus called because he was to be father of many nations, S. Peter has received this name because upon him as upon a firm rock was to be founded the multitude of Christians. And it is on account of this resemblance that S. Bernard [*] calls the dignity of Peter "patriarchate of Abraham."

When Isaias would exhort the Jews by the example of Abraham, the stock from which they sprang, he calls Abraham Peter: Look unto Abraham, *unto the rock (petram) whence you are hewn: . . . . look unto Abraham your father;* [†] where he shows that this name of rock very properly refers to paternal authority. This name is one of Our Lord's names; for what name do we find more frequently attributed to the Messias than that of rock? [‡] This changing and imposition of name is then very worthy of consideration. For the names that God gives are full of power and might. He communicates Peter's name to him; he has therefore communicated to him some quality corresponding with the name. Our Lord himself is by excellence called the rock, because he is the foundation of the Church, and the corner-stone, the support, and the firmness, of this spiritual edifice: and he has declared that on S. Peter should his Church be built, and that he would establish him in the faith: *Confirm thy*

---

[*] *de Consid.* ii.   [†] li. i, 2.
[‡] Eph. ii. 20; Ps. cxvii. 21; 1 Cor. x. 4.

brethren.* I am well aware that he imposed a name upon the two brothers John and James, *Boanerges, the sons of thunder;* † but this name is not one of superiority or command, but rather of obedience, nor proper or special but common to two, nor, apparently, was it permanent, since they have never since been called by it : it was rather a title of honour, on account of the excellence of their preaching. But in the case of S. Peter he gives a name permanent, full of authority, and so peculiar to him that we may well say : to which of the others hath he said at any time, Thou art Peter ? —showing that S. Peter was superior to the others.

But I will remind you that Our Lord did not change S. Peter's name, but only added a new name to his old one, perhaps in order that he might remember in his authority what he had been, what his stock was, and that the majesty of the second name might be tempered by the humility of the first, and that if the name of Peter made us recognise him as chief, the name of Simon might tell us that he was not absolute chief, but obeying and subaltern chief, and head-servant. S. Basil seems to have given support to what I am saying, when he said : ‡ " Peter denied thrice and was placed in the foundation. Peter had previously not denied, and had been pronounced blessed. He had said : *Thou art the Son of the living God,* and thereupon had heard that he was Peter. The Lord thus returned his praise, because although he was a rock, yet he was not the rock ; for Christ is truly the immovable rock, but Peter on account of the rock. Christ indeed gives his own prerogative to others, yet he gives them not losing them himself, he holds them none the less. He

* Luke xxii. 32.   † Mark iii. 17.   ‡ *Hom. d Pænit.* 4.

is a rock, and he made a rock; what is his, he communicates to his servants; this is the proof of opulence, namely, to have and to give to others." Thus speaks S. Basil.*

What does he [Christ] say? three things; but we must consider them one after the other: *Thou art Peter; and upon this rock I will build my church; and the gates of hell shall not prevail against it :* † he says, that Peter was a stone or rock, and that on this rock or this stone he would build his Church.

But here we are in a difficulty: for it is granted that Our Lord has spoken to S. Peter, and of S. Peter as far as this—*and upon this rock*—but, it is said that in these words he no longer speaks of S. Peter. Now I ask you:—What likelihood is there that Our Lord would have made this grand preface: *Blessed art thou Simon Bar-jona; because flesh and blood hath not revealed it to thee, but my Father who is in heaven: and I say to thee,* &c., in order to say no more than: *Thou art Peter,*—and then suddenly have changed his subject and gone on to speak of something else? And again, when he says: *And on this rock I will build my church,*—do you not see that he evidently speaks of the rock of which he had previously spoken? and of what other rock had he spoken but Simon, to whom he had said: *Thou art Peter?* But this is the ambiguity which may be causing hesitation in your mind; you perhaps think that as Peter is now the proper name of a man, it was so then, and that so we transfer the signification of Peter to rock by equivocation of masculine and feminine. But we do not equivocate here; for it is but one same word, and taken in the same sense, when

* Here there is an hiatus in the MS. [Tr.]   † Matt. xvi.

Our Lord said to Simon : *Thou art Peter,* and when he said: *and on this rock I will build my church.* And this name of Peter was not a proper name of a man, but was only [then] appropriated to Simon Bar-jona. This you will much better understand, if you take it in the language in which Our Lord said it; he spoke not Latin but Syriac. He therefore called him not Peter but Cephas, thus: *Thou art Cephas, and on this Cephas I will build:* as if one said in Latin: *Thou art saxum, and on this saxum;* or in French: *Thou art rocher, and on this rocher I will build my church.** Now what doubt remains that it is the same person of whom he says : *Thou art Rock,* and of whom he says : *And on this Rock?* Certainly there is no other Cephas spoken of in all this chapter but Simon. On what ground then do we come to refer this relative *hanc* to another Cephas besides the one who immediately precedes ?

You will say :—Yes, but the Latin says : Thou art *Petrus,* and not : Thou art *Petra:* now this relative *hanc,* which is feminine, cannot refer to *Petrus,* which is masculine. The Latin version indeed has other arguments enough to make it clear that this stone is no other than S. Peter, and therefore, to accommodate the word to the person to whom it was given as a name, who was masculine, there is given it a corresponding termination ; as the Greek does, which had put : *Thou art πετρος, and on this τῇ πέτρᾳ.* But it does not come out so well in Latin as in Greek, because in Latin *Petrus* does not mean exactly the same as *petra,* but in Greek *πετρος* and *πέτρα* is the very same thing. Similarly in French *rocher* and *roche*

* Or in English : *Thou art Rock, and on this Rock.* [Tr.]

is the same thing, yet still so that if I had to predicate
either word of a man, I would rather apply to him the
name of *rocher* than of *roche*, to make the masculine
word correspond with the masculine subject.   I have
only to add, on this interpretation, that nobody doubts
that Our Lord called S. Peter Cephas (for S. John
records it most explicitly, and S. Paul, to the Galatians), or that Cephas means a stone or a rock, as S.
Jerome says.*

In fine, to prove to you that it is really S. Peter of
whom it is said: *And on this rock,*—I bring forward
the words that follow.   For it is all one to promise
him *the keys of the kingdom of heaven,* and to say to
him: *Upon this rock;* now we cannot doubt that it is
S. Peter to whom he promises the keys of the kingdom
of heaven, since he says clearly: *And to thee will I
give the keys of the kingdom of heaven:* if therefore we
do not wish to disconnect this piece of the Gospel from
the preceding and the following words in order to place
it elsewhere at our fancy, we cannot believe but that
all this is said to S. Peter and of S. Peter: *Thou art
Peter, and on this rock I will build my church.*   And
this the Catholic Church, when, even according to
the admission of the ministers, she was true and pure,
has confessed loudly and clearly in the assembly of
630 Bishops at the Council of Chalcedon.†

Let us now see what these words are worth and
what they import.   (1.) We know that what the head
is to a living body, the root to a tree, that the foundation is to a building.   Our Lord then, who is comparing
his Church to a building, when he says that he will
build it on S. Peter, shows that S. Peter will be its

* In Gal. ii. 13.   † Act iii.

foundation-stone, the root of this precious tree, the head of this excellent body. The French call both the building and the family, house, on this principle, that as a house is simply a collection of stones and other materials arranged with order, correspondence and measure, so a family is simply a collection of persons with order and interdependence. It is after this likeness that Our Lord calls his Church a building, and when he makes S. Peter its foundation, he makes him head and superior of this family.

(2.) By these words Our Lord shows the perpetuity and immovableness of this foundation. The stone on which one raises the building is the first, the others rest on it. Other stones may be removed without overthrowing the edifice, but he who takes away the foundation, knocks down the house. If then the gates of hell can in no wise prevail against the Church, they can in no wise prevail against its foundation and head, which they cannot take away and overturn without entirely overturning the whole edifice.

He shows one of the differences there are between S. Peter and himself. For Our Lord is foundation and founder, foundation and builder; but S. Peter is only foundation. Our Lord is its Master and Lord in perpetuity; S. Peter has only the management of it, as we shall explain by and by.

(3.) By these words Our Lord shows that the stones which are not placed and fixed on this foundation are not of the Church, although they may be in the Church.

CHAPTER II.

RESOLUTION OF A DIFFICULTY.

BUT a great proof of the contrary, as our adversaries think, is that, according to S. Paul: *No one can lay another foundation but that which is laid: which is Christ Jesus;* * and according to the same we are *domestics of God; built upon the foundation of the Apostles and Prophets, Jesus himself being the chief corner-stone.*† And, in the Apocalypse,‡ the wall of the holy city had twelve foundations, and in these twelve foundations the names of the twelve Apostles. If then, say they, all the twelve Apostles are foundations of the Church, how do you attribute this title to S. Peter in particular? And if S. Paul says that no one can lay another foundation than Our Lord, how do you dare to say that by these words: *Thou art Peter, and on this rock I will build my church,* S. Peter has been established as foundation of the Church? Why do you not rather say, asks Calvin, that this stone on which the Church is founded is no other than Our Lord? Why do you not rather declare, says Luther, that it is the confession of faith which Peter had made?

But in good truth it is an ill way of interpreting Scripture to overturn one passage by another, or to strain it by a forced interpretation to a strange and unbecoming sense. We must leave to it as far as possible the naturalness and sweetness of the sense which belongs to it.

In this case, then, since we see that Scripture

* 1 Cor. iii. 11.   † Eph. ii. 19, 20.   ‡ xxi. 14.

teaches us there is no other foundation than Our
Lord, and the same teaches us clearly that S. Peter
is such also, yea and further that the Apostles are so,
we are not to give up the first teaching for the second,
the second for the third, but to leave them all three
in their entirety. Which we shall easily do if we
consider these passages in good faith and sincerely.

Now Our Lord is in very deed the only foundation
of the Church; he is the foundation of our faith, of
our hope and charity; he is the foundation of all
ecclesiastical authority and order, and of all the doctrine and administration which are therein. Who ever
doubted of this? But, some one will say to me, if
he is the only foundation, how do you place S. Peter
also as foundation? (1.) You do us wrong; it is not
we who place him as foundation. He, besides whom
no other can be placed, he himself placed him. So
that if Our Lord is true founder of the Church, as he
is, we must believe that S. Peter is such too, since
Our Lord has placed him in this rank. If any one
besides Our Lord himself had given him this grade
we should all cry out with you: *No one can lay
another foundation but that which is laid.* (2.) And
then, have you well considered the words of S. Paul?
He will not have us recognise any foundation besides
Our Lord, but neither is S. Peter nor are the other
Apostles foundations *besides* Our Lord, they are sub-
ordinate to Our Lord: their doctrine is not other
than that of their Master, but their very Master's
itself. Thus the supreme charge which S. Peter had
in the militant Church, by reason of which he is
called foundation of the Church, as chief and governor,
is not *beside* the authority of his Master, but is only

a participation in this, so that he is not the foundation of this hierarchy *besides* Our Lord but rather in Our Lord: as we call him most holy Father in Our Lord, outside whom he would be nothing. We do not indeed recognise any other secular authority than that of His Highness [of Savoy], but we recognise several under this, which are not properly other than that of His Highness, because they are only certain portions and participations of it. (3.) In a word, let us interpret S. Paul passage by passage: do you not think he makes his meaning clear enough when he says: *You are built upon the foundations of the Prophets and Apostles?* But that you may know these foundations to be no other than that which he preached, he adds: *Christ himself being the chief cornerstone.* Our Lord then is foundation and S. Peter also, but with so notable a difference that in respect of the one the other may be said not to be it. For Our Lord is foundation and founder, foundation without other foundation, foundation of the natural, Mosaic and Evangelic Church, foundation perpetual and immortal, foundation of the militant and triumphant, foundation by his own nature, foundation of our faith, hope and charity, and of the efficacy of the Sacraments.

S. Peter is foundation, not founder, of the whole Church; foundation but founded on another foundation, which is Our Lord; foundation of the Evangelic Church alone, foundation subject to succession, foundation of the militant not of the triumphant, foundation by participation, ministerial not absolute foundation; in fine, administrator and not lord, and in no way the foundation of our faith, hope and charity, nor of the

efficacy of the Sacraments.   A difference so great as
this makes the one unable, in comparison, to be called
a foundation by the side of the other, whilst, however,
taken by itself, it can be called a foundation, in order
to pay proper regard to the Holy Word.   So, although
he is the Good Shepherd, he gives us shepherds *
under himself, between whom and his Majesty there
is so great a difference that he declares himself to be
the only shepherd.†

At the same time it is not good reasoning to say :
all the Apostles in general are called foundations of
the Church, therefore S. Peter is only such in the
same way as the others are.   On the contrary, as Our
Lord has said in particular, and in particular terms,
to S. Peter, what is afterwards said in general of the
others, we must conclude that there is in S. Peter
some particular property of foundation, and that he
in particular has been what the whole college has
been together.   The whole Church has been founded
on all the Apostles, and the whole on S. Peter in
particular ; it is then S. Peter who is its foundation
taken by himself, which the others are not.   For to
whom has it ever been said : *Thou art Peter,* &c. ?
It would be to violate the Scripture to say that all
the Apostles in general have not been foundations
of the Church.   It would also be to violate the
Scripture to deny that S. Peter was so in particular.
It is necessary that the general word should produce
its general effect, and the particular its particular, in
order that nothing may remain useless and without
mystery out of Scriptures so mysterious.   We have
only to see for what general reason all the Apostles

* Eph. iv. 11.   † John x. 11 ; Ezech. xxxiv. 23.

are called foundations of the Church: namely, because
it is they who by their preaching have planted the
faith and the Christian doctrine; in which if we are
to give some prerogative to any one of the Apostles
it will be to that one who said: *I have laboured more
abundantly than all they.**

And it is in this sense that is meant the passage
of the Apocalypse. For the twelve Apostles are called
foundations of the heavenly Jerusalem, because they
were the first who converted the world to the Christian religion, which was as it were to lay the foundations of the glory of men, and the seeds of their
happy immortality. But the passage of S. Paul seems
to be understood not so much of the person of the
Apostles as of their doctrine. For it is not said that
we are built upon the Apostles, but upon the foundation of the Apostles—that is, upon the doctrine which
they have announced. This is easy to see, because
it is not only said that we are upon the foundation
of the Apostles, but also of the Prophets, and we
know well that the Prophets have not otherwise been
foundations of the Evangelical Church than by their
doctrine. And in this matter all the Apostles seem
to stand on a level, unless S. John and S. Paul go
first for the excellence of their theology. It is then
in this sense that all the Apostles are foundations of
the Church; but in authority and government S.
Peter precedes all the others as much as the head
surpasses the members; for he has been appointed
ordinary pastor and supreme head of the Church, the
others have been delegated pastors intrusted with as
full power and authority over all the rest of the

* 1 Cor. xv. 10.

Church as S. Peter, except that S. Peter was the head
of them all and their pastor as of all Christendom.
Thus they were foundations of the Church equally
with him as to the conversion of souls and as to
doctrine; but as to the authority of governing, they
were so unequally, as S. Peter was the ordinary head
not only of the rest of the whole Church but of the
Apostles also. For Our Lord had built on him the
whole of his Church, of which they were not only
parts but the principal and noble parts. " Although
the strength of the Church," says S. Jerome,* " is
equally established on all the Apostles, yet amongst
the twelve one is chosen that a head being appointed
occasion of schism may be taken away." " There are,
indeed," says S. Bernard to his Eugenius,† and we
can say as much of S. Peter for the same reason,
" there are others who are custodians and pastors of
flocks, but thou hast inherited a name as much the
more glorious as it is more special."

CHAPTER III.

THIRD PROOF.   OF THE SECOND PROMISE MADE TO S.
PETER : AND I WILL GIVE THEE THE KEYS OF
THE KINGDOM OF HEAVEN.

OUR adversaries are so angry at our proposing to them
the chair of S. Peter as a holy touchstone by which
we may test the meanings, imaginations and fancies
they put into the Scriptures, that they overthrow

* ad Jovin. i. 27.   † *de Consid.* ii. 8.

heaven and earth to wrest out of our hands the express words of Our Lord, by which, having said to S. Peter that he would build his Church upon him, in order that we might know more particularly what he meant he continues in these words: *And to thee I will give the keys of the kingdom of heaven.* One could not speak more plainly. He has said: *Blessed art thou, Simon Bar-jona, because flesh and blood,* &c. *And I say to thee that thou art Peter, . . . and to thee will I give,* &c. This *to thee* refers to that very person to whom he had said: *And I say to thee ;*—it is then to S. Peter. But the ministers try as hard as they can to disturb the clear fountain of the Gospel, so that S. Peter may not be able to find his keys therein, and that we may turn disgusted from the water of the holy obedience which we owe to the vicar of Our Lord.

And therefore they have bethought them of saying that S. Peter had received this promise of Our Lord in the name of the whole Church, without having received any particular privilege in his own person. But if this is not violating Scripture, never did man violate it. For was it not to S. Peter that he was speaking? and how could he better express his intention than by saying: *And I say to thee. . . . I will give to thee?* Put with this his having just spoken of the Church, and said: *The gates of hell shall not prevail against it,* which would have prevented him from saying: *And I will give to thee the keys of the kingdom,* if he had wished to give them to the whole Church immediately. For he does not say *to it,* but, *to thee, will I give.* If it is allowed thus to go surmising over clear words, there will be nothing in the

Scripture which cannot be twisted into any meaning whatever; though I do not deny that S. Peter in this place was speaking in his own name and in that of the whole Church, not indeed as delegated by the Church or by the disciples (for we have not the shadow of a sign of this commission in the Scripture, and the revelation on which he founds his confession had been made to himself alone—unless the whole college of Apostles was named Simon Bar-jona), but as mouth-piece, prince and head of the Church and of the others, according to S. Chrysostom and S. Cyril on this place, and " on account of the primacy * of his Apostolate," as S. Augustine says. It was then the whole Church that spoke in the person of S. Peter as in the person of its head, and not S. Peter that spoke in the person of the Church. For the body speaks only in its head, and the head speaks in itself not in its body ; and although S. Peter was not as yet head and prince of the Church, which office was only conferred on him after the resurrection of the Master, it was enough that he was already chosen out for it and had a pledge of it. As also the other Apostles had not as yet the Apostolic power, travelling over all that blessed country rather as scholars with their tutor to learn the profound lessons which afterwards they taught to others than as Apostles or Envoys, which they afterwards were throughout the whole world, when their sound went forth into all the earth.†
Neither do I deny that the rest of the prelates of the Church have a share in the use of the keys ; and as

* Ult. in Joan. The French text has *permanence*, probably a mis-reading for *primacie*. [Tr.]

† Ps. xviii. 5.

for the Apostles I own that they have every authority here. I say only that the giving of the keys is here promised principally to S. Peter, and for the benefit of the Church. For although it is he who has received them, still it is not for his private advantage but for that of the Church. The control of the keys is promised to S. Peter in particular, and principally, then afterwards to the Church; but it is promised principally for the general good of the Church, then afterwards for that of S. Peter; as is the case with all public charges.

But, one will ask me, what difference is there between the promise which Our Lord here makes to S. Peter to give him the keys, and that which he made to the Apostles afterwards? For in truth it seems to have been but the same, because Our Lord explaining what he meant by the keys said: *And whatsoever thou shalt bind upon earth, it shall be bound also in heaven, and whatsoever thou shalt loose,* &c.— which is just what he said to the Apostles in general: *Whatsoever you shall bind,* &c.* If then he promises to all in general what he promises to Peter in particular, there will be no ground for saying that S. Peter is greater than one of the others by this promise.

I answer that in the promise and in the execution of the promise Our Lord has always preferred S. Peter by expressions which oblige us to believe that he has been made head of the Church. And as to the promise, I confess that by these words: *And whatsoever thou shalt loose,* Our Lord has promised no more to S. Peter than he did to the others afterwards:

* Matt. xviii. 18.

Whatsoever you shall bind, &c. For the words are the
same in substance and in meaning in the two passages.
I admit also that by these words: *And whatsoever
thou shalt loose,* said to S. Peter, he explains the
preceding: *And I will give to thee the keys,* but I
deny that it is the same thing to promise the keys
and to say: *Whatsoever thou shalt loose.* Let us then
see what it is to promise the keys of the kingdom of
heaven. And who knows not that when a master,
going away from his house, leaves the keys with
some one, what he does is to leave him the charge and
governance thereof. When princes make their entrance
into cities, the keys are presented to them as an
acknowledgment of their sovereign authority.

It is then the supreme authority which Our Lord
here promises to S. Peter; and in fact when the
Scripture elsewhere wishes to speak of a sovereign
authority it has used similar terms. In the Apocalypse
(i. 17, 18), when Our Lord wishes to make himself
known to his servant, he says to him: *I am the first
and the last, and alive and was dead: and behold I
am living for ever and ever, and have the keys of death
and of hell.* What does he mean by *the keys of death
and of hell,* except the supreme power over the one
and the other? And there also where it is said:
*These things saith the Holy one and the True one, who
hath the key of David: he that openeth and no man
shutteth, shutteth and no man openeth* (Ibid. iii. 7)—
what can we understand but the supreme authority
of the Church? And what else is meant by what
the Angel said to Our Lady (Luke i. 32): *The Lord
God shall give unto him the throne of David his father,
and he shall reign in the house of Jacob for ever?*—the

Holy Spirit making us know the kingship of our Lord, now by the seat or throne, now by the keys. But it is the commandment which in Isaias (xxii.) is given to Eliacim which is parallel in every particular with that which Our Lord gives to S. Peter. In it there is described the deposition of a sovereign-priest and governor of the Temple: *Thus saith the Lord God of hosts: go get thee in to him that dwelleth in the tabernacle, to Sobna who is over the temple; and thou shalt say to him—what dost thou here?* And further on: *I will depose thee.* See there the deposition of one, and now see the institution of the other. *And it shall come to pass in that day that I will call my servant Eliacim the son of Helcias, and I will clothe him with thy robe, and will strengthen him with thy girdle, and will give thy power into his hand: and he shall be as a father to the inhabitants of Jerusalem, and to the house of Juda. And I will lay the key of the house of David upon his shoulder; and he shall open, and none shall shut: and he shall shut and none shall open.* Could anything fit better than these two Scriptures? For: *Blessed art thou, Simon Bar-jona, because flesh and blood have not revealed it to thee, but my Father who is in heaven*—is it not at least equivalent to: *I will call my servant Eliacim the son of Helcias?* And *I say to thee that thou art Peter, and upon this rock I will build my church, and the gates of hell,* &c.—does this not signify the same as: *I will clothe him with thy robe, and will strengthen him with thy girdle, and will give thy power into his hand, and he shall be as a father to the inhabitants of Jerusalem and to the house of Juda?* And what else is it to be the foundation or foundation-stone of a family than to be there as father, to have the superintendence, to be governor there? And if one has had this assurance: *I will lay the key of the house of David upon his shoulder,* the other has had no less, who had the promise: *And I will give to thee the keys of the kingdom of heaven.* And if when he has opened no one shall shut, when he has shut no one shall open; so, when the other shall have loosened no one shall bind, when he shall have bound no one shall loosen. The one is Eliacim son of Helcias, the other, Simon the son of Jonas; the one is clothed with the pontifical robe, the other with heavenly revelation; the one has power in his hand, the other is a strong rock; the one is as father in Jerusalem, the other is as foundation in the Church; the one has the keys of the kingdom of David, the other those of the Church of the Gospel; when one shuts nobody opens, when one binds nobody looses; when one opens no one shuts, when one loosens nobody binds. What further remains to be said than that if ever Eliacim son of Helcias was head of the Mosaic Temple, Simon son of Jonas was the same of the Gospel Church? Eliacim represented Our Lord as figure, S. Peter represents him as lieutenant; Eliacim represented him in the Mosaic Church, and S. Peter in the Christian Church. Such is what is meant by this promise of giving the keys to S. Peter, a promise which was never made to the other Apostles.

But I say that it is not all one to promise the keys of the kingdom and to say: *Whatever thou shalt loose,* although one is an explanation of the other. And what is the difference?—certainly just that which there is between the possession of an authority and the exercise of it. It may well happen that

while a king lives, his queen, or his son, may have
just as much power as the king himself to chastise,
absolve, make gifts, grant favours : such person, however, will not have the sceptre but only the exercise
of it. He will indeed have the same authority, but
not in possession, only in use and exercise. What
he does will be valid, but he will not be head or
king, he must recognise that his power is extraordinary, by commission and delegation, whereas the
power of the king, which may be no greater, is
ordinary and is his own. So Our Lord promising the
keys to S. Peter remits to him the ordinary authority,
and gives him that office in ownership, the exercise
of which he referred to when he said : *Whatsoever thou
shalt loose,* &c. Now afterwards, when he makes the
same promise to the other Apostles, he does not give
them the keys or the ordinary authority, but only
gives them the use and exercise thereof. This difference is taken from the very terms of the Scripture :
for *to loose and to bind* signifies but the action and
exercise, *to have the keys,* the habit. . . . See how
different is the promise which Our Lord made to S.
Peter from that which he made to the other Apostles.
The Apostles all have the same power as S. Peter,
but not in the same rank, inasmuch as they have it
as delegates and agents, but S. Peter as ordinary head
and permanent officer. And in truth it was fitting
that the Apostles who were to plant the Church
everywhere, should all have full power and entire
authority as to the use of the keys and the exercise
of their powers, while it was most necessary that
one amongst them should have charge of the keys by
office and dignity,—" that the Church, which is one,"

as S. Cyprian says,* "should by the word of the Lord be founded upon one who received the keys thereof."

CHAPTER IV.

FOURTH PROOF.　OF THE THIRD PROMISE MADE TO S. PETER: I HAVE PRAYED FOR THEE, &c.

To which of the others was it ever said: *I have prayed for thee, Peter, that thy faith fail not, and thou being once converted, confirm thy brethren?* (Luke xxii. 32). Truly they are two privileges of great importance, these. Our Lord, when about to establish the faith in his Church, did not pray for the faith of any of the others in particular, but only of S. Peter as head. For what could be the object of this prerogative? *Satan hath sought you* (*vos*)—you all; *but I have prayed for thee, Peter,*—is not this to place him alone as responsible for all, as head and guide of the whole flock? But who sees not how pregnant this passage is for our purpose? Let us consider what precedes, and we shall find that Our Lord had declared to his Apostles that there was one of them greater than the others: *He who is the greatest among you . . . and he that is the leader,*—and immediately Our Lord goes on to say to him that the adversary was seeking to sift them, all of them, as wheat, but that still he had prayed for him in particular that his faith should not fail. I pray you, does not this grace which was so peculiar to

---

* Ad *Jubaianum.*

III.

him, and which was not common to the others, according to S. Thomas, show that S. Peter was that one who was *greatest among* them? All are tempted, and prayer is made for one alone. But the words following render all this quite evident. For some Protestant might say that he prayed for S. Peter in particular on account of some other reason that might be imagined (for the imagination ever furnishes support enough for obstinacy), not because he was head of the others or because the faith of the others was maintained in their pastor. On the contrary, gentlemen, it is in order that *being once converted* he might *confirm* his *brethren.* He prays for S. Peter as for the confirmer and support of the others; and what is this but to declare him head of the others? Truly one could not give S. Peter the command to confirm the Apostles without charging him to have care of them. For how could he put this command in practice without paying regard to the weakness or the strength of the others in order to strengthen or confirm them? Is this not to again call him foundation of the Church? If he supports, secures, strengthens the very foundation-stones, how shall he not confirm all the rest? If he has the charge of supporting the columns of the Church, how shall he not support all the rest of the building? If he has the charge of feeding the pastors, must he not be sovereign pastor himself? The gardener who sees the young plant exposed to the continual rays of the sun, and wishes to preserve it from the drought which threatens it, does not pour water on each branch, but having well steeped the root considers that all the rest is safe, because the root continues to distribute the moisture to the rest of the plant. Our Lord also, having planted this holy assembly of the disciples, prayed for the head and the root, in order that the water of faith might not fail to him who was therewith to supply all the rest, and in order that through the head the faith might always be preserved in the Church.

But I must tell you, before closing this part of my subject, that the denial which S. Peter made on the day of the Passion must not trouble you here; for he did not lose the faith, but only sinned as to the confession of it. Fear made him disavow that which he believed. He believed right but spoke wrong.

CHAPTER V.

FIFTH PROOF.   THE FULFILMENT OF THESE PROMISES: FEED MY SHEEP.

WE know that Our Lord gave a most ample procuration and commission to his Apostles to treat with the world concerning its salvation, when he said to them (John xx.): *As the Father hath sent me I also send you . . . receive ye the Holy Ghost: whose sins you shall forgive,* &c. It was the execution of that promise of his which had been made them in general: *Whatsoever you shall bind,* &c. But it was never said to any one of the other Apostles in particular: *Thou art Peter, and upon this rock I will build my Church,* nor was it ever said to one of the others: *Feed my sheep* (John xxi. 17). S. Peter alone had this charge. They were equal in the Apostolate, but into the pastoral dignity S. Peter alone was instituted: *Feed my sheep.* There are other pastors in the Church; each must *feed the flock which is under* him, as S. Peter says (1 Ep. v. 2), or *that over which the Holy Ghost hath placed* him bishop, according to S. Paul (Acts xx. 28). But, "to which of the others," says S. Bernard,* "were ever the sheep so absolutely, so universally committed: *Feed my sheep?*"

And to prove that it is truly S. Peter to whom these words are addressed, I betake myself to the holy Word. It is S. Peter only who is called Simon son of John, or of Jona (for one is the same as the other, and Jona is but the short of Joannah); and in order that we may know that this Simon son of John is really S. Peter, S. John bears witness that it was Simon Peter—*Jesus saith to Simon Peter: Simon, son of John, lovest thou me more than these?* It is then S. Peter to whom in particular Our Lord says: *Feed my sheep.*

And Our Lord puts S. Peter apart from the others in that place where he compares him with them: *Lovest thou me,*—there is S. Peter on the one side—*more than these,*—there are the Apostles on the other. And although all the Apostles were not present, yet the principal ones were,—S. James, S. John, S. Thomas and others. It is only S. Peter who *is grieved*, it is only S. Peter whose death is foretold. What room is there then for doubting that it was to him alone that this word *feed my sheep* is addressed, a word which is united to all these others?

Now that to feed the sheep includes the charge of them, appears clearly. For what is it to have the charge of feeding the sheep, but to be pastor and shepherd; and shepherds have full charge of the sheep,

* *De Consid.* ii. 8.

and not only lead them to pasture, but bring them
back, fold them, guide them, rule them, keep them in
fear, chastise them and guard them.   In Scripture to
rule and to feed the people is taken as the same
thing, which is easy to see in Ezekiel (xxxiv.); in the
second Book of Kings (v. 2); and in several places of
the Psalms, where, according to the original there is
to feed, and we have *to rule:* and in fact, between
ruling and pasturing the sheep with iron crook there
is no difference.   In Psalm xxii., verse 1, *The Lord
ruleth me, i.e.,* as shepherd governeth me, and when it
is said that David had been elected *to feed Jacob his
servant and Israel his inheritance: and he fed them in
the innocence of his heart* (Ps. lxxvii. 71, 72), it is just
the same as if he said *to rule, to govern, to preside over.*
And it is after the same figure of speech that the
peoples are called *sheep of the pasture* of Our Lord
(Ps. xcix. 3), so that, to have the commandment of
feeding the Christian sheep is no other thing than to
be their ruler and pastor.

It is now easy to see what authority Our Lord
intrusted to S. Peter by these words: *Feed my sheep.*
For in truth the charge is so general that it includes
all the faithful, whatever may be their condition; the
commandment is so particular that it is addressed only
to S. Peter.   He who wishes to have this honour of
being one of Our Lord's sheep must acknowledge S.
Peter, or him who takes Peter's place, as his shepherd.
" *If thou lovest me* "—I quote S. Bernard *—"feed my
sheep.* Which sheep ?   The people of this or that
city or region or even kingdom ? *My sheep,* Christ
says.   Is it not clear to everybody that he did not

* *De Consid.* ii. 8.

mean some, but handed over all. There is no exception where there is no distinction. And perhaps the others, his fellow-disciples, were present when, giving a charge to one, he commended unity to all in one flock with one pastor, according to that (Cant. vi.): *One is my dove, my beautiful one, my perfect one.* Where unity is there is perfection."

When Our Lord said: *I know my sheep*, he spoke of all; when he said *feed my sheep*, he still means it of all; for Our Lord has but one fold and one flock. And what else is it to say: *feed my sheep*, but: Take care of my flock, of my pastures, or of my sheep and my sheepfold? It is then entirely under the charge of S. Peter. For if he said to him: *Feed my sheep*, either he recommended all to him or some only; if he only recommended some—which? I ask. Were it not to recommend to him none, to recommend to him some only without specifying which, and to put him in charge of unknown sheep? If all, as the Word expresses it, then he was the general pastor of the whole Church. And the matter is thus rightly settled beyond doubt. It is the common explanation of the Ancients, it is the execution of his promises. But there is a mystery in this institution which our S. Bernard does not allow me to forget, now that I have taken him as my guide in this point. It is that Our Saviour thrice charges him to do the office of pastor, saying to him first: *Feed my lambs;* secondly, *my lambs;* thirdly, *my sheep :*—not only to make this institution more solemn, but to show that he gave into his charge not only the people, but the pastors and Apostles themselves, who, as sheep, nourish the lambs and young sheep, and are mothers to them.

And it makes nothing against this truth that S. Paul and the other Apostles have fed many peoples with the Gospel doctrine, for being all under the charge of S. Peter, what they have done belongs also to him, as the victory does to the general, though the captains have fought: nor, that S. Paul received from S. Peter *the right hand of fellowship* (Gal. ii. 9), for they were companions in preaching, but S. Peter was greater and chief in the pastoral office; and the chiefs call the soldiers and captains comrades.

Nor that S. Paul was the Apostle of the Gentiles and S. Peter of the Jews; because it was not to divide the government of the Church, nor to hinder either the one or the other from converting the Gentiles and the Jews indifferently, nor because the chief authority was not in the hands of one; but it was to assign them the quarters where they were principally to labour in preaching, in order that each one attacking impiety in his own province the world might the sooner be filled with the sound of the Gospel.

Nor that he would seem not to have known that the Gentiles were to belong to the fold of Our Lord, which was confided to him: for what he said to the good Cornelius: *In truth I perceive that God is no respecter of persons; but in every nation he that feareth him and worketh justice is acceptable to him* (Acts x.), is nothing different from what he had said before: *Whosoever shall call upon the name of the Lord shall be saved* (ii.), and the prophecy which he had explained: *And in thy seed shall all the families of the earth be blessed* (iii.). He was only uncertain as to the time when the bringing back of the Gentiles was to begin, according to the holy Word of the Master: *You shall be witnesses unto*

*me in Jerusalem, and in all Judæa and Samaria, and
even to the uttermost part of the earth* (i.), and that of
S. Paul: *To you it behoved us to speak first the word
of God, but seeing you reject it, we turn to the Gentiles*
(xiii.), just as Our Lord had already opened the mind
of the Apostles to the intelligence of the Scriptures
when he said to them: *Thus it behoved . . . that
penance and remission of sins should be preached in his
name among all nations, beginning with Jerusalem*
(Luke *ult.*).

Nor that the Apostles instituted deacons without
the command of S. Peter, in the Acts of the Apostles
(vi.); for S. Peter's presence there sufficiently authorised that act; besides, we do not deny that the
Apostles had full powers of administration in the
Church, under the pastoral authority of S. Peter.
And we bishops, in union with the Holy See of Rome,
ordain both deacons and priests without any special
authorisation.

Nor that the Apostles sent Peter and John into
Samaria (Ib. viii.), for the people also sent Phinees,
who was the High Priest, and their superior, to the children of Ruben and Gad (Jos. xxii.); and the centurion
sent the chiefs and heads of the Jews, whom he considered to be greater than himself (Luke vii.); and S.
Peter being in the council, himself consented to and
authorised his own mission.

Nor finally, that which is made so much of—that
S. Paul *withstood* S. Peter *to the face* (Gal. ii.), for every
one knows that it is permitted to the inferior to correct
the greater and to admonish him with charity and
submission when charity requires; witness our S.
Bernard in his books *On Consideration;* and on this

subject the great S. Gregory * says these all golden words : " He became the follower of his inferior, though before him in dignity ; so that he who was first in the high dignity of the Apostolate might be first in humility."

CHAPTER VI.

SIXTH PROOF. FROM THE ORDER IN WHICH THE EVANGELISTS NAME THE APOSTLES.

IT is a thing very worthy of consideration in this matter that the Evangelists never name either all the Apostles or a part of them together without putting S. Peter ever at the very top, ever at the head of the band. This we cannot consider to be done accidentally ; for it is perpetually observed by the Evangelists ; and it is not four or five times that they are thus named together, but very often. And besides, as to the other Apostles, they do not keep any particular order.

The names of the twelve Apostles are these, says S. Matthew (x.): *The first, Simon who is called Peter, and Andrew his brother ; James the son of Zebedee and John his brother ; Philip and Bartholomew, Thomas and Mathew the publican, James of Alpheus and Thaddeus, Simon Chananeus, and Judas Iscariot.* He names S. Andrew the 2d; S. Mark names him the 4th ; and to better show that it makes no difference, S. Luke, who in one place has put him 2d, in another puts him 4th. S. Matthew puts S. John 4th; S. Mark

puts him 3d; S. Luke in one place 4th, in another
2d. S. Matthew puts S. James 3d; S. Mark puts
him 2d. In short, it is only S. Philip, S. James of
Alpheus and Judas who are not sometimes higher,
sometimes lower. When the Evangelists elsewhere
name all the Apostles together there is no principle
except as regards S. Peter, who goes first everywhere.
Well now, let us imagine that we were to see in the
country, in the streets, in meetings, what we read in
the Gospels (and in truth it is more certain than if we
had seen it)—if we saw S. Peter the first and all the
rest grouped together,—should we not judge that the
others were equals and companions, and S. Peter the
chief and captain.

But, besides this, very often when the Evangelists
talk of the Apostolic company they name only Peter,
and mention the others as accessory and following:
*And Simon and they who were with him followed after
him* (Mark i.): *But Peter and they that were with him
were heavy with sleep* (Luke ix.) You know well that
to name one person and put the others all together
with him, is to make him the most important and the
others his inferiors.

Very often again he is named separately from the
others, as by the Angel: *Tell his disciples and Peter*
(Mark xvi.): *But Peter standing up, with the eleven
. . . they said to Peter and the rest of the Apostles*
(Acts ii.): *Peter then answering and the Apostles said,
Have we not power to lead about a woman, a sister, as
well as the rest of the apostles, and the brethren of the
Lord and Cephas* (1 Cor. ix.)? What does this
mean, to say: *Tell his disciples and Peter—Peter and
the Apostles answered?* Was Peter not an Apostle?

Either he was less or more than the others, or he was equal. No man, who is not altogether mad, will say he was less. If he is equal and stands on a level with the others, why is he put by himself? If there is nothing particular in him, why is it not just as well to say: Tell his disciples and Andrew, or John? Certainly it must be for some particular quality which is in him more than in the others, and because he was not a simple Apostle. So that having said: *Tell his disciples,* or, *as the rest of the Apostles,* how can one longer doubt that S. Peter is more than Apostle and disciple? Only once in the Scriptures S. Peter is named after S. James, *James and Cephas and John gave the right hands of fellowship* (Gal. ii.) But in truth there is too much occasion to doubt whether in the original and anciently S. Peter was named first or second, to allow any valid conclusion to be drawn from this place alone. For S. Augustine, S. Ambrose, S. Jerome, both in the commentary and in the text, have written Peter, James, John, which they could never have done if they had not found this same order in their copies: S. Chrysostom has done the same in the commentary. All this shows the diversity of copies, which makes the conclusion doubtful on either side. But even if the copies we now have were originals, one could deduce nothing from this single passage against the order of so many others; for S. Paul might be keeping to the order of the time in which he received the hand of fellowship, or without concerning himself about the order might have written first the one which came first to his mind.

But S. Matthew shows us clearly what order there was

amongst the Apostles, that is, that one was first, and
the remainder were equal without 2d or 3d.   *First,*
says he, *Simon who is called Peter;* he does not say
2d, Andrew, 3d, James, but goes on simply naming
them, to let us know that provided S. Peter was
first all the rest were in the same rank, and that
amongst them there was no precedence.   *First,* says
he, *Peter,* and Andrew.   From this is derived the name
of Primacy.   For if he were first (*primus*), his place
was first, his rank first, and this quality of his was
Primacy.

It is answered to this that if the Evangelists here
named S. Peter the first, it was because he was the
most advanced in age amongst the Apostles, or on
account of some privilege which existed amongst them.
But what is the worth of such a reason as this, I
should like to know?   To say that S. Peter was the
oldest of the society is to seek at hazard an excuse for
obstinacy; and the Scripture distinctly tells us he was
not the earliest Apostle when it testifies that S.
Andrew led him to Our Lord.   The reasons are seen
quite clearly in the Scripture, but because you are
resolved to maintain the contrary, you go seeking
about with your imagination on every side.   Why say
that S. Peter was the oldest, since it is a pure fancy
which has no foundation in the Scripture, and is
contrary to the Ancients?   Why not say rather that
he was the one on whom Christ founded his Church,
to whom he had given the keys of the kingdom of
heaven, who was the confirmer of the brethren?—for
all this is in the Scripture.   What you want to maintain you do maintain; whether it has a base in
Scripture or not makes no difference.   And as to the

other privileges, let anybody go over them to me in order, and none will be found special to S. Peter but those which make him head of the Church.

CHAPTER VII.

SEVENTH PROOF.   OF SOME OTHER MARKS WHICH ARE SCATTERED THROUGHOUT THE SCRIPTURES OF THE PRIMACY OF S. PETER.

IF I wanted to bring together here all that is to be found, I should make this proof as large as I want to make all the section, and without effort on my part. For that excellent theologian, Robert Bellarmine, would put many things into my hands.   But particularly has Doctor Nicholas Sanders treated this subject so solidly and so amply that it is hard to say anything about it which he has not said or written in his books *On the Visible Monarchy.*   I will give some extracts.

Whoever will read the Scriptures attentively will see this Primacy of S. Peter everywhere.   If the Church is compared to a building, as it is, its rock and its secondary foundation is S. Peter (Matt. xvi.).

If you say it is like a family, it is only Our Lord who pays tribute as head of the household, and after him S. Peter as his lieutenant (Ib. xvii.).

If to a ship, S. Peter is its captain, and in it Our Lord teaches (Luke v.).

If to a fishery, S. Peter is the first in it; the true disciples of Our Lord fish only with him (Ib. and John xxi.).

If to draw-nets (Matt. xiii.), it is S. Peter who casts them into the sea, S. Peter who draws them; the other disciples are his coadjutors. It is S. Peter who brings them to land and presents the fish to Our Lord (Luke v., John xxi.).

Do you say it is like an embassy?—S. Peter is first ambassador (Matt. x.).

Do you say it is a brotherhood?—S. Peter is first, the governor and confirmer of the rest (Luke xxii.).

Would you rather have it a kingdom?—S. Peter receives its keys (Matt. xvi.).

Will you consider it a flock or fold of sheep and lambs?—S. Peter is its pastor and shepherd-general (John xxi.).

Say now in conscience, how could Our Lord testify his intention more distinctly. Perversity cannot find use for its eyes amid such light. S. Andrew came the first to follow Our Lord; and it was he who brought his brother, S. Peter, and S. Peter precedes him everywhere. What does this signify except that the advantage one had in time the other had in dignity?

But let us continue. When Our Lord ascends to heaven, all the holy Apostolic body goes to S. Peter, as to the common father of the family (Acts i.).

S. Peter rises up amongst them and speaks the first, and teaches the interpretation of weighty prophecy (Ib.).

He has the first care of the restoration and increase of the Apostolic college (Ib.). It is he who first proposed to make an Apostle, which is no act of light authority; for the Apostles have all had successors, and by death have not lost their dignity. But S. Peter teaching the Church shows both that Judas had lost his Apostolate and that another was needed in his place, contrary to the ordinary course of this authority, which in the others continues after death, and which they will even exercise on the Day of Judgment, when they shall be seated around the Judge, judging the twelve tribes of Israel.

The Apostles have no sooner received the Holy Ghost than S. Peter, as chief of the Evangelic Embassy, being with his eleven companions, begins to publish, according to his office, the holy tidings of salvation to the Jews in Jerusalem. He is the first catechist of the Church, and preacher of penance; the others are with him and are all asked questions, but S. Peter alone answers for all as chief of all (Acts ii.).

If a hand is to be put into the treasury of miracles confided to the Church, though S. John is present and is asked, S. Peter alone puts in his hand (Ib. iii.).

When the time comes for beginning the use of the spiritual sword of the Church, to punish a lie, it is S. Peter who directs the first blow upon Ananias and Saphira (Ib. v.): from this springs the hatred which lying heretics bear against his See and succession; because, as S. Gregory says,* " Peter by his word strikes liars dead."

He is the first who recognises and refutes heresy in Simon Magus (Ib. viii.): hence comes the irreconcileable hatred of all heretics against his See.

He is the first who raises the dead, when he prays for the devout Tabitha (Ib. ix.).

When it is time to put the sickle into the harvest of paganism, it is S. Peter to whom the revelation is made, as to the head of all the labourers, and the steward of the farmstead (Ib. x.).

* In Ezech. ii. 18.

The good Italian centurion, Cornelius, is ready to receive grace of the Gospel; he is sent to S. Peter, that the Gentiles may by his hands be blessed and consecrated: he is the first in commanding the pagans to be baptized (Acts x.).

When a General Council is sitting, S. Peter as president therein opens the gate to judgment and definition; and his sentence [is] followed by the rest, his private revelation becomes a law (Ib. xv.).

S. Paul declares that he went to Jerusalem expressly to see Peter, and stayed with him fifteen days (Gal i.). He saw S. James there, but to see him was not what he went for,—only to see S. Peter. What does this signify? Why did he not go as much to see the great and most celebrated Apostle S. James as to see S. Peter? Because we look at people in their head and face, and S. Peter was the head of all the Apostles.

When S. Peter and S. James were in prison the Evangelist testifies that *prayer was made without ceasing by the Church to God for S. Peter,* as for the general head and common ruler (Acts xii.).

If all this put together does not make you acknowledge S. Peter to be head of the Church and of the Apostles, I confess that Apostles are not Apostles, pastors not pastors, and doctors not doctors. For in what other more express words could be made known the authority of an Apostle and pastor over the people than those which the Holy Ghost has placed in the Scriptures to show that S. Peter was above Apostles, pastors, and the whole Church?

CHAPTER VIII.

EIGHTH PROOF.   TESTIMONIES OF THE CHURCH TO
THIS FACT.

It is true that Scripture suffices, but let us see who
wrests it and violates it.   If we were the first to
draw conclusions in favour of the Primacy of S. Peter,
one might think that we were wresting it.   But how
do things stand?   It is most clear on the point, and
has been understood in this sense by all the primitive
Church.   Those, then, force it who bring in a new
sense, who gloss it against the natural meaning of the
words, and against the sense of Antiquity.   If this be
lawful for everybody, the Scripture will no longer be
anything but a toy for fanciful and perverse wits.

What is the meaning of this—that the Church has
never held as patriarchal sees any but those of Alexandria, of Rome, and of Antioch?   One may invent a
thousand fancies, but there is no other reason than
that which S. Leo produces: *—because S. Peter
founded these three sees they have been called and
esteemed patriarchal, as testify the Council of Nice,
and that of Chalcedon, in which a great difference is
made between these three sees and the others.   As for
those of Constantinople and Jerusalem, the above-
named Councils show how differently they are considered from those three others founded by S. Peter.

Not that the Council of Nice speaks of the see of
Constantinople; for Constantinople was of no importance at all at that time, having only been built by the

* Ad *Anat.*

III.

great Constantine, who dedicated and named it in the twenty-fifth year of his Empire: but the Council of Nice treats of the see of Jerusalem, and that of Chalcedon of the see of Constantinople.

By the precedence and pre-eminence of these three sees, the ancient Church testified sufficiently that she held S. Peter for her chief, who had founded them. Otherwise why did she not place also in the same rank the see of Ephesus, founded by S. Paul, confirmed and assured by S. John; or the see of Jerusalem, in which S. James had conversed and presided?

What else did she testify, when in the public and patent letters which they anciently called *formatæ*, after the first letter of the Father, Son, and Holy Ghost, there was put the first letter of Peter, except that after Almighty God, who is the absolute King, the lieutenant's authority is in great esteem with all those who are good Christians?

As for the consent of the Fathers concerning this point, Surius, Sanders, and a thousand others have taken away from posterity all occasion of doubting it. I will only bring forward the names by which the Fathers have called him, which sufficiently show their belief concerning his authority.

Optatus of Milevis called him "the head of the Churches" (Contra Parm. ii.). They have called him "Head of the Church," as S. Jerome (adv. Jov. i.), and S. Chrysostom (Hom. 11 in Matt.). "Happy foundation of the Church," as S. Hilary (in Matt. xvi.), and "Janitor of heaven, the first of the Apostles," as S. Augustine (in J. 56) after S. Matthew. "Mouth and crown of the Apostles," as Origen (in Luc. xvii.), and S. Chrysostom (in Matt. 55). "Mouth and

prince of the Apostles," as the same S. Chrysostom
(in J. 87). "Guardian of the brethren, and of the
whole world" (Ib. ult.). "Pastor of the Church and
head stronger than adamant" (Id. in Matt. 55).
"The immovable rock, immovable pedestal, the
great Apostle, first of the disciples, first called and
first obeying" (Id. in Pœn. 3). "Firmament of the
Church, leader and master of Christians, column of
the spiritual Israel, guardian of the feeble, master of
the heavens, mouth of Christ, supreme head of the
Apostles" (Id. in ador. caten. et glad. Apost. princ.
Petri). "Prince of the Church, port of faith, master
of the world" (Id. in SS. P. et P. et Eliam). "First
in the supremacy of the Apostolate" (Greg. in Ezech.
xviii.). "High Priest of Christians" (Euseb. in Chron.
44). "Master of the army of God" (Id. Hist.
ii. 14). "Set over the other disciples" (Bas. de
Judic. Dei 9). "President of the world" (Chrys. in
Matt. 11). "The Lord of the house of God, and
prince of all his possession" (Bern. Ep. 137, ad
Eugen.).

Who shall dare to oppose this company? Thus
they speak, thus they understand the Scripture, and
according to it do they hold that all these names and
titles are due to S. Peter.

The Church then was left on earth by her Master
and Spouse with a visible chief and lieutenant of the
Master and Lord. The Church is therefore to be
always united together in a visible chief-minister
of Christ.

CHAPTER IX.

THAT SAINT PETER HAS HAD SUCCESSORS IN THE VICAR-
GENERALSHIP OF OUR LORD.   THE CONDITIONS
REQUIRED FOR SUCCEEDING HIM.

I HAVE clearly proved so far that the Catholic Church
was a monarchy in which Christ's head-minister
governed all the rest.   It was not then S. Peter only
who was its head, but, as the Church has not failed
by the death of S. Peter, so the authority of a head
has not failed; otherwise it would not be one, nor
would it be in the state in which its founder had
placed it.   And in truth all the reasons for which
Our Lord put a head to this body, do not so much
require that it should be there in that beginning
when the Apostles who governed the Church were
holy, humble, charitable, lovers of unity and concord,
as in the progress and continuation thereof, when
charity having now grown cold each one loves himself,
no one will obey the word of another nor submit to
discipline.

I ask you :——if the Apostles, whose understanding
the Holy Spirit enlightened so immediately, who were
so steadfast and so strong, needed a confirmer and
pastor as the form (*forme*) and visible maintenance of
their union, and of the union of the Church, how
much more now has the Church need of one, when
there are so many infirmities and weaknesses in the
members of the Church ?   And if the wills of the
Apostles, so closely united in charity, had need of an
exterior bond in the authority of a head, how much

more afterwards when charity has grown so cold is there need of a visible authority and ruler ?   And if, as S. Jerome says, in the time of the Apostles : " One is chosen from amongst all, in order that, a head being established, occasion of schism may be taken away," * how much more now, for the same reason, must there be a chief in the Church ?   The fold of Our Lord is to last till the consummation of the world, in visible unity : the unity then of external government must remain in it, and nobody has authority to change the form of administration save Our Lord who established it.†

All this has been well proven above, and it follows therefrom that S. Peter has had successors, has them in these days, and will have them even to the end of the ages.

I do not profess here to treat difficulties to the very bottom.   It is enough for my purpose to indicate some principal reasons and to expose our belief precisely. Indeed, if I were to take notice of the objections which are made on this point, while I should find small difficulty I should have great trouble, and most of them are so slight that they are not worth losing time over.   Let us see what conditions are required for succeeding to an office.

There can only be succession to one who, whether by deposition or by death, gives up and leaves his place ; whence Our Lord is always head and sovereign Pontiff of the Church, to whom no one succeeds, because he is always living, and has never resigned or quitted this priesthood [or] pontificate ; though here below, in the Church militant, he partly exercises it

* Adv. Jov. i. 26.   † See Preface.

by his ministers and servants, his authority, however, being too excellent to be altogether communicated. But these ministers and representatives, as
many pastors as ever there are, can give up and do
give up, either by deposition or by death, their offices
and dignities.

Now we have shown that S. Peter was head of the
Church as prime minister of Christ, and that this office
or dignity was not conferred on him for himself alone,
but for the good and profit of the whole Church; so
that Christianity being always to endure, this same
charge and authority must be perpetual in the Church
militant:—but how would it be perpetual if S. Peter
had no successor? For there can be no doubt that
S. Peter is pastor no longer, since he is no longer in
the Church militant, nor is he even a visible man,
which is a condition requisite for administration in
the visible Church.

It remains to learn how he made this quittance,
how he left this pontificate of his;—whether it was
by laying it down during his life or by natural death.
Then we will see who succeeded him and by what
right.

And on the one hand nobody doubts that S. Peter
continued in his charge all his life. For those words
of Our Lord: *Feed my sheep*, were to him not only
an institution into this supreme pastoral charge, but
an absolute commandment, which had no other
limitation than the end of his life, any more than
that other: *Preach the Gospel to every creature*,* which
the Apostles laboured in until death. Whilst therefore S. Peter lived this mortal life, he had no suc-

* Mark *ult.*

cessor,—he did not lay down his charge, and was not deposed from it. For he could not be so (except by heresy, which never had access to the Apostles, least of all to their head) unless the Master of the fold had removed him, which was not done.

It was death then which removed him from this guard and general watch which he was keeping as ordinary pastor over the whole sheepfold of his Master. But who succeeded in his place? As to this, all antiquity agrees that it was the Bishop of Rome, for this reason that S. Peter died Bishop of Rome—therefore the diocese of Rome was the last seat of the head of the Church: therefore the Bishop of Rome who came after the death of S. Peter, succeeded to the head of the Church, and consequently was head of the Church. Some one might say that he succeeded the head of the Church as to the bishopric of Rome, but not as to the kingship of the world. But such a one must show that S. Peter had two sees, of which the one was for Rome, the other for the universe, which was not the case. It is true that he had a seat at Antioch, but he who held it after him had not the Vicar-generalship, because S. Peter lived long afterwards, and had not laid down that charge; but having chosen Rome for his see he died Bishop thereof, and he who succeeded him, succeeded him simply, and sat in his seat, which was the general seat over the whole world, and over the bishopric of Rome in particular. Hence, the Bishop of Rome remained general lieutenant in the Church, and successor of S. Peter. This I am now about to prove so solidly that only the obstinate will be able to doubt it.

CHAPTER X.

THAT THE BISHOP OF ROME IS TRUE SUCCESSOR OF S. PETER, AND HEAD OF THE MILITANT CHURCH.

I HAVE presupposed that S. Peter was Bishop of Rome and died such. This the opposite party deny; many of them even deny that he ever was at Rome; but I am not obliged to attack all these negatives in detail, because when I shall have fully proved that S. Peter was and died Bishop of Rome, I shall have sufficiently proved that the Bishop of Rome is the successor of S. Peter. Besides, all my proofs and my witnesses state in express terms that the Bishop of Rome succeeded to S. Peter, which is my contention, and from which again will follow a clear certainty that S. Peter was at Rome and died there.

And now here is my first witness,—S. Clement, disciple of S. Peter, in the first letter which he wrote to James, the brother of the Lord; which is so authentic that Rufinus became the translator of it about twelve hundred years ago. Now he says these words: "Simon Peter, the chief apostle, brought the King of ages to the knowledge of the city of Rome, that it also might be saved. He being inspired with a fatherly affection, taking my hand in the assembly of the brethren, said: I ordain this Clement, Bishop, to whom alone I commit the chair of my preaching and doctrine." And a little further on: "to him I deliver the power of binding and loosing which was delivered to me by the Lord." And as to the authority of this epistle, Damasus in the Pontifical, in the life of Clement, speaks of it thus: "In the letter which was written to James you will find how to Clement was the Church committed by Blessed Peter." And Rufinus, in the preface to the book of the Recognitions of S. Clement, speaks of it with great honour, and says that he had turned it into Latin, and that S. Clement bore witness in it to his own institution, and said "that S. Peter had left him as successor in his chair." This testimony shows us both that S. Peter preached at Rome and that he was Bishop there. For if he had not been Bishop how would he have delivered to S. Clement a chair which he would not have held there?

The second, S. Irenæus (iii. 3): "To the greatest and oldest and most famous Church, founded by the two most glorious Apostles, Peter and Paul." And a little further on: "The blessed Apostles therefore, founding and instituting the Church, delivered to Linus the office of administering it as Bishop; to him succeeded Anacletus; after him, in the third place from the Apostles, Clement receives the episcopate.

The third, Tertullian (de Pr. xxxii.): "The Church also of the Romans publishes,"—that is, shows by public instruments and proofs—"that Clement was ordained by Peter." And in the same book (xxxvi.): "Happy Church, into which the Apostles poured with their blood their whole doctrine!"—and he speaks of the Roman Church, "where Peter's passion is made like to the Lord's." Whereby you see that S. Peter died at Rome and instituted S. Clement there. So that joining this testimony to the others, it is seen that he was Bishop there and died teaching there.

The fourth, S. Cyprian (Ep. 55, ad Corn.): "They dare to sail off to the chair of Peter, and to the head Church, whence the sacerdotal unity has come forth;"—and he is speaking of the Roman Church.

Eusebius (*Chron.* ann. 44): "Peter, by nation a Galilæan, the first pontiff of Christians, having first founded the Church of Antioch, proceeds to Rome, where, preaching the Gospel, he continues twenty-five years bishop of the same city."

Epiphanius (ii. 27): "The succession of bishops at Rome is in this order; Peter and Paul, Linus, Cletus, Clement, &c."

Dorotheus (in *Syn.*): "Linus was Bishop of Rome after the first ruler, Peter."

Optatus of Milevis (*de Sch Don.*): "You cannot deny that you know that in the city of Rome the episcopal chair was first intrusted to Peter, in which Peter, head of all the Apostles, sat." And a little further on: "Peter sat first, to whom succeeded Linus, to Linus succeeded Clement."

S. Jerome (ad Dam.): "With the successor of the fisherman and the disciple of the cross do I treat: I am united in communion with thy Blessedness, in the chair of Peter."

S. Augustine (Ep. 53, ad Gen.): "To Peter succeeded Linus, to Linus Clement."

In the Fourth General Council of Chalcedon (Act. iii.), when the legates of the Holy See would deliver sentence against Dioscorus, they speak in this fashion: "Wherefore, most holy and blessed Leo, of the great and older Rome, by us and by the present holy synod, together with the thrice blessed and ever to be praised Apostle Peter, who is the rock and the foundation of the Catholic Church, has stripped him of the episcopal dignity and also ejected him from the priestly ministry." Give a little attention to these particulars; that the Bishop of Rome alone deprives him, by his legates and by the Council; that they unite the Bishop of Rome with S. Peter. For such things show that the Bishop of Rome holds the place of S. Peter.

The Synod of Alexandria, at which Athanasius was present, in its letter to Felix II., uses remarkable words on this point, and amongst other things, relates that in the Council of Nice it had been determined that it was not lawful to celebrate any Council without the consent of the Holy See of Rome, but that the canons which had been made to that effect had been burnt by the Arian heretics. And in fact, Julius I., in the *Rescript against the Orientals in Favour of Athanasius* (cc. 2, 3), cites two canons of the Council of Nice which relate to this matter,—which work of Julius I. has been cited by Gratian, four hundred years ago, and by Isidore nine hundred: and the great Father, Vincent of Lerius, makes mention of it a thousand years back. I say this because all the canons of Nice are not in existence, only twenty remaining: but so many grave authors cite others beyond the twenty, that we are obliged to believe what is said by those good Fathers of Alexandria above-named, that the Arians have got the greater part destroyed.

For God's sake let us cast our eyes on that most ancient and pure Church of the first six centuries, and regard it from all sides. And if we find it firmly believes that the Pope was successor of S. Peter, what rashness will it be to deny it?

This, methinks, is a reason which asks no credit,

but pays in good coin. S. Peter has had successors in
his vicarship: and who has ever in the ancient Church
had the reputation of being successor of S. Peter, and
head of the Church, except the Bishop of Rome? In
truth all ancient authors, whosoever they be, all give
this title to the Pope, and never to others.

And how then shall we say it does not belong to
him? Truly it were to deny the known truth. Or
let them tell us what other bishop is the head of the
Church, and successor of S. Peter. At the Council of
Nice, at those of Constantinople and Chalcedon, it is
not seen that any bishop usurps the primacy for himself: it is attributed, according to ancient custom, to
the Pope; no other is named in equal degree. In
short, never was it said, either certainly or doubtfully,
of any bishop in the first five hundred years that he
was head or superior over the rest, except of the
Bishop of Rome; about him indeed it was never
doubted, but was held as settled that he was such.
On what ground, then, after fifteen hundred years
passed, would one cast doubt on this ancient tradition?
I should never end were I to try to catalogue all
the assurances and repetitions of this truth which we
have in the Ancients' writings: but this will suffice
just now to prove that the Bishop of Rome is the
successor of S. Peter, and that S. Peter was and died
Bishop at Rome.

CHAPTER XI.

SHORT DESCRIPTION OF THE LIFE OF S. PETER, AND OF THE INSTITUTION OF HIS FIRST SUCCESSORS.

THERE is no question which the ministers fight over so pertinaciously as this.   For they try by force of con-jectures, presumptions, dilemmas, explanations, and by every means, to prove that S. Peter was never at Rome:—except Calvin, who, seeing that this was to belie all antiquity, and that it was not needed for his opinion, contents himself with saying that at least S. Peter was not long Bishop at Rome: "On account of the consent of writers, I do not dispute that he was at Rome.   But that he was bishop, especially for a long time, I cannot admit."   But in truth, though he were Bishop of Rome for but a very short time, if he died there he left there his chair and his succession.   So that as to Calvin we should not have great cause for discussion, provided that he was resolved to acknow-ledge sincerely that S. Peter died at Rome, and that he was bishop there when he died.   And as to the others we have sufficiently proved above that S. Peter died Bishop of Rome.

The statements which are made to the contrary are more captious than hard to resolve; and because he who shall have the true account of the life of S. Peter before his eyes will have enough answer for all the objections, I will briefly say what I think the more probable, in which I will follow the opinion of that excellent theologian, Gilbert Genebrard, Archbishop of Aix, in his *Chronology*, and of Robert Bellarmine,

Jesuit, in his *Controversies*, who closely follow S. Jerome, and Eusebius *in Chronico*.

Our Lord then ascended into heaven in the eighteenth year of Tiberius, and commanded his Apostles to stay in Jerusalem twelve years, according to the ancient tradition of Thraseas, martyr, not all indeed but some of them (to verify the word spoken by Isaias,* and as SS. Paul and Barnabas seem to imply †), for S. Peter was in Lydda and in Joppa before the twelve years had expired:—it was enough that some Apostles should remain in Judæa as witnesses to the Jews.   S. Peter then remained in Judæa about five years after the Ascension, preaching and announcing the Gospel, and at the end of the first year, or soon afterwards, S. Paul was converted, who after three years went *to Jerusalem to see Peter,* ‡ with whom he stayed fifteen days.   S. Peter then having preached about five years in Judæa, towards the end of the fifth year went to Antioch, where he remained Bishop about seven years, that is, till the second year of Claudius, but meanwhile making evangelic journeys into Galatia, Asia, Cappadocia, and elsewhere, for the conversion of the nations.   From thence, having committed his episcopal charge to the good Evodius, he returned to Jerusalem, on his arrival in which place he was imprisoned by Herod *to please the Jews* § about the time of the Passover.   But escaping from the prison soon afterwards under the direction of the angel, he came, that same year, which was the second of Claudius, to Rome, where he established his chair, which he held about twenty-five years, during which he did not omit to visit various provinces, according

* lxv.   † Acts xiii. 46.   ‡ Gal. i. 18.   § Acts xii. 6.

to the necessity of the Christian commonwealth ; but amongst other things, about the eighteenth year of the Passion and Ascension of the Saviour, which was the ninth of Claudius, he was driven with the rest of the Hebrews from Rome, and went away to Jerusalem, where the Council of Jerusalem was celebrated, in which S. Peter presided.   Then Claudius being dead, S. Peter returned to Rome, taking up again his first work of teaching and of visiting from time to time various provinces, where at last Nero, having imprisoned him for death, with S. Paul his companion, Peter, yielding to the holy importunities of the faithful, was about to make his escape and get out of the city by night, when meeting Our Saviour by the gate he said to him : *Domine quo vadis ?*—Lord, whither goest thou ?   He answered : I go to Rome to be crucified anew : * an answer which S. Peter well knew pointed towards his cross.   So that, after having been about five years in Judæa, seven years in Antioch, twenty-five years at Rome, in the fourteenth year of Nero's empire he was crucified, head downwards, and on the same day S. Paul had his head cut off.

But before dying, taking by the hand his disciple S. Clement, S. Peter appointed him his successor, an office which S. Clement would not accept nor exercise till after the death of Linus and of Cletus, who had been coadjutors of S. Peter in the administration of the Roman bishopric.   So that to him who would know why some authors place S. Clement first in order after S. Peter, and others S. Linus, I will make him an answer by S. Epiphanius,

* Amb. contra Aux. ; Origen in Gen. iii ; Athan. *pro fugâ ;* Jerome *de Vir. ill. ;* Eusebius *in Chron ;* Ado ; Tertull. *de præscr.*

an author worthy of credit, whose words are these : *
" Let no man wonder that Linus and Cletus took up
the episcopate before S. Clement, he being a disciple
of the Apostles, contemporary with Peter and Paul;
for they also were contemporaries of the Apostles;
whether therefore whilst they were alive he received
from Peter the imposition of the hands of the episcopate, and refusing the office waited, or, after the
departure of the Apostles was appointed by the bishop
Cletus, we do not clearly know."

Because therefore S. Clement had been chosen by S.
Peter, as he himself testifies, and yet would not accept
the charge before the death of Linus and Cletus,
some, in consideration of the election made by S.
Peter, place him the first in order, others, looking at
the refusal he gave and at his leaving the exercise of
it to Linus and Cletus, place him the fourth.

Besides, S. Epiphanius may have had reason to
doubt about the election of S. Clement made by S.
Peter, for want of having had sufficient proofs; while
possibly Tertullian, Damasus, Rufinus, and others
may have had means of ascertaining the truth; and
this may be the reason why S. Epiphanius speaks thus
indecisively. Tertullian, who was more ancient, states
positively : " The Church of the Romans publishes
that Clement was ordained by Peter," that is, proves
by documents and public acts. As for myself I prefer,
and reasonably, to place myself on the side of those
who are certain; because he who doubts what a man
of probity and sense distinctly certifies contradicts the
speaker; on the contrary, to be sure of that which
another doubts about is simply to imply that the

* Hær. 27.

doubter does not know all, as indeed he has first confessed himself, by doubting,—for doubting is nothing but not certainly knowing the truth of a thing.

And now, having seen by this short account of the life of S. Peter, which bears every mark of probability, that S. Peter did not always stay in Rome, but, having his chair there, did not omit to visit many provinces, to return to Jerusalem and to fulfil the apostolic office, all those frivolous reasons which are drawn from the negative authority of the Epistle of S. Paul will no longer have entrance into your judgments. For if it be said that S. Paul, writing to Rome and from Rome, has made no mention of S. Peter, we need not be surprised, for, perhaps, he was not there at that time.

So, it is quite certain that the First Epistle of S. Peter was written from Rome, as S. Jerome witnesses : * "Peter," says he, "in his first Epistle, figuratively signifying Rome under the name of Babylon, says : *"The Church which is in Babylon, elected together, saluteth you."* This that most ancient man Papias, a disciple of the Apostles, had previously attested, as Eusebius records. But would this consequence be good—S. Peter, in that Epistle, gives no sign that S. Paul was with him, therefore Paul was never in Rome ? This Epistle does not contain everything, and if it does not say that he was there, it also does not say that he was not. It is probable that he was not there then, or that if he were it was not expedient to name him in that place for some reason. I say the same of S. Paul's letter.

Lastly, to adjust the times of the life of S. Peter to

* *De Vir. Ill.*

III.

the reigns of Tiberius, Caius Caligula, and Nero, we can lay them out something in this fashion. In the eighteenth year of Tiberius, Our Lord ascended into heaven, and Tiberius survived Our Lord in this world about six years; five years after the Ascension, in the last year of the Empire of Tiberius, S. Peter came to Antioch, where having stayed about seven years—that is, what remained of Tiberius, four years of Caius Caligula, and two of Claudius—towards the end of the second of Claudius he came to Rome, where he remained seven years, that is, till the ninth of Claudius, when the Jews were driven out of Rome, which caused S. Peter to withdraw into Judæa. About five years afterwards, Claudius being dead in the fourteenth year of his reign, S. Peter returned to Rome, where he stayed till the fourteenth and last year of Nero. This makes about thirty-seven years that S. Peter lived after the death of his Master, of which he lived twelve partly in Judæa partly in Antioch, and twenty-five he lived as Bishop of Rome.

CHAPTER XII.

CONFIRMATION OF ALL THE ABOVE BY THE TITLES WHICH ANTIQUITY HAS GIVEN TO THE POPE.

HEAR in few words what the Ancients thought of this matter, and in what rank they held the Bishop of Rome. This is the way they speak, whether of the See of Rome and its Church, whether of the Pope: for all comes to the same.

Chair of Peter	Cyp. Lib. i., Ep. 3 [Editio Erasmi].
Principal Church	Ib. 55 [ad Corn.]
Commencement of sacerdotal unity	Ib. iii. 13.
Bond of unity: sublime summit of the priesthood	Ib. iv. 2.
Church in which is the superior authority	Iren. iii. 3.
Root and matrix of the Church .	Cyp. iv. 8.
Seat on which our Lord established the whole Church . . .	Anac. Ep. 1, ad omnes Episc., &c.*
Hinge and head of all Churches .	Ib. 3.
Refuge of bishops	Marcellus, Ep. 1, ad Episc. Antioch.
Supreme Apostolic seat . . .	Syn. Alex. Ep. ad Fel. ubi Ath.
Head of the pastoral honour . .	Prosper *de Ingratis* [lin. 40].
Supremacy of the Apostolic chair .	Aug. Ep. 162 [Migne 43].
Principal dignity of the Apostolic priesthood	Prosper *de Voc. Gen.* ii. 16. In præf. Conc. Chal.; Valent. Imperator.
Head of all Churches . . .	Victor Ut. *de persec. Van.* ii.; Justinianus *de summa Trin.*
Head of the world, of the universe, by religion	Leo M. in Nat. SS. P. et P.; Prosper *de Ingratis.*
Set over the rest of the Churches .	Syn. Rom. sub Gelasio.
The presiding Church . . .	Ign. ad Rom. in inscriptione.
The first see to be judged by no one	Syn. Sinuessana 300 Episc.
First seat of all	Leo Ep. 61 [ad Theod.]
Most safe harbour of Catholic communion	Hieron. Ep. 16.
Apostolic fountain	Innoc. ad Patres Milev. inter Epist. S. Auf. 93 [Migne 182].

Thus do they name the Roman Church; now see how they style the Pope.

Bishop of the most holy Catholic Church	Cyp. iii. 11.
Most holy and most blessed Patriarch	Conc. Chalc., Act iii.

---

* This passage is from S. Siricius, Ep. 1, ad Himer. [Tr.]

Head of the Council of Chalcedon.	In relatione.
Head of the Universal Church .	Ibid. xvi.
Most blessed Lord ; elevated to the Apostolic Dignity ; father of fathers ; supreme pontiff of all prelates	Steph. Episc. Carthag. in Ep. ad Damas. nomine Conc. Carthag.
High Priest	Hieron. Præf. Evang. ad Dam.
Prince of Priests	Id testatur tota antiq. apud Valent. ep. ad Theodos. initio. Conc. Chalc.
Ruler of the house of the Lord .	Amb. in 1 Tim. iii.
Guardian of the Lord's vineyard .	Conc. Chalc. ep. ad Leon.
Vicar of Christ	Cy. i. 3.
Confirmer of the brethren . .	Bern. Ep. 190.
Great priest ; supreme pontiff ; prince of bishops ; heir of the Apostles ; Abel in primacy ; Noe in government ; Abraham in patriarchate ; Melchisedech in order ; Aaron in dignity ; Moses in authority ; Samuel in judgment ; Peter in authority ; Christian unction ; shepherd of the Lord's fold ; key-bearer of the Lord's house ; shepherd of all shepherds ; called in plenitude of power.	Ib. de Consid. ii. 8.

I should never end if I tried to heap together all the titles which the Ancients have given to the Holy See of Rome and to its Bishop. The above ought to suffice to make even the most perverse wits see the extravagant lie which Beza continues to tell after his master Calvin, in his treatise *On the Marks of the Church*, where he says that Phocas was the first to give authority to the Bishop of Rome over the rest, and to place him in Primacy.

What is the use of uttering so gross a lie ? Phocas lived in the time of S. Gregory the Great, and every one of the authors I have cited is earlier than S.

Gregory, except S. Bernard, whom I have quoted, from his books *On Consideration,* because Calvin holds these so true that he considers truth itself has spoken in them.*

It is objected that S. Gregory would not let himself be called Universal Bishop. But universal Bishop may be understood of one who is in such sort bishop of the universe that the other bishops are only vicars and substitutes,—which is not the case. For the bishops are truly spiritual princes, chiefs and pastors; not lieutenants of the Pope, but of Our Lord, who therefore calls them brethren. Or the word may be understood of one who is superintendent over all, and in regard of whom all the others who are superintendents in particular are inferiors indeed but not vicars or substitutes. And it is in this sense that the Ancients have called him Universal Bishop, while S. Gregory denies it in the other sense.

They object the Council of Carthage, which forbids that any one shall call himself Prince of Priests; but it is for want of something to go on with that they put this in:—for who is ignorant that this was a provincial Council affecting the bishops of that Province, in which the Bishop of Rome was not;—the Mediterranean Sea lies between them.

There remained the name of Pope, which I have kept for the ending of this part of my subject, and which is the ordinary one by which we call the Bishop of Rome. This name was common to bishops;

---

* In the 1st *title of the Fabrian Code,* the Saint gives as a further reason why he dwells on the testimony of S. Bernard the fact that Calvin and others have put him forward as an adversary of papal supremacy. [Tr.]

witness S. Jerome, who thus styles S. Augustine in an Epistle: * "May the Almighty keep thee safe, Lord, truly holy and reverend pope." But it has been made particular to the Pope by excellence, on account of the universality of his charge, whence he is called in the Council of Chalcedon, Universal Pope, and simply Pope, without addition or limitation. And this word means nothing more than chief father or grandfather. *Papos aviasque trementes anteferunt patribus seri novâ curâ nepotes.*†

And that you may know how ancient this name is amongst good men—[hear] S. Ignatius, disciple of the Apostles: "When thou wast," says he, "at Rome with Pope Linus." ‡ Already at that time there were papists, and of what sort!

We call him His Holiness, and we find that S. Jerome already called him by the same name: § "I beseech thy Blessedness, by the cross, &c. . . . I following Christ alone am joined in communion with thy Blessedness, that is, the chair of Peter." We call him Holy Father, but you have seen that S. Jerome so calls S. Augustine.

For the rest, those who, explaining chapter ii. of the 2d of Thessalonians, to make you believe the Pope is Antichrist, may have told you that he makes himself be called God on earth, or Son of God, are the greatest liars in the world: for so far are the popes from taking any ambitious title, that from the time of S. Gregory they have for the most part called themselves

---

* 97.

† "Late born grandsons, reversing the ordinary rule, cherish their trembling grandsires and grandames more than their parents."— Ausonius ad nep.

‡ Ad Mariam Zarbensem.   § Ad Dam. ep. 15.

Servants of the servants of God. Never have they
called themselves by such names as you say except
in the ordinary acceptation, as every one can be if
he keep the commandments of God, according to the
power given *to them that believe in his name* (John i.)
Rightly indeed might those call themselves children
of the devil who lie so foully as do your ministers.

———

CHAPTER XIII.

IN HOW GREAT ESTEEM THE AUTHORITY OF THE POPE OUGHT TO BE HELD.

IT is certainly not without mystery that often in the
Gospel where there is occasion for the Apostles in
general to speak, S. Peter alone speaks for all.   In
S. John (vi.) it was he who said for all: *Lord, to
whom shall we go ?   Thou hast the words of eternal
life.   And we have believed and have known that thou
art the Christ the Son of God.*   It was he, in S.
Matthew (xvi.), who in the name of all made that
noble confession : *Thou art Christ, the Son of the
living God.*   He asked for all: *Behold we have left all
things,* &c. (Matt. xxvii.)   In S. Luke (xii.): *Lord, dost
thou speak this parable to us, or likewise to all ?*

It is usual that the head should speak for the
whole body ; and what the head says is considered
to be said by all the rest.   Do you not see that in
the election of S. Matthias it is he alone who speaks
and determines ?

The Jews asked all the Apostles : *What shall we do, men and brethren* (Acts. ii.) ? S. Peter alone answers for all : *Do penance,* &c.   And it is for this reason that S. Chrysostom and Origen have called him " the mouth and the crown of the Apostles," as we saw above, because he was accustomed to speak for all the Apostles ; and the same S. Chrysostom calls him " the mouth of Christ," because what he says for the whole Church and to the whole Church as head and pastor, is not so much a word of man as of Our Lord : *Amen, I say to you he that receiveth whomsoever I send receiveth me* (John xiii.).   Therefore what he said and determined could not be false.   And truly if the confirmer be fallen, have not all the rest fallen ?—if the confirmer fall or totter, who shall confirm him ?—if the confirmer be not firm and steady, when the others grow weak who shall strengthen them ?   For it is written that if the blind lead the blind both shall fall into the ditch, and if the unsteady and the feeble would hold up and support the feeble, they shall both come to ground.   So that Our Lord, giving authority and command to Peter to confirm the others, has in like proportion given him the power and the means to do this ; otherwise vainly would he have commanded things that were impossible.   Now in order to confirm the others and to strengthen the weak, one must not be subject to weakness oneself, but be solid and fixed as a true stone and a rock.   Such was S. Peter, in so far as he was Pastor-general and governor of the Church.

So when S. Peter was placed as foundation of the Church, and the Church was certified that the gates of hell should not prevail against it,—was it not enough to say that S. Peter, as foundation-stone of the ecclesiastical government and administration, could not be crushed and broken by infidelity or error, which is the principal gate of hell? For who knows not that if the foundation be overthrown, if that can be sapped, the whole building falls. In the same way, if the supreme acting shepherd can conduct his sheep into venomous pastures, it is clearly visible that the flock is soon to be lost. For if the supreme acting shepherd leads out of the path, who will put him right? if he stray, who will bring him back?

In truth, it is necessary that we should follow him simply, not guide him; otherwise the sheep would be shepherds. And indeed the Church cannot always be united in General Council, and during the first three centuries none were held. In the difficulties then which daily arise, to whom could one better address oneself, from whom could one take a safer law, a surer rule, than from the general head, and from the vicar of Our Lord? Now all this has not only been true of S. Peter, but also of his successors; for the cause remaining the effect remains likewise. The Church has always need of an infallible * confirmer, to whom she can appeal; of a foundation which the gates of hell, and principally error, cannot overthrow; and has always need that her pastor should be unable to lead her children into error. The successors, then, of S. Peter all have these same privileges, which do not follow the person but the dignity and public charge.

S. Bernard calls the Pope another " Moses in

---

* Here the French editor had substituted *permanent* for *infallible.* [Tr.]

authority." Now how great the authority of Moses
was every one knows. For he sat and judged concerning all the differences amongst the people, and all
difficulties which occurred in the service of God : he
appointed judges for affairs of slight importance, but the
great doubts were reserved for his cognizance : if God
would speak to the people, it is by his mouth and
using him as a medium. So then the supreme pastor
of the Church is competent and sufficient judge for
us in all our greatest difficulties ; otherwise we should
be in worse condition than that ancient people who
had a tribunal to which they might appeal for the
resolution of their doubts, particularly in religious
matters. And if any one would reply that Moses was
not a priest, nor an ecclesiastical pastor, I would send
him back to what I have said above on this point. For
it would be tedious to make these repetitions.

In Deuteronomy (xvii.) : *Thou shalt do whatsoever
they shall say that preside in the place which the Lord
shall choose, and what they shall teach thee according to
his law : neither shalt thou decline to the right hand
nor to the left hand. But he that shall be proud, and
refuse to obey the commandment of the priest . . . that
man shall die.* What will you say to this necessity
of accepting the judgment of the sovereign pontiff ?—
that one was obliged to accept that judgment which
was according to the law, not any other ? Yes, but
in this it was needful to follow the sentence of the
priest ; otherwise, if one had not followed it but had
examined into it, it would have been vain to have
gone to him, and the difficulty and doubt would never
have been settled. Therefore it is said simply : *He
that shall be proud, and refuse to obey the commandment*

of the priest and the decree of the judge shall die. And
in Malachy (ii. 7): *The lips of the priest shall keep
knowledge ; and they shall seek the law at his mouth.*
Whence it follows that not everybody could answer
himself in religious matters, nor bring forward the
law after his own fancy, but must do so according as
the pontiff laid it down. Now if God had such great
providence over the religion and peace of conscience
of the Jews as to establish for them a supreme judge
in whose sentence they were bound to acquiesce, there
can be no doubt he has provided Christianity with a
pastor, who has this same authority, to remove the
doubts and scruples which might arise concerning the
declarations of the Scriptures.

And if the High Priest wore on his breast the
Rational of judgment (Ex. xxviii.), in which were the
Urim and the *Thummim*, doctrine and truth, as some
interpret them, or illuminations and perfections, as
others say (which is almost the same thing, since
perfection consists in truth and doctrine is only
illumination)—shall we suppose that the High Priest
of the New Law has not also the efficacy of them ?
In truth, all that was given out and out to the ancient
Church, and to the servant Agar, has been given in
much better form to Sara and to the Spouse. Our
High Priest then still has the Urim and the Thummim
on his breast.

Now whether this doctrine and truth were nothing
but these two words inscribed on the Rational, as S.
Augustine seems to think and Hugh of S. Victor
maintains, or whether they were the name of God, as
Rabbi Solomon asserts according to Vatablus and
Augustine bishop of Eugubium, or whether it was

simply the stones of the Rational, by which Almighty
God revealed his will to the priest, as that learned
man Francis Ribera holds;—the reasons why the
High Priest had doctrine and truth in the Rational on
his breast was without doubt because *he declared the
truth of judgment*, as by the Urim and Thummim the
priests were instructed as to the good pleasure of
God, and their understandings enlightened and per-
fected by the Divine revelation : thus the good Lyra
understood it, as Ribera has in my opinion sufficiently
proved.   Hence when David wished to know whether
he should pursue the Amalecites he said to the priest
Abiathar: *Bring me hither the ephod* (1 Kings
xxx. 7), or vestment for the shoulders, which was
without doubt to discover the will of God by means
of the Rational which was joined to it, as this Doctor
Ribera continues learnedly to prove.   I ask you,—if
in the shadow there were illuminations of doctrine
and perfections of truth on the breast of the priest
to feed and confirm the people therewith, what is
there that our High Priest shall not have, the priest
of us, I say, who are in the day and under the risen
sun ?   The High Priest of old was but the vicar and
lieutenant of Our Lord, as ours is, but he would seem
to have presided over the night by his illuminations,
and ours presides over the day by his instructions ;
both of them as ministering for another and by the
light of the Sun of Justice, who though he is risen is
still veiled from our eyes by our own mortality ;—for
to see him face to face belongs ordinarily to those
alone who are delivered from the body which goes to
corruption.   This has been the faith of the whole
ancient Church, which in its difficulties has always

had recourse to the Rational of the See of Rome to see therein doctrine and truth. It is for this reason that S. Bernard has called the Pope "Aaron in dignity," * and S. Jerome the Holy See "the most safe harbour of Catholic communion," and "heir of the Apostles," for he bears the Rational to enlighten with it the whole of Christendom, like the Apostles and Aaron, in doctrine and truth. It is in this sense that S. Jerome says to S. Damasus: "He who gathereth not with thee scattereth, that is, he who is not of Christ is of Antichrist;" and S. Bernard says †️ that the scandals which occur, particularly in the faith, must be brought before the Roman See:—"for I think it proper that there chiefly should the damage of faith be repaired where faith cannot fail; for to what other see was it ever said: *I have prayed for thee that thy faith fail not?*" And S. Cyprian: ‡️ "They dare to sail off to the Apostolic See and to the chief (*principalem*) Church, forgetting that those are Romans, to whom wrong faith cannot have access." Do you not see that he speaks of the Romans because of the Chair of S. Peter, and says that error cannot prevail there. The Fathers of the Council of Milevis with the Blessed S. Augustine demand help and invoke the authority of the Roman See against the Pelagian heresy, writing to Pope Innocent in these terms: "We beseech you to deign to apply the pastoral solicitude to the great dangers of the infirm members of Christ; since a new heresy and most

---

* See references previously. In margin here the Saint adds: " S. Bernard, in his letter to the Canons of Lyons, submits all his writings to the Roman Church." [Tr.]

† Ep. 190.   ‡ Ep. 55.

destructive tempest has begun to arise amongst the
enemies of the grace of Christ." And if you would
know why they appeal to him, what do they say?
"The Lord has by his highest favour placed thee in
the Apostolic See." This is what this holy Council
with its great S. Augustine believed, to whom S.
Innocent replying in a Letter which follows the one
just quoted amongst those of S. Augustine: "Carefully and rightfully," he says, "have you consulted the
secret oracles of the Apostolic honour: his, I say,
with whom, besides those things which are outside,
remains the solicitude of all the churches as to what
doctrine is to be held in doubtful things. For you
have followed the fashion of the ancient rule, which
you and I know to have been always held by the
whole world. But this I pass over, for I do not
believe that it is unknown to your wisdom; how indeed
have you confirmed it by your actions, save knowing
that throughout all the provinces answers to peti-
tioners ever emanate from the Apostolic See? Especially when questions of faith are discussed, I
consider that all our brethren and co-bishops must
refer to Peter only, that is, to the author of their
name and honour; even as your charity has now
referred that which may advantage all churches in
general throughout the whole world." Behold the
honour and credit in which was the Apostolic See
with the most learned and most holy of the Ancients,
yea with entire Councils. They went to it as to the
true Ephod and Rational of the new law. Thus did
S. Jerome go to it in the time of Damasus, to whom,
after having said that the East was cutting and tearing
to pieces the robe of Our Lord, seamless and woven

from the top throughout, and that the little foxes were spoiling the vineyard of the Master, he says: "As it is difficult, amongst broken cisterns that can hold no water, to discern where is that fountain sealed up, and garden enclosed, therefore I considered that I must consult the Chair of Peter and the faith praised by Apostolic mouth." I shall never end if I try to bring forward the grand words which the Ancients have uttered on this point: he who wishes can read them quoted in the great Catechism of Peter Canisius, in which they have been given in full by Busembaum. S. Cyprian refers all heresies and schisms to the contempt of this chief minister;* so does S. Jerome;† S. Ambrose holds for one same thing "to communicate and agree with the Catholic bishops and to agree with the Roman Church:"‡ he protests that he follows in all things and everywhere the form of the Roman Church. S. Irenæus will have every one be united to this Holy See, "on account of its principal power." The Eusebians bring before it the accusations against S. Athanasius; S. Athanasius, who was at Alexandria, a principal and patriarchal see, went to answer at Rome, being called and cited to appear there: his adversaries would not appear, "knowing," says Theodoret, "that their lies were manifested in open court." The Eusebians acknowledge the authority of the see of Rome when they call S. Athanasius thither, and S. Athanasius when he presents himself. But particularly do those Arian heretics the Eusebians confess the authority of the see of Rome when they dare not appear there for fear of being condemned.

---

* Ad Cornel. contra Feliciss. † Ep. 165 adv. Lucif.
‡ De excessu Fratris, 46.

But who does not know that all the ancient heretics tried to get themselves acknowledged by the Pope? Witness the Montanists or Cataphrygians, who so deceived Pope Zephyrinus, if we may believe Tertullian (not now the man he had been but become a heretic himself), that he issued letters of reunion in their favour, which, however, he promptly revoked by the advice of Praxeas. In fine, he who despises the authority of the Pope will restore the Pelagians, Priscillians and others, who were only condemned by provincial councils with the authority of the Holy See of Rome. If I wished to occupy myself in showing you how much Luther made of it in the beginning of his heresy I should astonish you with the great alteration in this old dotard. Look at him in Cochlæus: " Prostrate at the feet of Your Beatitude, I offer myself with all I am and have; give me life, slay me, call, recall, approve, reject; I shall acknowledge the voice of Christ presiding and speaking." These are his words in the dedicatory letter which he wrote to Pope Leo X. on certain conclusions of his, in the year 1518. But I cannot omit what this great arch-minister wrote in 1519, in certain other resolutions of other propositions; for in the thirteenth he not only acknowledges the authority of the Holy Roman See, but proves it by six reasons which he holds to be demonstrations. I will summarise them: 1st reason— the Pope could not have reached this height and this monarchy except by the will of God; but the will of God is always to be venerated, therefore the primacy of the Pope is not to be called in question. 2d. We must give in to an adversary rather than break the union of charity; therefore it is better to obey the

Pope than to separate from the Church.   3d. We must not resist God who wills to lay on us the burden of obeying many rulers, according to the word of Solomon in his Proverbs (xxviii. 2).   4th. There is no power which is not from God, therefore that of the Pope which is so fully established is from God. 5th. Practically the same.   6th. All the faithful so believe, and it is impossible that Our Lord should not be with them; now we must stay with Our Lord and Christians in all things and everywhere: He says afterwards that these reasons were unanswerable, and that all the Scripture comes to support them.   What do you think of Luther,—is he not a Catholic?   And yet this was at the beginning of his reformation.

Calvin gives the same testimony, though he goes on to embroil the question as much as he can; for speaking of the See of Rome he confesses that the Ancients have honoured and revered it, that it has been the refuge of bishops, and more firm in the faith than the other sees, which last fact he attributes to a want of quickness of understanding.

———

CHAPTER XIV.

HOW THE MINISTERS HAVE VIOLATED THIS AUTHORITY.

UNDER the ancient law the High Priest did not wear the Rational except when he was vested in the pontifical robes and was entering before the Lord.   Thus we do not say that the Pope cannot err in his private opinions, as did John XXII.; or be altogether a heretic,

III.

as perhaps Honorius was. Now when he is explicitly a heretic, he falls *ipso facto* from his dignity and out of the Church, and the Church must either deprive him, or, as some say, declare him deprived, of his Apostolic See, and must say as S. Peter did: *Let another take his bishopric.** When he errs in his private opinion he must be instructed, advised, convinced; as happened with John XXII., who was so far from dying obstinate or from determining anything during his life concerning his opinion, that he died whilst he was making the examination which is necessary for determining in a matter of faith, as his successor declared in the *Extravagantes* which begins *Benedictus Deus.* But when he is clothed with the pontifical garments, I mean when he teaches the whole Church as shepherd, in general matters of faith and morals, then there is nothing but doctrine and truth. And in fact everything a king says is not a law or an edict, but that only which a king says as king and as a legislator. So everything the Pope says is not canon law or of legal obligation; he must mean to define and to lay down the law for the sheep, and he must keep the due order and form. Thus we say that we must appeal to him not as to a learned man, for in this he is ordinarily surpassed by some others, but as to the general head and pastor of the Church: and as such we must honour, follow, and firmly embrace his doctrine, for then he carries on his breast the *Urim* and *Thummim*, doctrine and truth. And again we must not think that in everything and everywhere his judgment is infallible, but then only when he gives judgment on a matter of faith in questions

* Acts i.

necessary to the whole Church ; for in particular cases which depend on human fact he can err, there is no doubt, though it is not for us to control him in these cases save with all reverence, submission, and discretion.   Theologians have said, in a word, that he can err in questions of fact, not in questions of right; that he can err *extra cathedram,* outside the chair of Peter, that is, as a private individual, by writings and bad example.

But he cannot err when he is *in cathedra,* that is, when he intends to make an instruction and decree for the guidance of the whole Church, when he means to confirm his brethren as supreme pastor, and to conduct them into the pastures of the faith.   For then it is not so much man who determines, resolves, and defines as it is the Blessed Holy Spirit by man, which Spirit, according to the promise made by Our Lord to the Apostles, teaches all truth to the Church, and, as the Greek says and the Church seems to understand in a collect of Pentecost,* conducts and directs his Church into all truth : *But when that Spirit of truth shall come, he will teach you all truth,* or, *will lead you into all truth.*†   And how does the Holy Spirit lead the Church except by the ministry and office of preachers and pastors ?   But if the pastors have pastors they must also follow them, as all must follow him who is the supreme pastor, by whose ministry Our God wills to lead not only the lambs and little sheep, but the sheep and mothers of lambs ; that is, not the people only but also the other pastors : he succeeds S. Peter, who received this charge : *Feed my sheep.*   Thus it is that God leads his Church

* Wednesday in Whit-week.   † John xvi. 13.

into the pastures of his Holy Word, and in the exposition of this he who seeks the truth under other leading loses it. The Holy Spirit is the leader of the Church, he leads it by its pastor; he therefore who follows not the pastor follows not the Holy Spirit.

But the great Cardinal of Toledo remarks most appositely on this place that it is not said *he shall carry the Church into all truth*, but *he shall lead;* to show that though the Holy Spirit enlightens the Church, he wills at the same time that she should use the diligence which is required for keeping the true way, as the Apostles did, who, having to give an answer to an important question, debated, comparing the Holy Scriptures together; and when they had diligently done this they concluded by the—*It hath seemed good to the Holy Spirit and to us;* that is, the Holy Spirit has enlightened us and we have walked, he has guided us and we have followed him, up to this truth. The ordinary means must be employed to discover the truth, and yet in this must be acknowledged the drawing and presence of the Holy Spirit. Thus is the Christian flock led,—by the Holy Spirit but under the charge and guidance of its Pastor, who however does not walk at hazard, but according to necessity convokes the other pastors, either partially or universally, carefully regards the track of his predecessors, considers the *Urim* and *Thummim* of the Word of God, enters before his God by his prayers and invocations, and, having thus diligently sought out the true way, boldly puts himself on his voyage and courageously sets sail. Happy the man who follows him and puts himself under the discipline of his crook! Happy the man who embarks in his boat, for he shall feed on truth, and shall arrive at the port of holy doctrine!

Thus he never gives a general command to the whole Church in necessary things except with the assistance of the Holy Spirit, who, as he is not wanting in necessary things even to second causes, because he has established them, will not be more wanting to Christianity in what is necessary for its life and perfection. And how would the Church be one and holy, as the Scriptures and Creeds describe her? —for if she followed a pastor, and the pastor erred, how would she be holy; if she followed him not, how would she be one? And what confusion would be seen in Christendom, while the one party should consider a law good the others bad, and while the sheep, instead of feeding and fattening in the pasture of Scripture and the Holy Word, should occupy themselves in controlling the decision of their superior?

It remains therefore that according to Divine Providence we consider as closed that which S. Peter shall close with his keys, and as open that which he shall open, when seated in his chair of doctrine teaching the whole Church.

If indeed the ministers had censured vices, proved the inutility of certain decrees and censures, borrowed some holy counsels from the ethical books of S. Gregory, and from S. Bernard's *De Consideratione*, brought forward some good plan for removing the abuses which have crept into the administration of benefices through the malice of the age and of men, and had addressed themselves to His Holiness with humility and gratitude, all good men would have honoured them and favoured their designs. The good

Cardinals Contarini the Theatine, Sadolet, and Pole, with those other great men who counselled the refor- mation of abuses in this way, have thereby deserved immortal commendation from posterity. But to fill heaven and earth with invectives, railings, outrages,— to calumniate the Pope, and not only in his person, which is bad enough, but in his office, to attack the See which all antiquity has honoured, to wish to go so far as to sit in judgment upon him, contrary to the sense of the whole Church, to style his position itself anti-Christianism—who shall call this right ? If the great Council of Chalcedon was so indignant when the Patriarch Dioscorus excommunicated Pope Leo, who can endure the insolence of Luther, who issued a Bull in which he excommunicates the Pope and the bishops and the whole Church ? All the Church gives him (the Pope) patents of honour, speaks to him with reverence. What shall we say of that fine pre- face in which Luther addressed the Holy See : " Martin Luther to the most Holy Apostolic See and its whole Parliament, grace and health. In the first place, most holy see, crack but burst not on account of this new salutation in which I place my name first and in the principal place." And after having quoted the Bull against which he was writing, he begins with these wicked and vile words : " *Ego autem dico ad papam et bullæ hujus minas, istud : qui præ minis moritur ad ejus sepulturam compulsari debet crepitibus ventris.*" And when writing against the King of England,— " Living," said he, " I will be the enemy of the papacy, burnt I will be thy enemy." What say you of this great Father of the Church ? Are not these words worthy of such a reformer ? I am ashamed to read them, and my hand is vexed when it lays out such shameful things, but if they are hidden from you, you will never believe that he is such as he is,—and when he says: "It is ours not to be judged by him but to judge him."

But I detain you too long on a subject which does not require great examination. You read the writings of Calvin, of Zwingle, of Luther: take out of these, I beg you, the railings, calumnies, insults, detraction, ridicule, and buffoonery which they contain against the Pope and the Holy See of Rome, and you will find that nothing will remain. You listen to your ministers; impose silence upon them as regards railings, detraction, calumnies against the Holy See, and you will have your sermons half their length. They utter a thousand calumnies on this point: this is the general rendezvous of all your ministers. On whatever subjects they may be composing their books, as if they were tired and spent with their labour they stay to dwell on the vices of the Popes, very often saying what they know well not to be the fact. Beza says that for a long time there has been no Pope who has cared about religion or who has been a theologian. Is he not seeking to deceive somebody?—for he knows well that Adrian, Marcellus, and these five last have been very great theologians. What does he mean by these lies? But let us say that there may be vice and ignorance: "What has the Roman Chair done to thee," says S. Augustine,[*] "in which Peter sat and in which now Anastasius sits? . . . Why do you call the Apostlic Chair the chair of pestilence? If it is on account of men whom you consider to be declaring

[*] Contra lit. Petil. ii. 51.

and not keeping the law—did Our Lord, on account of
the Pharisees, of whom he said: *they say and do not*
do any injury to the chair in which they sat ?   Did
he not commend that chair of Moses, and reprove
them, saving the honour of their chair ?   For he says:
Super cathedram, &c. (Matt. xxiii. 2).   If you considered these things you would not, on account of
the men you speak against, blaspheme the Apostolic
Chair, with which you do not communicate.   But
what does it all mean save that they have nothing to
say, and yet are unable to keep from ill-saying."

ARTICLE VII.

*MIRACLES: THE SEVENTH RULE OF FAITH.**

CHAPTER I.

HOW IMPORTANT MIRACLES ARE FOR CONFIRMING OUR FAITH.

IN order that Moses might be believed God gave him
power to work miracles (Ex. iv.) ; Our Lord, says S.
Mark (ult.), confirmed in the same manner the Apostolic
preaching; if Our Lord had not done such miracles
men would not have sinned in not believing in him,

* The Saint has the following detached note : " I keep a place for
proving the faith by miracles, after the 'Rules of faith.'   This will
be a sort of 6th (7th) Rule, not ordinary but extraordinary, which
our adversaries have not, though they would need to have it, as they
despise the others which they lack.   I will there bring in the saying
of the Sr. des Montaignes."   He does not give this saying, see Preface.
[Tr.]

says the same Lord (John xv. 24); S. Paul testifies
that God confirmed the faith by miracles (Heb. ii. 4).
Therefore a miracle is a sound proof of the faith, and
an important argument for persuading men to believe;
for if it were not our God would not have made use
of it.

And it is needless to answer that miracles are no
longer necessary after the sowing of the faith, for I
have not only shown the contrary above, but I am
now not maintaining that they are necessary, but
simply that when it may please God to work them
for the confirmation of some article we are obliged to
believe it.   For either the miracle is rightly per-
suasive and confirmatory of belief or not: if not, then
Our Lord did not rightly confirm his doctrine; if it
be, then when miracles do take place they oblige us
to accept them as a most convincing reason,—which
of course they are.

Thou art the God who doest wonders, says David
(Ps. lxxvi. 15) to Almighty God, therefore that which
is confirmed by miracles is confirmed on the part of God;
now God cannot be author or confirmer of a lie, that
therefore which is confirmed by miracles cannot be
a lie, but must be absolute truth.

And, in order to obviate idle objections, I allow
that there are false miracles and true miracles, and
that among true miracles there are some which evidently argue the presence of God's power, and others
which do so only by their circumstances.   The
miracles which Antichrist will do will all be false,
both because his intention will be to deceive, and
because one part will only be illusions and vain
magical appearances, the other part not miracles *in*

nature but only miracles *to men,*—that is, on account
of being extraordinary they will seem miracles to
simple folk.   Such will be his making fire come down
from heaven *in the sight of men* (Apoc. xiii.), his
making the image of the beast speak, and healing a
mortal wound.   Of these, the descent of the fire upon
the earth and the speaking of the image will, as it
seems, be mere illusions, whence he adds *in the sight
of men;* they will be acts of magic.   The healing of
the mortal wound will be a popular not a philosopher's
miracle;—for when the people see what they think
impossible they take it to be a miracle, as they
consider many things impossible in nature which are
not so.   Now many cures are of this kind, and many
wounds are mortal and incurable to some doctors
which are not so to those who are more competent
and have some choicer remedy.   Thus that wound
will be mortal according to the ordinary course of
medicine; but the devil, who is more advanced in
the knowledge of the virtues of herbs, perfumes,
minerals, and other drugs than men are, will effect
this cure by the secret application of medicaments
unknown to men; and this will appear a miracle to
any one who is unable to distinguish between human
and diabolic knowledge,* between diabolic and divine;
whereas while the diabolic exceeds the human by a
great degree, the divine surpasses the diabolic by an
infinity.   Human science extends to but a little part
of the virtue which is in nature, diabolic goes much
further, but divine has no other limits, in dealing
with nature, but its own infinity.

* The following note is placed in the margin of the autograph:
Il faut abreger tout ceci à peu de paroles et scholastiques.   [Tr.]

I said that among true miracles there are some which furnish a certain knowledge and proof that the power of God is at work therein, others not so except by consideration and aid of the circumstances. This appears from what I have said; and, for example, the wonders which the Egyptian magicians did (Ex. iv.– viii.) were exactly like those of Moses as regards the external appearance, but he who considers the circumstances will very easily see that the one kind were true miracles, the others false; as the magicians themselves confessed, when they said: *The finger of God is here.* So might I say if Our Lord had never done other miracles than to tell the Samaritan woman that he whom she then had was not her husband (John iv. 18), or than to change the water into wine (Ib. ii.), it might have been possible to think that there was illusion and magic; but since these wonders proceeded from the same might which made the blind see, the dumb speak, the deaf hear, the dead live, there remained no room for doubt. For, to make things pass from privation and non-existence to actuality,* and to give to man the vital operations, are things impossible to all human powers; these are strokes of the sovereign Master; and when afterwards he pleases to effect cures or alterations in things by his almighty power, he still makes them to be recognised as miraculous even though secret nature may be able to do as much,—because, having done what surpasses nature, he has given us assurance of what he is and of the character of the [thing done].† As when a man has made a masterpiece, though he may after-

---

* *La privation en son habitude.*
† The line here ends with *de la.* [Tr.]

wards do some common works we still consider him a
master.

In a word, the miracle, the true miracle, is a very
certain proof, and a certain confirmation of belief,
and this at whatever time it may be worked, otherwise we must overthrow all the Apostolic preaching.
It was reasonable that faith being of things which
surpass nature, it should be certified by works which
surpass nature, and which show that the preaching or
announced word proceeds from the mouth and authority of the Master of nature, whose power is un-
limited, and who, by a miracle, makes himself witness
of the truth, subscribes and stamps the word delivered
by the preacher.

Now it seems that miracles are general attestations
for the simple and commoner sort; for not every one
can go so deep as to the admirable harmony there is
between the Prophets and the Gospel, to the great
wisdom of the Scriptures, or to similar striking marks,
which distinguish the Christian religion. This is an
examination for the learned to make; but there is no
one who does not comprehend the argument furnished
by a true miracle; everybody understands that language. Amongst Christians it seems as if miracles
are not necessary, but in reality they are; and it is
not without reason that the sweetness of Divine Providence supplies them to his Church at all seasons, for
in all there are heresies. These indeed are sufficiently
condemned, even according to the capacity of the less
gifted, by the antiquity, majesty, unity, Catholicity,
sanctity of the Church, but everybody cannot value
his inheritance (as Optatus says) according to its true
value. Everybody does not understand this language

in its full force, but when God speaks by works everybody understands—this is a language common to all nations. So the writing on letters of protection may not be recognised by everybody, but when the white cross, the arms of the Prince, are seen, all the world knows that sovereign approval and authority run there.

CHAPTER II.

HOW GREATLY THE MINISTERS HAVE VIOLATED THE FAITH DUE TO THE TESTIMONY OF MIRACLES.

THERE is scarcely any article of our religion which has not been approved of God by miracles. The miracles which take place in the Church, showing where the true Church is, sufficiently prove all the belief of the Church : for God would never bear witness to a Church which had not the true faith and was erring, idolatrous, and deceiving.

.   .   .   .

ARTICLE VIII.

HARMONY OF FAITH AND REASON : EIGHTH RULE OF FAITH.

CHAPTER I.

I HAVE put off the showing of the absurdities which are in the doctrine of our adversaries to the end of the treatise on the rules of faith, these absurdities being a consequence of their believing without rule and sailing without compass. And [put off showing] that they have not the efficacy of the doctrine of Catholicism; for not only are they not Catholics, but cannot be, effecting the destruction of the body of Our Lord, instead of acquiring new members for it.

Also when Luther says † that infants in Baptism have the use of their understanding and reason, and when the synod of Wittenberg says ‡ that infants in Baptism have movements and inclinations like to the movements of faith and charity, and this without understanding :—is not this to mock God, nature, and experience ?

And when it is said that " in sinning we are incited, pushed, necessitated by the will, ordinance, decree, and predestination of God,"—is this not to blaspheme against all reason, and against the majesty of the supreme goodness ? Such is the fine theology of

---

* In a detached note the Saint says : " A chapter must be composed on simplicity of faith and humility in believing." See Preface. [Tr.]

† Apud Cochl., ann. 1523.   ‡ Ann. 1536. L. 3 : Miscell. tract.

Zwingle, Calvin, and Beza.* " But," says Beza, " you will say that they could not resist the will of God, that is, the decree; I acknowledge it: but as they could not so they would not: they could not wish otherwise, I own, as to the event and working (*energiam*), but yet the will of Adam was not forced." Goodness of God, I call you as my witness! You have pushed me to do evil; you have so decreed, ordained, and willed; I could not act otherwise, I could not will otherwise,—what fault of mine is there? O God of my heart! chastise my will, if it is able not to will evil and wills to will it; but if it cannot help willing evil, and thou art the cause of its impossibility, what fault of mine can there be? If this is not contrary to reason, I protest that there is no reason in the world.

The law of God is impossible, according to Calvin and the others:† what follows, except that Our Lord is a tyrant who commands impossible things? If it is impossible, why is it commanded?

Works, good as ever they may be, rather deserve hell than Paradise: shall then the justice of God, which will give to every one according to his works, give to every one hell?

This is enough, but the absurdity of absurdities, and the most horrible unreason of all is this: that while holding that the whole Church may have erred for a thousand years in the understanding of the Word of God, Luther, Zwingle, Calvin can guarantee that they understand it aright: this absurdity is greater when

---

* Zw. *de prud.* 5, 6: Calv. *Instit.* I. 17, 18 ; *de Praed. ; Instruct. contra Lib. ; Beza contra Castal.*

† Calv. *ant. Sess.* 6, *conc. Tr. :* Luther *de lib. Christ.*

a mere wretched minister (*ministrot*), while preaching
as a word of God that all the visible Church has erred,
that Calvin and all men can err, dares to pick and
choose amongst the interpretations of the Scripture
that one which pleases him, and to certify and maintain it as the Word of God: and you yourselves carry
the absurdity still further when, having heard that
everybody may err in matter of religion—even the
whole Church—without trying to find for yourselves
some other religion amongst a thousand sects, which
all boast of rightly understanding the Word of God,
and rightly preaching it, you believe so obstinately
in the minister who preaches to you, that you will
hear no more ?   If everybody can err in the understanding of the Scripture, why not you and your
minister ?   I wonder that you do not always walk
trembling and shaking: I wonder how you can live
with so much assurance in the doctrine which you
follow, as if you could not err, and yet you hold as
certain that every one has erred and can err.

The Gospel soars far above all the most elevated
reasonings of nature ; it never goes against them, never
injures them nor dissolves them: but these fancies of
your evangelists obscure and destroy the light of
nature.

CHAPTER II.

THAT THE ANALOGY OF THE FAITH CANNOT SERVE AS
A RULE TO THE MINISTERS TO ESTABLISH THEIR
DOCTRINE.

It is a saying full of pride and ambition amongst
your ministers, and one which is ordinary with them,
that we must interpret the Scriptures and test the
exposition of them by the analogy of the faith. The
simple people when they hear this analogy of the
faith, think that it is some word of secret potency and
cabalistic virtue; and they wonderingly admire every
interpretation which is given, provided that this word
be brought into the field. In truth the ministers are
right when they say that we must interpret the
Scripture, and prove our expositions of it by the
analogy of faith; but they are wrong in not doing
what they say. The poor people hear nothing but
their bragging about this analogy of faith, and the
ministers do nothing but corrupt, spoil, force it, and
tear it to shreds. Let us look into this, I beg you.
You say that the Scripture is easy to understand, provided that one adjust it to the rule and proportion,
or analogy, of the faith. But what rule of faith can
they have who have no Scripture except one entirely
glossed, wrested, and strained by interpretations,
metaphors, metonymies? If the rule is subject to
irregularity, who shall regulate it? And what analogy
or proportion of faith can there be, if a man proportion the articles of faith with conceptions the most
foreign to their true sense? If the fact of proportion
with the articles of faith is to serve you to decide

III.

upon doctrine and religion, leave the articles of faith
in their natural shape; do not give them a form
different from that which they have received from
the Apostles. I leave you to guess what use the
Symbol of the Apostles can be to me in interpreting
the Scriptures, when you gloss it in such a way that
you put me in greater difficulties about its sense than
ever I was in about the Scriptures themselves.

If any one ask how the same body of Our Lord
can come to be in two places, I shall say that this is
easy to God, and I shall confirm it by this reason of
faith : *I believe in God the Father Almighty.* But if
you gloss both the Scripture and the article of faith
itself, how will you confirm your gloss ? At this
rate there will be no first principle except your
notions. If the analogy of faith be subject to your
glosses and opinions, you must say so openly, that we
may know what you are at, which will now be this—
to interpret Scripture by Scripture and analogy, adjusting everything to your own interpretations and
ideas. I apply the whole question [of the Real
Presence] * to the analogy of the faith : this explanation agrees perfectly with that first word of the Creed
where *Credo* takes away all difficulties of human
reason ; the *omnipotentem* strengthens me, the mention
of *creation* heartens me ;—for why shall he who
made all things out of nothing, not make the body of
Christ out of bread ? That name of *Jesus* comforts
me, for his mercy and his will to do great things for
me are there expressed. That he is the *Son*, consubstantial with the Father, proves to me his illimitable
power. His being *conceived of a Virgin*, against the

* See Preface.

course of nature; his not disdaining to lodge within
her for our sakes; his being *born* with penetration of
dimension, an act which goes beyond and above the
nature of a body—these things assure me both of his
will and of his power. His *death* supports me ;—
for he who died for us, what will he not do for us ?
His *sepulchre* cheers me, and his *descent into hell ;*—
for I shall not doubt his descent into the obscurity of
my body, &c. His *resurrection* gives me fresh life ;
for this new penetration of the stone, the agility,
subtlety, brightness, and impassibility of his body,
are no longer according to the grosser laws which we
conceive of. His *ascension* makes me rise to this
faith ;—for if his body penetrate matter, raise itself,
by his sole will, and place itself, without place, at the
right hand of the Father, why shall it not, here below,
be where seems good to him, and occupy space only
as he wills it to do ?   His being *seated at the right
hand of the Father* shows me that everything is put
under him, heaven, earth, distances, places, dimensions.
That *from thence he shall come to judge the living and
the dead,* urges me to the belief of the illimitability of
his glory, and [teaches me] therefore that his glory is
not attached to place, but that wherever he goes he
carries it with him ;—he is, then, in the most holy
Sacrament without quitting his glory or his perfections.   That *Holy Ghost,* by whose operation he was
conceived and born of a Virgin, can equally well by
his operation effect this admirable work of Transub-
stantiation.   *The Church,* which is *holy* and cannot
lead us into error, which is *Catholic* and therefore is
not restricted to this miserable world, but is to extend
in length from the Apostles, in breadth throughout

the world, in depth as far as to Purgatory, in height
to heaven, including all nations, all past ages,
canonised saints, our forefathers of whom we have
hope, prelates, councils old and recent—[she, through
all these her members] sings in every place, *Amen,
Amen,* to this holy belief.

This is the perfect *Communion of Saints,* for it is
the food common to angels, and sainted souls in
Paradise, and ourselves; it is the true bread of which
all Christians participate. The *forgiveness of sins,* the
author of forgiveness being there, is confirmed; the
seed of our *resurrection* sown, *life everlasting* bestowed.
Where do you find contradiction in this holy analogy
of faith? So much the reverse, that this very belief
in the most holy Sacrament, which in truth, reality,
and substance, contains the true and natural body of
Our Lord, is actually the abridgment of our faith,
according to that of the Psalmist : * *He hath made a
memory* [*of his wonderful works*]. O holy and perfect
memorial of the Gospel! O admirable summing up
of our faith! He who believes, O Lord, in Your
presence in this most holy Sacrament, as Your holy
Church proposes it, has gathered and sucked the sweet
honey of all the flowers of Your holy Religion : hardly
can he ever fail in faith.

But I return to you, gentlemen, and simply ask
what passages you will any longer oppose to me against
such clear ones as these—*This is my body.* That
the flesh profiteth nothing ? †—no, not yours or mine,
which are but carrion, nor our carnal sentiments;
not mere flesh, dead, without spirit or life; but that
of the Saviour which is ever furnished with the life-

* cx. 4. † John vi.

giving Spirit, and with his Word. I say that it profits unto life eternal all who worthily receive it: what say you?—that *the words of Our Lord are spirit and life?* *—who denies it save yourselves, when you say they are but tropes and figures? But what sense is there in this consequence:—the words of Our Lord are spirit and life, therefore they are not to be understood of his body? And when he said: *The Son of man shall be delivered up to be mocked and scourged,* &c.† (I take as examples the first that come), were his words not spirit and life?—say then that he was crucified in figure. When he said: *If therefore you see the Son of man ascending where he was before* (John vi.), does it follow that he only ascended in figure? And still these words are comprised among the rest, of which he said: *They are spirit and life.* Finally, in the Holy Sacrament, as in the holy words of our Lord, the spirit is there which vivifies the flesh, otherwise it would profit nothing; but none the less is the flesh there with its life and its spirit. What further will you say?—that this Sacrament is called bread? So it is; but as Our Lord explains: *I am the living bread* (Ib.) These are fully sufficient examples:—as for you, what can you show like these? I show you an *is,* show me the *is not,* which you maintain, or the *signifies.* I have shown you the *body,* show me your effectual sign; seek, turn, turn again, make your spirit spin as fast as you like, and you shall never find it. At the very most you will show that when the words are somewhat strained, a few phrases in the Scriptures may be found like those you pretend to find here; but to *esse* from *posse* is a

* Ib.   † Luke xviii. 32.

lame consequence: I say that you cannot make them
fit; I say that if everybody takes them as he likes,
the greater number will take them wrongly. But let
us just see a piece of this work while it is being done.
You produce for your belief: *The words which I speak
are spirit and life;* and this you fasten on: *As often
as you shall eat this bread;* you add: *Do this in commemoration of me;* you bring up: *You shall show forth
the death of the Lord until he comes;* * *But me you
shall not have always.* But consider a little what
reference these words have to one another. You
adjust all this to the anomology † of your faith, and
how? Our Lord is *seated at the right hand,* therefore
he is not here. Show me the thread with which you
sew this negative to this affirmative:—because a body
cannot be in two places. Ah! you said you would
join your negative with analogy by the thread of
Scripture:—where is this Scripture, that a body
cannot be in two places? Just observe how you
mingle the profane employment of a merely human
reason with the Sacred Word? But, say you, Our
Lord will come to judge the living and the dead from
the right hand of his Father. What does this prove?
If it were necessary for him to come, in order to
become present in the Holy Sacrament, your analogy
would have some speciousness, though not even then
any reality,—for when he does come to judge nobody
says that it will be on earth; the fire will precede.
There is your analogy: in good earnest which has
worked the better, you or I?

---

* 1 Cor. xi ; John xii.

† Ανομολογια, *i.e.,* disproportion. A play on the word Analogy.
[Tr.]

If we let you interpret the Descent of Our Lord into hell as of the Sepulchre, or as of a fear of hell and of the pains of the damned,—the sanctity of the Church as the sanctity of an invisible and unknown Church,—its universality as that of a secret and hidden Church,—the Communion of Saints as simply a general benevolence,—the remission of sins as only a non-imputation;—when you shall have thus proportioned the Creed to your judgment, it will certainly be in good proportion with the rest of your doctrine, but who does not see the absurdity? The Creed, which is the instruction of the most simple, would be the most obscure doctrine in the world, and while it has to be the rule of faith, it would have to be regulated by another rule. *The wicked walk round about.** One infallible rule of our faith is this: God is All-mighty. He who says all excludes nothing, and you would regulate this rule, and would limit it so that it should not extend as far as absolute power, or the power of placing a body in two places, or of placing it in one without its occupying exterior space. Tell me, then —if the rule need regulation, who shall regulate it? Similarly the Creed says that Our Lord descended into hell, and Calvin would rule that this is to be understood of an imaginary descent; somebody else refers it to the sepulchre. Is not this to treat the rule as a Lesbian one, and to make the level bend to the stone instead of cutting the stone by the level. Indeed as S. Clement † and S. Augustine ‡ call it rule, so S.

---

* Ps. xi.

† We do not find this passage in any authentic work of S. Clement [Tr.]

‡ Serm. 213, alias 119.

Ambrose * calls it key.   But if another key be required to open this key where shall we find it ?   Is
it to be the fancy of your ministers, or what ?   Will
it be the Holy Spirit ?—but everybody will boast that
he has a share in this.   Good heavens ! into what
labyrinths do they fall who quit the path of the
Ancients !   I would not have you think me ignorant
of this, that the Creed alone is not the whole rule
and measure of faith.   For both S. Augustine † and
the great Vincent of Lerins ‡ also call the sense of
the Church (*sentiment Ecclesiastique*) rule of our faith.
The Creed alone says nothing openly of the Consub-
stantiality, of the Sacraments, or of other articles of
faith, but comprehends the whole faith in its root and
foundation, particularly when it teaches us to believe
the Church to be holy and Catholic ;—for by this it
sends us to what the Church shall propose.   But as
you despise the whole of the doctrine of the Church,
you also despise this noble, this notable and excellent
part of it, which is the Creed, refusing belief in it
until you have reduced it to the petty scale of your
conceptions.   Thus do you violate this holy measure
and proportion which S. Paul requires to be followed,
yea, even by the prophets themselves.§

* Appendix, Serm. 33. More probably belongs to S. Maximus of
Turin. [Tr.]

† Contra Ep. Fund 4, 5.   ‡ Comm. c. ii.   § 1 Cor. xiv.

CHAPTER III.

CONCLUSION OF THE WHOLE OF THIS SECOND PART BY
A SHORT ENUMERATION OF MANY EXCELLENCES
WHICH ARE IN THE CATHOLIC DOCTRINE AS COM-
PARED WITH THE OPINION OF THE HERETICS OF
OUR AGE.*

SAILING thus then without needle, compass or rudder
on the ocean of human opinions, you can expect
nothing but a miserable shipwreck. Ah! I implore
you, while this day lasts, while God presents you the
opportunity, throw yourselves into the saving bark of
a serious repentance, and take refuge on the happy
vessel which is bound under full sail for the port of
glory.

If there were nothing else, do you not recognise
what advantages and excellences the Catholic doctrine
has beyond your opinions ? The Catholic doctrine
makes more glorious and magnificent the goodness and
mercy of God, your opinions lower them. For example,
is there not more mercy in establishing the reality of
his body for our food than in only giving the figure
and commemoration thereof and the eating by faith
alone ? *All seek the things that are their own, not the
things that are Jesus Christ's* (Phil. ii. 21). Is it not
more honourable to concede to the might of Jesus

* This chapter seems to fulfil the design referred to in the following
detached note of the Saint's : "A chapter is also to be composed on the
greater glory of the Gospel in the faith of Catholics than in the faith
of the heretics. Where reference is to be made to what was said at
the end of the chapter *de visibili* [Pt. I. c. 6.], viz., that in the visible
Church the eye of mind and of body is fed, in the invisible neither."
[Tr.]

Christ the power to make the Blessed Sacrament, as the Church believes it, and to his goodness the will to do so, than the contrary? Without doubt it is more glorious to Our Lord. Yet because our mind cannot comprehend it, in order to uphold our own mind, *all seek the things that are their own, not the things that are Jesus Christ's.* Is it not more, in justifying man, to embellish his soul with grace, than without embellishing it to justify him by a simple toleration (*connivence*) or non-imputation? Is it not a greater favour to make man and his works agreeable and good than simply to take man as good without his being so in reality? Is it not more to have left seven Sacraments for the justification and sanctification of the sinner than to have left only two, one of which serves for nothing and the other for little? Is it not more to have left the power of absolving in the Church than to have left it not? Is it not more to have left a Church visible, universal, of striking aspect, perpetual, than to have left it little, secret, scattered and liable to corruption? Is it not to value more the travails of Jesus Christ when we say that a single drop of his blood suffices to ransom the world, than to say that unless he had endured the pains of the damned he would have done nothing? Is not the mercy of God more magnified in giving to his saints the knowledge of what takes place here below, the honour of praying for us, in making himself ready to accept their intercession, in having glorified them as soon as they died, than in making them wait and keeping them in suspense, according to Calvin's words, until the judgment, in making them deaf to our prayers and remaining himself inexorable to theirs. This will be seen more clearly in our treatment of particular points. Our doctrine [then] makes more admirable the power of God in the Sacrament of the Eucharist, in justification and inherent justice, in miracles, in the infallible preservation of the Church, in the glory of the Saints.

The Catholic doctrine cannot have its source in any passion, because nobody follows it save on this condition, of captivating his intelligence, under the authority of the pastors. It is not proud, since it teaches not to believe self but the Church. What shall I say further? Distinguish the voice of the dove from that of the crow. Do you not see this Spouse, who has nought but honey and milk under her tongue, who breathes only the greater glory of her Beloved, his honour and obedience to him? Ah! then, gentlemen, be willing to be placed as living stones in the walls of the heavenly Jerusalem. Take yourselves out of the hands of these men who build without a rule, who do not adjust their conceptions to the faith, but the faith to their conceptions. Come and offer yourselves to the Church, who will place you, unless you prevent her, in the heavenly building, according to the true rule and proportion of faith. For never shall any one have a place there above who has not been worked and laid, according to rule and square, here below.

[The following detached notes of the Saint bear upon the matter of the foregoing chapter. Tr.]

All the ancient sacrifices of a farinaceous nature were as it were the condiment of the bloody sacrifices. So the Sacrifice of the Eucharist is as it were the condiment of the Sacrifice of the Cross, and with most excellent reason united to it.

The Church is a mountain, heresy a valley: for heretics go down, from the Church that errs not to an erring one, from truth to shadow.

Ismael, who signified the Jewish synagogue (Gal. iv), was cast out when he would play with Isaac, that is, the Catholic Church. How much more heretics, &c.

That of Isaias (liv. 17) agrees excellently with the Church as against heresy: *No weapon that is formed against thee shall prosper; and every tongue that resisteth thee in judgment thou shalt condemn. This is the inheritance of the servants of the Lord, and their justice with me, saith the Lord.*

PART III.

Church Doctrines and Institutions.

INTRODUCTION.

THESE two fundamental faults into which your ministers have led you, namely, the having abandoned the Church and the having violated all the true rules of the Christian religion, make you altogether inexcusable, gentlemen. For they are so gross that you cannot but know them, and so important that either of the two suffices to make you lose true Christianity : since neither faith without the Church nor the Church without faith can save you, any more than the eye without the head or the head without the eye could see the light. Whoever would separate you from union with the Church should be suspected by you, and whoever should so greatly infringe the holy rules of the faith ought to be avoided and disregarded, whatever his appearance might be, whatever he might allege. You should not have so lightly believed. Had you been prudent in your way of acting you would have seen that it was not the Word of God they brought forward but their own ideas veiled under words of Scripture, and you would have known well that so rich a dress was never made for covering so worthless a body as this heresy is.

For, by supposition, let us say that there was never Church, nor Council, nor pastor, nor doctor, since the Apostles, and that the Holy Scripture contains only those books which it pleases Calvin, Beza, and Martyr to acknowledge; that there is no infallible rule for understanding it rightly, but that it is at the mercy of the notions of everybody who likes to maintain that he is interpreting Scripture by Scripture, and by the analogy of the faith,—as one might say he would get to understand Aristotle by Aristotle and by the analogy of philosophy. Only let us acknowledge that this Scripture is divine. And I maintain before all equitable judges that if not all, at least those amongst you who had some knowledge and ability, are inexcusable, and cannot defend their choice of religion from lightness and rashness.

And here is what I come to. The ministers will only fight on Scripture; I am willing. They will only have such parts of Scripture as they chose; I ageee. And still I say that the belief of the Catholic Church beats them completely, since she has more passages in her favour than the contrary opinion has, and her passages are more clear, more simple, more pure, interpreted more reasonably, more conclusive, and more apt. This I believe to be so certain that every one may come to know and recognise it. But if we would show this in minute detail we should never finish; it will be quite enough, I think, to show it in some of the chief articles.

It is this then that I profess to do in this Third

Part, in which I shall attack your ministers on the
Sacraments in general, and in particular on those of
the Eucharist, Confession, and Marriage ; on the honour
and invocation of the saints ; on the propriety of
ceremonies in general; then in particular on the
merit of good works, on justification, and on indul-
gences. In this I will employ nought but the pure
and simple Word of God; with which alone I will
make you see, by examples, your fault so clearly that
you will be bound to repent of it. And meantime
I beg of you, that if you see me engage, and at length
overcome the enemy with Scripture alone, you will
then represent to yourselves that great and honourable
succession of martyrs, pastors, and doctors, who have
testified by their teaching and at the price of their
blood that this doctrine for which we now fight was
the holy, the original, the Apostolic; which will be as
it were a superfluity of victory ; so that if we found
ourselves on an equality with our enemies by Scripture alone, the antiquity, the agreement, the holiness
of our authors would still make us triumph. And in
doing this I will ever adjust the sense and bearing of
the Scriptures which I shall produce to the rules which
I have established in the Second Part, although my
chief design is only to give you a proof of the hollow-
ness of your ministers, who do nothing but cry out
Holy Scripture, Holy Scripture, yet all they effect is
to contradict its clearest statements. In the assembly
of the Princes which took place at Spires, in the year
1526, the Protestant ministers wore these letters on
the right sleeve of their dress: V. D. M. I. Æ., by
which they meant to declare *Verbum Domini manet
in æternum* [the Word of the Lord remaineth for ever].

Would you not say that they had a monopoly of Holy
Scripture ?   They quote indeed morsels of it, and on
every occasion, " in public and in private," says the
great Lirinensis,* " in their discourses, in their books,
in the streets, and at banquets. . . . Read the works
of Paul of Samosata, of Priscillian, of Eunomius, of
Jovinian, and of those other pests : you will see a great
heap of examples, and scarcely a page which is not
painted and adorned with sentences out of the Old
and the New Testament. . . . They act like those do
who, wishing to get little children to take some bitter
potion, rub and cover with honey the rim of the cup,
in order that infant simplicity tasting the sweet first
may not be frightened of the bitter."   But he who
sounds the depths of their doctrine will see clearly as
the day that it is but a painted sham, like what the devil
brought forward when he tempted Our Lord.   For he
quoted Scripture to his purpose.   " What," says the
same Lirinensis,† " will he not do with wretched man,
when he dares to attack with words of Scripture the very
Lord of majesty ?   Let us look closely at the doctrine of
this passage. . . . For as then the head of one party
spoke to the head of the other, so now members speak
to members ; namely, the members of the devil to the
members of Jesus Christ, unbelievers to the faithful,
the sacrilegious to the religious—in a word, heretics to
Catholics."   But as the head answered the head, so
can we members answer the non-members.   Our head
repulsed their chief with passages of the Scripture,
let us repulse them in like fashion, and by solid and
plain consequences, deduced from Holy Scripture, let
us show their falseness and deceitfulness in covering

* Comm. xxxv.   † Ib. xxxvii.

their fancies with the words of Scripture. This is what I intend to do here, but briefly, and I protest that I will produce most faithfully what seems to me to be most in their favour, and convict them from the Scripture itself. Thus will you come to see that though they and we use and fight with the Scripture, yet we have the reality and right usage of them, and they only have the vain and illusive appearance. So both Aaron and the magicians changed their rods into living serpents, but the rod of Aaron devoured the rods of the others.

ARTICLE I.

OF THE SACRAMENTS.

CHAPTER I.

OF THE NAME OF SACRAMENT.

THIS word Sacrament is explicitly used in Scripture in the meaning which it has in the Catholic Church, since S. Paul, speaking of marriage, calls it clearly and precisely Sacrament.* But we shall see this by and by. It is enough now, against the insolence of Zwingle † and others who would reject this name, that the whole ancient Church has used it. For it is not by any greater authority that the words Trinity, consubstantial, person, and a hundred others, have been received in the Church as holy and legitimate. But it is a most unprofitable and foolish rashness to

---

* Eph. v.   † *De verâ et fals. relig.*

III.

attempt to change the Ecclesiastical words which antiquity has left us: to say nothing of the danger that there might be, after changing the words, of going on to the change of the meaning and belief,—as we see to be ordinarily the aim of these innovators on words. Now since the pretended reformers for the most part, though not without grumbling, leave this word in use in their books, let us enter into the difficulties we have with them over the causes and effects of the Sacraments, and let us see how they in this point despise the Scripture and the other rules of faith.

CHAPTER II.

OF THE FORM OF THE SACRAMENTS.

LET us begin with this: The Catholic Church holds as form of the Sacraments consecratory words; the pretended ministers, wishing to reform this form, say * that the consecrating words are charms, and that the true form of the Sacraments is preaching. What do the ministers produce from Holy Scripture for the support of this reformation? Two passages only as far as any one knows ; the one from S. Paul, the other from S. Matthew. S. Paul, speaking of the Church, says † that Our Lord sanctified it, *cleansing it by the laver of water in the word of life ;* and Our Lord himself, in S. Matthew,‡ gives this commandment to his disciples : *Teach all nations, baptizing them in the*

---

* Calv. Instit. iv. 14 ; in Eph. v.   Beza in sum. doctr. *de re sacram.*
† Eph. v. 26.   ‡ Ult. 19.

*name of the Father, and of the Son, and of the Holy
Ghost.* These two passages most clearly prove that
preaching is not the true form of the Sacraments.
But whoever told them that there was no other
" word of life " than preaching ? I maintain, on the
contrary, that this holy invocation : *I baptize thee in
the name of the Father, and of the Son, and of the Holy
Ghost,* is also a word of life ; as S. Chrysostom and
Theodoret say.* Just as the other prayers and the
other invocations of God's name are ; which, however,
are not sermons. And if S. Jerome,† following the
mystical sense, would have preaching to be a sort of
cleansing water, he does not therefore set himself
against the other Fathers who have understood the
laver of water to be Baptism precisely, and the word
of life to be the invocation of the most holy Trinity,
in order to interpret the passage of S. Paul by the
other of S. Matthew : *Teach all nations, baptizing
them in the name of the Father, of the Son, and of the
Holy Ghost.* And as to this latter, nobody ever
denied that instruction should precede Baptism in the
case of those who are capable of it, according to the
words of Jesus Christ, who places the instruction first
and the Baptism afterwards. But keeping within the
same words, we place the previous instruction by
itself, as a disposition requisite to him who has the
use of reason, and Baptism also apart : so that the
one cannot be the form of the other. Indeed Baptism would rather be the form of preaching than
preaching of Baptism, if one must be the form of the
other ; since the form cannot precede but must follow
the matter, and preaching precedes Baptism, while

* In Eph. v.   † In idem.

Baptism follows upon the preaching. Wherefore S. Augustine would not have spoken correctly when he said: "the word comes to the element and the Sacrament is made;"* for he would rather have had to say: the element comes to the word.

These two passages then are wholly inapplicable to your reformed teaching; yet they are all you have.

At the same time your pretensions would be somewhat more tolerable if we had not in the Scripture contrary reasons more express beyond all comparison than yours are. They are these. He who *believes and is baptized:* do you see this belief which springs in us by preaching separated from Baptism?—they are then two distinct things, preaching and Baptism. Who doubts but that S. Paul catechised and instructed in the faith many Corinthians who were baptized? But if instruction and preaching were the form of Baptism, S. Paul was not right in saying:† *I give God thanks that I baptized none of you but Crispus and Caius,* &c. For to give the form to a thing, is it not to do it? The case is made stronger still in that S. Paul separates baptizing from preaching: *Christ sent me not to baptize but to preach the Gospel.* And to show that the Baptism is Christ's, not his who administers it, he does not say: are you baptized in the preaching of Paul? but rather: *are you baptized in the name of Paul?*—showing that though preaching goes before still it is not of the essence of Baptism, as if the Baptism were to be attributed to the preacher and catechist in the same way that it is attributed to him whose name is invoked in it.

Certainly any one who nearly examines the first

* In Joan. lxxx.   † 1 Cor. i. 14.

Baptism administered after Pentecost * will see as
clearly as the day that preaching is one thing and
Baptism another. *When they had heard these things*
—see on the one hand the preaching—*they had com-
punction in their hearts, and said to Peter and the rest
of the Apostles: What shall we do, men brethren ?
But Peter to them: do penance* (said he), *and be
baptized every one of you in the name of Jesus Christ,
for the remission of your sins :*—see on the other hand
the Baptism, put by itself. One may see as much
in the Baptism of that pious eunuch of Ethiopia
(Acts viii.), in that of S. Paul (Ib. ix), in which there
was no preaching, and in that of the good and
religious Cornelius (Ib. x.)

And as to the most holy Eucharist, which is the
other Sacrament which the ministers make pretence
of receiving,—where do they ever find that Our Lord
made use of preaching ? S. Paul teaches the Corinthians how the Supper should be celebrated, but we
do not find that there is any command to preach;
and in order that nobody should doubt but that the
rite he was expounding was legitimate, he says that
he had so learnt it from Our Lord: *For I have received
of the Lord that which also I delivered to you.*† Our
Lord indeed made an admirable discourse, related by
S. John; but this was not for the mystery of the
Supper, which was already completed.

We do not say that it is not becoming to instruct
the people about the Sacraments conferred upon them,
but only that this instruction is not the form of the
Sacraments. So that if in the institution of these
divine mysteries, and in the very practice of the

* Acts ii. 37, 38.   † 1 Cor. xi. 23.

Apostles, we find a distinction between preaching and the Sacraments, by what authority shall we confound them together ?

In this point, then, according to the Scriptures, we are absolutely victorious, and the ministers are convicted of violating the Scriptures, since they would change the essence of the Sacraments contrarily to their institution.

Again, they violate Tradition, the authority of the Church, of Councils, of the Popes, and of the Fathers, who have all believed and do believe that the Baptism of little children is true and legitimate. But how would we have preaching employed therein ? Infants do not understand what one says to them ; they are not capable of using reason ; what is the use of instructing them ? We might indeed preach before them, but it would be of no use ; for their understanding is not yet open to receive instruction, as instruction ; it touches them not, nor can it be applied to them,—what effect then can it have on them ? The Baptism therefore would be vain, since it would be without form, and therefore the form of Baptism is not preaching. Luther answers * that infants do feel the actual movements of faith, by preaching. This is to violate and belie experience and also common sense.

Further, the greater part of the Baptisms which are administered in the Catholic Church are administered without any preaching : they are therefore not true Baptisms, since the form is lacking to them. Why then do you not rebaptize those who go from our Church to yours ? It would be an anabaptism.

So then behold how, according to the rules of the

* Contra Coch. an. 1523.

faith, and principally according to Holy Scripture,
your ministers err, when they teach you that preaching is the form of the Sacraments. But let us see
if what we believe be more conformable to the Holy
Word. We say that the form of the Sacraments
is a consecratory word, a word of benediction or
invocation. Is there anything so clear in Scripture?
*Teach all nations, baptizing them in the name of the
Father, and of the Son, and of the Holy Ghost.* Is not
this form—*in the name of the Father*—invocative?
Certainly the same S. Peter who says to the Jews:*
*Do penance and be baptized every one of you in the name
of Jesus Christ for the remission of your sins,* says
shortly afterwards to the lame man at the Beautiful
Gate of the Temple: *In the name of Jesus Christ of
Nazareth, rise up and walk.* Who does not see that
this last prayer is invocative, and why not the first,
which is in substance the same? So S. Paul does
not say: The chalice of preaching of which we preach
is it not the communication of the blood of Christ?
—but, on the contrary: *The chalice of benediction
which we bless.*† They consecrated it then and blessed
it. So at the Council of Laodicea (c. 25): "The
deacon may not bless the chalice." S. Denis calls
them consecratory,‡ and in his description of the
Liturgy or Mass, he does not mention preaching, so
far was he from considering it to be the form of the
Eucharist. In the Council of Laodicea, where the
order of the Mass is spoken of, nothing is said of
preaching, which was, therefore, a thing of propriety,
but not of the essence of this mystery. Justin Martyr
(*Apol.* I. 65), describing the ancient office which the

* Acts ii.   † 1 Cor. x. 16.   ‡ *De Eccl. Hier.* ult.

Christians performed on Sundays, amongst other things
says that after the general prayers they offered bread,
wine, and water ; then the prelate made earnest prayers
and thanksgivings [*eucharistias*] to God; the people
gave thanks, saying, Amen : " these things being
consecrated, with the Eucharist, every one participates,
and the same things are given to the Deacons, to be
carried to the absent." * Several things are noticeable
here : water was mingled with the wine, they offered,
they consecrated, they carried it to the sick. But if our
reformers had been there, it would have been necessary
to carry the preaching to the sick, or nothing would
have been done. For as John Calvin says : † " The
simple explanation of the mystery to the people,
makes a dead element begin to be a sacrament." S.
Gregory of Nyssa says : ‡ " I consider that now the
bread is sanctified by the Word of God ; " and—he is
speaking of the Sacrament of the Altar,—" we believe that it is changed into the body of the Word."
And afterwards he says that this change is made " in
virtue of the benediction." " How," says the great
S. Ambrose,§ " can that which is bread become the
body of Christ ?—by consecration : " and further on :
" It was not the body of Christ before consecration,
but, after the consecration, I tell thee it now is the
body of Christ ; "—and you may see him at great
length. But I reserve myself on this subject for
when we shall be treating of the holy Mass.

* We translate the Saint's quotation as it stands. In the text of
S. Justin the word *eucharista* is certainly used in a technical sense.
He speaks particularly of " the bread, wine, and water *in which* thanks-
giving (or eucharist) is made." [Tr.]

† In Ep. ad Eph. v.   ‡ Orat. Catech. mag. cap. 37.
§ De Sac. iv. 14, 16.

I would finish with this signal sentence of S.
Augustine : * "Paul could preach the Lord Jesus
Christ by signs of three kinds; in one way by his
tongue, in another by an Epistle, in a third by the
Sacrament of his body and blood: but neither his
tongue nor his ink, nor significant sounds uttered
by his tongue, nor the signs of letters traced on
parchments do we say to be the body and blood of
Christ, but that only which, taken from the fruits
of the earth and consecrated by mystic prayer, we
duly receive." And if S. Augustine says : † "Whence
such a power in water that touching the body it
should wash the heart, unless by the effect of the
word, not inasmuch as it is said but inasmuch as
it is believed :"—we say nothing different. For in
truth the words of benediction and sanctification with
which we form and perfect the Sacraments, have no
virtue save when uttered under the general intention
and belief of the Church. For if any one said them
without this intention, they would indeed be spoken, but
for nothing, because it is "not what is said but what
is believed," &c.

CHAPTER III.

OF THE INTENTION REQUIRED IN THE ADMINISTRATION OF THE SACRAMENTS.

I HAVE never been able to find any proof taken from
Scripture of the opinion which your preachers have
on this point. They say that though the minister

* De. Trin. iii.   † In Joan. lxxx.

may have no intention of effecting the Supper or baptizing, but simply acts in mockery or in joke, yet still, provided he does the exterior action of the Sacrament, the Sacrament is completed.*

All this is said without reason given, without bringing forward anything but certain consequences unsupported by no word of God, mere quibbles. On the contrary, the Council of Florence † and that of Trent ‡ declare that if any one says that at least the intention of doing what the Church does is not required in the ministers when they confer the Sacraments, he is anathema. These are the words of the Council of Trent. The Council does not say that it is necessary to have the particular intention of the Church (for otherwise Calvinists, who have no intention in Baptism of taking away original sin, would not baptize rightly since the Church has that intention) but only the intention of doing in general what the Church does when she baptizes, without particularising or determining the what or the how.

Again, the Council does not say that it is necessary to mean to do what the Church of Rome does, but only in general what the Church does, without particularising which is the true Church. Yea if a man, thinking that the pretended Church of Geneva was the true Church, should limit his intention to the intention of the Church of Geneva, he would indeed be in error if ever man was in error, in his knowledge of the true Church; but his intention would be sufficient in this point, since, although it would point to the idea of a counterfeit Church, still

* Luther *in Cap. Bab.* de Bapt; Calv. *in Ant.* 7.
† In Instr. Arm. ‡ Sess. vii. 11.

it would only have its real significance in the idea of
the true Church, and the error would only be material,
not, as our Doctors say, formal.

Further, it is not required that we have this intention actually, when we confer the Sacrament, but it
is enough that we can say with truth that we are
performing such and such ceremony, and saying such
and such word,—as pouring water, saying: I baptize
thee in the name of the Father, &c.—with the intention of doing what true Christians do, and what Our
Lord has commanded, although at the moment we
may not be attentive to this or thinking of it.   As
it is enough to enable me to say, I am preaching for
the service of God and the salvation of souls, if
when I begin to get ready I have that intention,
although when I am in the pulpit I may think of
what I have to say and be keeping this in memory,
thinking no more of that first intention : or as it is
with one who has resolved to bestow a hundred
crowns for the love of God, then goes out of his
house to do it, and thinking of other things distributes
that sum ; for although he keep not his thoughts
actually addressed to God, yet it cannot be said that
his intention is not on God, by virtue of his first
determination, nor that he is not doing this work of
charity deliberately and intentionally.   Such intention
at least is required, and also suffices, for the conferring
of the Sacraments.

Now that the proposition of the Council is made
clear, let us go on to see whether it is, like that of
our adversaries, without foundation in Scripture.
One cannot reasonably doubt but that to perform
the Lord's Supper, or Baptism, it is necessary to do

what Our Lord has commanded to this end, and not only to do it but to do it in virtue of this commandment and institution;—for these actions might be done in virtue of another commandment than Our Lord's; as, for instance, if a man were asleep and baptized in a dream, or if he were drunk. The words indeed would be there and the matter, but they would have no power, as not proceeding from the command of him who could render them vigorous and effective. Just as not all that a judge says and writes are judicial sentences, but only what he says as a judge. Now how could one make a difference between sacramental actions done in virtue of the commandment which makes them fertile, and these same actions done for another end? Questionless the difference can only be in the intention with which one does them. It is necessary then that not only should the words be pronounced, but also that they should be pronounced with the intention of obeying the command of Our Lord:—in the Supper,—*Do this;* in Baptism,—*Baptizing them in the name of the Father, and of the Son, and of the Holy Ghost.* But, to speak plainly, is not this command, *do this,* addressed properly to the minister of the Sacrament? Without doubt. Now it is not said simply *do this,* but, *do this for a commemoration of me.* How can one do this sacred action in commemoration of Our Lord, without having the intention of thereby doing what Our Lord has commanded, or at least of doing what Christians the disciples of Our Lord do; in order that if not immediately, at least by means of Christtians or of the Church, this action may be done in commemoration of Our Lord? I think it is impossible to imagine that a man can perform the Supper in commemoration of Our Lord if he have not the intention of doing what Our Lord has commanded, or at least of doing what those do who do it in commemoration of Our Lord. It is then not enough to do what Our Lord has commanded when he says *do this;* but we must do it for the intention that Our Lord has commanded; that is, *in commemoration of him;* if not with this intention in particular yet with it in general, if not immediately yet at least mediately, meaning to do what the Church does, and she having the intention of doing what Our Lord has done and commanded. So that one refers one's intention to that of the Spouse, which is accommodated to that of the Beloved. In a similar way, Our Lord does not say that we are to say these words, *I baptize thee,* simply, but commanded that the whole action of Baptism should be done *in the name of the Father.* So that it is not enough to say *in the name of the Father,* but the washing or aspersion itself must be done in the name of the Father, and this authority must give life and power not only to the word but also to the whole action of the Sacrament, which of itself would have no supernatural virtue. Now how can an action be done in the name of God which is done in mockery of God? In truth the action of Baptism does not so much depend on the words that it cannot be done with a power and an authority quite contrary to the words, if the heart which is the mover of words and action address it to a contrary intention. Yea more, for these words *in the name of the Father,* &c., can be said in the name of the enemy of the Father; as these words, in truth, can be,

and often are, said in lying.   If then Our Lord does
not simply command that we do the action of Baptism,
nor simply say the words, but that we do the action
and say the words *in the name of the Father,* &c.; we
must have at least the general intention of performing
the Baptism in virtue of the command of Our Lord,
in his name, and for him.   And as for absolution,
that the intention is required there is still more
expressly stated.   *Whose sins you shall forgive they are
forgiven them.**   I leave this to their consideration.

And it is in this connection that S. Augustine
says : †   " Whence is there such power in water that
touching the body it should wash the heart except by
the action of the word, not inasmuch as it is said but
inasmuch as it is believed ? "—that is, the words of
themselves being pronounced without any intention
or belief have no virtue, but being said with power
and faith, and according to the general intention of
the Church, they have this salutary effect.   And if
it is found in history that some Baptisms given in
sport have been approved, we must not think it
strange, because one can do many things in play, and
yet have the intention of truly doing what one has
seen done.   But we say that is done in sport which
is done out of season and indiscreetly, when not done
by malice or involuntarily.

[The following detached notes of the Saint bear
upon the matter of this Third Part.   Tr.]

On the Episcopal blessing with the sign of the
cross we find in the life of S. Hilarion (fol. 29):
Resalutatis omnibus, manuque eis benedicens.

* John xx. 23.   † See end of last chapter.   [Tr.]

On the intercession of Saints we must not forget
the saying of Luther, which he wrote to George Duke
of Saxony (an. 1526 apud Coch.): *Initio rogabo
prœterea et certissime impetrabo remissionem apud
Dominum meum J. C., super omnibus quæcumque Il.
Clem. vestra contra verbum ejus facit ac fecit.* I ask
you, if this monk &c. [how much more men of
holiness might beseech God] ?

On the veneration of the Saints, or of the Pope,
that must not be forgotten which he said to the King
of England in a letter of the year 1525, found in
Cochlæus in the acts of the year 26. *Quare his
litteris prosterno me pedibus majestatis tuæ quantum
possum humillime.*

ARTICLE II.

PURGATORY.

INTRODUCTION.

THE Catholic Church has been accused in our age of
superstition in the prayer which she makes for the
faithful departed, inasmuch as by this she supposes
two truths which, it is maintained, do not exist,
namely : that the departed are in punishment and
need, and that they can be helped. Whereas, the
departed are either damned or saved ; the damned are
in pain, but it is irremediable ; and the saved enjoy
perfect bliss:—so the latter have no need and the
former have no means of receiving help ; wherefore

it is useless to pray to God for the departed. Such is the summing up of the accusation. It ought surely to suffice anybody who wishes to frame a right judgment of this accusation to know that the accusers were private persons and the accused the universal body of the Church. But still, as the temper of our age has led to the submitting all things, however sacred, religious, and authoritative they may be, to the control and censure of everybody, many persons of honour and eminence have taken the cause of the Church in hand to defend it, considering that they could not better employ their piety and learning than in the defence of her, at whose hands they had received all their spiritual good,—Baptism, Christian doctrine, and the Scriptures themselves. Their reasons are so convincing that if they were properly balanced and weighed against those of the accusers their validity would at once be recognised. But unhappily, sentence has been given without the party being heard. Have we not reason, all we who are domestics and children of the Church, to make ourselves appellants, and to complain of the partiality of the judges, leaving on one side for the present their incompetence? We appeal then from the judges not instructed to themselves instructed, and from judgments given, the parties not heard, to judgments, parties heard. Let us beg all those who wish to judge of this difference to consider our allegations and proofs so much the more attentively as there is question not of the condemnation of the accused party who cannot be condemned by her inferiors, but of the condemnation or salvation of the judges.

CHAPTER I.

OF THE NAME OF PURGATORY.

WE maintain, then, that we may pray for the faithful departed, and that the prayers and good works of the living greatly relieve them and are profitable to them: —for this reason, that all those who die in the grace of God, and consequently in the number of the elect, do not go to Paradise at the very first moment, but many go to Purgatory, where they suffer a temporal punishment, from which our prayers and good works can help and serve to deliver them. There lies the point of our difference.

We agree that the blood of Our Redeemer is the true purgatory of souls; for in it are cleansed all the souls in the world; whence S. Paul speaks of it, in the 1st of Hebrews, as *making purgation of sins.* Tribulations also are a purgatory, by which our souls are rendered pure, as gold is refined in the furnace. *The furnace trieth the potter's vessels, and the trial of affliction just men.** Penance and contrition again form a certain purgatory, as David said of old in the 50th Psalm: *Thou shalt wash me, O Lord, with hyssop, and I shall be cleansed.* It is well known also that Baptism in which our sins are washed away can be again called a purgatory, as everything can be that serves to purge away our offences: but here we take Purgatory for a place in which after this life the souls which leave this world before they have been perfectly cleansed from the stains which they have contracted— since nothing can enter Paradise which is not pure

* Ecclus. xxvii.

and undefiled—are detained in order to be washed and purified. And if one would know why this place is called simply Purgatory more than are the other means of purgation above-named, the answer will be, that it is because in that place nothing takes place but the purgation of the stains which remain at the time of departure out of this world, whereas in Baptism, Penance, tribulations, and the rest, not only is the soul purged from its imperfections, but it is further enriched with many graces and perfections; whence the name of Purgatory has been limited to that place in the other world which, properly speaking, is for no purpose but the purification of souls. And agreeing as to the blood of Our Lord, we so fully acknowledge the virtue thereof, that we protest by all our prayers that the purgation of souls, whether in this world or in the other, is made solely by its application:—more jealous of the honour due to this precious medicine than those who so highly value it that they undervalue the using of it. Therefore by Purgatory we understand a place where souls for a time are purged of the spots and imperfections they carry with them from this mortal life.

CHAPTER II.

OF THOSE WHO HAVE DENIED PURGATORY: AND OF THE MEANS OF PROVING IT.

It is not an opinion adopted lightly—this article of Purgatory. The Church has long maintained this belief to all and against all, and it seems that the first who impugned it was Aerius, an Arian heretic, as S. Epiphanius testifies (Hær. 75), and S. Augustine (Hær. 53), and Socrates (ii. 35)—about twelve hundred years ago. Afterwards came certain persons who called themselves *Apostolics*, in the time of S. Bernard. Then the Petrobusians, about five hundred years back, who also denied this same article, as S. Bernard (sermons 65 and 66 on the Cant. of Cant. and ep. 241) and S. Peter of Cluny (epp. 1, 2, and elsewhere) record. This same opinion of the Petrobusians was followed by the Vaudois, about the year 1170, as Guidon says in his *Summa;* and some Greeks were suspected on this matter, justifying themselves in the Council of Florence, and in their apology presented to the Council of Basle. In fine, Luther, Zwingle, Calvin, and those of their party, have altogether denied the truth of Purgatory : for although Luther, *in disputatione Lipsicâ*, says that he firmly believed, yea certainly knew, that there was a Purgatory, still he afterwards retracted this in the book, *De Abrogandâ Missâ Privatâ*. And it is the custom of all the factions of our age to laugh at Purgatory, and despise prayers for the dead. But the Catholic Church has strongly opposed all these, each in its time, having in her hand the Holy Scripture, out of which our forefathers have drawn many good reasons.

For (1.) she has proved that alms, prayers, and other holy actions can help the departed : whence it follows that there is a Purgatory, for those in hell can have no help in their pains, and into Paradise, all good being there, we can convey none of ours for those who are therein ; wherefore it is for those who are in

a third place, which we call Purgatory. (2.) She has
proved that in the other world some of the departed
have been delivered from their punishments and sins ;
and since this cannot be done either in hell or in
Paradise, it follows that there is a Purgatory. (3.)
She has proved that many souls, before arriving in
Paradise, passed through a place of punishment, which
can only be Purgatory. (4.) Proving that the souls
below the earth gave honour and reverence to Our
Lord, she at the same time proved Purgatory, since
this cannot be understood of those poor wretches who
are in hell. (5.) By many other passages, with a
variety of consequences, but all very apposite. In these
one ought so much the more to defer to our doctors,
because the passages which they allege now have been
brought forward for the same purpose by those great
ancient fathers, without our having to make new
interpretations in order to defend this holy article ;
which sufficiently shows how candidly we act in this
matter : whereas our adversaries draw conclusions
from the Holy Scripture which have never been
thought of before, but are quite freshly started simply
to oppose the Church.

So our reasons will be in this order, (1.) We will
quote the passages of Holy Scripture, then (2.)
Councils, (3.) ancient Fathers, (4.) all sorts of
authors. Afterwards we will bring forward reasons,
and at last we will take up the arguments of the
opposite party and will show them not to be sound.
Thus shall we conclude by the belief of the Catholic
Church. It will remain for the reader to avoid looking at things through the medium of passion, to think
attentively over the soundness of our proofs, and to

throw himself at the feet of the divine goodness, crying out in all humility with David: *Give me understanding and I will search thy law, and I will keep it with my whole heart.** And then I doubt not that such men will return into the bosom of their grandmother the Church Catholic.

CHAPTER III.

OF SOME PASSAGES OF THE SCRIPTURE IN WHICH MENTION IS MADE OF A PURGATION AFTER THIS LIFE, AND OF A TIME AND A PLACE FOR IT.

THIS first argument is irrefragable. There is a time and a place of purgation for souls after this mortal life. Therefore there is a Purgatory; since hell cannot allow any purgation, and Paradise can receive nothing which needs purgation. Now that there is a time and place of purgation after this life, here is the proof.

(1.) In Psalm lxv. 12: *We have passed through fire and water, and thou hast brought us out into a refreshment.* This place is brought in proof of Purgatory by Origen (Hom. 25 *in Numeros*), and by S. Ambrose (in Ps. xxxvi., and in sermon 3 on Ps. cxviii.), where he expounds the water of Baptism, and the fire of Purgatory.

(2.) In Isaias (iv. 4): *If the Lord shall wash away the filth of the daughters of Sion, and shall wash away*

* Ps. cxviii. 34.

the blood of Jerusalem out of the midst thereof by the spirit of judgment and the spirit of burning. This purgation made in the spirit of judgment and of burning is understood of Purgatory by S. Augustine, in the 20th Book of the *City of God*, ch. 25. And in fact this interpretation is favoured by the words preceding, in which mention is made of the salvation of men, and also by the end of the chapter, where the repose of the blessed is spoken of; wherefore that which is said—*the Lord shall wash away the filth*—is to be understood of the purgation necessary for this salvation. And since it is said that this purgation is to be made in the spirit of heat and of burning, it cannot well be understood save of Purgatory and its fire.

(3). In Micheas, in the 7th chapter (8, 9): *Rejoice not, thou my enemy, over me, because I am fallen: I shall arise, when I sit in darkness, the Lord is my light. I will bear the wrath of the Lord, because I have sinned against him, until he judge my cause and execute judgment for me: he will bring me forth into the light, I shall behold his justice.* This passage was already applied to the proof of Purgatory amongst Catholics from the time of S. Jerome, 1200 years ago, as the same S. Jerome witnesses by the last chapter of Isaias; where he says that the—*when I shall sit in darkness . . . I will bear the wrath of the Lord . . . until He judge my cause*—cannot be understood of any pain so properly as of that of Purgatory.

(4.) In Zachary (ix. 11): *Thou also by the blood of thy testament hast sent forth thy prisoners out of the pit wherein is no water.* The pit from which these prisoners are drawn is the Purgatory from which Our

Lord delivered them in his descent into hell, and cannot be understood of Limbo, where the Fathers were before the resurrection of Our Lord in Abraham's bosom, because there was water of consolation there, as may be seen in Luke xvi. Whence S. Augustine, in the 90th Epistle, to Evodius, says that Our Lord visited those who were being tormented in hell, that is, in Purgatory, and that he delivered them from it; whence it follows that there is a place where the faithful are held prisoners and whence they can be delivered.

(5.) In Malachy (iii. 3): *And he shall sit refining and cleansing the silver: and he shall purify the sons of Levi, and shall refine them as gold and as silver*, &c. This place is expounded of a purifying punishment by Origen (Hom. 6 on Exodus), S. Ambrose (on Ps. xxxvi.), St. Augustine (*de civ. Dei* xx. 25), and S. Jerome (on this place). We are quite aware that they understand it of a purgation which will be at the end of the world by the general fire and conflagration, in which will be purged away the remains of the sins of those who will be found alive; but we still are able to draw from this a good argument for our Purgatory. For if persons at that time have need of purgation before receiving the effects of the benediction of the supreme Judge, why shall not those also have need of it who die before that time, since some of these may be found at death to have remains of their imperfections. In truth if Paradise cannot receive any stains at that time, neither will it receive them any better at present. S. Irenæus in this connection, in chapter 29 of Book V., says that because the militant Church is then to mount up to the heavenly palace of the Spouse, and will no longer have time for purgation, her faults and stains will there and then be purged away by this fire which will precede the judgment.

(6.) I leave on one side the passage of Psalm xxxvii. —*O Lord, rebuke me not in thine indignation nor chastise me in thy wrath:*—which S. Augustine interprets of hell and Purgatory in such sense that to be rebuked in indignation refers to the eternal pains, and to be chastised * in wrath refers to Purgatory.

CHAPTER IV.

OF ANOTHER PASSAGE OUT OF THE NEW TESTAMENT, TO THIS EFFECT.

In the 1st Corinthians (iii. 13, 14, 15): *The day of the Lord shall declare (every man's work), because it shall be revealed by fire, and the fire shall try every man's work, of what sort it is. If any man's work abide which he hath built thereupon, he shall receive a reward. If any man's work burn, he shall suffer loss: but he himself shall be saved, yet so as by fire.* This passage has always been held as one of the important and difficult ones of the whole Scripture. Now in it, as is easily seen by one who considers the whole chapter, the Apostle uses two similitudes. The first is of an architect who with solid materials builds a valuable house on a rock: the second is of one who on the

----

* *Corripi; i.e.,* to be corrected by chastisement. [Tr.]

same foundation erects a house of boards, reeds, straw.
Let us now imagine that a fire breaks out in both the
houses.   That which is of solid material will be out of
danger, and the other will be burnt to ashes.   And if
the architect be in the first he will be whole and safe ;
if he be in the second, he must, if he would escape,
rush through fire and flame, and shall be saved yet so
that he will bear the marks of having been in fire :
he himself shall be saved, yet so as by fire.   The foundation spoken of in this similitude is Our Lord, of whom
S. Paul says : *I have planted* . . . and *as a wise
architect I have laid the foundation :* . . . and then
afterwards : *For no one can lay another foundation but
that which is laid ; which is Christ Jesus.*   The archi-
tects are the preachers and doctors of the Gospel, as
may be known by considering attentively the words of
this whole chapter.   And as S. Ambrose interprets,
and also Sedulius on this place, the day of the Lord
which is spoken of means the day of judgment,
which in the Scripture is ordinarily called the day
of the Lord,—as in Joel ii. : *the day of the Lord ;* in
Sophonias i. : *the day of the Lord is near ;* and in the
word that follows in our passage : *the day of the Lord
shall declare it ;* for it is on that day that all the
actions of the world will be declared in fire.   When
the Apostle says *it shall be revealed by fire,* he sufficiently shows that it is the last day of judgment ; [as]
in the Second to the Thessalonians i. : *when the Lord
Jesus shall be revealed from heaven with the angels of
his power, in a flame of fire ;* and in Psalm xcvi. : *fire
shall go before his face.*   The fire by which the architect is saved—*he himself shall be saved yet so as by
fire*—can only be understood of the fire of Purgatory.

For when the Apostle says *he shall be saved*, he excludes the fire of hell in which no one can be saved ; and when he says *he shall be saved by fire*, and speaks only of him who has built on the foundation, wood, straw, stubble, he shows that he is not speaking of the fire which will precede the day of judgment, since by this will pass not only those who shall have built with these light materials, but also those who shall have built in gold, silver, &c. All this interpretation, besides that it agrees very well with the text, is also most authentic, as having been followed with common consent by the ancient Fathers. S. Cyprian (Bk. iv. ep. 2) seems to make allusion to this passage. S. Ambrose, on this place, S. Jerome on the 4th of Amos, S. Augustine on Psalm xxxvi., S. Gregory (*Dial.* iv. 39), Rupert (in Gen. iii. 32), and the rest, are all express on the point; and of the Greeks, Origen in the 6th Homily on Exodus, Ecumenius on this passage (where he brings forward S. Basil), and Theodoret quoted by S. Thomas in the 1st *Opusculum contra errores Græc.*

It may be said that in this interpretation there is an equivocation and impropriety, inasmuch as the fire spoken of is taken now for that of Purgatory, now for that which will precede the day of judgment. We answer that it is a graceful manner of speech, by the contrasting these two fires. For notice the meaning of the sentence : the day of the Lord shall have light from the fire which will go before it, and as this day shall be lighted up by the fire, so this same day by the judgment shall cast light on the merit and defect of each work; and as each work shall be brought clearly out, so the workers who will have worked with imperfection shall be saved by the

fire of Purgatory. But besides this, if we should say
that S. Paul uses the same word in different senses
in the same passage it would be no new thing, for he
employs words in this way in other places, but so
properly that this serves as an ornament to his
language: as in the 2d of Corinthians, 5th chapter:
Him who knew no sin for us he hath made sin:—where
who sees not that *sin* in the first part is taken in its
proper sense, for iniquity ; and the second time
figuratively, for him who bears the penalty of sin ?

It may be said again that it is not said that he
will be saved *by fire*, but *as by fire*, and that therefore
we cannot conclude there is a Purgatorial fire. I
answer that there is a true similitude in this passage.
For the Apostle means to say that he whose works
are not absolutely solid will be saved, like the
architect who escapes from the fire, but at the same
time not without passing through the fire ; a fire of a
different quality from that which burns in this world.
It is enough that from this passage we evidently conclude that many who will gain possession of the
kingdom of paradise will pass through fire: now
this will not be the fire of hell, nor the fire which
will precede the judgment ; it will therefore be the
fire of Purgatory. The passage is difficult and
troublesome, but well considered it gives us a manifest
conclusion for our contention ;—so that we have here
two places by which we can learn that after this life
there are a time and a place of purgation.

CHAPTER V.

OF SOME OTHER PASSAGES BY WHICH PRAYER, ALMS-
DEEDS AND HOLY ACTIONS FOR THE DEPARTED
ARE AUTHORISED.

THE second argument which we draw from the Holy
Word in favour of Purgatory is taken from the
Second of the Machabees, chapter xii.; where the
Scripture relates that Judas Machabæus sent to Jerusalem twelve thousand drachms of silver for sacrifice
to be offered for the sins of the dead, and afterwards
it says: *It is therefore a holy and wholesome thought
to pray for the dead, that they may be loosed from sins.*
For thus do we argue. It is a holy and wholesome
thought to pray for the dead that they may be loosed
from their sins; therefore after death there will be
time and place for the remission of sins; but this
place cannot be either hell or Paradise, therefore it is
Purgatory. This argument is so correct that to
answer it our adversaries deny the authority of the
Book of Machabees, and hold it to be apocryphal, but
in reality this is for lack of any other answer. For
this Book has been held as authentic and sacred by
the third Council of Carthage (c. 47), which was held
about 1200 years ago, and at which S. Augustine
assisted, as Prosper says (*in Chron.*); and by Innocent
I. in the Epistle to Exuperius; and by S. Augustine
in the 18th Book of the *City of God*, c. 36,—whose
words are these: "It is the Catholic Church which
holds these books canonical, and not the Jews;"
and by the same S. Augustine, in the book *De Doctrinâ*

Christiana, chap. viii. ; and by Damasus, in the decree
on the canonical books which he made in a council
of seventy bishops ; and by many other Fathers whom
it would be long to cite.   So that to answer by denying the authority of the book, is to deny at the same
time the authority of antiquity.

We know how many things are alleged in support
of this negation, which things for the most part only
show the difficulty there is in the Scriptures, not any
falsehood in them.   It only seems to me necessary to
answer one or two objections that are made.   They first
say that the prayer was made to show the kind feeling
those persons had towards the departed, not as if they
thought the dead had need of prayer :—but this the
Scripture contradicts by those words : *that they may
be loosed from sins.*   Secondly, they object that it is a
manifest error to pray for the resurrection of the dead
before the judgment ; because this is to presuppose
either that souls rise again and consequently die, or
that bodies do not rise again unless by means of the
prayers and good actions of the living, which would
be against the article *I believe in the resurrection of
the dead :* now that these errors are presupposed in
this place of the Machabees appears by these words :
*For if he had not hoped that they that were slain should
rise again, it would have seemed superfluous and vain
to pray for the dead.*   The answer is that in this place
they do not pray for the resurrection either of the
soul or of the body, but only for the deliverance of
souls.   In this they presuppose the immortality of
the soul.   For if they had believed that the soul was
dead with the body they would not have striven to
further their release.   And because among the Jews

the belief in the immortality of the soul and the belief in the resurrection of bodies were so connected together that he who denied one denied the other;—to show that Judas Machabæus believed the immortality of the soul, it is said that he believed the resurrection of bodies. And in the same way the Apostle proves the resurrection of bodies by the immortality of the soul, although it might be that the soul was immortal without the resurrection of bodies. The following occurs in the 1st of Corinthians, chapter xv. : *What doth it profit me if the dead rise not again ? Let us eat and drink, for to-morrow we shall die.* Now it would not at all follow that we might thus let ourselves run riot, even if there was no resurrection : for the soul, which would remain in existence, would suffer the penalty due to sins, and would receive the guerdon of her virtues. S. Paul then in this place takes the resurrection of the dead as equivalent to the immortality of the soul. There is therefore no ground for refusing the testimony of the Machabees in proof of a just belief. But if, in the very last resort, we would take it as the testimony of a simple but great historian—which cannot be refused us—we must at least confess that the ancient synagogue believed in Purgatory, since all that army was so prompt to pray for the departed.

And truly we have marks of this devotion in other Scriptures which ought to make easier to us the reception of the passage which we have just adduced. In Tobias, chap. iv. : *Lay out thy bread and thy wine on the burial of a just man ; and do not eat or drink thereof with the wicked.* Certainly this wine and bread was not placed on the tomb save for the poor, in order that the soul of the deceased might be helped thereby, as the interpreters say commonly on this passage. It will perhaps be said that this Book is apocryphal, but all antiquity has always held it in credit. And indeed the custom of putting meat for the poor on sepulchres is very ancient even in the Catholic Church. For S. Chrysostom, who lived more than twelve hundred years ago, in the 32d Homily on the Book of S. Matthew, speaks of it thus: "Why on your friends' death do you call together the poor? Why for them do you beseech the priests to pray?" And what are we to think of the fasts and austerities which the ancients practised after the death of their friends? The men of Jabes Galaad, after the death of Saul, fasted seven days over him. David and his men did the same, over the same Saul, and Jonathan, and those who followed him, as we see in this [last] chapter of 1st Kings, and in the 1st chapter of 2d Kings. One cannot think that it was for any other purpose than to help the souls of the departed; —for to what else can one refer the fast of seven days? So David, who, in the 2d Kings, chapter xii., fasted and prayed for his sick son, after his death ceased to fast, showing that when he fasted it was to obtain help for the sick child, which, when it died, dying young and innocent, had no need of help;— wherefore David ceased fasting. Bede, more than 700 years ago, interprets thus the end of the 1st Book of Kings.* So that in the ancient Church, the custom already was to help by prayer and holy deeds the souls of the departed:—which clearly implies a faith in Purgatory.

* In Sam. L. iv. c. 10.

And of this custom S. Paul speaks quite clearly in the 1st of Corinthians, chap xv., appealing to it as praiseworthy and right. *What shall they do who are baptized for the dead, if the dead rise not again at all ? Why then are they baptized for them ?* This passage properly uuderstood evidently shows that it was the custom of the primitive Church to watch, pray, fast, for the souls of the departed. For, firstly, in the Scriptures to be baptized as often taken for afflictions and penances ; as in S. Luke, chap xii., where Our Lord speaking of his Passion says : *I have a baptism wherewith I am to be baptized, and how am I straitened until it be accomplished !*—and in S. Mark, chap x., he says : *Can you drink of the chalice that I drink of ; or be baptized with the baptism wherewith I am baptized ?*—in which places Our Lord calls pains and afflictions baptism. This then is the sense of that Scripture : if the dead rise not again, what is the use of mortifying and afflicting oneself, of praying and fasting for the dead ? And indeed this sentence of S. Paul resembles that of Machabees quoted above : *It is superfluous and vain to pray for the dead if the dead rise not again.* They may twist and transform this text with as many interpretations as they like, and there will be none to properly fit into the Holy Letter except this. But [secondly] it must not be said that the baptism of which S. Paul speaks is only a baptism of grief and tears, and not of fasts, prayers, and other works. For thus understood his conclusion would be very false. The conclusion he means to draw is that if the dead rise not again, and if the soul is mortal, in vain do we afflict ourselves for the dead. But, I pray you, should we not have more occasion to

afflict ourselves by sadness for the death of friends if
they rise no more—losing all hope of ever seeing them
again—than if they do rise? He refers then to the
voluntary afflictions which they undertook to impetrate
the repose of the departed, which, questionless, would
be undergone in vain if souls were mortal and the dead
rose not again. Wherein we must keep in mind what
was said above, that the article of the resurrection of
the dead and that of the immortality of the soul were
so joined together in the belief of the Jews that he
who acknowledged the one acknowledged the other,
and he who denied the one denied the other. It
appears then by these words of S. Paul that prayer,
fasting, and other holy afflictions were practised for
the departed. Now it was not for those in Paradise,
who had no need of it, nor for those in hell, who
could get no benefit from it; it was, then, for those
in Purgatory. Thus did S. Ephrem expound it twelve
hundred years ago, and so did the Fathers who disputed
against the Petrobusians.

The same can one deduce from the words of the
Good Thief, in S. Luke, chap. xxiii., when, addressing
Our Lord, he said : *Remember me when thou comest into
thy kingdom.* For why should he have recommended
himself, he who was about to die, unless he had
believed that souls after death could be succoured
and helped? S. Augustine (Contra Jul., B. vi.) proves
[from] this passage that sins are pardoned in the
other world.

III.

CHAPTER VI.

OF CERTAIN OTHER PLACES OF SCRIPTURE BY WHICH
WE PROVE THAT SOME SINS CAN BE PARDONED
IN THE OTHER WORLD.

IF there are some sins that can be pardoned in the
other world it is neither in hell nor in heaven, therefore it is in Purgatory. Now, that there are sins which
are pardoned in the other world we prove, firstly, by
the passage of S. Matthew in chap. xii., where Our
Lord says that *there is a sin which cannot be forgiven
either in this world or in the next*: therefore there are
sins which can be forgiven in the other world. For
if there were no sins which could be forgiven in the
other world, it was not now necessary to attribute
this property of not being able to be forgiven in the
next world to one sort of sins, but it sufficed to say it
could not be forgiven in this world. When Our
Lord had said to Pilate: *My kingdom is not of this
world,* in S. John, chap. xviii., Pilate drew this conclusion: *Art thou a king, then?* Which conclusion was
approved by Our Lord, who assented thereto. So
when he said that there is one sin which cannot be
forgiven in the other world, it follows very properly
that there are others which can. They try to say
that these words, *neither in this world nor in the world
to come,* only signify, for ever, or, never; as S. Mark
says in chap. iii., *shall never have forgiveness.* That
is quite true; but our reason loses none of its force
on that account. For either S. Matthew has properly
expressed Our Lord's meaning or he has not: one

would not dare to say he has not, and if he has, it still follows that there are sins which can be forgiven in the other world, since Our Lord has said that there is one which cannot be forgiven in the other world. And please tell me—if S. Peter had said in S. John, chap. xiii.: *Thou shalt never wash my feet either in this world or in the other,*—would he not have spoken [properly], since in the other world they might be washed?—and indeed he does say: *thou shalt not wash my feet for ever.* We must not believe then that S. Matthew would have expressed the intention of Our Lord by these words, *neither in this world nor in the next,* if in the next there cannot be remission. We should laugh at a man who said: I will not marry either in this world or in the next, as if he supposed that in the next one could marry. He then who says a sin cannot be forgiven either in this world or in the next, implies that there may be remission of some sins in this world and also in the other. I am well aware that our adversaries try by various interpretations to parry this blow, but it is so well struck that they cannot escape from it, unless by starting a new doctrine. And in good truth it is far better, with the ancient Fathers, to understand properly and with all possible reverence the words of Our Lord, than, in order to found a new doctrine, to make them confused and ill-chosen. S. Augustine (*de Civ. Dei,* lib. xxi., c. 24), S. Gregory (Hom. 7, *de Dec.,* c. 39), Bede (in Marc. iii.), S. Bernard (Hom. 66 in Cant.), and those who have written against the Petrobusians, have used this passage in our sense, with such assurance that S. Bernard to declare this truth brings forward nothing more, so much account does he make of this.

In S. Matthew (v.), and in S. Luke (xii.): *Make an agreement with thy adversary quickly, while thou art in the way with him ; lest perhaps the adversary deliver thee to the judge, and the judge deliver thee to the officer, and thou be cast into prison. Amen, I say to thee, thou shalt not go out from thence till thou pay the last farthing.* Origen, S. Cyprian, S. Hilary, S. Ambrose, S. Jerome, and S. Augustine say that the way which is meant in the *whilst thou art in the way* is no other than the passage of the present life : the *adversary* will be our own conscience, which ever fights against us and for us, that is, it ever resists our bad inclinations and our old Adam for our salvation, as S. Ambrose expounds, [and] Bede, S. Augustine, S. Gregory, and S. Bernard. Lastly, the judge is without doubt Our Lord in S. John (v.): *The Father has given all judgment to the Son.* The *prison*, again, is hell or the place of punishment in the other world, in which, as in a large jail, there are many buildings ; one for those who are damned, which is as it were for criminals, the other for those in Purgatory, which is as it were for debt. The *farthing*, of which it is said *thou shalt not go out from thence till thou pay the last farthing*, are little sins and infirmities, as the farthing is the smallest money one can owe. Now let us consider a little where this repayment of which Our Lord speaks —*till thou pay the last farthing*—is to be made. And (1.) we find from most ancient Fathers that it is in Purgatory : Tertullian (Lib. *de Animâ* c. x.), Cyprian (Epist., lib. iv. 2), Origen (Hom. 35 on this place of Luke), with Emissenus (Hom. 3 *de Epiph.*), S. Ambrose (in Luc. xii.), S. Jerome (in Matt. v.), S. Bernard (*serm. de obitu Huberti*). (2.) When it is

said *till thou pay the last farthing*, is it not implied
that one can pay it, and that one can so diminish
the debt that there only remains at length its last
farthing ?   But just as when it is said in the Psalm
(cix.) : *Sit at my right hand until I make thy enemies,*
&c., it properly follows that at length he will make
his enemies his footstool ; so when he says *thou shalt
not go out till thou pay*, he shows that at length he
will pay or will be able to pay.   (3.) Who sees not
that in S. Luke the comparison is drawn, not from a
murderer or some criminal, who can have no hope of
escape, but from a debtor who is thrown into prison
till payment, and when this is made is at once let
out ?   This then is the meaning of Our Lord, that
whilst we are in this world we should try by penitence
and its fruits to pay, according to the power which we
have by the blood of the Redeemer, the penalty to
which our sins have subjected us ; since if we wait
till death we shall not have such good terms in
Purgatory, when we shall be treated with severity of
justice.

All this seems to have been also said by Our Lord
in the 5th of S. Matthew, where he says : *He who is
angry with his brother shall be guilty of the judgment ;
and he who shall say to his brother, Raca, shall be guilty
of the council ; but he who shall say, thou fool, shall be
guilty of hell fire :* now it is only the third sort of
offence which is punished with hell ; therefore in the
judgment of God after this life there are other pains
which are not eternal or infernal,—these are the
pains of Purgatory.   One may say that the pains
will be suffered in this world ; but S. Augustine and
the other Fathers understand them for the other

world.   And again may it not be that a man should
die on the first or second offence which is spoken of
here ?   And when will such a one pay the penalty
due to his offence ?   Or if you will have that he pays
them not, what place will you give him for his retreat
after this world ?   You will not assign him hell,
unless you would add to the sentence of Our Lord,
who does not assign hell as a penalty save to those
who shall have committed the third offence.   Lodge
him in Paradise you must not, because the nature of
that heavenly place rejects all sorts of imperfections.
Allege not here the mercy of the Judge, because he
declares in this place that he intends also to use
justice.   Do then as the ancient Fathers did, and say
that there is a place where they will be purified, and
then they will go to heaven above.

In S. Luke, in the 16th chapter, it is written :
*Make unto yourselves friends of the mammon of iniquity,
that when you shall fail they may receive you into
eternal tabernacles.*   To *fail*,—what is it but to die ?
—and the *friends*,—who are they but the Saints ?
The interpreters all understand it so ; whence two
things follow,—that the Saints can help men departed,
and that the departed can be helped by the Saints.
For in what other way can one understand these
words : *make to yourselves friends who may receive you ?*
They cannot be understood of alms, for many times
the alms is good and holy and yet acquires us not
friends who can receive us into eternal tabernacles,
as when it is given to bad people with a holy and
right intention.   Thus is this passage expounded by
S. Ambrose, and by S. Augustine (*de Civ. Dei* xii. 27).
But the parable Our Lord is using is too clear to

allow us any doubt of this interpretation; for the similitude is taken from a steward who, being dismissed from his office and reduced to poverty, begged help from his friends, and Our Lord likens the dismissal unto death, and the help begged from friends unto the help one receives after death from those to whom one has given alms. This help cannot be received by those who are in Paradise or in hell, it is then by those who are in Purgatory.

CHAPTER VII.

OF SOME OTHER PLACES FROM WHICH BY VARIOUS CON-
SEQUENCES IS DEDUCED THE TRUTH OF PURGATORY.

S. PAUL to the Philippians (ii.) says these words : *That in the name of Jesus every knee may bow, of things in heaven, of things on earth, and of things under the earth* (*infernorum*). In heaven we find the Saints on their knees, bending them at the name of the Redeemer. On earth we find many such in the militant Church, but in hell where shall we find any of them ? David despairs of finding any when he says: *Who shall confess to thee in hell?* (Ps. vi.) So Ezechias in Isaias (xxxviii.): *For neither shall hell confess to thee.* To which that also ought to be referred which David sings elsewhere (xlix. 16): *But to the sinner God hath said: Why dost thou declare my justices and take my covenant in thy mouth?* For if God will receive no praise from the obstinate sinner, how should he permit

the wretched damned to undertake this holy office.
S. Augustine makes great account of this place for this
purpose in the 12th book on Genesis (xxxiii.).   There
is a similar passage in the Apocalypse (v.): *Who is
worthy to open the book, and to loose the seven seals thereof?
And no man was able neither in heaven, nor in earth,
nor under the earth.*   And further down in the same
chapter : *And every creature which is in heaven, and on
the earth, and under the earth . . . I heard all saying :
To him that sitteth upon the throne and to the Lamb,
benediction and honour and glory and power for ever and
ever.   And the four living creatures said Amen.*   Does
he not hereby uphold a Church, in which God is praised
under the earth ?   And what else can it be but that
of Purgatory ?

CHAPTER VIII.

OF THE COUNCILS WHICH HAVE RECEIVED PURGATORY AS AN ARTICLE OF FAITH.

AERIUS, as I have said above, was the first to teach
against Catholics that the prayers they offered for the
dead were superstitious.   He still has followers in our
age in this point.   Our Lord in his gospel (Matt. xviii.)
furnishes us our rule of action on such occasions.   *If
thy brother shall offend thee . . . tell the Church.   And if
he will not hear the Church let him be to thee as the heathen
and the publican.*   Let us hear then what the Church
says on this matter, in Africa, at the 3d Council of
Carthage (c. 29), and at the 4th (c. 79); in Spain, at

the Council of Braga (cc. 34, 39); in France, at the
Council of Chalons (de cons. d. 2, Can. *visum est*), and
at the 2d Council of Orleans (c. 14); in Germany,
at the Council of Worms (c. 20); in Italy, at the 6th
Council under Symmachus; in Greece, as may be seen
in their synods, collected by Martin of Braga (c. 69).
And by all these Councils you will see that the Church
approves of prayer for the departed, and consequently
of Purgatory.   Afterwards, what she had defined by
parts she defined in her general body at the Council
of Lateran under Innocent III. (c. 66), at the Council
of Florence in which all nations assisted (Sess. *ult.*),
and lastly at the Council of Trent (Sess. 25).

But what more holy answer from the Church would
one have than that which is contained in all her
Masses?   Examine the Liturgies of S. James, S. Basil,
S. Chrysostom, S. Ambrose, which all the Oriental
Christians still use; you will there see the commemoration of the dead, almost as it is seen in ours.   If
Peter Martyr, one of the learned men belonging to
the adverse party, confesses, on the 3d chapter of the
1st of Corinthians, that the whole Church has followed
this opinion, I have no need to dwell on this proof.
He says it has erred and failed,—ah! who would
believe that!   Who art thou that judgest the Church
of God?   *If any one hear not the Church, let him be
to thee as the heathen and the publican.   The Church is
the pillar and ground of truth, and the gates of hell shall
not prevail against it.   If the salt lose its savour wherewith shall it be salted;* if the Church err by whom shall
she be set right?   If the Church, the faithful guardian
of truth, lose the truth, by whom shall the truth be
found?   If Christ cast off the Church, whom will he

receive,—he who admits no one but through the Church? And if the Church can err, can you not also, O Peter Martyr, fall into error?—without doubt: I will then rather believe that you have erred than the Church.

CHAPTER IX.

OF THE TESTIMONY OF THE ANCIENT FATHERS TO THE TRUTH OF PURGATORY.

IT is a beautiful thing, and one full of all consolation, to see the perfect correspondence which the present Church has with the ancient, particularly in belief. Let us mention what makes to our purpose concerning Purgatory. All the ancient Fathers have believed in it, and have testified that it was of Apostolic faith. Here are the authors we have for it. Among the disciples of the Apostles, S. Clement and S. Denis. Afterwards, S. Athanasius, S. Basil, S. Gregory Nazianzen, Ephrem, Cyril, Epiphanius, Chrysostom, Gregory Nyssen, Tertullian, Cyprian, Ambrose, Jerome, Augustine, Origen, Boethius, Hilary,—that is, all antiquity as far back as 1200 years ago, which was the time before which these Fathers lived. It would have been easy for me to bring forward their testimonies, which are accurately collected in the books of our Catholics;—of Canisius, in his Catechism, of Sanders *On the Visible Monarchy*, of Genebrard in his Chronology, of Bellarmine in his Controversy on Purgatory, of Stapleton in his Promptuary. But particularly let those who would see at

length and faithfully quoted the passages of the ancient
Fathers, take up the work of Canisius, revised by
Buzæus. Certainly, however, Calvin spares us this
trouble, in Book iii. of his Institutions (c. 5, § 10),
where he thus speaks: " More than 1300 years ago
it was received that prayers should be offered for the
dead ; " and afterwards he adds : " But all, I confess,
were dragged into error." We need not then seek out
the names and the localities of the ancient Fathers
to prove Purgatory, since in reckoning their value
Calvin puts them at zero. What likelihood that one
single Calvin should be infallible and that all antiquity
should have gone wrong ! It is said that the ancient
Fathers have believed in Purgatory to accommodate
themselves to the vulgar. A fine excuse ! was it not
for the Fathers to correct the people's error if they
saw them erring, not to keep it up and give in to it ?
This excuse then is but to accuse the Ancients. But
how shall we say the Fathers have not honestly believed in Purgatory, since Aerius, as I have said
before, was held to be a heretic because he denied it ?
It is a shame to see the audacity with which Calvin
treats S. Augustine, because he prayed and got prayers
for his mother S. Monica ; and the only pretext he
brings forward is that S. Augustine, in Book 21 of
the *de Civitate,* seems to doubt about the fire of Purgatory. But this is nothing to the purpose ; for it is
true that S. Augustine says one may doubt of the fire
and of the nature thereof, but not of Purgatory. Now
whether the purgation is made by fire or otherwise,
whether or no the fire have the same qualities as that
of hell, still there ceases not to be a purgation and
a Purgatory. He puts not then Purgatory in question

but the quality of it; as will never be denied by those who will look how he speaks of it in chapters 16 and 24 of the same Book of the *de Civitate*, and in the work *De Curâ Pro Mortius Agendâ*, and a thousand other places. See then how we are in the track of the holy and ancient Fathers, as to this article of Purgatory.

CHAPTER X.

OF TWO PRINCIPAL REASONS, AND OF THE TESTIMONY OF OUTSIDERS IN FAVOUR OF PURGATORY.

HERE are two invincible proofs of Purgatory. The first:—there are sins which are light in comparison with others, and which do not make man guilty of hell. If then a man die in them, what will become of him? Paradise receives nothing defiled (Apoc. xxi.): hell is too extreme a penalty, it is not deserved by his sin: it must then be owned that he will stay in a Purgatory, where he will be duly purified, and afterwards go to heaven. Now that there are sins which do not make man deserving of hell, Our Saviour says in Matthew (v.): *Whosoever is angry with his brother shall be guilty of the judgment; and whosoever shall say to his brother, Raca, shall be guilty of the council; and whosoever shall say, thou fool, shall be guilty of hell fire (gehennœ ignis).* What, I pray you, is it to be guilty of the *gehenna* of fire but to be guilty of hell? Now this penalty is deserved by those only who call their brother, *thou fool.* Those who get angry, and those who express their anger in words not injurious and defamatory, are not in the same rank; but one deserves judgment, that is, that his anger should be brought under judgment, like the idle word (Matt. xii.) of which Our Lord says man *shall render an account in the day of judgment,*— account must be rendered of it: the second deserves the council, that is, deserves to be deliberated about whether he shall be condemned or not (for Our Lord accommodates himself to men's way of speaking): the third alone is the one who, without question, infallibly shall be condemned. Therefore the first and second kinds of sin do not make man deserving of eternal death, but of a temporal correction; and therefore if a man die with these, by accident or otherwise, he must undergo the judgment of a temporal punishment, and when his soul is purged thereby he will go to heaven, to be with the blessed. Of these sins the Wise Man speaks (Prov. xxiv.): *The just shall fall seven times a day:* for the just cannot sin, so long as he is just, with a sin which deserves damnation; it means then that he falls into sins to which damnation is not due, which Catholics call venial, and these can be purged away in the other world in Purgatory.

The second reason is, that after the pardon of sin there remains part of the penalty due to it. As for example, in the 2d of Kings, chap. xii., the sin is forgiven to David, the Prophet saying to him: *The Lord hath also taken away thy sin: thou shalt not die. Nevertheless, because thou hast given occasion to the enemies of the Lord to blaspheme for this thing, thy child shall die the death.*

APPENDIX.

———•———

Original text of hitherto unpublished fragment on the authority of the Pope, from the Annecy autograph, Englished on pp. 299–311 of this work.

[Combien on doit faire d'état de l'autorité du Pape.]

· · · · · ·

Or soit que ceste doctrine et verité ne fut autre que ces deux mots écrits au rational, comme semble croire St. Augustin, et Hugues de St. Victor l'assure, ou que ce fut le nom de Dieu, comme veut Rab. Salomon au récit Vatable et Augustin évêque d'Eugubhe, ou que ce fussent les seules pierres du rational par les quelles Dieu Tout Puissant révélait ses volontés au prêtre comme veut ce docte homme Francois Ribera : La raison pour la quelle le grand prêtre avait au rational sur sa poitrine la doctrine et la verité, était sans doute parce que *Indicabat iudicii veritatem*, mesme que par le Urim et Thummim, les prêtres étaient instruits au bon plaisir de Dieu et leurs entendements éclairés et perfectionnés par la revelation divine, comme le bon de Lyra l'a entendu, et Ribera l'a assez suffisamment prouvé a mon avis.   Donc quand David voulait savoir s'il devait poursuivre les Amalécites il dit au prestre Abiathar : *Applica ad me Ephod* ou le super huméraire, ce qui fut sans doute pour reconnaître la volonté de Dieu, au rational qui y était joint comme va déduisant doctement ce docteur Ribera.   Je vous prie

L. 3 de temph. c. XII.

Deut. 17, v. 9,

si en l'ombre il y avait des illuminations de doctrine et
des perfections de verité en la poitrine du prêtre pour en
repaître et raffermir le peuple, qu'est ce que nostre grand
prêtre n'aura pas, de nous, dis-je, qui sommes au jour et
au soleil levé. Le grand prêtre ancien n'était que vicaire
et lieutenant de N. Sgr. non plus que le notre, mays il
semble qu'il présidat a la nuit par ses illuminations et le
notre préside au jour par ses instructions, ministerielle-
ment tous deux et par la lumière du soleil de justice, le
quel bien qu'il soit levé est néammoins voilé a nos yeux
par notre propre mortalité, car le voir face à face ordinairement n'appartient qu'à ceux qui sont délivrés du corps
qui se corrompt. Ainsi a cru toute l'Eglise ancienne la
quelle en ses difficultés a toujours eu recours au rational
du siège de Rome pour y voir la doctrine et verité. C'est

St. Bernard
in epistola
ad canoni-
cos Lug-
dunenses
soumet à
l'Eglise ro-
maine tous
ses écrits.
pour ce sujet que St. Bernard a appellé le pape *Dignitate
Aaron* et St. Hierosme le St. Siége *tutissimum coitionis
catholicæ portum*, et heritier des Apostres car il porte le
rational pour en éclairer tout le Christianisme, comme les
Apôtres et Aaron, de doctrine et verité. C'est à ce propos
que St. Hierosme dit au pape Damase *qui tecum non*

Epistola ad
Dam.
*colligit spargit, hoc est qui Christi non est anti-Christi
est* et St. Bernard dit qu'il faut rapporter les scandales
qui se font, principalement en la foy, au siège de Rôme
*dignum namque arbitror ibi potissimum resarcire dam-
num fidei ubi non possit fides sentire defectum, cui
enim alteri sedi dictum est aliquando: Ego pro te rogavi*

Epistola
190.
ut non deficiat fides tua. St. Cyprien: *Navigare audent
ad Cathedram Petri atque ad ecclesiam principalem nec
cogitare eos esse romanos ad quos perfidia habere non
possit accessus.* Ne voyez vous pas qu'il parle des Romains
à cause de la chaire de St. Pierre et dit que l'erreur ne
peut rien. Les Pères du concile milévitain avec le bien-

Epistola 92.
heureux St. Augustin demandent secours et implorent
l'autorité du siège de Rome contre l'hérésie pelagienne
écrivant au pape Innocent en cette sorte: *Magnis peri-*

*culis infirmorum membrorum Christi pastoralem diligen-
tiam quaesumus adhibere digneris ; nova quippe haeresis
et nimium perniciosa tempestas surgere inimicorum gratiae
Christi coepit.* Que si vous voulez savoir pourquoi ils
s'adressent à lui : Que disent-ils? *Te Dominus gregi suo
praecipuo munere in Sede Apostolica collocavit.* Voilà
ce que croyait ce saint concile avec son grand St. Augustin
au quel St. Innocent rendant en une épître qui suit la
précédente parmi celles de St. Augustin *Diligenter et
congrue,* disent-ils, *apostolico consulistis honoris arcana.
Inquam illius, quem praeter illa quae sunt extrinsecus
solicitudo manet omnium Ecclesiarum super anxiis rebus
quae sit tenenda sententia. Antiquae scilicet regulae
formam scecuti quam toto semper ab orbe mecum nostis
esse servatam. Verum haec missa facio neque enim hoc
vestram credo latere prudentiam ; quid enim actione
firmastis nisi scientes quod per omnes provincias de apostolico fonte petentibus responsa semper emanent? Praeser-
tim quoties fidei ratio ventilatur, arbitror omnes fratres et
coepiscopos nostros nonnisi ad Petrum, id est sui nominis
et honoris auctorem referre debere, velut nunc retulit
vestra dilectio, quod per totum mundum possit omnibus
ecclesiis in commune prodesse.* Voyez vous l'honneur et
le crédit au quel était le siège apostolique vers les anciens
les plus doctes et saints, voire même vers les conciles
entiers. On y allait comme au vrai Ephod et rational de
la nouvelle loi. Ainsy y alla saint Hierosme du temps
de Damase au quel après avoir dit que l'Orient rompait et
mettait en pièce la roubbe entière et tissue par dessus de
N. S. et que les renardeaux gataient la vigne du Maître
ut inter lacus contritos, dict-il, *qui aquam non habent,
difficile, ubi fons signatus et hortus ille conclusus sit, possim
illigi. Ideo mihi Cathedram Petri et fidem apostolico ore
laudatam censui consulendam.* Je n'aurai jamais fait si
je voulais produire les belles sentences que les anciens
ont dites sur ce fait. Qui voudra les lise fidèlement

III.

cottées au grand catechisme de Pierre Canisius où elles

Epistola
165, p. 69
advers. Lu-
ciferianos.
ont été étendues au long par Busem. St. Cyprien rap-
porte toutes les hérésies et schismes au mépris qu'on fait
de ce chef ministérial. Aussi fait bien St. Hierosme;

Oratione
de obitu
fratris.
Satira de
sacram.
l. 3, c. 1.
St. Ambroise tient pour une même chose *Communicare
et convenire cum episcopis catholicis est convenire cum
Ecclesia Romana.* Il proteste de suivre en tout et par
tout la forme de l'Eglise Romaine. St. Irénée veut que
chacun vienne joindre à ce Saint Siège *Propter potentiorem
principalitatem.* Les Eusebiens y portent les accusations
contre St. Athanase. St. Athanase qui était en Alex-
andrie siège principal et patriarchal vint répondre a Rome
y éstant appelé et cité, les adversaires n'y voulurent pas
comparoistre sachant dict Theodoret *mendacia sua mani-
festo fore detecta.* Les Eusebiens confessent l'authorité
du siège de Rome quand ils y appellent St. Athanase et
St. Athanase quand ils s'y presente. Mais surtout les
Eusebiens hérétiques arriens confessent assez combien
son jugement est infaillible quand ils n'y osent comparoistre de peur d'y être condamnés. Mais qui ne scait
que tous les anciens hérétiques taschoyent à se faire

l. q. p. xca.
avouer par le pape, tesmoins les Montanistes on Cata-
phryges qui déçurent tellement le pape Zephirin, s'il faut
croire a Tertullien (non plus celui d'autrefois mais devenu
hérétique en son faict propre) qu'il lascha des traits de
reunion en leur faveur, les quels néammoins il révoca
promptement par l'avis de Praxéas. Enfin qui méprisera
l'authorité du pape remettra sur les pélagiens priscilliens
et autres qui n'ont esté condamnés que par les conciles
provinciaux avec l'autorité du St. Siège de Rome. Que
si je voulais m'amuser à vous montrer combien Luther en
faysait état au commencement de son hérésie je vous
ferois esbahis d'une si grande mutation de ce viel grand-
père. Voyez-le chez Cocleus, *Prostratum me pedibus tuae
Beatitudinis offero cum omnibus quae sunt et habeo, vivi-
fica, occide, voca, revoca, approba, reproba, voces Christi*

in te praesidentes et loquentes agnoscam. Ce sont ses
paroles en l'espitre dédicatoire, qu'il escrit au Pape Léon
X sur certaines siennes resolutions l'an 1518. Mays je
ne puis laisser en arrière ce que ce grand archiministre
escrivit l'an 1519 en certaines autres resolutions d'autres
propositions, car en la 13me non seulement il reconnait
l'authorité du St. Siège romain mays la prouve par six
raisons qu'il tient pour démonstrations. Je le mettrai en
sommaire. La 1re : Le pape ne pourrait être venu à ce
grade et a ceste monarchie sans le vouloir de Dieu, mays
le vouloir de Dieu est toujours vénérable donc il ne faut
pas contrevenir à la primauté du pape. La 2me : Il faut
plutôt céder a son adversaire que de rompre l'union de
charité, donques il vaut mieux obéir au pape que de se
séparer de l'Eglise. La 3me : Parce qu'il ne faut résister
à Dieu qui nous veut presser et charger de plusieurs
princes selon le dire de Salomon en ses proverbes. La
4me : Il n'y a point de puissance qui ne soit de Dieu,
donques celle du pape qui est tant établie est de Dieu.
La 5me : N'est que la même. La 6me : Parce que tous les
fidèles le croyent ainsi entre les quels il est impossible
que N. S. ne soit, or il faut arreter avec N. S. et les
chrétiens en tout et partout ; il dit par après que ces
raisons sont insolubles ; et que toute l'escriture y vient
battre. Que vous semble de Luther est-il pas catholique ?
Et neammoins c'était au commencement de sa reformation.

Calvin vient à ce point quoyqu'il l'aille embrouillant la
matière tant qu'il peut, car parlant du siège de Rome il
confesse que les anciens l'ont honoré et révéré qu'il a
été le refuge des evesques et plus constant en la foy que
les autres sièges ce qu'il attribue à faute de vivacité
d'entendement.

14. c. 8 n.
103.

Combien les Ministres ont violé cette Autorité.

En l'ancienne loy le grand prêtre ne portait pas le rational si non quand il estoit revestu des habits pontificaux et qu'il entroit devant le Seigneur. Ainsi ne disons nous pas que le pape en ses opinions particulières ne puisse errer comme fit Jean XXII, ou être du tout hérétique comme peut être fut Honorius. Or quand il est hérétique exprès *ipso facto* il tombe de son grade hors de l'Eglise et l'Eglise le doit ou priver comme disent quelques uns, ou le declarer privé de son siège apostolique et dire comme fit St. Pierre : *Episcopatum eius accipiat alter.* Quand il erre en sa particulière opinion il le faut enseigner, adviser, convaincre comme on fit à Jean XXII le quel tant s'en faut qu'il mourut opiniatre ou que pendant sa vie il determina aucune chose touchant son opinion, que pendant qu'il faysoit l'inquisition requise pour determiner en matière de foy, il mourut, au recit de son successeur en l'extravagante qui se commence *Benedictus Deus.* Mais quand il est revestu des habits pontificaux, je veux dire, quand il enseigne toute l'Eglise comme pasteur ès choses de la foy et des moeurs générales, alhors il n'y a que doctrine et vérité. Et de vrai tout ce que dict un roy n'est pas loy ni édict, mais seulement ce que le roy dict comme roy et déterminant juridiquement. Ainsy tout ce que dict le pape n'est pas droit canon ni loy, il faut qu'il veuille determiner et donner loy aux brebis et qu'il y garde l'ordre et forme requise. Ainsy disons nous qu'il faut avoir recours a luy non comme à un docte homme, car en cela il est ordinairement devancé par plusieurs autres, mays comme au chef et pasteur général de l'Eglise et comme tel honorer, suivre et embrasser fermement sa doctrine, car alors il porte en sa poitrine *le Urim et Thummim* la doctrine et vérité. Et ne faut pas non plus penser qu'en tout et partout son

Act. I.

jugement soit infaillible. Mais lhors seulement qu'il
porte sentence en matière de foy en des actions nécéssaires
à toute l'Eglise, car ès cas particuliers qui dependent du
faict humain, il y peut errer sans doute, quoyque nous
autres ne devions le controller en cest endroit qu'avec
toute révérence submission et discrétion. Les theologiens
ont dit tout en mot qu'il peut errer *in quaestionibus facti
non iuris.* Qu'il peut errer *extra cathedram* hors la
chaire de St. Pierre c'est-à-dire comme homme particulier
par escrits et mauvais exemples.

Mais non pas quand il est *in cathedra*, c'est-a-dire
quand il veut faire une instruction et décret pour enseigner
toute l'Eglise, quand il veut confirmer ses frères comme
suprème pasteur et les veut conduyre ès paturages de la
foy. Car alors ce n'est pas tant l'homme qui détermine,
resoult et définit que c'est le bénit St. Esprit, par l'homme,
lequel, selon la promesse faite par N. S. à ses apôtres
enseigne toute la vérité à l'Eglise et comme dit le Grec
et semble que l'Eglise l'entende en une collecte de Pente-
coste, conduit et meyne son Eglise en toute vérité *cum
autem venerit ille Spiritus veritatis docebit vos omnem
veritatem* ou *deducet vos in omnem veritatem.* Et comment est ce que le St. Esprit conduit l'Eglise si non par
le ministère et office de predicateurs et pasteurs. Mais
si les pasteurs ont des pasteurs encore ils les doivent
suivre, ainsy tous doivent suivre celui qui est le suprème
pasteur par le ministère duquel notre Dieu veut conduire
non les agneaux seulement et brebiettes, mays les brebis
et mères des agneaux c'est-a-dire non les peuples seulement mays les autres pasteurs encore, celui succède a St.
Pierre qui eut cette charge *Pasce oves meas.* C'est ainsi
que Dieu conduit son Eglise ès paturages de sa sainte
parole, et en l'exposition d'icelle, qui cherche la vérité
sous autre conduite la perd. Le St. Esprit est conducteur
de l'Eglise il la conduit par son pasteur; qui donques ne
suit le pasteur ne suit pas le St. Esprit.

Mais le grand cardinal de Tolède remarque tres-bien à propos sur ce lieu qu'il n'est pas dit *portabit Ecclesiam in omnem veritatem*, mais *deducet* pour montrer, que quoy que le St. Esprit esclaire l'Eglise si veut-il qu'elle use de la diligence requise à tenir le bon chemin comme firent les Apostres qui, ayant à répondre sur une question importante débattirent de part et d'autre, conférant les escritures ensemble ce qu'ayant faict diligemment ils conclurent par le *Visum est Spiritui Sancto et nobis* c'est-à-dire le St. Esprit nous a esclairé et nous avons marché, il nous a guidé, nous l'avons suivi, jusques a ceste vérité. Il faut employer les moyens ordinaires pour la recherche de la vérité et néammoins reconnoistre la trenne et l'abord en icelle de l'assistance du St. Esprit. Ainsi est conduit le troupeau chretien, par le St. Esprit, mais sous la charge et conduite de son Pasteur, le quel néammoins ne court pas à la volée, mays selon la necessité convoque les autres pasteurs, ou en partie, ou généralement, regarde soigneusement la piste des devanciers, considère le *Urim et Thummim* de la parole de Dieu, entre devant son Dieu par ses prières et invocations et s'estant ainsy diligemment enquesté du vrai chemin se met en campaigne hardiment et faict voile de bon cœur. Heureux qui le suit et se range à la discipline de sa houlette. Heureux qui s'embarque en son navire car il repaistra de vérité et naviguera au port de la sainte doctrine.

Ainsi ne faict-il jamais commandement général à toute l'Eglise es choses nécessaires, qu'avec l'assistance du St. Esprit le quel ne manquant mesme pas aux especes des affaires et choses nécessaires parce qu'il les a établies, ne manquera pas aussi au christianisme en ce qui lui est necessaire pour sa vie et perfection. Et comment serait l'Eglise une et sainte telle que les escritures et symboles la descrivent, car si elle suivait un pasteur et que le pasteur erra, comme serait elle sainte? si elle ne le suivoit pas comme serait elle une? Et quelle débauche verroit-on parmi le christianisme pendant que les uns trouveront et jugeront une loy mauvaise les autres bonne, et que les brebis au lieu de paistre et s'engraisser es pasturages de l'Escriture et sainte parole s'amuseroyent à controller les jugements du superieur?

Reste donq que selon la divine Providence nous tenions pour fermé ce que St. Pierre fermera avec ses clefs et pour ouvert ce qu'il ouvrira étant assis en la chaire instruisant toute l'Eglise.

Que si les ministres eussent tansé les vices, remonstré l'inutilité de quelques decrets et censures, emprunté quelques saints advis des livres moraux de St. Gregoire et de ceux de St. Bernard, *de consideratione,* produit quelque bon moyen de lever les abus qui sont survenus en le pratique bénéficiaire par la malice du temps et des hommes et se fussent adressés a Sa Sainteté avec humilité et reconnaissance, tous les bons les eussent honorés et caressé leurs desseins. Les bons cardinaux Contareno Theatmo * et Sadolet et Polus avec ces autres grands personnages qui présentèrent le conseil de réformer les abus en ceste sorte, en ont merité une immortelle récommandation de la postérité. Mays remplir l'air et la terre d'injures, invectives, outrages, calomnier le pape, et non seulement en sa personne ce qui ne se doit jamais faire, mays en sa dignité, attaquer le siége que toute l'antiquité a honoré, le vouloir juger contre le conseil de toute l'Eglise, appeler la dignité même antichristianisme; qui sera celui qui le pourra trouver bon? Le grand concile de Calcédoine trouva si étrange que Dioscorus patriarche excommunia le pape Léon, et qui pourra souffrir l'insolence de Luther qui fit une bulle ou il excommunie et le pape et les évesques et toute l'Eglise. Toute l'Eglise lui donne des lettres honorables, lui parle avec reverence. Que dirons-nous de ce beau commencement de livre que Luther adressa au St. Siège : *Martinus Luther Sanctis-*

Cod. Quartis anni 39.

Art. 3.

Anno 22 apud Cocleus.

* Theatino? [Tr.]

simae Sedi Apostolicae et toti eius parlamento meam gratiam et salutem. Imprimis sanctissima sedes crepa et non frangere ob novam istam salutationem in qua nomen meum primo et in supremo loco pono. Et après avoir récité la bulle contre la quelle il écrivait il commence par ces iniques et vilaines paroles : *Ego autem dico ad papam et bullae huius minas, istud, qui prae minis moritur ad eius sepulturam compulsari debet crepitibus ventris.* . . . Et quand écrivait contre le roy d'Angleterre *Vivens,* dit-il, *papatus hostis ero, exustus tuus hostis ero.* Que dites-vous de ce grand Père? sont-ce pas des paroles dignes d'un tel réformateur? J'ai honte de les lire et ma main se fache de presenter ces vilaynies, mays qui vous les cachera, vous ne croiez jamais qu'il soit tel qu'il est. Et quand il dit : *Nostrum est non iudicari ab ipso sed ipsum iudicare.* . . .

THE END.

APPENDIX II

Parallel References between the French and English Editions of This Book

* Note—In the English translation, material is divided into: Parts, Articles and Chapters; in the French Edition, into Parts, Chapters and Articles.

TOPICAL INDEX

INDEX OF NAMES

NAMES OF HERETICS

SCRIPTURAL INDEX

If you have enjoyed this book, consider making your next selection from among the following . . .

Prices subject to change.

Stories of Padre Pio. *Tangari* 9.00
Miraculous Images of Our Lady. *Joan Carroll Cruz*. 21.50
Miraculous Images of Our Lord. *Cruz* 16.50
Brief Catechism for Adults. *Fr. Cogan* 12.50
Raised from the Dead. *Fr. Hebert* 18.50
Autobiography of St. Margaret Mary 7.50
Thoughts and Sayings of St. Margaret Mary 6.00
The Voice of the Saints. *Comp. by Francis Johnston* 8.00
The 12 Steps to Holiness and Salvation. *St. Alphonsus*. 9.00
The Rosary and the Crisis of Faith. *Cirrincione/Nelson* 2.00
Sin and Its Consequences. *Cardinal Manning* 9.00
St. Francis of Paola. *Simi & Segreti* 9.00
Dialogue of St. Catherine of Siena. *Transl. Thorold* 12.50
Catholic Answer to Jehovah's Witnesses. *D'Angelo* 13.50
Twelve Promises of the Sacred Heart. (100 cards). 5.00
Life of St. Aloysius Gonzaga. *Fr. Meschler* 13.00
The Love of Mary. *D. Roberto*. 9.00
Begone Satan. *Fr. Vogl*. 4.00
The Prophets and Our Times. *Fr. R. G. Culleton* 15.00
St. Therese, The Little Flower. *John Beevers* 7.50
Mary, The Second Eve. *Cardinal Newman*. 4.00
Devotion to Infant Jesus of Prague. *Booklet* 1.50
The Wonder of Guadalupe. *Francis Johnston*. 9.00
Apologetics. *Msgr. Paul Glenn* 12.50
Baltimore Catechism No. 1 .... 5.00
Baltimore Catechism No. 2 .... 7.00
Baltimore Catechism No. 3 .... 11.00
An Explanation of the Baltimore Catechism. *Kinkead* 18.00
Bible History. *Schuster* 16.50
Blessed Eucharist. *Fr. Mueller* 10.00
Catholic Catechism. *Fr. Faerber* 9.00
The Devil. *Fr. Delaporte* 8.50
Dogmatic Theology for the Laity. *Fr. Premm* 21.50
Evidence of Satan in the Modern World. *Cristiani* 14.00
Fifteen Promises of Mary. (100 cards) 5.00
Life of Anne Catherine Emmerich. 2 vols. *Schmoeger* 48.00
Life of the Blessed Virgin Mary. *Emmerich* 18.00
Prayer to St. Michael. (100 leaflets) 5.00
Prayerbook of Favorite Litanies. *Fr. Hebert* 12.50
Preparation for Death. (Abridged). *St. Alphonsus* 11.00
Purgatory Explained. *Schouppe* 16.50
Purgatory Explained. (pocket, unabr.). *Schouppe* 12.00
Spiritual Conferences. *Tauler*. 15.00
Trustful Surrender to Divine Providence. *Bl. Claude* 7.00

Prices subject to change.

Prices subject to change.

Holy Eucharist—Our All. *Etlin* 3.00
Glories of Divine Grace. *Fr. Scheeben* 18.00
Saint Michael and the Angels. *Approved Sources* 9.00
Dolorous Passion of Our Lord. *Anne C. Emmerich* 18.00
Our Lady of Fatima's Peace Plan from Heaven. *Booklet* 1.00
Three Conversions/Spiritual Life. *Garrigou-Lagrange* 7.00
Mystical Evolution. 2 Vols. *Fr. Arintero, O.P.* 42.00
St. Catherine Labouré of the Mirac. Medal. *Fr. Dirvin* 16.50
Manual of Practical Devotion to St. Joseph. *Patrignani* 17.50
The Active Catholic. *Fr. Palau* 9.00
Ven. Jacinta Marto of Fatima. *Cirrincione* 3.00
Reign of Christ the King. *Davies* 2.00
St. Teresa of Ávila. *William Thomas Walsh* 24.00
Isabella of Spain—The Last Crusader. *Wm. T. Walsh* 24.00
Characters of the Inquisition. *Wm. T. Walsh* 16.50
Blood-Drenched Altars—Cath. Comment. Hist. Mexico 21.50
Self-Abandonment to Divine Providence. *de Caussade* 22.50
Way of the Cross. *Liguorian* 1.50
Way of the Cross. *Franciscan* 1.50
Modern Saints—Their Lives & Faces, Bk. 1. *Ann Ball* 21.00
Modern Saints—Their Lives & Faces, Bk. 2. *Ann Ball* 23.00
Divine Favors Granted to St. Joseph. *Pere Binet* 7.50
St. Joseph Cafasso—Priest of the Gallows. *St. J. Bosco* 6.00
Catechism of the Council of Trent. *McHugh/Callan* 27.50
Why Squander Illness? *Frs. Rumble & Carty* 4.00
Fatima—The Great Sign. *Francis Johnston* 12.00
Heliotropium—Conformity of Human Will to Divine 15.00
Charity for the Suffering Souls. *Fr. John Nageleisen* 18.00
Devotion to the Sacred Heart of Jesus. *Verheylezoon* 16.50
Sermons on Prayer. *St. Francis de Sales* 7.00
Sermons on Our Lady. *St. Francis de Sales* 15.00
Sermons for Lent. *St. Francis de Sales* 15.00
Fundamentals of Catholic Dogma. *Ott* 27.50
Litany of the Blessed Virgin Mary. (100 cards) 5.00
Who Is Padre Pio? *Radio Replies Press* 3.00
Child's Bible History. *Knecht* 7.00
St. Anthony—The Wonder Worker of Padua. *Stoddard* 7.00
The Precious Blood. *Fr. Faber* 16.50
The Holy Shroud & Four Visions. *Fr. O'Connell* 3.50
Clean Love in Courtship. *Fr. Lawrence Lovasik* 4.50
The Secret of the Rosary. *St. Louis De Montfort* 5.00

At your Bookdealer or direct from the Publisher.
Call Toll Free 1-800-437-5876

Prices subject to change.

NOTES

NOTES

NOTES

NOTES